D0844180

Private Property and the Limits of American Constitutionalism

Private Property and the Limits of American Constitutionalism

The Madisonian Framework and Its Legacy

JENNIFER NEDELSKY

THE UNIVERSITY OF CHICAGO PRESS
CHICAGO AND LONDON

Jennifer Nedelsky is associate professor of law and political science at the University of Toronto. Her current work on feminist theory has appeared in the *Yale Journal of Law and Feminism* and in *Representations*.

The University of Chicago Press, Chicago 60637
The University of Chicago Press, Ltd., London

Printed in the United States of America
99 98 97 96 95 94 93 92 91 90 5 4 3 2 1

Library of Congress Cataloging-in-Publication Data

Nedelsky, Jennifer.
Private property and the limits of American constitutionalism : the Madisonian framework and its legacy / Jennifer Nedelsky.
p. cm.
Includes bibliographical references and index.
ISBN 0-226-56970-5 (clothbound)
1. Right of property—United States—History. 2. United States—Constitutional history. 3. Property—Social aspects—United States—History. I. Title.
KF562.N43 1990
342.73'029—dc20
[347.30229] 90-37127
CIP

∞ The paper used in this publication meets the minimum requirements of the American National Standard for Information Sciences—Permanence of Paper for Printed Library Materials, ANSI Z39.48-1984.

For Joe

Contents

Acknowledgments

> How much it takes to be a writer. Bent (far more common than we assume), circumstances, time, development of craft—but beyond that: how much conviction as to the importance of what one has to say, one's right to say it. And the will, the measureless store of belief in oneself to be able to come to, cleave to, find the form for one's own life comprehensions. Difficult for any male not born into a class that breeds such confidence. Almost impossible for a girl, a woman . . . . What was needed to confirm and vivify has been meager—and occasional, accidental. The compound of what denies, vitiates, actively discourages, has been powerful—and continous, institutionalized.
>
> TILLIE OLSEN, "One Out of Twelve: Women Who Are Writers in Our Century" (A Talk to College Teachers of Literature, 1971)[1]

I have been exceptionally fortunate in having resources and people around me to "confirm and vivify." Over the long years of working—and not working—on this book, I have become increasingly conscious of the forces to which Tillie Olsen so eloquently refers and of the good fortune that has enabled me to survive them. Someday I hope to write about those forces. Here, I want to gratefully acknowledge not only those I name, but all the others who, in sometimes fleeting, but important ways, have contributed the support, encouragement, and validation that made it possible for me to persevere.

This project began long ago as a dissertation for the Committee on Social Thought at the University of Chicago. I had three advisers—Hannah Arendt, Herbert Storing, and Stanley Katz—whom I found inspiring and admirable. They treated me with respect and provided both help and encouragement. I still think of what I learned from

1. Sara Ruddick and Pamela Daniels, eds., *Working it Out: 23 Women Writers, Artists, Scientists, and Scholars Talk about Their Lives and Work* (New York: Pantheon Books, 1977), pp. 326–27, 329, n. 7. It is a sad situation that despite all the things that *have* changed, Tillie Olsen's observations of almost twenty years ago still ring so true today.

them as I try to help students, particularly women, struggle with the challenges of writing. Stan Katz later became a colleague and continued to provide help and advice. John O'Brien and my parents, Ruth and Leo Nedelsky, were also important sources of support while I worked on the dissertation.

I have also been extremely fortunate in the financial support I have had over the years. A Killam Post-Doctoral Fellowship at the Faculty of Law, Dalhousie University, made it possible for me to get a grounding in law and begin research in legal history, which provided important dimensions to my understanding of constitutionalism. A grant from Project '87 together with a paid leave from Princeton University gave me a year's relief from teaching, which allowed me to write the first new sections of the book. The NEH-sponsored Legal History Workshop at the University of Wisconsin at Madison provided both financial support for a summer and an exceptional group of colleagues to discuss this project with. I felt honored to get comments from Willard Hurst and delighted to have the time for sustained conversations with Morton Horwitz and Bob Gordon—conversations which then continued over the years. The Russell Sage Foundation gave me still another year of research time, during which I worked out the basic framework of the book. At Russell Sage I found a wonderfully stimulating environment, a model of collegial exchange and support for young scholars. And I had the benefit of Robert Merton's extraordinary capacities as interlocutor, reader, and editor of my work. His detailed and thoughtful advice made a lasting difference in my capacity to write. At the University of Toronto, I received a University Research Grant and grants from the Connaught Program in Legal Theory and Public Policy for this and a related project, most of which was ultimately absorbed into the present book. The Faculty of Law also provided me with funding for research assistants.

At Princeton University I taught Constitutional Interpretation with Walter Murphy and an impressive, shifting group of colleagues including William Harris, Clement Vose, and Thomas Wright. This collective teaching was a stimulating introduction to contemporary constitutional law and theory, which provided a foundation for the arguments I have developed here. And, of course, being at Princeton opened doors for me. Beginning my teaching career there made it easier for me to establish the wide-ranging network of collegial friendships and contacts that has been so helpful to me as my work has developed over the years. Finally, at Princeton I gained a new understanding of the institutionalized "compound" of negation to which Tillie Olsen refers and of the importance of sisterly solidarity in mitigating its impact. Lynn Gordon and Barbara Nelson have my lasting gratitude for the support they provided in the years we were together there.

When I came to the University of Toronto, I found the intellectual home in which I was finally able to finish this book. The Faculty of Law has an ethos of collegiality that is both stimulating and supportive. The Departments of Political Science and Philosophy have provided me with an impressive variety of interesting and appreciative colleagues. Robert Prichard, then dean of the Faculty of Law, not only orchestrated my appointment but continued to provide active encouragement and support. Among many other tangible and intangible contributions, he made available to me the services of a fine editor, Diane Yew, who was extremely helpful in the final stages of organizing the manuscript.

Over the years I have accumulated such a large "support staff" that it is impossible to mention them all. But even an imperfect effort at acknowlegment seems important. The librarians at Princeton and at Russell Sage were very helpful, and Ann Morrison and the exceptional staff at the Faculty of Law Library at the University of Toronto have saved me endless hours tracking down elusive references. And they have done so with a good cheer, promptness, and efficiency that never ceases to amaze me. Over the years, I have also had very bright and helpful research assistants, including Linda Fitzgerald, Adam Sloan, Allison Hudgins, and Shauna Van Praagh. Kathleen Gallivan provided particularly important help and substantive research in the final stages of completing the manuscript. Numerous secretaries have labored away at successive drafts. I would particularly like to thank Tsiporah Lipton, Kathy Tzimika, and Ellen Downer.

Partial versions of this manuscript have been floating around for so long that I cannot remember all the helpful criticisms, suggestions, and encouraging remarks I have received. Nevertheless, they all mattered. I especially appreciated the generous notes I got from colleagues I had never met when I published the first little pieces of the argument in a review essay in the *Harvard Law Review*. And, of course, there have been a few people whose interest in my work has been particularly important. Early on, Morton Horwitz's work gave me a whole new perspective on property. His encouragement to pursue legal history (with some legal training) meant a lot to me, as did our conversations off and on over the years. Frank Michelman has responded to my work with an extraordinary spirit of generosity and openness. His public engagement with my work when it was still in manuscript (and when no one was sure it would ever proceed beyond manuscript) gave me an extremely important sense of validation. He has consistently made time to help me and offered thoughtful comments on the penultimate draft of the book. And he has done all this with a rare capacity to inspire admiration, while never expecting deference. I was also fortunate in having extremely helpful reviewers for this manuscript. Carey McWilliams (for a different press) offered not only perceptive comments but remarks on the political importance of the book which were important to me in sustaining my own belief in its usefulness. Cass Sunstein, who, like McWilliams, first saw the manuscript in very rough form, was able to see the basic argument and to see what it needed to make it work. His long, thoughtful set of questions and comments provided a framework for my revisions and for the new chapters I wrote. As I transformed the initial draft into a book, it was a great help to know that the (then still anonymous) reader was both appreciative and discerning. With the last draft, he offered still another set of suggestions with the same spirit and acuity. Sandy Levinson, like Cass, not only read the manuscript with unheard-of promptness but provided both helpful comments and encouraging remarks. The final product has benefited immensely from their help.

I turn finally to some of my most important debts, which fit into no neat category. I want to mention five friends and colleagues who, in very different ways, over different periods of time have shown an interest in my intellectual pursuits and a confidence in me that has sustained me in important ways: Joseph Cropsey, Edwin Haefele, Donna Freireich, Cheryl Noble, and Lynn Gordon. And I want to thank Betsy Halpern and Lucinda Sykes for helping me untangle the paralyzing ways in which I had internalized Tillie Olsen's "compound of what denies, vitiates, actively discourages." But even with their liberating help, I think I might have remained at an impasse if it had not been for the arrival of my son, Michael. I think my connection with him finally made me believe that I could finish my book and pursue an academic career without losing my soul. Once I had Michael, I finally sat down, focused my energies, and wrote the book.

At the heart of what made all of this possible is my husband, Joe Carens. First, he persuaded me that we could go ahead and have a child (whether the book got finished or not). Then he took on household responsibilties in ways that cleared the space for me to focus my energies on writing. And he not only made it possible for me to finish the book, he helped me to believe it was possible. When I finally did finish a draft, he had still more to offer: enthusiastic admiration together with expert editorial advice and substantive questions, criticisms, and suggestions. The hours he spent with me discussing the arguments and going over countless revisions have contributed more than anything else to the nuance and clarity of the final version. It is a special pleasure to dedicate this book to him. He made it possible, but he didn't require it.

Finally, I owe a debt of thanks to Merilyn Johnson, whose loving care and attentive responsibility enabled me to both focus on my work and enjoy being at home with Michael.

The length of these acknowledgments reflects not only the number of debts one incurs when a project takes as long as this one, but my sense that without such support, I would not have been able to write this book. The responsibility for errors, however, I claim as mine alone.

1 Introduction

I. Private Property and American Constitutional Government

Private property has shaped the structure of the American political system. The framework of our political institutions and the categories through which we understand politics developed around the problems of making popular government compatible with the security of property. This focus on property has been the source of the greatest strengths of the American Constitution, of its greatest weaknesses, and of the distorted quality even of its strengths.

Our Constitution maintains a working tension between democratic values and the privileged status of private rights. This impressive achievement has its roots in the Framers' concern with protecting property from democratic incursion. Their sense of the vulnerability of property in a republic became the focus for the broader task of securing individual rights against the tyranny of the majority. This focus, in turn, led to the greatest weakness of our system: its failure to realize its democratic potential. The Framers' preoccupation with property generated a shallow conception of democracy and a system of institutions that allocates political power unequally and fails to foster political participation. Finally, the focus on property distorted the very strength it provided: the conception and institutionalization of rights as limits to the legitimate scope of the state. With property as the paradigmatic instance of the vulnerability of rights in a democracy, inequality became both a presumption and an object of protection which skewed the conception of limited government that underlies our Constitution. Both the skewed conception and the stunted forms of democracy have outlasted the primacy of property itself as a constitutional barrier to democratic action.

To understand the enduring significance of property in our system, we must understand the original formation of the United States Constitution: the Federalist victory at the Constitutional Convention in 1787, ratified in 1788 and consolidated with the rise of judicial review in the first decades of the nineteenth century. The struggles over the formation involved fundamental choices about the allocation of power, the hierarchy of values the system would foster and protect, and the relation between citizens and their government. And the terms in which the choices were framed were as important as the choices themselves. The choices shaped our institutions; the categories and priorities still shape our perception of alternatives and the grounds on which we choose among them.

The core of my argument is that those who won the formative contests over the nature of the new republic were preoccupied with the protection of private property. This is not a repetition of the Progressives' claim that "the new government was a republic rigged up with contrivances to protect the interests of the propertied minority."[1] That claim is crudely true, but it misses what is most important about property in the formation of the Constitution: the distortion of the problems and potential of republican government. My emphasis is not on economic interest, but on the structure of ideas and institutions.[*2]

In the 1780s, the urgent sense that property rights had to be protected from democratic legislatures became the focus for formulating the principle that individual rights set limits to the legitimate power of government. That property-centred formulation shaped the Constitution in 1787 and then hardened into a notion of rights as judicially enforced boundaries dividing the legitimate scope of government from the protected sphere of individual liberty. This formative focus on property resulted in the neglect of two crucial issues: the means of fostering popular participation in government and the relationship between economic and political power. Both our institutions and our tradition of political thought still betray this original neglect.

These neglected issues are part of the basic problem: the original focus on property placed inequality at the center of American constitutionalism. For the Framers, the protection of property meant the protection of *unequal* property and thus the insulation of both property and inequality from democratic transformation. Effective insulation, in their view, required wealth-based inequality of access to political power. It also meant that the illegitimacy of redistribution defined the legitimate scope of the state. The inherent vulnerability of all individual rights became transformed into a fear of "the people" as a threatening propertyless mass whose power must be contained. The lesson of the formation is that when inequality is built into the conception of rights as limits to legitimacy, both our institutions and our understanding of constitutionalism must be distorted. Those distortions remain to be grappled with in the post-New Deal era of contested egalitarianism.

The modern welfare state does not fit easily within the Federalists' conceptual framework. Property once provided the conceptual boundary to the legitimate scope of government. That boundary is now threatened by the changing meaning of property and the demands of equality which simultaneously challenge traditional rights of property and the traditional scope of the state. In many crucial respects, we have accepted the New Deal but rejected its conceptual underpinnings. As a country, we routinely engage in redistribution to ameliorate social ills, but we have not simply accepted property as a mere social construct to be redefined or redistributed without constraint. The status of property as boundary lingers despite its disintegration as a constitutional concept. We countenance redistribution as a means, but we have no consensus on a vision of the state that clearly defines redistribution as a legitimate goal. And we tacitly rely upon, but have no clear means of justifying, this distinction between means and goal. In short, because the original structure of constitutionalism rested on an effort to prevent democratic control of property, our post-New Deal state requires a rethinking not just of the meaning of property, but also of the scope and purpose of the state. As such, it requires new foundations for constitutionalism.

I should clarify my claims about property: I do not claim that any particular property regime has inevitable consequences for democracy and constitutionalism. The links I do claim are the following: the Federalists' focus on protecting property from redistribution and, more broadly, from democratic redefinition, led to a misunderstanding of both the problems and the potential of democracy; and treating the protection of unequal property as the paradigm case of the problem of protecting individual rights in a democracy led to a misconception of the complex relation between democracy and individual autonomy, which is the true problem of constitutionalism. It was thus not property as such, but the effort to protect property and inequality from democratic revision, that has had distorting consequences.

II. The American Conception of Limited Government

The American conception of limited government developed and changed between 1787 and 1830, as did the institutional solutions to what were seen as its essential problems. The story of that development forms the conceptual framework for this book.

I will sketch this framework in advance, because it provides the thread of connection running through three detailed historical chapters, a chapter assessing the Constitution as it emerged from its formation, and the concluding argument about the contemporary significance of property. I should emphasize at the outset that the emergence of the American conception of limited government is a story of contests, not of monolithic forces. No one strain of thought, no single set of ideas or interests entirely shaped the American Constitution. But despite ongoing conflict and even accommodation, one strain of thought, that of the Federalists,*[3] won out. And in that dominant mode of thought, property was the focus around which the basic issues of limited government were worked out. The story of limited government in America is thus, in part, the story of the triumph of the Federalist perspective and of the priority it accorded to property.

I begin the story with the era of the American revolution.*[4] The principle of consent was the core of political discourse in the debates over independence and the early discussions of the new forms of government for the former colonies. There was a consensus that men*[5] had the right to be bound only by laws to which they had consented,*[6] and that consent was essential to republican government. The agreement on this general principle was deep and broad enough to obscure the uncertainties and disagreements about just what consent should mean in practice.

By the 1780s, the confidence of the revolutionary era had waned, and the emphasis on consent had shifted. Almost all the new state governments had issued paper money and passed debtor relief laws which were widely perceived as attacks on property rights.*[7] These events appeared to many as dramatic evidence of the limits of the principle of consent as the foundation for good and just government. The revolutionary claim that a man is a slave if his property can be taken without his consent gave way to the grim realization that consent alone was not adequate protection; property was now threatened by duly elected republican legislatures. The first stage in the development of limited government was characterized by a focus on this threat.

For many of the leading figures in American politics, the events of the 1780s signaled the need to replace the Articles of Confederation with a central government strong enough to take a respected place among the nations of the world and capable of avoiding and controlling the unjust propensities of the state governments. The Federalists were the chief proponents of such views in the debates over the Constitution. To say that they treated republican principles primarily as a problem, rather than a goal, would be a slight overstatement. It would, however, capture an important matter of emphasis: they took the principle of consent as a given and turned their attention to the dangers inherent in governments based on such principles. The result was a subtle but important shift in focus from the promise of republican government to the containment of its threats.

James Madison provided the most thoughtful formulation of the basic problem which republican government posed for the Federalists. Good government must be able to protect both the "rights of persons" and the "rights of property."[8] In republican government, those two objectives were in tension with one another because of a third category of rights, the right of all men to be governed only by those laws to which they consent. The problem was that if political rights were granted equally to all, the rights of persons and the rights of property would not be equally protected. The propertied could be relied upon to respect the rights of persons, in which they also had an interest. But the propertyless had no corresponding interest in property. The rights of property would thus be at risk whenever the sheer numerical advantage of the poor was translated into political power through equal political rights. The threat to property in America was particularly insidious because it took indirect forms such as depreciation of currency rather than direct expropriation. No one denied that property was a basic right, but the propertyless majority would nevertheless demand measures that destroyed the security of property.*[9] The problem of providing equal protection for the rights of persons and the rights of property in a manner consistent with republican principles was, Madison said, the most difficult of all political problems.

Part of the American solution to this problem was the formulation of important categories and hierarchies of rights. Civil rights, which included both the rights of persons and of property, were to be distinguished from political rights. Political rights, moreover, were conceived of as mere means to the true end of government, the protection of civil rights. In this view, political rights had no intrinsic value. By designating political rights as means, it was possible to treat them as purely instrumental and entirely contingent, and thus to make compromises of these rights appear not to involve compromise of principle.

In 1787, however, the choice implicit in these categories was still preliminary, its precise formulation and implementation unclear. The constitutional convention of that year can be seen as an effort to create a government which could protect all the competing rights of citizens: political rights as well as the rights of persons and property. Madison and his fellow Federalists were certain in their conviction that civil rights provided independent standards by which to measure the outcome of democratic processes. They felt acutely that when property rights were infringed by legislatures—that is, were infringed with the consent of the governed—such consent did not make the infringements legitimate. There was, however, no comparable certainty among the Framers about the way to give effect to those independent standards. In a republic where the people are, in principle, their own governors, the question of limited government becomes a question of *self*-limiting government—which, as we shall see, poses the irreducible problem of a government setting and enforcing its own limits.

The solution that emerged from the 1787 convention was one which did not rely heavily on limits as such.*[10] State governments were limited by specific prohibitions, but the Federal government would rely primarily on a structure of institutions designed to check each other and to minimize the likelihood of effective majoritarian tyranny. This solution had several advantages. It sustained the tensions between the competing categories of civil and political rights, as well as the particular tensions among the rights of persons, property, and participation. The Constitution of 1787 could encompass all of the competing values by avoiding a clear subordination of one to the other. It provided a fluid kind of solution which left somewhat vague whether the conceptual primacy of civil over political rights was to be translated into an institutionalized hierarchy of enforceable limits. It was important to the development of limited government in America that the Constitution of 1787 left the tensions between competing values open and alive. It was equally important that the balance struck between them was skewed by the Framers' preoccupation with property.

For those whose views prevailed at the Convention, property was the central instance of rights at risk in a republic. It was property that alerted them to the inherent vulnerability of minority rights in popular government, and thus property that became the focal point for the broader problem. And property was not just an abstract symbol. It was a right whose security was essential to the economic and political success of the new republic. If property could not be protected, not only prosperity, but liberty, justice, and the international strength of the nation would ultimately be destroyed. The focus on property bred a general suspicion of the people. Influential Framers, such as Madison, foresaw a permanent propertyless majority which would be fluid in its composition, but fixed in its inevitability. "The people" thus posed a permanent threat to the rights of property, rights whose protection was demanded not only by "the rules of justice,"[11] but by the requirements of political and economic stability.

Under the Constitution of 1787, the people were to be the base of the government, but their participation and efficacy was to be controlled, channeled, and contained by the structure of government. Both Federalists and Anti-Federalists agreed that the structure of the institutions outlined in the Constitution would draw the elite into the government. The people would have the role of periodically selecting among those elite and trying to evaluate their performance, but the ongoing control of public affairs would be left in the hands of the suitable (and propertied) few. The Anti-Federalists raised what we would today call democratic objections.[12] But the potential value of active self-governance never engaged the attention of the Federalists.

They were committed to republican government, which they thought allowed for the highest degree of popular participation possible without disintegration into anarchy or oligarchy. But theirs was not a literal vision of self-governance. They wanted the elite to rule. They treated the ability to govern as essentially fixed (rather than as a capacity that could be developed) and as class-based. Thus they were not concerned with expanding or enhancing the people's competence and involvement in public affairs. For the Federalists, the challenge was to make republican government compatible with the security of rights, not to design institutions that would foster men's ability to govern themselves. The democratic values that prevailed in 1787 were shallow values, and, in the subsequent tradition of American political thought, they have remained so.

The preoccupation with property had another important consequence for the structure of American government and the dominant tradition of political thought: the neglect of the problems arising from the relationship between economic and political power. For those preoccupied with containing the popular threat to property, the dangers posed by wealth commanded little attention; the problem of economic power remained submerged.

In sum, the Constitution of 1787 institutionalized the principle of consent in ways that left open important questions about what to do in a conflict between the rights of the people to implement their will through their representatives and the independent rights of property.*[13] The Constitution did not simply give precedence to property (or other private rights) over the republican principles of government by consent. However, the primacy of the Federalist concern with protecting property so shaped the structure of the Constitution that it was characterized as much by this implicit priority as by the absence of its formal institutionalization. The tensions remained, but the balance was tipped.

The remaining step in the formation of the Constitution,*[14] the rise of judicial review, tipped the balance further. The establishment of judicial review may be seen as the culmination and consolidation of the Federalist conception of politics. The Marshall Court took the Federalist hierarchy of rights to its logical, institutional conclusion (a conclusion which Madison resisted, preferring balanced tensions to logical consistency).[15] By the end of the 1820s, the American approach to limited government had come to be characterized by its focus on clear limits, by its vision of hard boundaries as giving meaning and efficacy to the idea of limited government.

Judicial review was established in the context of the rise of early party divisions, the battles between the Hamiltonian Federalists and the Jeffersonian Republicans. With the victory of the Jeffersonians in 1800, it seemed clear to the Federalists that winning in 1787 had not been enough.*[16] The carefully crafted federal structure alone was not sufficient protection for certain basic rules and rights—property and contract in particular. Property was thus one of the crucial issues around which judicial review and the law-politics distinction was built. The courts could make a strong claim that property belonged in a distinctly legal realm, which had the sanction of the long and honorable tradition of common law. The need for the judiciary to protect this venerable realm from legislative encroachment could then be seen to rest on a neutral legal tradition rather than on the fear and suspicion of the people. Once the crucial boundaries were defined as a matter of law, the judiciary's claim to draw them was virtually unassailable.

Limited government thus took the form of judicially enforced boundaries. The dilemma of self-limiting government—of the political entity requiring limits being the one to set those limits—was "solved" by placing those limits in an arena declared to be outside of politics. The bifurcation of law and politics separated the limits from their object while giving the judicial source of limits a status exalted enough to stand against the claims of democracy. The neutrality of law stood above the petty squabbles of politics. The particular American dilemma of circumscribing the democratic power of a sovereign could thus also be evaded by recourse to a distinct legal arena which provided an ostensibly apolitical basis for defining and enforcing limits. Law, according to the model, did not thwart the will of the people; law gave effect to it in a loftier, truer way than politics.

The idea of boundaries and of a sharp distinction between law and politics has been central to the American conception of limited government. Property was for 150 years the quintessential instance of rights as boundaries. It has been the symbol and source of a protected sphere into which the state cannot enter. Property has also carried with it the paradox of self-limiting government: it is the limit to the state; it is also the creature of the state. In property, the state sets its own limits.

Despite all the ways in which the state has changed those limits when it has suited some "public purpose," the paradox has been kept obscured by the distinction between law and politics. This distinction has sustained a mythic quality of property as not merely a social construct, but a basic right, linked in powerful ways to cherished values of freedom and autonomy. The myth of property and the image of the law-politics distinction have sustained each other and have together provided the foundation for the American conception of limited-government.

Property remains central to our conception of government. The basic issues of the legitimate scope of government, indeed the desirable nature of government, continue to be fought over the issue of property. From the early challenges to workmen's compensation, to the continuing regulation-vs-market debate, to new claims for equal protection on the grounds of wealth, property has stood at the center of conflicts that shape the kind of political system we have. The context for these contests continues to be the property-centered ideas and institutions shaped during the formation of the Constitution.

This enduring importance of property coexists, however, with a major shift in its constitutional status. Since the New Deal, the position of property in our constitutional language and institutions has so changed that the notion of limited government which has long sustained American Constitutionalism may now be at risk. Put more starkly, the foundation of American constitutionalism is shifting with the modern disintegration of property as a constitutional barrier. That shift may demand a new conception of limited government.

The story of limited government in America begins with private property as the clear, compelling, even defining, instance of the limits that private rights place on legitimate government. The story concludes with the dilemmas of a tradition facing fundamental challenges to its founding concepts.*[17]

III. The Lessons of the Formation

The formation of the Constitution is my focus for understanding the centrality of property in American constitutionalism. Despite important changes, such as the direct election of the Senate, the Civil War Amendments, and the extension of the franchise to women, the basic constitutional structure is that outlined in the Constitution of 1787 and consolidated in the rise of judicial review. The formation is therefore a useful key, although it is, of course, neither the only one, nor the key to everything about American constitutional government.

The Constitution was formed in a series of battles over the nature and structure of the new republic. The contestants were concerned with designing institutions capable of generating a particular kind of polity. Because many of them were men of extraordinary thoughtfulness and political acuity, the debates over the Constitution offer exceptionally illuminating commentary on the ways different institutional forms promote varying kinds of behaviour, values, and policies.[18]

The arguments did not reflect a simple faith that written outlines of political institutions could encompass or control all practices within those institutions. On the contrary, the arguments are of interest because they present a dynamic vision of institutions developing and generating patterns of behavior which, in turn, shape the development of those institutions. The contestants did assume that the basic structure of government would follow the written outline. But they were interested in the subtle and complex ways in which the formal structures of institutions outlined in the Constitution would foster patterns of relationships among citizens—such as forms of inequality and attachment to private interest—and between citizens and their government—such as forms of political participation. This attention to the ways institutions affect what we might call the "political culture" of a society is among the most valuable contributions of the Framers.

They also help us understand the structure of the system because they saw it as a whole. The Federalists, for example, wanted to implement republican principles through a highly mediated structure that would promote stability and justice. They were not only concerned with such issues as the capacity of the House and Senate to refine the public's views and filter their passions, but also with the way the structure as a whole would contain the dangers of democracy while providing the power necessary for effective national government.

The Constitutional Convention of 1787 produced a document that laid out the framework of our political system, and my primary sources of insights into its structure and institutions are the debates in and around that convention. I have, however, defined my subject as the "formation" rather than the writing of the Constitution because the constitutional structure was, in important ways, not completed until judicial review was firmly in place. Whatever the Framers' expectations about judicial review, its powerful role in American government was not established with the writing of the Constitution in 1787, but with the Marshall Court in the first decades of the nineteenth century.

The Federalists had a notion of the primary objectives and values of politics, of the role of popular participation, of ways of ranking competing values, and of managing the tensions between them. Their conception of politics triumphed in 1787, and again with the establishment of judicial review, and has continued to affect the way we perceive political problems—both what counts as political and what counts as a problem.

IV. The Focus on the Framers: Madison, Morris, and Wilson

The writing of the Constitution was an extraordinary collective act of creation. Fifty-five men participated in the Constitutional Convention, and at every stage compromise and collaboration characterized the proceedings. To understand that process of collective determination and the decisions that emerged from it, it is extremely useful to understand the competing interests at stake and the coalitions formed to promote them. The great divisive issues of small-vs.-large states and Northern-vs.-Southern economic interests (including the highly charged issue of slavery) pervaded virtually every debate. These interests intersected in various and shifting ways with the conflicts over the degree of power that should be centralized in the federal government. And the different visions of the kind of economy, international power, and citizenry the new republic should have, crosscut all of these conflicts in still other ways.

We have excellent studies that provide us with various angles on the conflicts which were both the context and the substance of the debates over the Constitution.[19] These studies tell us about the forces at work in the convention as a whole. They provide important background and overviews, and I rely on them. My effort is, however, different. My objective is to take a close look at how the idea of property shaped the political thought of the Framers and the institutions they designed. I examine the way they conceived of property, why they thought it was important, how their views on property affected their perception of the problems at hand, and the institutional solutions they offered. To answer these questions in detail, I have chosen to examine three of the most influential delegates to the 1787 convention: James Madison, Gouverneur Morris, and James Wilson.

Madison is an obvious choice and the primary focus of this study. The common characterization of him as "Father of the Constitution" is apt, for the Constitution is very largely a Madisonian document. Madison was one of the chief actors in setting the agenda the convention followed, and although he did not prevail in every instance, the Constitution as a whole has a Madisonian structure. It reflects the tensions within his ideas, the concerns that preoccupied him, and his most creative contributions to republican government. The Constitution also reflects the limitations of his thought.*[20]

Madison's astute and subtle analyses of the problems and potential of republican government make his strengths clear. The weaknesses of Madisonian political thought and the Madisonian Constitution are best revealed by the ideas of two of his allies at the convention, James

Wilson and Gouverneur Morris. They were, like Madison, staunch Federalists who shared the goal of creating a strong central government. All three worked together in the convention and voted together on most major issues. But their understanding of republican government differed in important respects, and the differences were closely linked to their individual approaches to property.

Wilson, Madison, and Morris encompassed the spectrum of views on property at the convention. Madison's political thought was characterized by an often agonized effort to find a working balance between the rights of property and republican principles. Gouverneur Morris, by contrast, asserted a clear, unequivocal priority of property, which simply subordinated competing values. Wilson, on the other end of the continuum, was the only member of the convention to proclaim that property was not the object of government.[21] The comparison of their views reveals the ways in which the strengths and weaknesses of each was related to his views on property. Most importantly, the respective strengths of Morris and Wilson reveal the limitations of Madison's thought and, thus, of the Madisonian tradition of constitutionalism.

Morris's chief contribution to the convention and to our critical appraisal of the Madisonian Constitution, was his argument that in a commercial republic the wealthy and not the poor would hold the power, and that the Constitution should be designed to contain the threat from the few as well as the many. It was as though the lack of ambivalence he felt toward the priority of property allowed him to see the danger in the power of wealth. His arguments about the threat from the propertied few show the comparative neglect of this issue by those whose views prevailed in 1787. Wilson provides an implicit critique from the other direction. Free of a preoccupation with property, he was one of the few Federalists to turn his mind to the potential rather than to the dangers of popular participation. He was interested in designing institutions that would foster the political capacity of the people. As with Morris, his insights reveal the skewed quality of the property-dominated thought of his fellow Federalists. The fact that Wilson and Morris were themselves Federalists who shared the prevailing Madisonian goals makes their implicit critiques particularly useful. They serve as internal critics who accepted the dominant Federalist perspective and could challenge its weaknesses on its own terms.[22] Wilson is particularly important because he understood the problem of majority tyranny differently than Madison, and because he offered a vision of a democratic solution to this basic problem of republican government. While Morris's contribution lies in his critique, Wilson has substantively important alternatives to offer. Wilson's different presuppositions, values, and perceptions of democracy permit us to see the underlying conceptual framework of the Madisonian vision that triumphed. The aspirations Wilson shared with his fellow Federalists make clear that an alternative was available to them; their failure to recognize it rests heavily on the role of property in the Madisonian approach they adopted.

The critical insights of Morris and Wilson, as well as Madison's own contributions to our understanding of the Constitution, emerge from an analysis of their "political theory" and constitutional proposals. I present their conceptions of the basic principles and most pressing problems of republican government, as well as their understanding of how particular institutions could implement those principles and solve those problems. My analysis focuses on how each Framer's views on property fit within his institutional and theoretical frameworks. Finally, I use the critique their views provide of each other to assess the Constitution of 1787—its strengths, its weaknesses, and the extent to which these strengths and weaknesses suggest that it was a Madisonian document.

This approach presumes an understanding of their political thought and what it can tell us that requires some explanation. The obvious problem is this: although these men were thoughtful, insightful, sometimes profound statesmen, they were not primarily theorists. Is it possible to use their political thought in the ways I propose without imputing a philosophical mission and a theoretical coherence which they never had? My answer is that despite their pragmatic nature, they came to the convention with a coherent set of principles and ideas about politics which they wanted to implement in the new Constitution. Their ideas had, to a large extent, developed in an effort to solve the problems—both immediate and long-run—of their fledgling republic. Their conceptions of republican principles and theories of government were thus intertwined with the institutional designs they proposed. Their views on the proper nature of representation, for example, were refined as well as concretized in the process of deciding on the optimal form of the legislature—the size of election districts, the length of terms, the modes of selection. Moreover, principle merged with practical politics, such as competing economic interests, in the collaboration and compromise that produced the Constitution. Nevertheless, the constitution-making these men engaged in is best understood as an effort to design institutions in accordance with deeply held political principles and with general conceptions of how institutions do and should work.

Their ideas do not constitute political theory on the order of Locke, but they have sufficient coherence to allow us to analyze them as systems of thought. We can see the relations between their views on property and their other ideas and values, and thus assess how central property was to their political thought as a whole and to the Constitution they helped produce. The comparisons among Madison, Morris, and Wilson make this assessment clearer still; the relations between their views on private property and the comparative strengths and weaknesses of their thought show us not only how property was important, but what difference that importance made.

Together, these three Framers provide a critical perspective on the significance of property in the ideas and institutions which became the foundation of our political system. The juxtaposition of their ideas shows property as part of our very ideals of justice, liberty, and democracy. Their debates suggest the ways our institutions were designed to protect property and the consequences of the choices involved in those designs. In short, these Framers provide a perspective on the subtle ways property is an integral part of our Constitution.

V. The Structure

Chapters two, three, and four provide a detailed examination of each of these Framers' theories and designs for the new Constitution. Madison remains the central focus, with the chapters on Morris and Wilson organized around their contributions to understanding the strengths and weaknesses of the Madisonian approach. Chapter five argues that the Constitution produced by the convention of 1787 was indeed Madisonian. I use the direct juxtaposition of the three Framers to examine the strengths and weaknesses of both the institutional and conceptual framework established in 1787. A brief look at the Anti-Federalists' objections to the new Constitution confirms the critical insights provided by Wilson and Morris. My argument throughout is that the Federalists' preoccupation with property distorted not just the institutions they designed, but the conceptual legacy they provided. I use the current debate over the "republican" nature of our tradition to clarify the contours as well as the context of this conceptual framework, and the debates that it has provoked from 1787 to the present. Finally, I argue that the rise of judicial review was both a consolidation and a subtle transformation of the Madisonian Constitution. This final section on the formation of the Constitution is, in part, about the complex ways judicial review removes basic issues from popular comprehension and control. It is thus the conclusion to the story of the original structuring (and confining) of democratic politics to serve the complex set of values associated with, and symbolized by, private property.

This story ends one hundred and fifty years ago in a still largely agrarian society with a pre-civil war Constitution and economy, a huge disenfranchised population (women, blacks, and native peoples), and a federal government whose size and scope were a mere fraction of what it is today. The conclusion to the book turns to the question of what this long distant formation tells us about the political system that has evolved from it.

I begin with contemporary concerns about democracy and economic power and argue that these problems are best understood not as anomalous failures, but as integral parts of the coherent system of ideas and institutions I have described as Madisonian federalism. I then turn to my primary focus, the twin challenges to our traditional conception of limited government: the demise of property as a constitutional limit to legislative power and the pressures of egalitarianism. Together they demand a new understanding of the purposes and limits to government. This demand provides the opportunity not simply to overcome the weaknesses of the tradition—which are not as easily separable from its strengths as reformers like to hope. The transformations already underway invite us to transcend the failings of the tradition's greatest strength: the (mis)understanding of the vulnerability of individuals and minorities to the collective power of democracy. When we understand the distortions rooted in the original focus on property, we can more clearly see the real problems Madison so brilliantly and imperfectly grappled with, and we can begin to envision alternatives to the concepts and institutions he bequeathed us.

2 The Madisonian Vision: The Republican Solution to the Republican Problem

James Madison not only established the agenda for the Constitutional Convention of 1787; he provided the formulation of the problems our Constitution was designed to solve. This formulation set an inspiring challenge, but one that was, on his own terms, impossible to meet. Both our institutions and our conceptual legacy continue to reflect the tensions in his thought, his impressive effort to resolve them, and his ultimate failure to do so. At the heart of these tensions is the priority he accorded to property despite his assertion that the rights both of persons and of property were cardinal objects of government and despite his uneasy sense that protecting property required compromising republican principles.

These tensions are the source of the depth and richness of Madison's thought as well as its limitations. We can thus best understand his most important contributions and his most enduring failures by focusing on his own perspective: how he saw the problems of republican government and why he structured his arguments and his institutions the way he did. In addition, the framework we use today for understanding republican government is in crucial ways the one we inherited from him. It is therefore important to remain within that framework so that we may understand its internal strengths and weaknesses. Later we move to the criticisms additional perspectives provide and to the present-day implications of his arguments.

We begin with the dilemma that framed Madison's approach to republican government. We look at why protecting both the rights of persons and property was a problem. And we see that we should take seriously Madison's efforts to make republican principles compatible with both: despite the priority he accorded to property in practice and emphasis, he never treated it as a priority in principle. His efforts to achieve all of his objectives provides the context in which to understand the priority he did accord to property.

I. The Dilemma of Republican Government

Madison considered property so important that he would have returned property to the trilogy of rights Jefferson had amended in the Declaration of Independence; life, liberty, and the pursuit of happiness were incomplete without property. The declaration Madison wanted to prefix to the Constitution stated that

> government is instituted and ought to be exercised for the benefit of the people; which consists in the enjoyment of life and liberty, with the right of acquiring and using property and generally of pursuing and obtaining happiness and safety.[1]

And, in what was probably Madison's single most important statement on republican government, he asserted that "the first object of government" was "the protection of different and unequal faculties of acquiring property."[2] This carefully stated claim was a central part of his argument in *The Federalist*, No. 10. The priority claimed for property rights must, therefore, be taken very seriously. But Madison also argued that there were not one, but two "cardinal objects of government: the rights of persons, and the rights of property,"*[3] and that, consequently, "the most either can claim, is such a structure [of government] as will leave a reasonable security for the other."[4] Achieving this dual object was, he said, "the most difficult of all political arrangements."[5]

The immediate question raised by Madison's different statements of the object of government is whether the claim that property is the *first* object of government represents a choice of property over the rights of persons. Much of this chapter will deal with variants of this question. First, however, we need to understand why he saw a problem in protecting the rights both of persons and of property.

Why did Madison believe that security for one would threaten the other? An obvious guess would be that Madison saw some inherent tension or incompatibility between the two. Protecting both sets of rights would, for example, be a problem if the full exercise and security of the rights of property would necessarily infringe on the rights of persons, or vice versa. In fact, however, Madison gave no indication that he saw such a conflict. He never suggested that the rights either of persons or of property involved an intrinsic threat or limit to the other. The problem with protecting both persons and property lay not in the characteristics of the rights, but in the practical problems of securing them, given the inevitable inequality and conflict of a free society.

Madison saw the problems as he did because he saw America as a divided society. He believed that the United States would ultimately be subject to the age-old division between the rich and the poor. It was true that in 1787 America had "not reached that stage of Society in which conflicting feelings of the Class with, and the Class without property have the operation natural to them in Countries fully peopled."[6] In future times, however, "a great majority of people will not only be without landed, but without any other sort of property."[7] And when that time arrived the "conflicting feelings" would certainly emerge: "an increase of the population will of necessity increase the proportion of those who will labor under all the hardships of life, and secretly sigh for a more equal distribution of its blessings."[8]

The protection both of persons and of property was a problem because of this inevitable division between those with and those without property. It was the conflict between these two classes that required the statesman to treat the two sets of rights as separate and in tension with one another. Madison suggested that both classes would, if given the power, be likely to violate the rights of the other: "Give all power to property, and the indigent will be oppressed. Give it to the latter and the effect may be transposed."*[9] But the rights of property were more vulnerable in a republic than the rights of persons. In the first place, the propertied class would inevitably be the minority: "It is now observed that in all populous countries, the smaller part only can be interested in the rights of property."[10] The majority, having no property, would have no interest in protecting the rights of property and, indeed, were likely to think they had an interest in violating those rights. The propertyless majority could only be relied on to protect the rights they had a direct interest in: the rights of persons.[11] Madison thought that the interests of the propertied, on the other hand, were such that those with property were less likely to violate the rights of others: "As the holders of property have at stake all the other rights common to those without property, they may be the more restrained from infringing, as well as the less tempted to infringe the rights of the latter."[12] It would nevertheless not be safe to entrust them with exclusive power.

The problem of how to balance these two classes in order to protect the rights of both—to weigh their power, their threat, and the importance of each set of rights—was compounded by the matter of republican principles. Madison recognized a "fundamental principle that men cannot be justly bound by laws in making of which they have no part,"[13] that is, men have a fundamental right to suffrage. But if this right were extended equally to all, the controlling power in the government would be the majority "not interested in the rights of property."[14] If property rights were to be secured, therefore, some restriction of this fundamental right was required. Madison was thus faced with the problem of balancing not only the rights of property and the rights of persons, but political rights as well: in principle, there was no conflict between the rights of persons and the rights of property; in principle, suffrage was the right of all; but in practice, if political rights were given equally to all, the rights of persons and the rights of property would not be equally protected.

Madison faced this problem in the concrete form of qualifications for suffrage under the Constitution. As he succinctly put it when reconsidering the issue in 1821:

> In a just and free, Government, . . . the rights both of property and of persons ought to be effectually guarded. Will the former be so in case of universal and equal suffrage? Will the latter be so in case of a suffrage confined to the holders of property?[15]

At the time of the convention, Madison was prepared to risk the rights of persons and restrict the political rights of a future majority in order to protect property; with a reluctant afterthought about republican principles he concluded that freehold suffrage would be best.[16]

In discussing the problems of protecting persons and property, Madison never said that the security of property was more important. When considering both sets of rights, he was never willing to accord priority to property in principle. He was nevertheless willing to give it priority in practice (freehold suffrage), to declare it to be the first object of government (in *The Federalist*, No. 10),*[17] and to make it the center of his attention at the time of the convention. This study of property in Madison's thought begins therefore with a problem and not a principle: if property was not in fact first in principle, if it was only one of two cardinal objects, why did it assume such primacy in his thinking about the new Constitution?

The puzzle I pose is a real one only if we give credence to Madison's claims about persons as well as those about property. Only if we take seriously the dilemma as he presented it, does it provide a useful framework of analysis. There are, of course, compelling reasons for accepting his proclaimed commitment to protecting property: his repeated explicit statements of its importance; its recurrent centrality in his arguments (which will become clearer in the course of my discussion) and in *The Federalist*, No. 10, in particular; and his preference for freehold suffrage in the House, representation of property in the Senate, and election of the President by the "qualified part" of the people. Moreover, in 1787 every major political figure in America treated property as at least one object of government.

The obvious question is whether Madison's claims for the rights of persons deserve equal credence. If not, of course, the dilemma of persons, property, and political rights dissolves into mere rhetoric. It becomes a clever device for making his preference for property appear to be the outcome of a troubled struggle over irreconcilable principles. But that interpretation would be a mistake. To dismiss Madison's formulation as empty rhetoric would be to misunderstand a problem that focused and shaped his political thought.

There are several reasons to believe that Madison saw the problem in the terms he stated. First, he used the persons and property formulation in both private letters and in the debates at the 1787 convention (a semipublic forum). It was in the document most clearly intended for wide public circulation, *Federalist*, No. 10, that he proclaimed the faculties for acquiring property as the first object of government. It hardly makes sense therefore to construe his presentation of the dilemma as a rhetorical device to disguise the priority he accorded to property.

Another reason to believe that Madison was struggling with an issue that he took seriously is that he returned to it again, using the same formulation, almost forty years later. In 1821, when he was preparing his notes of the debates for publication, he added a long note on the difficulties of protecting both persons and property, and the disadvantages of each of the solutions. In 1821 he gave more weight than he had in 1787 to the issue of political rights, beginning his discussion with the statement that "the right of suffrage is a fundamental Article of Republican Constitutions." But the dilemma was the same one he had grappled with in 1787. Finally, as elder statesman at the convention to revise the Virginia Constitution, Madison said that the rights of persons and the rights of property "cannot well be separated," but he returned to his basic argument that the rights of suffrage must be assigned so as to afford adequate protection for property as well as persons. (In this case it was property in slaves that he thought was at risk from the majority "who have no interest in this species of property.")[18] Whenever Madison was confronted with the basic problem of structuring a republican government, he saw the dilemma of protecting the rights of persons and property without violating political rights. He always presented the predicament as a troubling one, and he was never entirely satisfied with the solutions he arrived at.

There is a final reason for taking seriously each component of the dilemma Madison presented. While his emphasis in 1787 was on property, he offered reasons why the particular historical context of the convention made that emphasis necessary: the political thought of the American Revolution had given rise to an understandable, but dangerous neglect of property rights.

> The necessity of thus guarding the rights of property was for obvious reasons unattended to in the commencement of the Revolution. In all the Governments which were considered as beacons to republican patriots and lawgivers the rights of persons were subjected to those of property. The poor were sacrificed to the rich. In the existing state of American population and American property the two classes of rights were so little discriminated that a provision for the rights of persons was supposed to include of itself those of property, and it was natural to infer from the tendency of republican laws, that these different interests would be more and more identified. Experience and investigation have however produced more correct ideas on the subject.[19]

Madison thought that the revolutionary principles of government assured respect for the rights of persons, but left the rights of property vulnerable to the excesses of popular government. He therefore took the importance of personal rights for granted and turned his energies to emphasizing that "property as well as personal rights" deserved protection.[20]

The contingency of his emphasis is, moreover, supported by a shift in his language in 1792. By the 1790s, Madison was shocked and frightened by the direction governmental policy was taking under the influence of Alexander Hamilton. Madison thought Hamilton's plans for the redemption of public securities and for the national bank would favor the wealthy few.[21] Worse still, these policies reflected the power of the "monied interests" and their unholy collusion with government. Now the many were victims of the few.[22] Under these circumstances, Madison shifted the emphasis of his arguments. Property now seemed the dominant interest, and the rights of persons in need of special emphasis. In 1792, the climate of the times led him to presume a respect for property, as he had earlier assumed a respect for personal rights.

> In a word, as a man is said to have a right to his property, he may equally be said to have a property in his rights . . . . Government is instituted to protect property of every sort; as well that which lies in the various rights of individuals, as that which the term particularly expresses.[23]

In this often quoted but quite atypical passage Madison was trying to draw on the accepted importance of property to lend its sanctity to individual rights more generally. The era immediately following the revolution had presented the opposite and, for republics, characteristic problem of the disregard of property rights. But when a perversion of republican government brought a reversal of this problem—when the personal rights of the many, rather than the property rights of the few, were particularly at risk—Madison was true to his proclaimed concern with both sets of rights. In 1792, as in 1787, he placed his emphasis on the rights most at risk.

Madison's dilemma was, then, a real one, and finding a balanced solution was the challenge he set for himself and for the new Constitution. The vulnerability of property in 1787 was, however, not merely an historical accident of the immediate revolutionary past. Madison's comments in 1792 were atypical because the problems he was responding to were not those he thought characteristic of republican government. In his view, property would always be at risk in a republic and thus always the proper subject of emphasis for republican statesmen.

Having seen that Madison's commitment to the rights of persons as well as property was not mere rhetoric, we can return to the puzzle of why he accorded property a priority. The mere fact of its vulnerability is not a sufficient explanation. We turn now to unpacking Madison's vision of the nature of the threats to property and their implications and consequences for republican government. Following the emphasis of his own presentation, we begin with his arguments about why property was important, and then turn to the implicit questions that he did not address directly: Just what were the rights of property? What intrinsic importance did they have? What role should government have with respect to property? What part does inequality play in Madison's conception of property? Finally, we turn to how he reconciled the protection he wanted for property with republican principles and, in particular, majority rule.

A. THE PROBLEM OF PROPERTY

Property and the problem of republican government

As a Framer of the new government, Madison saw the protection of property as both an immediately pressing concern and as indicative of larger problems. He thought that state legislatures under the Articles of Confederation had repeatedly violated the rights of property through depreciating paper money and through debtor relief laws, particularly those requiring paper money to be accepted in payment of debts. He urged the Virginia legislature to see that paper money "affects rights of property as taking away equal value in land; [and] . . . affects property without trial by jury."[24] Such unjust laws were a reality in many states and a threat everywhere. They were distressing evidence that even though the majority were not yet propertyless, the rights of property were already precarious.

The dangerous prevalence of those laws was, in Madison's view, largely responsible for the crisis that brought delegates to the constitutional convention.

> [He argued for] the necessity of providing more effectually for the security of private rights, and the steady dispensation of justice. Interferences with these were evils which had more perhaps than anything else, produced this convention.[25]

Those evils arose, he reminded his fellow delegates, because property had become the target of majorities using their legislative power to enhance their interests at the expense of the rights and interests of others.

> What has been the major source of those unjust laws . . . Has it not been the real or supposed interest of the major number: Debtors have defrauded their creditors. The landed interest has borne hard on the mercantile interest. The holders of one species of property have thrown a disproportion of taxes on the holders of another species.[26]

The government that was to replace the Articles of Confederation had to be able to solve this pressing problem of legislative injustice.

The legislative violations of property rights were, moreover, not simply an immediate problem. They brought "into question the fundamental principle of republican government, that the majority who rule in such governments are the safest Guardians both of the Public Good and private rights."[27] In Madison's eyes the popular attacks on property become proof that a majority as well as a minority could pursue injustice, violate individual rights, and undermine the public good.

Madison's concern with property thus stood in a special relation to individual rights generally. "Property" for Madison did not incorporate or symbolize all individual rights;*[28] but the problem of protecting property rights in a republic pointed to, and was part of, the more general problem of the security of private rights. While Madison did not use the term property to stand for all individual rights (as in the Lockean sense of life, liberty, and estate), the reverse often appears to be the case: when Madison spoke of individual rights, it was property he had in mind. It is certainly true that over and over again when Madison made arguments for the urgent necessity of securing individual rights, the context of the argument or the specifics he mentioned had to do with property rights. Property provided Madison with the crucial example of the vulnerability of all individual rights, and that example was clearly uppermost in his mind when he discussed the general problem.

The finest expression of the relation between property and individual rights in Madison's thought is, of course, *The Federalist*, No. 10. This was his most refined and most general statement of the basic problem of republican government. He identified the vulnerability of all minorities, the possibility and danger of a variety of majority factions, and the inevitability of factions of all kinds. But property was his chief concern: "the most common and durable source of factions has been the various and unequal distribution of property." And the conflict over property would be the chief concern of government: "The regulation of these various and interfering interests forms the principal task of modern legislation." He both posed the problem and offered the solution in a way that was applicable to all individual rights; but it was property that stood at the center of the discussion.

Madison thought the fate of republican government depended on the ability of the new Constitution to protect the rights that had been violated under the Articles of Confederation. If the new government could not prove that it could protect property, people would reject it as incapable of providing justice or security. Madison believed that rejection was a real possibility. He saw republican government in America as a precarious experiment which, in 1787, had come to a crucial turning point. He spoke of the "mortal diseases of the existing constitution," and warned that the situation was "marked by symptoms which are truly alarming, which have *tainted the faith of the most orthodox republicans*, and which challenge from the votaries of liberty every concession in favor of stable Government not infringing fundamental principles, as the only security against an *opposite extreme of our present situation*."[29] Madison was convinced that republican government could not survive if it could not prevent the abuses to which it was prone: "Was it to be supposed that republican liberty could long exist under the abuses of it practiced in some of the States?"[30] People would, finally, not tolerate such abuses and would look to other, non-republican, forms of government for a remedy. Attacks on property would, in the end destroy republican liberty itself.

For Madison, the capacity of the new government to protect property took on a still larger significance. If republican liberty failed in America, it might fail forever.

> [Hamilton] concurred with Mr. Madison that we were now to decide forever the fate of Republican government; and that if we did not give to that form due stability and wis-

> dom, it would be disgraced and lost among ourselves, disgraced and lost to mankind forever.[31]

The protection of property was a test by which the republican form of government would stand or fall.

In sum, Madison saw property as central to the critical problems he faced as a Framer of the new Constitution: property was under attack in 1787; property would always be at risk in a republic because it would always be vulnerable to the dissatisfaction of the (inevitable) propertyless majority; and the vulnerability of property rights revealed the nature of the republican threat to individual rights, oppression by the majority. If the new government could not protect property, it could not meet either its immediate challenge or its most fundamental objectives. Property was thus, in a particularly immediate way, the paradigmatic instance of the central problem of republican government. Madison turned his most creative energies to solving that problem, and property was the example he held before him as the framed his questions and worked out his answers.

Property, stability and republican liberty

Most of Madison's arguments about securing property are efforts to impress upon his audience the dire consequences of threats to property. He clearly did not think it was necessary to argue that property was a fundamental right, or a component of individual liberty, or the basis for it. It was not property's status as a basic right that he thought was challenged, or doubted, or misunderstood. What was misunderstood was the nature and significance of the threats republican government posed to property, and the threat violations of property, in turn, posed to republican government.

The aspect of those reciprocal threats that Madison emphasized most was the threat to stability. In his view, the protection of property rights was essential to the stability of society and government, and stability, in turn, was necessary if republican government was to endure.

> The instability, injustice and confusion introduced into the public councils have, in truth, been the mortal diseases under which popular governments have everywhere perished.[32]

Madison warned that "the enemies of republican government" had always alleged stability "to be inconsistent with its nature."[33] The state governments during the confederation had done little to prove these enemies wrong. It was now essential that the new government show that a republic could overcome the problem of instability.

> He conceived it to be of great importance that a stable and firm Government organized in the republican form should be held out to the people. If this be not done, and the people left to judge of this species of Government by the operations of the defective systems under which they now live, it is much to be feared the time is not distant when in universal disgust, they will renounce the blessings which they purchased at so dear a rate, and be ready for any change.[34]

Madison repeatedly instructed his audiences on the importance of stability and the threats posed by legislative attacks on property.

> [S]tability in government is essential to national character and to the advantages annexed to it, as well as to that repose and confidence in the minds of the people, which are among the chief blessings of civil society. An irregular and mutable legislation is not more an evil in itself than it is odious to the people . . . [the people] will never be satisfied till some remedy be applied to the vicissitudes and uncertainties which characterize the State administrations.*[35]

He was certain the readers of *The Federalist* would know what those "vicissitudes" referred to: paper money schemes and debtor relief laws. We can see the connection in his mind between paper money, vacillating state policy, and instability in three different descriptions of the benefits of a federal veto on state legislation. To Jefferson he said that this would prevent the states from "oppressing the minority within themselves by paper money and other unrighteous measures which favor the interest of the majority."[36] To Edmund Randolph he wrote, "it will also give internal stability to the States. There has been no moment since the peace at which the Federal assent would have been given to paper money, etc., etc., . . . "[37] To Washington he argued that it would be a "control on the internal vicissitudes of State policy, and the aggressions of interested majorities on the rights of minorities and of individuals."[38]

Laws that interfered with personal property rights necessarily led to "vicissitudes" in state policy: "One legislative interference is but the first link of a long chain of repetitions, every subsequent interference being naturally produced by the effects of the preceding."[39] And the shifting interferences with the laws governing property would bring a devastating instability into the economic order.*[40] They would undermine confidence both in public engagements and in private contracts, and thus erode the prerequisites for long-term enterprise.

The republic required the proper legal framework for its economy. Neither public nor private projects could flourish unless the laws guaranteed the security of both possession and transaction. To do so the laws had to be stable as well as just. If perpetuated, the fluctuating injustice of state legislation of the 1780s would destroy the very "national character" necessary for an effective market economy: a character that honored the obligations of contract and respected the rights of property.

This connection between individual property rights and stability was central to Madison's dominant concern with each. This connection, he argued, was the lesson of the confederation.

> The sober people of America are weary of the fluctuating policy which has directed the public councils. They have seen with regret and with indignation that sudden changes and legislative interferences, in cases affecting personal rights, become jobs in the hands of enterprising and influential speculators, and snares to the more industrious and less informed part of the community . . . some thorough reform is wanting, which will banish speculations on public measures, inspire a general prudence and industry, and give a regular course to the business of society.*[41]

Instability would in the end be intolerable because it would disrupt the economy and destroy the citizens' sense of security in their rights. Only the effective protection of property from legislative infringement could prevent the instability that would ultimately destroy the republic.

There was also another way in which the protection of property was necessary to prevent popular liberty from destroying itself. If the people were able to use their power to attack property, they would soon find that they had lost their power in that pursuit.

> Liberty not less than justice pleads for the policy here recommended [providing protection for property rights by annexing a property qualification to the right to vote for senators]. If *all* power be suffered to slide into hands not interested in the rights of property, which must be the case whenever a majority fall under that description, one of two things cannot fail to happen; either they will unite against the other description and become the dupes and instruments of ambition, or their poverty and dependence will render them the mercenary instruments of wealth. In either case liberty will be subverted: in the first by a despotism growing out of anarchy, in the second, by an oligarchy founded on corruption.[42]

Madison was not simply afraid that the propertyless majority would legislate an alternative distribution of property. He saw no possibility that efforts of the poor to attain a "greater share of the blessings of life" could produce a viable alternative. The result would be anarchy. The majority were not just misguided, they were incapable of pursuing their objectives. If the propertyless should unite against the propertied, they would become the "dupes and instruments of ambition." Others would use them and their hopeless desires to rise to political power. The anarchy of the propertyless would give way to despotism. The only other possibility Madison could envision was that the propertyless would simply sell their power to the wealthy. In that case republican liberty would be replaced by oligarchy. Madison concluded, therefore, that the structure of the political system had to be able to protect property from the numerical strength and political incompetence of the propertyless. A failure to do so would mean the failure of republican government.

The arguments presented so far are compelling reasons why Madison thought the protection of property should be a central concern for republican government. But they leave open the more fundamental question of the intrinsic importance of property rights. Was property one of the two cardinal objects of government because it was as intrinsically important as the rights of persons? There is also a prior question: exactly what were the "rights of property?" Madison did not address either question directly. He spoke as though the basic meaning and value of property rights were obvious. In urging people to recognize that laws like paper money constituted a violation of property rights and to realize the consequences of such violations, he never felt called upon to define or defend those rights as such. Nevertheless, we must try to reconstruct Madison's conception of property rights in order to understand his dilemma and his choices.

The meaning of property

Madison's claim for the priority of property in *The Federalist*, No. 10, is very special and precise: the first object of government is the protection of "the faculties of men from which the rights of property originate," namely, "the different and unequal faculties of acquiring property." The context of this claim suggests a great deal about his conception of property rights. First, his argument implies that the free exercise of these faculties is a basic aspect of man's liberty. He argued that there were two ways to remove the cause of faction: one was to destroy liberty; the second was to give to every citizen the same opinions, the same passions, and the same interests. The argument ran that, if you did not destroy liberty, there were two aspects of man's exercise of liberty that would make this latter attempt impracticable: the free exercise of man's reason and the free exercise of his faculties for acquiring property. The very pairing of these aspects suggests that the restriction of the free exercise of man's faculties for acquiring property would be as fundamental a limitation on his liberty as the restriction of his use of reason would be. Despite the fact that "the most common and durable source of factions has been the various and unequal distribution of property," Madison did not seriously consider the possibility of limiting the exercise of the faculties which lead to this unequal distribution. As he had said at the outset, to cure faction by destroying liberty would be a remedy worse than the disease.

But what did it mean to protect "the different and unequal faculties of acquiring property"? Madison gave some indication in his 1792 article on property: "That is not a just government, nor is property secure under it, where arbitrary restrictions, exemptions, and monopolies deny to part of its citizens that free use of their faculties and free choice of occupations which . . . are the means of acquiring property. . . ."[43] Government should, apparently, ensure the free exercise of the faculties of acquisition by preventing unwarranted or discriminatory restrictions on this freedom. It was thus opportunity and, implicitly, equal opportunity that the phrase "faculties for acquiring property" suggested. But it was explicitly opportunity for *unequal* faculties. Madison even suggested that the rights of property had their origin in this natural inequality among men: it was the *diversity* of the faculties of men from which the rights of property originate. Madison's conception of property thus appears rooted in inequality. He was in any case explicit that, "from the protection of different and unequal faculties of acquiring property, the possession of different degrees and kinds of property immediately results."[44]

This then raises the question of what the right to acquire property meant for the right to possession. Note that Madison said that possession resulted from the protection, not from the exercise, of these faculties. The implication is that the protection of the faculties must involve protection of possession: the protection of the faculties to acquire would have no meaning if acquisition, that is, possession, did not result. And possession is only a fragile and limited physical relation to an object unless it is transformed into a right with a claim to protection. In fact, Madison explicitly said that there was a "principle of natural law, which vests in individuals an exclusive right to the portions of ground with which he has incorporated his labors."*[45] He also made the more general claim that "the personal right to acquire property, which is a natural right, gives to property, when acquired, a right to protection, as a social right."*[46]

Possession was merely a social right, but the thrust of Madison's arguments was to invest it with the sanctity of the natural right from which it derived. As *The Federalist*, No. 10, made clear, unequal possessions were the natural result of liberty; the protection of liberty implied the protection of possessions. We can thus best understand Madison's view of redistributive schemes as not simply disastrous policy, but as iniquitous violations of both liberty and justice. He referred to "a rage for paper money, for an abolition of debts, for an equal division of property, or for any other improper or wicked project."[47] Even something short of equal distribution of property looked suspect to him. He warned of Shay's Rebellion, "they profess to aim only at a reform of their constitution, and of certain abuses in the public administration, but an abolition of debts public and private, and a new division of property are strongly suspected to be in contemplation."[48]

Madison did not, however, have a simple conception of property as land or even material goods. The "faculties for acquiring property" emphasized a subtle, nonmaterial dimension of property. And the legislàtive injustice he feared was not straightforward confiscation, but the more indirect infringements inherent in paper money and debtor relief law. Those interferences with the security of expectation and transaction were the dangers to be apprehended in the new republic. They were both more likely and more invidious because they were less overt violations of property. Madison's concept of property thus had a modern, sophisticated quality that went far beyond the focus on land that we associate with the traditional image of the yeoman farmer.

Property and government

We are left with two questions about Madison's understanding of property. The first is what the proper role of the government was with respect to property. I have argued that Madison opposed laws with redistributive consequences. But we know that he did not envision a government that simply took a hands-off attitude toward property. On the contrary, "the regulation of those various and interfering [property] interests forms the principal task of modern legislation." Government had to make laws that mediated competing interests in the public good and provided the legal framework necessary to foster economic enterprise. He thought that he knew the difference between laws affecting property that amounted to unjust interferences with rights and those that constituted appropriate regulation. He did not, however, try to offer a systematic explanation of the difference. Similarly, he did not offer a theory to distinguish the redistributive schemes he branded as theft from the assistance to the indigent that he approved or from the indirect redistribution that might accompany taxation, regulation, or promotion of economic activities. Indeed, he never suggested that the need to articulate such distinctions occurred to him. I think his tacit distinction was something like the following. Tax policies and economic regulation might have some redistributive consequences, but it should not be their *objective* to benefit some at the expense of others. That was the sort of partial, self-interested legislation to be avoided. Similarly, the poor laws (about which I have found only one passing reference)[49] provided minimal assistance to the indigent out of local taxes. But the marginal redistribution involved in this sort of state-administered charity did nothing to threaten the basic security of property rights. The poor laws entailed no change in the meaning of entitlement (charity is a moral obligation on the donor with no parallel entitlement of the recipient), no instability, and, most important, an aim only to ameliorate, not redistribute as such. I think that what seemed so clearly iniquitous about the debtor relief schemes was that their purpose was redistribution—and substantial redistribution—using the power of the state to change the terms of exchange and entitlement in order to take from some and give to others. Of course, the debtors demanding relief argued that they were in a condition requiring amelioration. But Madison was certain that their demands entailed illegitimate incursions on property rights. In the end, I think the only thing that is really clear about these distinctions is that Madison thought they were clear and would be obvious to enlightened statesmen (although they would be misunderstood by the people). As we shall see, Madison tried to make sure that the sort of people who would know the difference would hold office under the new government.

Property and inequality

The second question has to do with the implications of his choice of the phrase "faculties for acquiring property." The phrase is important; it is the only formulation of the rights of property that truly applies to all. (The rights of use, possession, and transfer, for example, are applicable only to those who already have property). The first object of government is thus, at least in the first instance, not the protection of rights enjoyed only by the few. Moreover, the phrase implied equality of opportunity. From the perspective of the late twentieth century, that implies an effort to equalize opportunity. No such implication should be read into Madison's position. Madison did expect a society of great opportunity and economic mobility that would give a far more equal opportunity to all than, say, the countries of Europe, and he thought that was desirable. But he showed no evidence of concern that even in such a fluid society the inevitable inequality of possession could lead to inequality of opportunity. For Madison, the inequality of property and its advantages were part of the natural order of a free society. Madison's choice to make faculties, rather than possession or use, the starting point of his discussion was important. But it would be a mistake to import twentieth-century equalitarianism into a conception of property to which inequality was central.

We now have a clearer sense of what Madison meant by property and why he would have treated it as a priority for the new government. The inevitable inequality of property made it peculiarly vulnerable in a republic: the protection of property was part of the larger problem of protecting minority rights; property was essential to the stability and endurance of republican government; and the right of property was tied to republican liberty. We can understand why Madison would designate property as the first object of government even though he never argued that in principle the rights of property took priority over the rights of persons.

But Madison was willing to do more than direct the Framers' (and the people's and their representatives') attention to the prime importance of property. He wanted to design a government that could permanently frustrate the majority's ongoing wishes with respect to property. We thus encounter the third component of Madison's challenge, republican principles. What made Madison sufficiently confident of his judgement about the importance of property to set it above the lasting wishes of the majority? The arguments we have seen so far are compelling, but not dispositive, and, in any case, not the only components of Madison's understanding of property and republican principles.

Property and republican principles

First, it is important that in his willingness to thwart the majority's will to redistribute property, he did not have to contend with any unease about whether the presence of poverty might itself challenge the legitimacy of the property rights he was fixed on protecting. The idea that the need of the many might give them a legitimate claim against the rights of the few—and thus a moral foundation for using political power to give effect to that claim—is not simply a twentieth-century notion. We know that Madison encountered and rejected a forceful version of the contingency of property rights.

Madison's close and respected friend, Thomas Jefferson, wrote from France about his dismay over the plight of the poor and his conclusions about the necessary modifications of property rights. Madison responded with his own thoughts about the problem of the poor. Jefferson's correspondence deserves lengthy quotation because it is important to see exactly what suggestions Madison had to consider and how he chose to respond to them.

> I am conscious that an equal division of property is impracticable, but the consequences of this enormous inequality producing so much misery to the bulk of mankind, [is that] legislators cannot invent too many devices for subdividing property, only taking care to let their subdivisions go hand in hand with the natural affections of the human mind. The descent of property of every kind therefore to all the children, or to all the brothers and sisters, or other relations in equal degree is a politic measure, and a practicable one. Another means of silently lessening the inequality of property is to exempt all from taxation below a certain point, and to tax the higher portions of property in geometrical progression as they rise. Whenever there is in any country, uncultivated lands and unemployed poor, it is clear that the laws of property have been so far extended as to violate natural right. The earth is given as a common stock for man to labour and live on. If, for encouragement of industry we allow it to be appropriated, we must take care that other employment be furnished to those excluded from the appropriation. If we do not the fundamental right to labor the earth returns to the unemployed.[50]

Jefferson suggested here that property originated as a means to an end; men allowed the earth to be appropriated in order to encourage industry, which, presumably, would be to the advantage of all. But this appropriation necessarily excluded some, and Jefferson argued that the use of this means carried a responsibility to provide employment for those excluded. The rights of property were contingent on the fulfillment of this responsibility. Jefferson also suggested that since the rights of property were only a means, they must be judged by their results; they must be measured against other rights.

Madison did not comment directly on any of these suggestions.*[51] But he respectfully implied that Jefferson's perception of both the problem and the solution was too simplistic. It failed to go to the root of the problem, which was that "[a] certain degree of misery seems inseparable from a high degree of populousness." Even if the unemployed did reclaim their right to labor the earth, the problem would not be solved: "If the lands in Europe which are now dedicated to the amusements of the idle rich, were parcelled out among the idle poor, I readily conceive the happy revolution which would be experienced by a certain proportion of the latter. But still would there not remain a great proportion unrelieved?" Madison suggested that the difficulty should be seen not in terms of property laws but in terms of population.

> No problem in political economy has appeared to me more puzzling than that which relates to the most proper distribution of the inhabitants of a country fully peopled. Let the lands be shared among them ever so wisely, and let them be supplied with laborers ever so plentifully; as there must be a great surplus of subsistence, there will also remain a great surplus of inhabitants, greater by far than will be employed in clothing both themselves and those who feed them, and in administering to both, every other necessary and even comfort of life. What is to be done with this surplus?[52]

Many would be absorbed into undesirable occupations, such as domestics and soldiers, but even these occupations would not absorb them all. Once a certain level of population had been reached, even with the wisest distribution of the land and employment on the land, there would be unemployed poor left over.

An unjust system of property could, of course, exacerbate the problem, and such a system should be changed.*[53] Madison suggested in passing that a reform of the gross inequities in France was "necessary and desirable." And he said that "a more equal partition of property" would have the (presumably desirable) results of "a greater simplicity of manners, consequently a less consumption of manufactured superfluities, and a less proportion of idle proprietors and domestics." (Although his point was that this would, in fact, only make the problem of the surplus population worse, because there would be less employment for them.) But the thrust of his argument was that overpopulation, not property laws, caused poverty. One should not, therefore, draw any sweeping conclusions about the necessity or advantages of equalizing property. He implicitly warned that the suffering of the poor must itself not be taken as evidence that property should be redistributed. Since property laws were not the cause of poverty, the existence of poverty did not suggest to Madison that the laws of property ought to be reevaluated. Since the misery of some was inevitable, their needs were not rights against which the rights of property had to be balanced. In short, poverty and its attendant misery were not evidence of injustice in the system of property.

Madison could say in passing that government should do what it could to minimize poverty. And he thought a thriving commercial republic *would* minimize it. But the central issue poverty posed for a republic was not amelioration, but protecting property from the impoverished.*[54]

However confident Madison was of the inevitability of poverty and of the ineffectiveness and injustice of redistribution as a solution, he still faced the problem of setting that judgment above the will of the majority. Madison recognized that problem and struggled with it. As he saw it, the underlying issue was this:

> True it is that no other rule exists, by which any question which may divide a society, can be ultimately determined, but the will of the majority; but it is also true that the majority may trespass on the rights of the minority.[55]

Majority rule was a political principle, but it conflicted with the basic value of justice. And injustice perpetrated by a majority had no higher moral status than the injustice of a minority.

> It is well understood that interest leads to injustice as well where the opportunity is presented to . . . an interested majority in a Republic, as to the interested minority in any other form of Government.[56]

Majority rule was not itself a standard of legitimacy. Madison suggested that the majority should be prevented not only from trespassing on the rights of individuals, but from changing the form of government.

> At first view, it might not seem to square with republican theory to suppose . . . that a majority have not the right . . . to subvert a government . . . . But theoretic reasoning, in this as in most other cases, must be qualified by the lessons of practice. Why may not illicit combinations, for purposes of violence, be formed as well by a majority of a State, especially a small State, as by a majority of a county or a district of the same State . . . . [57]

But what constituted an "illicit" combination? On what principle could the majority be prevented from implementing its will, from taking steps to achieve its desire for a larger share of the benefits, or indeed, from reordering the society however it chose? Madison's answer was clear: there were "rules of justice"[58] which stood above the will of the majority. And it was clear that the rules of justice required the protection of property. The rights of property were based on natural rights. Majority rule on the other hand, "does not result . . . from a law of nature, but from compact founded on utility."[59]

The rules of justice provided Madison with a political standard of right and wrong. Majorities had the power in republican government, but force and right were not necessarily on the same side.[60] To decide that the best government was one in which the will of the majority was the final arbiter was not to declare that their will determined what was right.

> [T]here is no maxim in my opinion which is more liable to be misapplied, and which therefore more needs elucidation than the current one that the interest of the majority is the political standard of right and wrong. Taking the word "interest" as synonymous with "ultimate happiness," in which sense it is qualified with every necessary moral ingredient, the proposition is no doubt true. But taking it in the popular sense, as referring to immediate augmentation of property and wealth, nothing can be more false. In the latter sense it would be in the interest of the majority of every community to despoil and enslave the minority of individuals; . . . In fact, it is only re-establishing under another name and a more specious form, force as the measure of right.*[61]

This statement rests on Madison's understanding of "ultimate happiness." He was not simply making the distinction between permanent and temporary interests; the majority would always want the property of the minority, and efforts to give effect to such desires could never be for their "ultimate happiness." Madison built into that concept "every necessary moral ingredient." By definition, then, nothing that conflicted with the rules of justice could contribute to "ultimate happiness." This was, however, not simply a question of definitions. Madison was certain that it was *true* that unjust actions could not advance any group's ultimate happiness. Because Madison was certain that (at least in America) individuals had a just right to their property, he could unequivocally reject the idea that it might be in the true interest of the majority to claim a share of the property held by the minority. Majority rule had limited weight because the majority could not always determine their own true interest.

Where does this leave us in terms of the status of property and of republican principles in Madison's political thought? As I have suggested, the question of property can be translated into the broader terms of Madison's view of justice. Although *The Federalist*, No. 10, reflected an important connection between property and liberty, Madison more consistently spoke of infringements on property rights in terms of justice rather than liberty. The issue of justice allows us to understand how he resolved the tension between republican principles and the need to protect property.

The core of Madison's views is revealed in his claim in *The Federalist*, No. 51: "Justice is the end of government. It is the end of civil society. It ever has been and ever will be pursued until it be attained, or until liberty be lost in the pursuit."[62] Madison never defined justice. As with property, he seemed to consider the meaning of these central concepts unproblematic. Indeed, it was because they were unproblematic that property and, more broadly, justice could stand as clear limits to the legitimacy of the will of the majority. Had Madison seen these concepts as fundamentally contested—rather than merely misunderstood or neglected—the problems of treating them as standards against which to measure the will of the majority would have been far more obvious and troubling.*[63]

Despite the significant lack of definition, it is quite clear from what Madison denounced as unjust that he believed that justice entailed the security of the rights of persons and property, what we might call civil rights. If justice, the security of civil rights, was the end of government, were political rights merely the means? Were the principles of government by consent and majority rule subordinate therefore to the end of government, the security of rights required by justice? Once again, Madison did not make quite such explicit pronouncements, but we can deduce the answers.

It is clear that Madison was committed to republican government. The whole object of his efforts to form a new Constitution was to find a way to make republican government work. The question is why. What was the nature of his attachment to republican government? His arguments about representation in the new government suggest that he thought men had some intrinsic right to be bound only by those laws to which they had consented. There is the further suggestion that all men had this right equally and that, therefore, a minority could never legitimately rule the majority. But we have also seen that Madison had some ambivalence about the status of majority rule. He said both that "no other rule exists, by which any question which may divide a society, can be ultimately determined," and that majority rule was merely a "compact founded on utility." I think that Madison's views about the intrinsic value of political rights were uncertain and unexamined.

He did not inquire closely into the ways political rights might be required by the basic equality of men. He was committed to republican government primarily because it was the form best suited to achieve the basic objects of government: the welfare of the great body of the people; and justice, the protection of the rights both of persons and of property. This view of republican government is reflected in a statement quoted earlier: "the fundamental principle of republican government," which the unjust laws of the confederation period brought into question, was not that men had a right to govern themselves, but that "the majority who rule in such governments are the safest Guardians both of the public good and private rights." Madison treated the republican principles of consent and majority rule primarily as instrumental values—and instrumental not to a more general principle of self-governance, but to the objects of government. He retained his belief that republican government was the best means for securing the rights and welfare of all, but only if its dangers could be controlled. The ultimate ends of government justified modifications of what might naively be assumed to be the best means. Republican liberty had to be given effect in ways that would foster the great objects of government and thus make possible the endurance of republican government itself. To return to Madison's terms in *The Federalist*, No. 51, the purpose of political liberty was to achieve justice, and liberty would only survive to the extent that it succeeded in that purpose. To set property above the will of the majority was thus in keeping with his view that justice was the object of political liberty and, therefore, the ultimate condition for its endurance.

We thus find a coherent set of beliefs and ideas behind Madison's emphasis on the protection of property rights. The free exercise of men's different and unequal faculties for acquiring property was a basic part of their liberty. From the right to exercise these faculties followed the right to unequal amounts of property acquired, and the "rules of justice" required the protection of these, as all, individual rights. The majority had the final power in a republic, but wise policy would be made according to the rules of justice and consideration of the public good, not according to the "interests" of the majority. This was not in conflict with a commitment to the will of the majority because the "ultimate happiness" of the majority would not conflict with the rules of justice. The majority must be prevented from misguided attempts to oppress the minority on the grounds of liberty as well as justice: a society which could not secure individual rights would destroy its own liberty. Finally, the rights the majority were most likely to attack, and which were central both to man's liberty and to the stability of society, were the rights of property. It followed that the first object of republican government was to protect the rights of property.

B. The Divided Society, Public Good, and Representation

The previous section focused on property as an individual right in order to understand the value Madison accorded it. In Madison's own arguments, however, he rarely talked about individual rights (including property) separately from the public good. Indeed, implicit in the views discussed above are conceptions of the public good and of the nature of society. This section tries to render these ideas more explicit and to examine their relation to Madison's understanding of political representation. We can then see the full dimensions of Madison's theory of republican government and the role of property in it.

The divided society

For Madison, the division between the rich and the poor was one among many inevitable in civilized society. The splits would vary with circumstances, but they would always emerge.

> All civilized societies would be divided into different Sects, Factions, and Interests, as they happened to consist of rich and poor, debtors and creditors, the landed, the manufacturing, the commercial interests, the inhabitants of this district or that district, the followers of this political leader or that political leader, the disciples of this religious sect or that religious sect.[64]

As Madison saw it, this inevitable fact of divisions arose not from the particular structure of societies or governments, but from human nature itself: "The latent causes of faction are thus sown in the nature of man," although they are "brought into different degrees of activity, according to the different circumstances of civil society."[65] A statesman committed to free government had to accept the fact of conflict and division, for they could not be eliminated without eliminating liberty. Perfect harmony could only be achieved through perfect uniformity, which was impossible among free men.[66] The object of the statesman was, then, not to eliminate differences, but to understand their nature and to design a structure of government that could control their effects.

The most important divisions republican statesmen had to deal with were, as we have seen, those arising from property.[67] In America, the stark reality of a society divided between the rich and the poor could be mitigated by the economic mobility of open opportunity and by inheritance laws favoring a dispersion of property. "[I]n a government like ours a constant rotation of property results from the free scope of industry, and from the laws of inheritance . . . It does not require a long life to witness these vicissitudes of fortune."[68] Those vicissitudes would not, however, alter the basic problem of the conflict between the rich and the poor.

Madison also saw important divisions between those holding different kinds of property. "The landed, the manufacturing, the commercial" would always favor different economic and trade arrangements, and would see their interests in conflict. In Madison's view, however, the "various" distribution of property would not give rise to the same hard, inevitable line of division that the "unequal" distribution would create.[69] One split over a kind of property was, however, a serious threat. Rejecting the idea that there was an important conflict between the large and small states, he argued that "the real difference of interests lay . . . between the Northern and Southern States. The institution of slavery and its consequences formed the line of discrimination."[70] As he made clear later in his life, this division was particularly dangerous because it formed along the lines of both property and geography.

> Parties under some denominations or other must always be expected in a government as free as ours. When the individuals belonging to them are intermingled in every part of the whole Country, they strengthen the Union of the Whole, while they divide every part. Should a State of parties arise, founded on geographical boundaries and other physical and permanent distinctions which happen to coincide with them, what is to control those great repulsive Masses from awful shocks against each other?[71]

Madison considered the elimination of slavery, and thus of the dangerous division between the North and the South, as ultimately possible and extremely desirable. But at the time of the convention (and, in fact, as late as 1829 at the convention to amend the Virginia Constitution), Madison treated slavery as a political reality that could not be immediately removed. As with other divisions in society, the central task of government was not to eliminate the conflict, but to prevent one interest from oppressing the other.

The inevitable divisions in society were the source of the basic problems and tasks confronting republican government. From the "regulation of the various and interfering interests"[72] to the protection of the rights of persons and property, Madison's views of society as divided shaped his approach to republican government. Yet there was an important ambiguity about whether he saw the divisions as irreconcilable. The problems a divided society poses to republican government depend, after all, on the nature of the conflicts. Did Madison see a society in which the choice to pursue the interest of one group would entail a sacrifice of another? Did republican government have to choose between the rich and the poor?

The ambiguity over these questions arose from his use of the phrase "real or supposed" differences. For example, "What has been the source of those unjust laws complained of among ourselves? Has it not been the real or supposed interest of the major number?"[73] and ". . . as the ultramontane states may either have or suppose they have a less similitude of interests to the Atlantic states than these have to one another."[74] Because of this consistent usage it is often hard to tell whether Madison believed various groups to be in genuinely irreconcilable conflict, or merely blind to the mutuality of their interests. The North-South difference over slavery was the exception; he called it a real difference and never used the phrase "real or supposed" when referring to slavery. The divisions between different kinds of property, "the landed, the manufacturing, the commercial," Madison seemed to view as more supposed than real. He saw an ultimate mutuality of interests among them; in the long run an advantage to one would be an advantage to the others. The conflict of interests between those with and those without property was critically divisive, but even here Madison used the phrase "real or supposed," at least with respect to the interest in redistributive schemes.

> Hence the liability of rights of property, and of the impartiality of laws affecting it, to be violated by legislative majorities having an interest real or supposed in the injustice: Hence agrarian laws, and other levelling schemes: Hence the cancelling and evading of debts and other violations of contracts.[75]

In fact, as we saw earlier, Madison did not believe it was in the interest of the poor to violate the rights of the rich; it was finally in the interest of both to respect all individual rights. Madison thought that even specific measures, such as the canceling or evading of debts, were of no lasting benefit to debtors. In the long run, debtors shared with their creditors an interest in the secure protection of property and economic transactions.

> To those . . . who are involved in such encumbrances [debt], relief cannot be granted. Industry and economy are the only resources.—It is vain to wait for money, or temporize. The great desiderata are public and private confidence. . . . where justice is administered with celerity . . . confidence produces the best effects. . . . The establishment of confidence will raise the value of property and relieve those who are so unhappy as to be involved in debts. If this be maturely considered, I think it will be found that as far as it will establish uniformity of justice, it will be of real advantage to such persons.*[76]

A proper legal framework, providing just and stable laws of property and contract, would ultimately be to the benefit of all. And indeed, only such a framework could serve the long-run interests of the poor.

In the final analysis, Madison did believe that those with different kinds and amounts of property ultimately shared a common interest.

Republican government was not faced with a "zero sum" society; it did not have to choose between the rich and the poor. Why then did he consistently use the seemingly evasive phrase "real or supposed" differences? The explanation seems to be that it was inevitably the *perception* of differences that was politically relevant. As he explained to Jefferson,

> However erroneous or ridiculous these grounds of dissention and faction may appear to the enlightened statesman or the benevolent philosopher, the bulk of mankind who are neither statesmen nor Philosophers, will continue to view them in a different light.[77]

In particular, people holding different kinds and amounts of property would always perceive differences among themselves. And in the short run they would be right; any given measure was likely to be of immediate benefit to one and to the disadvantage of the other. In the case of apportionment of taxes, for example, "every shilling with which they overburden the inferior number is a shilling saved to their own pockets."[78] And again,

> Although the mutuality of interest in the interchanges useful to both [agriculture and manufacturing] may, in one view, be a bond of amity and union, yet when the imposition of taxes whether internal or external takes place, as it must do, the difficulty of equalizing the burden and adjusting the interests between the two classes is always more or less felt.[79]

The inevitability of conflict, whether over real or supposed differences, was the central political reality. And the central task of government was to deal effectively and fairly with those conflicts.

The public good

Given Madison's vision of society as characterized by both pervasive conflict and underlying common interest, it is not surprising that he saw the public good in terms of "the permanent and aggregate interests of the community."[80] In Madison's discussions, the public good emerges as the opposite of the temporary and partial objectives of men of narrow vision. The pursuit of the public good required an enlarged vision; it required seeing all the elements of the community and considering the lasting interests of this aggregate. Madison's language consistently suggested that despite the conflicts, it was possible to take a perspective that encompassed the interests of all: "The public good, the real welfare of the great body of the people, is the supreme object to be pursued." Indeed, that goal was the measure of a government's legitimacy: "no form of government whatever has any other value than as it may be fitted for the attainment of this object."[81]

The central requirement for the perception and pursuit of the public good was impartiality: "The public good is most essentially promoted by an equal attention to the interest of all." Indeed, Madison's arguments often suggest that impartiality was not merely a requirement for the public good, but the essence or content of the concept. He often spoke of the public good as though it would emerge if only the government would refrain from being partial to any one interest. In fact, however, I think Madison had a more substantive notion of the public good. He certainly believed that prosperity and national strength were essential to the public good. More particularly, the principal task of modern legislation, the regulation of the various and conflicting interests, required some judgement about which balance of these interests would promote the common good. It is also implicitly clear that not just any rules of entitlement and exchange would foster the commerce and prosperity Madison saw as part of the public good. The right kind of laws of property and contract were necessary. Madison also implied that he saw the necessity of such substantive judgments in his arguments that the discernment of the public good required wisdom as well as virtue.*[82]

It may be that Madison offered no substantive definitions of the public good, because, as with his other basic concepts, he saw its meaning as self-evident. (Although, as with property and justice, the public good was likely to be misunderstood by men who were ignorant, corrupt, or blinded by self-interest.) It may even be that he focused so heavily on impartiality because he was certain that his vision of the public good had an inherent truth to it, and that it was in fact neutral with respect to conflicting interests. If his vision was true, others (at least those with the basic political abilities) would see it, if only they looked away from their partial interests. In such a conception, the distinction between the substantive vision of the public good and the impartiality needed to achieve it disappears. The qualification, as I implied above, was that despite the objective truth of his vision, not everybody could be relied on to see it that way. The chief requirement for the public good was therefore to ensure that government was composed of men who could recognize and promote the public good.

Government in the divided society

Madison's conception of the public good and of the divided society also raises the question of what he thought government should do in response to the conflict between the propertied and those laboring under all the hardships of life. We know that government had a special responsibility to protect property rights. Did "the real welfare of the great body of the people" also entail a special responsibility to the propertyless majority? No. The only thing government could do for the propertyless was, as we have seen, ensure a prosperous economy—which meant preventing them from implementing their ill-conceived demands. The impartial pursuit of the public good, not a special concern for the propertyless, was what good government should provide. But the fact that good government must prevent the majority from implementing their unjust schemes, did not mean that Madison thought society had no collective responsibility for the indigent. Poor laws were common in most states, including Virginia, and we have some reason to believe that Madison approved of such institutions. We have one specific indication from his later years that he felt society should make some provision for the poor. In a veto message for an act incorporating the Protestant Episcopal Church in Alexandria, Madison wrote that he opposed it, because "the bill vests in the said incorporated church an authority to provide for the support of the poor and the education of poor children of the same, an authority which . . . would be a precedent for giving to religious societies as such a legal agency in carrying into effect a *public and civil duty.*"[83]

Such duties (almost certainly the duties of *state* governments) were, however, incidental to the great objects of designing a new government. Responsibility for the poor was not a subject of debate at the convention nor of Madison's writings at the time.

If Madison's conceptions of impartiality and the public good meant that government should neither try to eliminate poverty nor accede to the demands of the poor, that did not mean that the wealthy should be able to use the government to advance their interests. We know this not from his discussions of the new constitution, but from his response to Hamilton's plans in the 1790s. At the time of the convention Madison devoted almost no attention to the potential threat of the wealthy using their power to promote their own unjust plans. He saw the major threat to justice and the public good as coming from those who did not adequately respect property rights. But he thought Hamilton's plans for redemption of public securities would unjustly favor wealthy speculators. And he not only opposed Hamilton's plan for the bank as unconstitutional, he was appalled at the spectacle of men within the government deriving personal gain from governmental measures, and the wealthy successfully exerting pressure from without. The shock of his reaction is eloquent evidence that he had not foreseen, and certainly did not condone, the corrupt reciprocity that enabled the rich to use the government for their own ends.

> [M]y imagination will not attempt to set bounds to the daring depravity of the times. The stock-jobbers will become the pretorian band of the Government, at once its tool and its tyrant; bribed by its largesses and overawing it by its clamours and combinations.[84]

And again:

> It pretty clearly appears . . . what sort of hands hold [the public debt], and by whom the people of the United States are to be governed. Of all the shameful circumstances of this business, it is among the greatest to see the members of the Legislature who were the most active in pushing this Job openly grasping its emoluments.[85]

In 1791 he wrote to Jefferson that the abuses involved in the creation of the national bank and the redemption of government securities made it "a problem whether the system of the old paper under a bad Government, or of the new under a good one, be chargeable with the greater substantial injustice. The true difference seems to be that by the former the few were the victims of the many; by the latter the many to the few."[86] Both were equally abhorrent to him. His concern was with justice, and while that involved a commitment to the property rights of the minority unaffected by the inevitable misery of those without property, it forbade any favoring of the well-to-do. By 1791 he had become aware that republican government as it was constituted in the United States allowed for unjust collusion between the government and the wealthy at the expense of the public in general and the poor in particular.*[87] In response, he urged that the antagonism between the well-off and the unfavored class of the community be minimized. The evil of party divisions should be combatted:

> 1. By establishing political equality among all. 2. By withholding *unnecessary* opportunities from a few, to increase the inequality of property, by an immoderate, and especially unmerited, accumulation of riches. 3. By the silent operation of laws, which, without violating the rights of property, *reduce extreme wealth towards a state of mediocrity, and raise extreme indigence towards a state of comfort.* 4. By abstaining from measures which operate differently on different interests, and particularly such as favor one interest, at the expense of another.[88]

He made it clear that while the existence of divisions was inevitable, and his theory of the virtues of the extended republic was based on their existence, he never intended that these divisions should be increased or hardened.

> In all political societies, different interests and parties arise out of the nature of things, and the great art of politicians lies in making them checks and balances to each other. Let us then not increase these *natural distinctions* by favoring an inequality of property; . . . This is as little the voice of reason as it is of republicanism.[89]

For the first time he directly (though still not very specifically) suggested lessening the inequality of property, that is, reducing the extremes of wealth and indigence. The idea of "immoderate" accumulation of riches implied that some limit was appropriate. He took up Jefferson's phrase, "silently" operating laws, which in 1786 he had chosen not to pursue or comment upon. This was also the first time he discussed the possibility of government taking steps to mitigate the plight of the indigent, to raise them towards a state of comfort.

I think it is fair to say that Madison's concept of justice and sense of humanity always had room for such concerns, but that at the time of the convention he had not developed them. He did not see the need for addressing the problem of reducing the gap between the rich and the poor. He seems to have accepted the inevitability of the division and first turned his attention to it seriously when he saw an attempt to increase it.

It is as though he saw a natural inequality, and thus division, between the rich and the poor, that posed inevitable problems for republican government. Attempts to increase that inequality were "unnatural" and brought problems that republican government could and should avoid. His emphasis on protecting the rights of property from encroachments by the propertyless, and his comparative neglect of the potential danger of the wealthy, made sense in terms of his conception of republican government: the capacity of the wealthy to use the government for their own ends entailed a perversion of republican government, while the problem of a threat from a majority without property was inherent. His concern in the 1790s with the plight of the indigent, immoderate wealth, and a growing inequality of property were responses to perverse and unforeseen twists of governmental policy. His concern with the security of property rights was a fundamental and integral part of his theory of republican government.

The divided society in government

We turn now from the question of what government was to do about the divisions in society, to what role the divided groups should play in government. As a theorist of republican government, Madison treated this problem primarily in terms of representation, the formal institutional mechanism for allowing the different elements in society to participate in, or become a part of, the government.

Madison argued that all the various groups in society should be represented: "It is politic as well as just that the interests and rights of every class should be duly represented and understood in public councils." The representative body should be designed so that it "might equally understand and sympathize with the rights of the people in every part of the community" and that "every class of citizens should have an opportunity of making their rights felt and understood in public councils." Madison emphasized that it was necessary for all classes to be represented so that they did not have to rely on the benevolence or disinterestedness of others for the protection of their interests: "The three principal classes into which our citizens were divisible were the landed, the commercial, and the manufacturing . . . It is particularly requisite therefore that the interests of one or two of them should not be left entirely to the care or the impartiality of the third."[90]

It was even more critical that the rights and interests of the most basically divided classes, those with and those without property, not be left to the care and impartiality of the other: "Give all power to property and the indigent will be oppressed. Give it to the latter and the effect may be transposed. Give a defensive share to each and each will be secure."[91] But as we have seen, Madison thought that in popular government the rights of property were in particular need of protection. A defensive share for property could best be provided by giving it direct weight in the scheme of representation. Madison did not go so far as to say that those with property had a right to have their property as well as their persons represented. Representation of property was, however, more than simply a wise expedient; it would be appropriate: "In a general view I see no reason why the rights of property *which chiefly bears the burden of government* and is so much an object of legislation should not be represented as well as personal rights in the choice of Rulers."[92] Further, property holders deserved to have a greater role in government, because they had the most at stake. If a system of representation gave weight to property and thus gave property holders a twofold share of representation, that was proper because they had a twofold stake in society. Moreover, Madison suggested that, "In a certain sense the Country may be said to belong to [the owners of the soil]."[93]

Madison was primarily interested in the security for rights a system of representation should provide. He did speak of the justice of representation and, indeed, went so far as to say that it was a fundamental principle that "men cannot be justly bound by laws in making of which they have no part." But that principle was not as fundamental as the right to security: "Persons and property being both essential objects of Government, the most that either can claim, is such a structure of it as will leave reasonable security for the other."[94] Entitlement to representation was limited by the consequences for the security of rights. A system of representation should therefore be designed in light of the security it would provide, not on the basis of some abstract theory of entitlement.

For Madison the central question of representation was as he posed it to Caleb Wallace: "Whether . . . a representation according to numbers, or property or in a joint proportion of both [is] the most safe."[95]

> It would be happy if a State of Society could be found, or framed, in which an equal voice in making laws might be allowed to every individual bound to obey them. But this is a theory, which like most theories, confessedly requires limitations and modifications, and the only question to be decided in this as in other cases, turns on the particular degree of departure, in practice, required by the essence and object of the theory itself.[96]

We may conclude that these modifications were not disturbing to Madison because representation was first a means to secure rights and only secondly a right itself. But we may also take this philosophically resigned statement as another indication of the priority of property rights in his system; it is hard to imagine Madison making a similarly complacent statement about practical limitations of the theory of private property.*[97]

Although Madison was satisfied that it was no violation of principle to limit the rights of those without property to participate, he did indicate that there is a limit to how many people a republican government could safely exclude.[98] He discussed this most explicitly in a later statement.

> What is to be done with this unfavored class [who are "reduced by the competition for employment to the bare necessities of life"] of the community? If it be, on one hand, unsafe to admit them to a full share of political power, it must be recollected, on the other, that it cannot be expedient to rest a Republican Government on a portion of the society having a numerical and physical force excluded from, and liable to be turned against it; and which would lead to a standing military force, dangerous to all parties and to liberty itself.[99]

In considering who should be included and who excluded, Madison did not discuss the benefit to the state or the citizen of participation in public affairs. He made only two oblique references to this. He said at one point that "the more extensive a country, the more insignificant is each individual in his own eyes.—This may be unfavorable to liberty."[100] That was not said in the context of representation, and we do not have any indication that he made a connection between this insight and the sense of insignificance that might result from being excluded from a "full share of political power." Touching on the benefits of participation he said, "To the security for such a Government afforded by these combined numbers [those with and those without property] may be further added the political and moral influence emanating from the actual possession of authority and a just and beneficial exercise of it."[101] Madison did not, however, elaborate on this idea and it did not play a part in his discussion of systems of representation.

Representation and the public good

Madison's emphasis on ensuring that all groups had the necessary representation did not mean that his vision of representation consisted of the promotion of constituents' interests. His derogatory description of the members of Congress in 1785 was that they were merely "advocates for the respective interests of their constituents."[102] The higher responsibility of representatives was to promote the public good, which could not be furthered if representatives simply considered the rights and interests of their own constituents.

> The evil is fully displayed in the County representations, the members of which are everywhere observed to lose sight of the aggregate interests of the Community, and even to sacrifice them to the interests or prejudices of their respective constituents. In general these local interests are miscalculated. But it is not impossible for a measure to be accommodated to the particular interests of every County or district, when considered by itself, and not so when considered in relation to each other and to the whole State.[103]

The public good, which meant the true interest of all groups, could only be furthered by taking a view of the whole and looking toward the good of this whole. Finding a system of government in which this would be done was one of Madison's most difficult problems: "the great desideratum which has not yet been found for Republican Governments seems to be some disinterested and dispassionate umpire in disputes between different passions and interests in the State."[104] But how was this possible in a divided society with a system of representation which gave a voice to every interest and in which those who were to balance and adjudicate between conflicting interests were also the representatives of those interests? Madison defined this problem as a central one. He declared that "the regulation of these various and interfering interests forms the principal task of modern legislation and involves the spirit of party and faction in the necessary and ordinary operations of government."[105]

Madison said that a system cannot rely on enlightened statesmen to "adjust these clashing interests and render them all subservient to the public good."[106] But while he thought it would be unwise for a system of government to rely solely on having enlightened statesmen, "[T]he aim of every political constitution is, or ought to be, first to obtain for rulers men who possess most wisdom to discern, and most virtue to pursue the common good of the society."[107] Madison was quite explicit that representatives should be "guardians of the public weal,"[108] men able to take into view "indirect and remote considerations,"[109] men whose "enlightened views and virtuous sentiments render them superior to local prejudices."[110] He repeatedly referred to both wisdom and virtue; virtue alone was not sufficient.

> A good government implies two things: first, fidelity to the object of government, which is the happiness of the people; secondly a knowledge of the means by which that object can be best obtained. . . . Most governments are deficient in the first. I scruple not to assert that in American governments too little attention has been paid to the last.[111]

For Madison, the business of governing required more than good intentions. In particular, the framing of laws required talent and education,[112] and could best be done by a "few select and skillful individuals."[113] He later said explicitly that an advantage of "learned institutions" is that they "multiply the educated individuals from among whom the people may elect a due portion of their public Agents of every description; more especially of those who are to frame the laws."[114]

The guardians of the public weal must, then, be specially qualified. Here the question of property entered the issue of representation once again. Madison never said explicitly that it was men of property who had the necessary qualifications. But if we look at the language he used, we see that the attributes of those best suited to govern were those he associated with the property holders.*[115] Education and "superior information" are clearly "incident" to property holders.[116] The connection Madison made between respectability and property holding appears most clearly when we see that the mechanisms (such as large election districts) which would select men of respectability were also those which would select men sympathetic to the rights of property (who, we have seen, could only be property holders). We see the connection clearly drawn again when he described different groups' responses to the Constitution. He spoke of "the men of intelligence, patriotism, property and independent circumstances,"[117] and again, "men of abilities, of property, and of influence."[118] He clearly thought that men of property were generally those best suited to govern. He also expected that the voters would think so and take that into consideration: voters would "discriminate between real and ostensible property" in the candidates for office more effectually than property qualifications for office could do.[119]

The role Madison envisioned for the propertied also went beyond his hopes that they would hold office. He also recognized that their formal participation in government would be augmented by their informal influence.

> States have not like individuals, an influence over each other arising from superior advantages of fortune. If the law allows an opulent citizen but a single vote in the choice of his representative, the respect and consequence which he derives from his fortunate situation very frequently guide the votes of others to the objects of his choice.[120]

That informal influence would add a salutory counterweight to the numerical power of the poor.[121]

The different ways in which Madison talked about the nature and function of government in a divided society reveal a tension between his image of the men of property as those most likely to understand the public good and his presentation of property as an interest in need of protection and capable of oppression. Sometimes Madison emphasized the importance of representing all competing interest groups (as we would call them today). At other times he painted a picture of impartial and enlightened statesmen who could transcend mere interests to pursue the public good. Although he warned against relying on enlightened statesmen, he consistently focused on how to get them in office. He did not try to work out the tensions between his interest group approach and his vision of enlightened statesmen. The regulation of competing interests would involve the "spirit of party and faction in the necessary and ordinary operations of government," but he wanted representatives who could rise above party and faction so that the regulation would be in the public interest. The problem proved to be a serious one because property was both an interest competing with others and a right whose protection was essential for the public good. When Madison focused, as he most often did, on the sort of men capable of promoting the public good, the interest group status of property became submerged in the twin images of property's relation to the public good and to the prerequisites of leadership. Republican government had to deal with a perpetually divided society. And there was no simple mesh between Madison's objectives of providing an effective defense for all classes and ensuring a government capable of promoting the public good and providing the security for property necessary for liberty, justice, and the endurance of republican government. Without fully recognizing the tensions, Madison set himself the challenge of achieving these objectives while implementing republican principles.

II. The Republican Solution to Republican Problems

A. The House

The basic republican principle that all power should be derived from the great body of the people, not from any favored class of it,[122] was to be implemented in the popular election of the first branch of the legislature. Madison considered "the popular election of one branch of the national Legislature as essential to every plan of free Government."[123] Without this direct election, "the people would be lost sight of altogether; and the necessary sympathy between them and their rulers and officers, too little felt."[124] Madison also wanted to insure both this sympathy and adequate local information by doubling the number of representatives the convention had agreed on.[125] "He was an advocate for the policy of refining the popular appointments by successive filtrations, but thought it might be pushed too far."[126] He thought that the government would be more secure if based on the popular election of one branch: "[T]he great fabric to be raised would be more stable and durable if it should rest on the solid foundation of the people themselves, than if it should stand merely on the pillars of the [state] Legislatures."[127]

For Madison the popular election of the first branch ensured that the people would be given an opportunity to make their wishes felt in the government. They would have the share of political liberty that justice and policy required. This achieved, Madison devoted his attention to the inherent problems of republican government. While the popular base would in some sense be the root of these problems, Madison also thought that the direct election of a national legislature would itself mitigate the danger of faction. It was the first step in framing a "republican system on such a scale and in such a form as will control all the evils which have been experienced."[128] Election by the people of the whole nation would render the national legislature less susceptible to the factions that flourished in the more contracted sphere of the state governments. In a truly national government, as opposed to a government based on the state governments, the community would be divided into "so great a number of interests and parties," that it would be unlikely and difficult for a majority to unite in pursuit of an "interest separate from that of the whole or of the minority."[129]

Nevertheless, Madison thought additional precautions were necessary. He was intent upon removing the first branch of the legislature as much as possible from the passions and excesses of the people. The first means of achieving this was to have large election districts. Representatives elected by large numbers of electors would be the most independent and the least susceptible to undue influence.[130] And the best men were more likely to prevail in large districts.

> [I]t will be more difficult for unworthy candidates to practice with success the vicious arts by which elections are too often carried; and the suffrages of the people being more free, will be more likely to center on men who possess the most attractive merit and the most diffusive and established characters.[131]

In Madison's mind the best men were those "whose enlightened views and virtuous sentiments render them superior to local prejudices and to schemes of injustice."[132] Such independent and enlightened men would be capable of fulfilling their true task as representatives, which was not simply to implement, but to refine the views of their constituents. In particular, men of "established characters" would be the most likely to resist unjust schemes that would violate the rights of property. In 1821, he was particularly explicit that large election districts would favor those attached to the rights of property (the propertied).

> A resource favorable to the rights of landed and other property, when its possessors become the minority, may be found in an enlargement of the Election districts for one branch of the Legislature . . . large districts are manifestly favorable to the election of persons of general respectability, and of probable attachment to the rights of property . . . .[133]

Despite his view that men of property were the best suited to govern, Madison did not favor qualifications of property in the members of the Legislature. He expected the voters to do a better job of discerning whether candidates were men of substantial property than formal qualifications could.[134] Appropriate qualifications would be difficult to specify in a simple rule, for "if a small quantity of land should be made the standard, it would be no security—if a large one, it would exclude the proper representatives of those classes of Citizens who were not landholders."[135] (By the latter he meant not the propertyless, but the merchants and manufacturers.)

Madison also rejected the apportionment of representatives in the House on the basis of wealth as well as population. This plan, too, was not wrong, just unnecessary. The principled argument for basing apportionment on wealth was that "[r]epresentation and taxation were to go together; that taxation and wealth ought to go together, that population and wealth were not measures of each other." Madison did not reject the relation between representation and wealth in principle; but he argued that although the number of inhabitants was never an accurate measure of wealth, "in the United States it was sufficiently so for the object in contemplation."[136]

In designing the House, Madison focused on the less direct, more general, and, he thought, more effective protections provided by large election districts, with the additional precaution of a relatively long term. A three-rather than two-year term would help remedy "one of the greatest vices of our republics," instability.

> The tendency of longer period of service would be, to render the Body more stable in its policy, and more capable of stemming popular currents taking a wrong direction, till reason and justice could regain their ascendancy.[137]

Property rights in particular would benefit because they were especially subject to wrong-headed popular currents and because reason and justice were clearly on their side. Madison seemed to have some confidence that the unjust passions of the people were likely to pass and that, given time, reason and justice would prevail. It would thus be an advantage to the propertied and ultimately, of course, to all, if the representatives were removed from the immediate pressure of the people's demands.

For Madison, the greatest difficulty in designing the House was the question of suffrage. Here the goals of implementing republican principles and solving the problems inherent in republican government seemed incompatible. On the one hand there was "the fundamental principle that men cannot be justly bound by laws in making of which they have no part,"—a principle that would not be satisfied by "an indirect share of representation," such as the appointment of senators by directly elected state legislatures. On the other hand, "the freeholders of the Country would be the safest depositories of Republican liberty," both public and private. It was the latter point that he stressed to the convention.

> In future times a great majority of the people will not only be without landed, but any other sort of, property. These

> will either combine under the influence of their common situation; in which case, the rights of property and the public liberty will not be secure in their hands: or which is more probable, they will become the tools of opulence and ambition, in which case there will be equal danger on another side.[138]

Madison then continued on to rebut George Mason's objections to a freehold qualification. Madison presented freehold suffrage as the best plan. But he also suggested that its merits were not the only consideration: "Whether the Constitutional qualification ought to be a freehold would with him much depend on the probable reception such a change would meet with in States where the right was now exercised by every description of people."[139] There is no record of whether he voted for what he considered the best plan (as he so often urged his fellow delegates to do) or whether in this instance he felt it necessary to support a position which would give the Constitution the support of the people.*[140]

Although Madison did argue for freehold suffrage, he was uneasy about it. In a footnote to his notes on the debate over suffrage, he wrote that "[t]he most difficult of all political arrangements is that of so adjusting the claims of the two Classes as to give security to each, and to promote the welfare of all." He suggested that the federal structure of the American republic offered a solution that did not require infringement on republican principles.

> The federal principle, which enlarges the sphere of power without departing from the elective basis of it, and controls in various ways the propensity in small republics to rash measures and the facility of forming and executing them, will be found the best expedient yet tried for solving the problem.[141]

B. The Senate

Madison had a clear sense of the structure of the federal government necessary to complement the advantages of an extended sphere. It required first a divided legislature. The division itself would "protect the people against their rulers." But Madison also wanted the second branch designed to "protect the people against the transient impressions into which they themselves might be led."[142] The first branch, despite the advantages of large election districts, was likely to partake of the weaknesses of the people. The people were "liable to temporary errors through want of information as to their true interest, and . . . men chosen for a short term [two years had been agreed upon], and employed but a small portion of that in public affairs, might err from the same cause." Both the people and "a numerous body of Representatives, were liable to err also, from fickleness and passion."[143] Madison wanted the Senate to counterbalance these weaknesses. It should first of all be small, for "the more the representatives of the people were multiplied, the more they partook of the infirmities of their constituents."[144] A small Senate could be "a more select body . . . generally a more capable set of men."[145] It should also have a long term (Madison proposed nine years without re-eligibility)[146] in order to give the government essential stability the first branch would lack. The long term would also give the Senate the opportunity to acquire "a competent knowledge of the public interests,"[147] as opposed to the mistaken understanding the people and their representatives in the House were likely to have.

Madison particularly wanted the Senate to prevent the popular branch from violating property rights. It was in discussing the function of the Senate that he gave the warning noted earlier: "an increase in population will of necessity increase the proportion of those who will labor under all the hardships of life, and secretly sigh for a more equal distribution of its blessings."[148] When these became the majority, all power would slide into their hands, and the warning of the dangers this would bring was already to be seen in the "leveling spirit" which had appeared in certain quarters. The Senate was to guard against this danger and against all "interested coalitions to oppress the minority" as "a body sufficiently respectable for its wisdom and virtue, to aid on such emergencies, the preponderance of justice by throwing its weight into that scale."[149]

Madison also suggested that since the second branch was to protect property, it should represent property. He always considered it a good idea to have one branch particularly protect the rights of persons, and the other, the rights of property.[150] He generally spoke of this in terms of restricting the suffrage for one branch, an issue that did not come up because the convention adopted the plan of appointment by state legislatures. Rufus King quotes Madison as opposing this plan on the grounds that "the Senate ought to come from and represent the wealth of the nation."[151] The specific proposal Madison offered for representing property was not in terms of suffrage, but apportionment: "He suggested that . . . in the first branch the States should be represented according to their number of free inhabitants; And in the second which had for one of its primary objects the guardianship of property, according to the whole number, including slaves."*[152] In *The Federalist*, No. 54, Madison put a similar argument in the mouth of a hypothetical Southerner defending the three-fifths clause in the apportionment of the first branch. He began by asserting again that "[g]overnment is instituted no less for protection of the property than the persons of individuals." In some states, therefore, "one branch of the government is intended more especially to be the guardian of property and is accordingly elected by that part of the society which is most interested in this object of government." This policy did not, however, prevail in the federal Constitution. "The rights of property are committed into the same hands with the personal rights. Some attention ought, therefore, to be paid to property in the choice of those hands."

Once it was clear that the Senate was to be composed of an equal number of members from each state, appointed by the state legislatures, both of Madison's plans for *representing* property through suffrage or apportionment became irrelevant. The capacity of the Senate to *protect* property remained an objective, to be achieved by the small size of the body and the length of the term.

C. The Executive

Madison wanted to provide yet another check on the legislature through an executive veto. He argued, therefore, that the tenure and mode of election of the executive had to give him the independence necessary to stand up against legislative injustice. In making these arguments, Madison warned again that republican government could not survive if it could not provide a solution to the injustice and instability witnessed during the confederation.

> Experience had proved a tendency in our governments to throw all power into the Legislative vortex . . . . If no effectual check can be devised for restraining the instability and encroachments of the latter, a revolution of some kind or other would be inevitable.[153]

The object of the veto was both to protect the executive from encroachments on his power and to "control the National Legislature, so far as it might be infected with a . . . propensity" like that of the state legislatures to "a variety of pernicious measures."[154] In particular, a "negative in the Executive is . . . necessary . . . for the safety of a minority in Danger of oppression from an unjust and interested majority."[155]

Madison did not, however, support an absolute veto. He thought a qualified veto would serve the same purpose; it would make it more difficult for the legislature to pass unjust laws. And in any case, he thought "it would rarely if ever happen that the Executive, constituted as ours is proposed to be, would have firmness enough to resist the Legislature, unless backed by a certain part of the body itself."*[156]

Madison clearly advocated a strong and independent executive, but he was not certain about the means to achieve this. He was certain, however, that election by the national legislature would make the executive too dependent to exercise his veto power (or any other power) wisely and forcefully.*[157] He advocated either election by "the people or rather by the qualified part of them" or by electors chosen by the people.[158] He thought the former "the fittest in itself."

> It would be as likely as any [means] that could be devised to produce an Executive Magistrate of distinguished Character. The people generally could only know and vote for some Citizen whose merits had rendered him an object of general attention and esteem.[159]

There was, however, an important practical problem with direct election of the executive. The Northern states would have a greater weight in such an election because "the right of suffrage was more diffusive in the Northern than the Southern states."[160] A system of electors would even out the disparities between the proportion of qualified voters in the two sections of the country. Madison was not worried that this system would fail to foster a close tie between the citizens and the executive and thus would be less desirable than direct elections. His arguments in favor of direct election were not based on such ties, but on the best means of selecting a man who could fulfill the responsibilities of office.

Madison also did not seem to have a firm idea about what tenure would be best. He rarely participated in the debates on the subject. But he did seem willing to consider even tenure during good behavior in order to get a strong and independent executive (provided there was an impeachment procedure, which Madison strongly advocated in any case).[161] King's notes of the convention debates for 2 June say that Madison favored a term of "seven years and an exclusion forever—or during good behaviour."[162] He also lent support to McClurg's motion for such tenure by arguing strenuously for the need of an independent executive who would be more than the "Cyphers" the state executives were. But he added that the "genuine principles" of republican government "should be kept in view" and noted that he had contributed his support primarily out of respect for Dr. McClurg. The real choice came to be, as he described it to Jefferson, between a short term with a capacity to be reelected or a longer term with subsequent ineligibility. The problem was which would be safer and more likely to result in an "independent administration, and a firmer defence of the constitutional rights of the department."[163]

D. The Council of Revision

Madison thought that in either case the executive alone would be too weak to stand up to the encroachments or the injustice of a popular legislature. It was in the nature of republican government that it could not give "to an individual citizen that settled pre-eminence in the eyes of the rest, that weight of property, that personal interest against betraying the National interest, which appertain to an hereditary magistrate."[164] He was vulnerable therefore to both attack and corruption, and he could not therefore be relied on to fulfill his vital function of checking the legislature. Madison's solution was to give the judiciary a share in the revisionary power. This would both "double the advantage and diminish the danger."[165] It would "inspire" the executive with "additional confidence and firmness in exerting the revisionary power."[166]

The joint council of revision would also have only a qualified veto in Madison's scheme.

> [A]ll acts before they become laws should be submitted both to the Executive and Supreme Judiciary Departments . . . if either of these should object 2/3 of each House, if both should object, 3/4 of each House, should be necessary to overrule the objections and give to the acts the force of law.[167]

It seems likely that Madison advocated the council of revision because he preferred it to judicial invalidation of laws. John Francis Mercer supported Madison's proposal[168] with an argument that Madison made explicitly later: "He disapproved of the Doctrine that the Judges as expositors of the Constitution should have authority to declare a law void. He thought laws ought to be well and cautiously made, and then to be uncontrollable."[169]

The joint council of revision was one of Madison's most cherished ideas. He argued that,

> whether the object of the revisionary power was to restrain the Legislature from encroaching on the other co-ordinate Departments, or on the rights of the people at large; or from passing laws unwise in their principle, or incorrect in their form, the utility of annexing the wisdom and weight of the Judiciary to the Executive seemed incontestable.*[170]

Madison planned to ensure that the judges would have the wisdom and uprightness to veto unjust laws by excluding the first branch from the appointment of the judges.[171]

The judicial role in a council of revision would not only give added weight and firmness to the executive in exercising revisionary powers,

> it would be useful to the Legislature by the valuable assistance it would give in preserving a consistency, conciseness, perspicuity and technical propriety in the laws, qualities peculiarly necessary; and yet shamefully wanting in our republican Codes. It would moreover be useful to the Community at large as an additional check against a pursuit of those unwise and unjust measures which constituted so great a portion of our calamities.[172]

Madison was unswayed by his colleagues' arguments that judges should not be involved in legislation. Elbridge Gerry argued that "it was quite foreign from the nature of [the judicial] office to make them judges of the policy of public measures."[173] Rufus King made the point that "judges ought to be able to expound the law as it should come before them, free from the bias of having participated in its formation."[174] But Madison rejected the idea that giving the judiciary a role in the council of revision would violate the separation of powers. On the contrary, he argued, this additional check would give real effect to the separation of powers by enabling the judiciary to defend itself from encroachments.

> If a Constitutional discrimination of the departments on paper were a sufficient security to each against encroachments of the others, all further provisions would indeed be superfluous. But experience has taught us that it is necessary to introduce such a balance of powers and interests, as will guarantee the provisions on paper.[175]

Madison was, in effect, trying to explain to his colleagues that the system they were designing relied not only on a separation of powers, but on checks and balances, and that implementing both involved a complex tension between the two. The checks the different branches were designed to provide against each other would only work if they were not strictly excluded from each other's sphere. The very capacity to check the legislature meant intervening in the legislative sphere (e.g., through a veto), which was what would give the executive—and, Madison hoped, the judiciary—the ability to ensure that the separation of powers would not be destroyed by legislative encroachment. Madison tried to get his colleagues to see that, logically, the executive veto involved the same sort of blurring of separate spheres as an executive-judicial veto, and that only such blurring could sustain the separation that was crucial. (His colleagues had no answers to these subtle arguments. But it was clear to them that the judiciary should be separate from the legislature, and they simply voted Madison's proposal down.)

Madison kept returning to the idea of a joint council of revision, arguing for it strenuously. He believed that only the combined weight of the executive and the judiciary could provide the necessary multiple checking function. Only this joint strength could counteract the injustice and instability of the legislature. And only an effective veto could uphold the balanced structure of government necessary for both public and private liberty.

E. The National Veto

The institutions discussed above form the basic structure Madison advocated for the new government. It was, in essence, a carefully designed, *republican* system of checks on the people. The great body of the people would, indeed, be the basis of the government, but their views would be refined and improved upon in the first branch and controlled by the greater stability, wisdom, and justice in the second. If that failed, the council of revision would give their considered and informed advice and put at least a temporary halt to unjust or ill-conceived measures.

This careful federal structure was, however, not alone sufficient to meet Madison's objectives. He not only wanted to make it difficult for the people to perpetrate injustice at the national level, he wanted to *prevent* them from doing so in the states. Before, during, and after the convention Madison consistently argued that the national legislature should be given a veto over state laws. The factional conflict which had caused injustice and instability would continue to flourish at the state level, whereas the national government would have the advantages of an extended sphere and a structure of "successive filtrations." It should therefore use its advantages to act as an umpire for the conflicts within and between the states.[176]

> The great desideratum which has not yet been found for Republican Governments seems to be some disinterested and dispassionate umpire in disputes between different passions and interests in the State. . . . Might not the national prerogative here suggested be found sufficiently disinterested for the decision of local questions of policy, whilst it would itself be sufficiently restrained from the pursuit of interests adverse to the whole society.[177]

The national government could then protect property and other minority rights within the jurisdiction of state law as well; a national veto would be a "control on the internal vicissitudes of State policy, and the aggressions of interested majorities on the rights of minorities and of individuals."[178] He thought such a restraint was necessary both because it was part of the responsibility of the new government to ensure stability and the steady dispensation of justice, and because injustice within the states critically affected the national interest. States were likely to disrupt the national economy directly by violating treaties and harassing each other with "rival and spiteful measures dictated by mistaken views of interest."[179] Equally important, unjust practices within the states, such as depreciating currency and debtor relief laws, would not only undermine the economy internally, but would give the whole nation a bad reputation abroad. It was essential that the basic rules necessary for a thriving economy were observed throughout the country. Only a broadly defined national veto could exert the kind of ongoing control over internal state practices necessary to ensure the proper rules of economic conduct. Madison's original proposal would have given the national legislature the power to "negative all laws passed by the several States contravening in the opinion of the National Legislature the articles of the Union."[180] Specific prohibitions, such as that on impairment of contracts, were inadequate: "Evasions might and would be devised by the ingenuity of the Legislatures."[181] The judicial process was too slow: the states "can pass laws which will accomplish their injurious objects before they can . . . be set aside by the National Tribunals."[182]

Finally, the veto on state laws was necessary for justice and stability in yet a more general way. Since the most important part of Madison's solution to the problem of faction and majority oppression was the extended republic, it was essential that the general government actually have the power to govern over the entire country.*[183] In Madison's view the veto was a necessary part of that power; it was "essential to the efficacy and security of the General Government."[184] It would allow the federal government to prevent encroachments by the states and to enforce its basic law and treaties without resort to force.[185]

The national veto was one more means of protecting the federal government from encroachments that would undermine the very structure upon which Madison placed so much reliance. In a republic, the legislatures, both state and federal, threatened not only unjust and unwise laws, but an expansion of power that would suck all other branches into their "vortex." Like the council of revision, the national veto was therefore aimed not only at directly preventing unjust legislation, but at ensuring that the careful federal structure of institutional power would survive the inevitable pressure from state and federal legislatures.

III. Conclusion

Madison designed a structure of government to meet demanding objectives: to establish a strong national government capable of providing justice, security, stability, and prosperity. The government had to be strong enough to defend its interests abroad and to assure the stability and justice at home necessary for a prosperous and enduring republic. These objectives were to be met in the context of the challenge Madison posed to himself: to design a government true to republican principles that could protect the rights of both persons and property. I close with the question of whether his proposal for the new government succeeded by his own standards.

In some ways, Madison's national objectives were distinct from his attempt to design a republican government in which the rights of persons and property were secure. He wanted a government that could hold its own among other nations, that could both defend itself and secure the credit necessary for public and private enterprise. The new government should not have the dependence on the states or the limits to its power that had paralyzed and humiliated the government under the Articles of Confederation. And the federal government should be able to ensure a thriving economy in a truly national market. These goals were basic to Madison's vision of the new republic, and they were not derived from his concern with the problem of rights in a republic. But these concerns also overlapped in ways that shaped the structure Madison designed.

As we have seen, justice, security, stability, and prosperity all either entailed or required the protection of both persons and property. And these objectives stood in a reciprocal relation to a strong national government. Only a central government with sufficient scope and power could prevent the instability and injustice that had characterized the Articles of Confederation. Conversely, if the federal government did not promote just and stable policies, then it would lose its power: its strength, efficacy, and international reputation would be eroded and ultimately destroyed. The federal government could only serve the multiple purposes Madison envisioned if it had the power to pursue national objectives and secure rights without itself becoming a threat. Every aspect of Madison's carefully constructed structure was designed to further these ends. The separation of powers, the differently structured branches of the legislature, the system of representation, and the mutual checking function of the legislative, executive, and judiciary were all designed both to give the government adequate power and to contain the threats inherent in republican government.

One of those threats was the traditional one posed by any system of government: the rulers pursuing their own power or advantage. Madison was confident that his structure would make it difficult for those in office to usurp power or promote their interests at the expense of the people. But his primary concern was not this conventional problem, but the special challenge of republican government. The political liberty that made a government "republican" was itself a threat to the purpose of that liberty, the security of rights. Madison's effort to make republican liberty compatible with that security was guided by his focus on the vulnerability of property as the paradigmatic republican problem. His solution could not be simply to give the federal government so little power or efficacy that it could pose no serious threat. Not only did his national objectives require strong, effective government, but the security of rights did as well. The source of republican problems was faction, particularly majority faction, and the federal government was uniquely suited to solve that problem. A federal government designed to take advantage of its extended sphere was the essence of Madison's republican solution. It was truly a republican solution in that it relied on the structure of representative institutions rather than limits to those institutions.

The "successive filtrations," beginning with the refinement of the people's views by representatives capable of an enlarged and enlightened perspective, were checks that largely built upon, rather than stood in opposition to, republican principles. Madison was intent upon making it as difficult as possible for the people to use their political power in ways that threatened property or, more generally, individual rights or the public good. But his solution was not to try to establish the rights either of property or of persons as enforceable limits to the sovereignty of the people. He was not in favor of what we have come to know as the chief institutional means of protecting individual rights from democratic excess: the power of the federal judiciary to overturn both state and federal laws on constitutional grounds.

> In the State Constitutions and indeed in the Federal one also, no provision is made for the case of a disagreement in expounding them; and as the Courts are generally the last in making the decision, it results to them by refusing or not refusing to execute a law, to stamp it with its final character. This makes the Judiciary Department paramount in fact to the Legislature, which was never intended and can never be proper.[186]

Madison's preferred plan of a council of revision would have put a significant check on the ability of the legislature to implement its will, but would have left the final authority with the representatives of the people. He did seem to expect that the federal judiciary would have the power to invalidate *state* laws, but preferred a national legislative veto as more effective.[187] Such a veto would have placed the primary responsibility for overseeing state laws in a legislature, rather than in a judiciary empowered to treat rights as limits to legislative authority.

The genuinely republican character of Madison's solution does not, however, answer the question of whether it met his own standards. The problem with Madison's admirable plan of government lies in the guiding force of his preoccupation with protecting property from the inevitable threat of the majority. This preoccupation—justified from his perspective in the numerous ways outlined above—led to his perception of the people as a threat and thus to his persistent preoccupation with containing, confining, and channeling their power. His concern with protecting property focused his attention on the *problems* of republican government, leaving republican principles as largely unexamined assumptions. "Public liberty" was an inherent part of Madison's conception of republican government, but he treated the political rights it entailed as the source of the problems he had to solve, rather than as an objective he sought to achieve. The center of his attention was not on the forms of participation required by republican principles, but on how to achieve justice without sacrificing liberty. At each step of his plan, he paused to make sure it was consistent with republican principles, but the objective of each institution was to promote stability and justice. Madison's plan did not thwart republican principles; rather it subtly undermined them in its allocation of effective political power.*[188]

If all of his preferences had prevailed, the federal system would have "modified" political rights in important ways. Madison would have given property weight in the Senate and restricted the suffrage for the direct election of the executive, and he thought a restriction of suffrage in the House was preferable. Thus, at best, only the House would have been selected by the great body of the people. And even the House can hardly be said to have been "drawn" from the great body of the people, since it, like all the branches, was designed to put men of property in office. Madison acknowledged the need for the modification of political rights. But these modifications had consequences for the rights of the propertyless that he did not acknowledge.

Under Madison's plan, would not the interests of the propertyless be "left to the care and impartiality" of the propertied, a situation he condemned with respect to competing property interests?[189] Was this a system of institutions designed so that the officers of government would "equally understand and sympathize with the rights of the people in every part of the community" and in which "every class of citizens [would] have an opportunity of making their rights be felt and understood in public councils?"[190] Clearly it was not for the propertyless. By limiting their participation, Madison chose property not only over political rights, but over the security of the rights of persons to which the propertyless were entitled. Madison's understanding of the importance of property rights and what was required to protect them made it impossible for the propertyless to have the power within the government necessary either to secure their rights or to enjoy a full share of political liberty.

In 1787 the importance of the rights of persons and the right to participate in the making of the laws were assumptions in the back of Madison's mind. The protection of property was the object he held steadily before him as he worked on the Constitution. This focus cast "the people," the future majority, in the role of a problem to be contained, and tipped the balance among the competing values he sought to implement.

Madison set an exacting challenge for himself and for the new republic: to protect the rights of persons and of property and to implement the political rights required by republican principles. Madison's proposal for the new Constitution was an impressive effort, but it did not meet the challenge he set.

3 Aristocratic Capitalism: The Federalist Alternative of Gouverneur Morris

Gouverneur Morris was one of Madison's most important and interesting allies at the Constitutional Convention of 1787. He was an ardent Federalist and a strong supporter of the Constitution. Indeed, he is credited with writing the final version of the document. But he also disagreed with Madison and his fellow Federalists over crucial issues. In retrospect, he serves as a particularly forthright and insightful critic whose observations go to the heart of the Constitution's values and weaknesses.

He thought his fellow Framers had misunderstood the problem posed by the central fact of political life: the conflict between the rich and the poor, the few and the many. The Constitution was designed to contain the threat of the many: the danger of democratic excess and the tyranny of the majority. But the most serious danger in a *commercial* republic was, Morris argued, the power of the wealthy; the new institutions would only exacerbate that danger.

Morris was a true student of political economy. His most important contribution was his keen sense of the interaction between economic and political power and of the need to provide mutually sustaining institutions in the two realms. His vision of the new republic was that of a market economy. The government should ensure the necessary stability and legal framework for such an economy, and the resulting prosperity would give the new nation strength and respect at home and abroad. Morris's candor and bluntness make it particularly easy to see the implications of his positions for the dominant mode of thought at the convention and for the Constitution it produced. He frequently articulated values and assumptions which were left unstated and unexamined in the thought of his fellow Federalists. In other instances, such as his commitment to a market economy, his ideas were starker and more settled than those which prevailed. He provides a counterpoint against which the ambiguities and confusions of other views stand out. His clear and unqualified positions illuminate some of the most important and contested issues in American political thought: the status our Constitution accords to political liberty and to private property, the relation between the values of republicanism and those of capitalism, and the distribution of economic and political power our system fosters.

I. The Priority of Property in the Market Republic

Gouverneur Morris was unhesitating in his conviction that property was the primary object of government. "Life and liberty," he told his fellow Framers, "were generally said to be of more value than property." This was, however, mistaken:

> [P]roperty was the main object of Society. The savage state was more favorable to liberty than the Civilized; and sufficiently so to life. It was preferred by all men who had not acquired a taste for property; it was only renounced for the sake of property which could only be secured by the restraints of regular Government.[1]

Whatever their intrinsic values, life and liberty were not the reasons men joined together in societies and formed governments. It was only for the sake of property that men gave up the greater freedom of the state of nature and submitted themselves to the constraints of society and government. For Morris, this "fact" gave property an absolute primacy among the objects of government. And this primacy was the theoretical foundation he claimed for all his arguments.

Property was not only the origin of society, it was the source of all the benefits of civilization. The value of property lay in its security, and it was for security that men joined together, and security which civilization required.

> Property in Goods is the first Step in Progression from a State of Nature to that of Society. Till property in Lands be admitted Society continues rude and barbarous. After the Lands are divided a long Space intervenes before perfect Civilization is effected. Progress will be accelerated in Proportion as the Administration of Justice is more or less exact . . . . This Conclusion results that the State of Society is perfected in Proportion as the Rights of Property are secured.*[2]

The relation between justice and the security of property is central to Morris's political thought. Although he prided himself on his hard-nosed realism, he insisted that justice and morality were essential to the objects of government. "What constitutes the Happiness of a Man, of all the World ? The same applies to each. Virtue. Obedience to the moral law . . . Justice."[3] He did not treat this as a mere platitude. "Virtue once gone," he wrote to Thomas Jefferson, "freedom is but a name; for I do not believe it to be among possible contingencies, that a corrupted people should be for one moment free."[4] And again: "If Government dispenses with the Rules of Justice, it impairs the Object for which it was ordained [human happiness]."[5]

The content of Morris's conception of justice and morality is that suggested in the above quote on civilization and in the following: "Obedience to moral Law should be inculcated" by making sure that the laws "compel the Performance of Contracts, give Redress for Injuries, and punish crimes."[6] It was no accident that he cited performance of contracts first. The values Morris wanted the government to instill and protect were the values of a market economy. To achieve the society he envisioned, it was essential that the laws and policy affecting the security of property have the sanction of justice and morality—the kind of justice and morality requisite for a market society. A basic part of the task that Morris undertook was to teach the lessons of market morality and ensure that government would enforce them.

In keeping with the individualism of market values and with the need to emphasize their sanctity, Morris insisted that the object of government was the happiness of individuals, not the "public good." This latter indeterminate concept could be the source of much misguided evil if used to justify infringements on individual rights. "In the sincere Desire to promote it, just men may be proscribed, injustice be declared, property be invaded and violence patronized."*[7] And the "Compact which in all societies is implicit" did not authorize governments to sacrifice the rights of individuals for some notion of the collective good. No individual would have entered society on those terms. Each person's purpose in joining was "the increase of his own Felicity . . . . Hence he would reject every condition incompatible with that Object; and exact for its security every stipulation."[8]

Morris was probably overstating his case in implying that individual rights were never limited by or subject to the needs of the society. Eminent domain was an obvious limitation on the private rights of property, the very sphere Morris was most concerned about. But his message was clear. The "public good" was the most compelling, and therefore the most dangerous, basis for challenging property rights. He was prepared to meet this challenge by asserting the absolute rights of individuals in general and of property in particular.

The absolute rights of property were the underpinning of another of Morris's important contributions: his analysis of liberty. Morris took this centerpiece of republican rhetoric and broke it down into categories—civil and political—with a clear priority between them. He began by emphasizing restrictions: "When Society is established natural liberty must cease. It must be restricted. He who wishes to enjoy natural rights must establish himself where natural rights are admitted. He must live alone. If he prefers Society the utmost Liberty he can enjoy is political."[9] But political liberty must also, by its nature, be limited. If political liberty is "the Right of assenting or dissenting from every Public Act by which a Man is bound," then "the perfect enjoyment of it presupposes a Society in which unanimous Consent is required to every public act." But this means that the majority would be bound by the minority, even of one. Perfect political liberty, Morris concluded, is "a contradiction in terms. Its limitation is essential for its existence."[10]

The question for Morris was what degree of political liberty was appropriate for a given society, and property provided the answer: "Where political liberty is in Excess Property must be insecure and where Property is not secured Society cannot advance."[11] When a society did advance, its benefits required the continued restriction of political liberty.

> The most rapid Advances in the State of Society, are produced by Commerce. Commerce once begun is from its own Nature progressive . . . . It requires not only the perfect Security of property but perfect good Faith. Hence its Effects are to increase civil and diminish political liberty.[12]

Diminished political liberty was not, however, a drawback, but an advantage of commercial society. The true object of government was not political, but civil liberty: "Political liberty considered separately from civil liberty can have no other Effect than to gratify Pride. . . . If we consider political in connection with civil Liberty we place the former as the guard and Security to the latter. But if the latter be given up for the former we sacrifice the ends to the means." Morris not only clearly stated the priority between the two, he explicitly acknowledged that "Civil Liberty itself restricts political. Every Right of the Subject with Respect to the Government must derogate from its authority or be thereby destroyed."[13] And in a commercial republic this meant that the rights of property set limits to what the majority could do.

> If the public be in Debt to an Individual political Liberty enables a majority to cancel the obligation, but the Spirit of Commerce exacts punctual payment . . . . The Spirit of Commerce requires that property be sacred . . . . It requires that every Citizen have the Right freely to use his property.[14]

The proper protection for civil liberty, and property in particular, would prevent the people from using their political liberty to perpetrate injustice and would ensure the virtues of the market society Morris envisioned. Property, as the origin and purpose of government, should provide its ethic and limit.

Private property, a market society, and limited political liberty were the building blocks of Morris's political economy. He went beyond merely asserting their value to explaining the nature of property rights, the advantages of a market economy, and the importance of government policies that would foster both. Morris's earliest public writings were a series of newspaper articles warning against bad economic policy.[15] His message was that the productive use of property should be the criterion for all good policy.

> Unless the rewards of industry are secure, no one will be industrious; for the motive which prompts the toils of a laborious man, is the hope of enjoying what those toils produce. This produce is wealth, and whether it be in one shape or another, *so long as it is employed for the purpose of increasing the commodities in a country is it beneficial and no longer.*[16]

Morris urged his readers to consider the consequences of measures which might look superficially desirable. One of his chief targets was depreciating currency, which would have the result that "those who have industriously added to the wealth of the state would lose the fruits of their industry for the sake of the lazy and dissolute."[17] The justification of the depreciation as a tax on money was, he argued, completely misconceived. There were two uses of wealth:

> the one to let it out on interest to the industrious, and the other to purchase uncultivated land; the former is far more beneficial to the community than the latter. Now as a tax on money must produce the latter, if it produces anything, . . . such tax must be unwise.[18]

The main thrust of Morris's arguments was to counter the persistent notions of economy and morality that were antithetical to a market society. Money lenders might, for example, be unattractive characters, but it was a mistake to import such moral judgment into economic policy. The new republic required a modern, realistic approach which recognized that money lenders were necessary for new, productive enterprises. Similarly, the criterion for tax policy should be whether it fostered productive uses of wealth. A tax on fancy furniture, for example, might seem a suitable charge on the rich. But if such a tax discouraged the well-off from putting their money into this form of property, those who would have been productively employed making the furniture would be idle.[19] The questions of a "balance of trade"[20] and national debt should also be appraised not in terms of traditional goals, but on the realistic basis of their contribution to productivity.

Morris warned that a failure to adopt this modern approach, to attend to the effects of government policy on the uses of property, could have serious consequences for the whole society: "Above all things government should never forget that restrictions of the use of wealth may produce a landed monopoly, which is most thoroughly pernicious."[21] Sumptuary laws, for example, "tended to create a landed nobility, by fixing in the great landholders and their posterity their present possessions."[22] Economic policy should be designed to prevent this dangerous concentration of property: "A monopoly of the soil is pernicious or even destructive to society, let taxes, therefore, compel the owner, either to cultivate it himself or sell it to those who will cultivate it."*[23]

Implicit in all of Morris's economic arguments is a vision of a dynamic society. He suggested not only that productivity made property valuable to society, but that a society in which property was used productively was superior to one in which it was not. A society in which taxes encouraged productivity and the investments of the wealthy created jobs was a society of opportunity and fluidity. Men with talent and energy would prosper unimpeded by those with entrenched advantages. Morris wanted a society which was not only prosperous, but open and free.

Morris's vision required a modern conception of property rights. He needed to persuade people to think in terms of productivity rather than outmoded morality or mercantilist economics when making public policy. Moreover, he had to convince them that the free use of property was a basic right and the foundation of a successful republic. Morris repeatedly tried to clarify what constituted violations of property rights, and that such violations would have dire consequences both economically and politically. The price regulations and restrictions imposed on commerce to secure provisions during the Revolutionary War were, Morris argued, a clear instance of the violation of property rights—and of its inevitable stupidity and danger.

> The whole system of commerce hath been inverted, the laws of property invaded, the laws of justice infringed, every absurdity practiced, and every impossibility tried, to get a little beef and a little bread which would almost have come forward of themselves if things had been left to their natural course, if honest labor had been permitted to reap the blushing clusters of plenty in the lap of freedom.[24]

Morris's arguments were almost always a mixture of prudence and principle. Economic regulation was not only doomed to be unsuccessful in achieving its aims, it was fundamentally dangerous as a violation of rights: "The tyranny of . . . [price regulations] now appeared in its proper garb. The invasion of rights of property was clothed with every necessary circumstance of violence."[25] And the damage done was likely to be permanent: "Above all things government should never forget that . . . if the rights of property are invaded, order and justice will at once take their flight and perhaps forever."[26]

Morris relied on a consensus that property rights should be securely protected. He tried to build on that consensus and get people to expand their conception of property and acknowledge its implications for government policy. Depreciating currency together with legal tender laws should, for example, be seen as attacks on property: "Those who had been compelled to accept the paper would be as effectively robbed by the two acts of government taken together as they would have been by the one act of a highway man or house breaker."[27]

Similarly, Morris wanted to invest contractual obligations with all the accepted sanctity of property. The revocation of a state charter, he argued, constituted a violation of property rights. In admonishing the representatives of the Pennsylvania General Assembly not to abolish the bank charter, he urged them to consider that as a violation of private property "it must sully the Reputation of the State." Foreigners would certainly see it so and ask, "If your government so little respects the Property of their own Citizens as to overturn an Institution like the bank, how can our Property be safe among you?" "Beware," he warned, "how you lay the Foundation for future Encroachments. While Justice is the Principle of Government to be innocent is to be secure." By implication, once justice was abandoned, nothing was secure.[28]

Justice was the concept Morris used to encompass the value and importance of protecting the rights of property necessary for a market economy. Injustice was his focus when explaining the political consequences of a failure to provide this protection. Morris's basic precept was that "The tranquility and liberty of nations can only be sustained upon justice."[29]

A government which perpetrated injustice undermined the very character of its citizens. In 1781 Morris wrote in despairing tones to John Jay, "if our Governments are driven by necessity to have recourse to Expedients and Chicanery, . . . new Emissions and Depreciations [will] so impair our Morals, that the Country will not be worth fighting for, nor its Inhabitants worth preserving."[30] Unjust policy also undermined the strength and authority of government.

> [The regulation of prices] sapped the foundations of civil authority, for the temptation of interest to contravene or elude the law was too great to be resisted. Of consequence

> the legislature fell into contempt, because it made manifest that they were not possessed of that superior wisdom and power, which are sources of reverence and respect.[31]

Laws that violated the rights of property also exacerbated a basic weakness of republics, their tendency to a multiplicity and variability of laws. Unjust policy was inherently unstable: "that which is not right cannot last."[32] One bad law would generate another.

The justice of a nation's policies also determined its international reputation. Morris believed there was an inherent respectability in just policy. He spoke of the "dignity" acquired by "wise and honest measures."[33] A government that committed official acts of injustice announced to all that it could not be trusted, that it did not scruple to violate honor and principle. The regulation of prices, for example, "gave a woeful impression of the new governments, by laying down a violation of the rights of property as the corner stone on which they were to be erected."[34] It was particularly damaging when a government committed breaches of public faith by failing to meet its own obligations.

> Financial policy must be strictly just for if there be an object in the world for which the very existence of a republic should be staked, it is for the preservation of her public faith, particularly in an infant republic just emerging from subjection and claiming the aid, alliance and confidence of other powers.[35]

A nation with a reputation for unjust policies would destroy its public credit. It would be unable to borrow money at home or abroad either for peacetime projects or wartime emergencies. It would be essentially helpless. And it would destroy the capacity of its citizens to embark on new enterprises. No one would want to risk money in ventures in a country whose government could not be relied upon to uphold the just rights of property. The consequences of such a situation in a capital-scarce economy such as America's were dire.

Government had an obligation to ensure the conditions for prosperity not only because it contributed directly to the happiness of the citizens, but because prosperity was a source of strength, and commerce the basis for greatness.[36] "Let our public credit be well established and supported and in a very few years our commercial resources will astonish the world."[37] From such a position of strength and prosperity, America would be able to negotiate favorable terms in treaties for both trade and defence. Other nations would not only desire connections with America, but they would be wary about violating their agreements.[38] All these advantages would, however, be destroyed by official injustice. America would be reduced to an insignificant and vulnerable country: her economy would crumble, her government lose its authority, and in her poverty and weakness she would be at the mercy of other nations in both war and peace.*[39]

Finally, Morris thought there was another reason why it was important for America in particular to follow policies which would earn her a good reputation: it would determine the sort of men who would immigrate.

> [I]t might indeed be convenient that wealthy men should cross the Atlantic to become citizens of Pennsylvania. And so they will if equal Just laws and a mild just Administration give that security to property without which it is a Curse instead of a Blessing. But if bad laws be made . . . the wise and the good will avoid us as they would the pestilence.[40]

In short, as Morris presented it, the political success of the new republic was dependent on its economic policy. Morris's vision of republican government required a market economy.

II. Divisions in Society: The Poor versus the Rich

It was no accident, in Morris's view, that in the early years of the republic the question of just economic policy had come up over and over again in the form of paper money, taxes, price regulations, and the bank charter. Just economic policy would always be a fundamental and contested issue because society would always be divided between the many who were poor and the few who were rich. Class conflict was therefore the central concern of Morris's political thought. Morris articulated the fears and perceptions shared by most of his fellow Federalists and unrelentingly faced the implications of their views. The conflict between the rich and the poor was inevitable and ultimately irreconcilable; a successful republic would prevent the poor from claiming an equal share of wealth or power.

The split was inevitable because "the severe law of property is, that in any well settled country a few must soon possess all, and the majority, the great majority nothing."[41] Efforts to equalize the distribution of property were likely to be pointless and certain to be harmful: "unless by agrarian laws the fabric of society be demolished, some individuals will become rich."[42]

Morris did not think that most Americans really wanted to see property divided equally, but in a republic the rhetoric of equality could be dangerous.

> Man is a creature of sense, and governed invariably by his feelings. Now you can easily make him feel, that in point

> of right he is equal to every other man. Vanity may even whisper to him that he is so in point of talent, and if vanity were remiss, the prompter flattery is at hand. But the more he feels his equality of rights and talents, the more must he feel his inequality in point of possessions. Where these are wanting, he has rights which he cannot exercise, talents which he cannot employ, desires which he cannot gratify, and in consequence, resentments he cannot allay.[43]

This candid acknowledgment of the consequences of economic inequality was not intended, of course, to question their propriety, but to point to their danger. Morris was unusually astute about both the implications of economic inequality for other rights and about the implications for property of claims for equality of rights. He likened the proponents of equality who denied any implied threat to property to "a robber who should say, bless me why so much apprehension, I don't mean to deprive you of your Property, but only to share."[44] In a republic, the danger of egalitarian rhetoric was immediate. The poor were likely to express their envy and discontent in pressure for misguided and unjust economic policies.

> It is common that those who labor, should feel some enmity towards those who do not. It is also very common for those who feel supposed grievances to take the most direct road for getting rid of them. Mankind are generally wrong in both instances, but never more so than in the question before us [the taxation of money]. . . . Monied men being odious, the plain method of dealing with them seems to be by taxing their money, and this is particularly agreeable when that money hath been acquired in a mean or wicked manner. But this is far from operating the desired effect.[45]

Morris was under no illusion about the hostility the poor felt for the rich: "It will perhaps be sufficient to say that it [a tax] will fall principally on the Rich; a Sort of creatures which are considered by some, as Lawful Game to be hunted like Deer or destroyed like wolves."[46] He treated this deep, hostile, and inevitable conflict between the two classes as the crucial problem of republican government.

The political significance Morris saw in the conflict had much to do with his perception of the two classes. His starting point was his opinion of mankind in general: "Men must be treated as men, and not as machines, much less as philosophers, and least of all things as reasonable creatures, seeing that in effect they reason not to direct, but to excuse their conduct."[47] Political theories which failed to take this realistic approach could do nothing but harm. Morris expressed the greatest contempt for Jefferson's "Faith": "He believes in the perfectability of man, the wisdom of mobs, and the moderation of Jacobins."[48]

One of Morris's descriptions of the people was so colorfully vitriolic that it became famous. While it is not entirely characteristic, it captures so many of his basic views that it is worth quoting at length. The subject of his comments was a public gathering in response to the closing of Boston's port in 1774. "It is needless to premise," he began, "that the lower orders of mankind are more easily led by specious appearances, than those of a more exalted station." The people having been roused to action, "there is no ruling them . . . the heads of the mobility grow dangerous to the gentry, and how keep them down is the question." He described his observations as follows:

> I stood in the balcony and on my right hand were ranged all the people of property, with some few poor dependents, and on the other all the tradesmen, etc., who thought it worth their while to leave their daily labor for the good of the country . . . . The mob begin to think and reason. Poor reptiles! It is with them a vernal morning, they are struggling to cast off their winter's slough, they bask in the sunshine and before noon they will bite, depend upon it. The gentry begin to fear this. Their committee will be appointed, and they will deceive the people, and again forfeit a share of their confidence. And if these instances of what with one side is policy, and the other perfidy, shall continue to increase, and become more frequent, farewell aristocracy. I see, and I see it with fear and trembling, that if the disputes with Britain continue, we shall be under the worst of all possible dominions. We shall be under the domination of a riotous mob.[49]

Morris's distaste for the mob, his fear of politically active lower classes, and his concern about how much control the men of property would be able to maintain were all important elements of his political thought. Morris did not, however, generally speak of the people in such hostile and disparaging terms. Only a tiny fraction of America's population was the "scum" Morris despised (primarily, he seemed to think, recent immigrants). This fraction was to become of concern to him later as the number of immigrants increased,[50] but around the time of the convention, he could confidently assert that the people of America were not the populace, the mob, of Europe. "Thank God, we have no populace in America, and I hope education and manners will long prevent that evil."*[51] Part of the reason for this was that in America the division between the rich and the poor was not that between those with property and those with none. In 1787 Morris estimated that nine-tenths of the American people were freeholders.[52] In

Morris's view America did have lower classes whose envy and hostility toward the rich posed a serious problem, but it was not the problem of a "riotous mob."

What brought forth Morris's hostility and contempt in the letter quoted above was the sight of the common people acting in a political capacity. Morris always treated with ironic suspicion "tradesmen, etc. who thought it worth their while to leave their daily labor for the good of the country." Morris had a characteristically derogatory remark about juries, one of the institutions most cherished by those who sought to promote democracy: "The only sensible man at the bar is C, for he speaks nonsense to the common jury."[53] When discussing the American people in the practice of their daily labor, on the other hand, he was generally laudatory. Particularly when drawing a comparison with European populations, he liked to portray the American working people as a manly and independent lot.*[54]

On the subject of the rich as a class, Morris's few direct comments had to do with the danger they posed politically: "Wealth tends to corrupt the mind and to nourish its love of power, and to stimulate it to oppression." Morris took this inclination to oppress very seriously, but he implied in all his writings that he considered the upper class to be generally superior to the lower classes. His "serious opinion," he confided to John Jay, was that "there is a less proportion of rogues in coaches than out of them."[55]

The fact that Morris saw American society split into two basic groups meant that he did not pay close attention to the gradations in the class structure of America. Nor did he try to define carefully the composition of the two groups with which he was concerned. His designation of the "lower orders" as the "poor" or the "people" was particularly vague. This vagueness reflects his judgment that the significant political distinction was between the many and the few. He was not concerned with conflict between the wealthy few and the poverty-stricken few, but with that between the wealthy few and all those beneath them, most of whom were not impoverished, but all of whom might envy the wealthy.

However imprecise his terms, Morris saw important class differences and clashes in America in 1787. He was not blinded by the absence of the extremes of poverty and wealth found in Europe, and he did not think that class conflict was a problem only for the future (although he did think it would get worse). All the Framers recognized the danger of the "democratic element," its instability, and its threat to property. But Morris treated the problem explicitly in terms of conflict between classes and as a two-way problem: the hostility and envy of the poor (the people) toward the rich, and the inclination of the rich to oppress the people. Morris did not treat the differences between the rich and the poor as misunderstandings that could be reconciled in favor of some common good; he treated the differences as real and inevitable. The task which faced the Framers, then, was not to eliminate or even reconcile these differences, but to design a structure of government capable of withstanding the strain of a divided body politic. The institutions of government had to be such that neither group could usurp power to oppress the other or destroy republican government.

III. The Institutions of Government

> Let the rich mix with the poor and in a Commercial Country, they will establish an Oligarchy. Take away commerce, and the democracy will triumph.[56]

Morris's proposals for the new Constitution were built around his most important insight: the relation between economic and political power. Morris was a thoughtful elitist who always asked to whom an institution would allocate effective power. His blunt arguments reveal his assumptions about the political capacity of the people and about where real dangers to the republic lay. We have seen his arguments about the political significance of economic policy. Let us turn now to the kinds of political institutions he wanted to sustain his vision of a market republic—and the consequences of this vision for the people.

Morris's plan for the legislature was to institutionalize class conflict in the two houses of Congress: the House was to be a democratic branch exclusively for the people and the Senate an overtly aristocratic body composed of the rich. Such an institutionalization of class divisions would serve first to check the vices of the democratic branch that republican government required. "Every man of observation had seen in the Democratic branches of the State Legislatures, precipitation—in Congress changeableness—in every department excesses against personal liberty private property and personal safety."[57] Mere virtue and ability in the second branch could not provide an adequate check. A balance of conflicting interests was necessary. "The checking branch must have a personal interest in checking the other branch. One interest must be opposed to another interest. Vices as they exist, must be turned against each other."[58] Opposing vices meant, of course, that there was to be no attempt to mitigate the hostility between the rich and the poor. On the contrary, the full strength of the conflict was to be used to establish balanced institutions. To balance the democratic branch, Morris wanted an "aristocratic body" which would "love to lord it through pride." This body had to have not only "great personal property," but "the aristocratic spirit."[59] Morris further wanted to entrench the Senate firmly by making its membership for life. Only then could it have the independence necessary to check the House. Recent history had shown that other devices were inadequate: "All the guards contrived by America have not restrained the Senatorial branches from a servile complaisance to the democratic."[60]

Of course Morris anticipated objections that such an aristocratic body would try to oppress the poor. This he argued was a misunderstanding of the problem. The issue was not *whether* the rich would try to oppress the poor: "[This aristocratic body] will do wrong, it will be said. He believed so: He hoped so. The Rich will strive to establish their dominion and enslave the rest. They always did. They always will."[61] The issue was what should be done about their inevitable attempts at oppression. The appropriate solution, according to Morris, was to isolate the rich, to identify them as having interests separate from and threatening to the people. It was as though the isolation of the rich in an explicitly aristocratic body would alert the people to their threats; it would be harder for the wealthy to pass off their interests as the public interest. "By thus combining and setting apart the aristocratic interest, the popular interest will be combined against it. There will be a mutual check and a mutual security."[62]

To ensure that the Senate would be composed only of the rich, Morris suggested that the senators not be paid: "They will pay themselves if they can. If they can not they will be rich and can do without it. Of such the second branch ought to consist; and none but such can compose it if they are not to be paid."[63] Morris did not address the more difficult problem of how the rich were to be excluded from the first branch.

The danger of the "democratic element" was taken as a given by most of the Framers. What made Morris's proposals unusual was that they were based on a clear perception of the power and potential danger of the rich. His plan was designed as much to secure a voice for the people as to prevent popular excesses. If, from some misguided notions of democracy, the rich and the poor were not given separate institutions, the rich would be able to overwhelm the poor with their power and influence. Morris perceived that it was a mistake to think that the people, by virtue of their numbers, held all the important power in a republic. This was to ignore the powerful advantages of the rich.

> [Morris] fears the influence of the rich. They will have the same effect here as elsewhere if we do not by such a Government [as proposed] keep them within their proper sphere. We should remember that the people never act from reason alone. The rich will take advantage of them. The result will be a violent aristocracy or a violent despot-

> ism. The schemes of the Rich will be favored by the extent of the Country. The people in such distant parts cannot communicate and act in concert. They will be dupes of those who have more knowledge and intercourse.[64]

It was not the rich but the poor who would be threatened by an unbalanced, democratic legislature. The passions of the poor, their tendency toward precipitation and excess, might be the vehicle of their undoing, but it was the rich who would engineer the oppression. The only way the people stood a chance of countering the advantages of the rich was to institutionalize the conflict in the structure of the legislature.

Morris also thought that giving the Senate to the rich would bring out the best in the elite.

> Men of large property will uniformly endeavor to establish tyranny. How then shall we ward off this evil: Give them the second branch, and you secure their weight for the *public good*. They become responsible for their conduct.[65]

He seemed to believe that the very fact that the rich would be publicly and visibly accountable for their conduct would inspire behavior in the public interest. Once in a permanent position of public honor and trust, and prevented from pursuing their private interests by the check in the House, the wealthy elite would, he thought, turn their talents to the good of the whole.

This idea of a wealthy, patriotic elite suggests a certain confusion in Morris's understanding of the Senate as an aristocratic body. On the one hand, he hoped it would "do wrong," that it would try to promote the interests of the rich. Only then could it serve to match and counter the democratic interest. This was in keeping with his idea of achieving stability by balancing conflicting interests. On the other hand, he argued that "the only security against encroachments will be a select and sagacious body of men, instituted to watch against them on all sides."[66] He seemed to intend the Senate not only to guard against encroachments by the first branch (a task compatible with the balance of interest theory); he implied that the Senate should also guard against attempts of the rich to dupe the people and exert their influence through the first branch. Morris wanted the structure of the system, and its stability, to rest on the constructive use of the basic conflict in society. At the same time, he hoped that the members of the Senate would, by virtue of their position, rise above the conflict and, in the public interest, protect the balance of the system itself.

Morris's argument hides the fact that these two functions of the Senate rested on opposing claims about the behavior to be expected from senators. I do not think, however, that Morris was being devious. I think his argument reflects an ambivalence in his views on the rich. On the one hand, they were a powerful class whose tyrannical designs had to be guarded against; on the other, the rich were the class from which men could be drawn who had the necessary qualities to be guardians of the public interest. They were both the most likely statesmen and the most likely demagogues and tyrants.

Morris could not persuade the convention to accept his plan for an upper chamber exclusively for the rich to counterbalance a first branch for the people. The design of the House thus posed the problem that the rich and the poor would mix with the result that the rich would be in a position to take advantage of the poor: "one of his principal objections to the Constitution as it is now before us, is that it threatens this Country with an Aristocracy. The aristocracy will grow out of the House of Representatives."[67]

Morris wanted the House of Representatives to be the "people's" branch. Having lost on trying to exclude the rich, he worked on excluding the poor. Once again he thought that it was only by taking account of the power of the rich that the genuinely democratic element in the government could be preserved.

> The strongest aristocratic feature in our political organization is that, which democrats are most attached to, the right of universal suffrage. This takes from men of moderate fortune their proper weight; and will, in process of time, give undue influence to those of great wealth.[68]

The feature Morris was taking exception to was the lack of property qualifications for electors of the House. Morris urged the convention to recognize that under universal suffrage the wealthy would be able to enhance their power by effectively controlling the votes of the poor. He wanted property qualifications not because he wanted only the interests of property represented, but because he believed such qualifications were the only means of ensuring genuine representation of the people.

> Give the votes to the people who have no property, and they will sell them to the rich who will be able to buy them. We should not confine our attention to the present moment. The time is not distant when this Country will abound with mechanics and manufacturers who will receive their bread from their employers. Will such men be the secure and faithful guardians of liberty? Will they be the impregnable barrier against aristocracy?[69]

Giving the vote to the economically dependent would not give them political power; it would give power to their employers. (This was a particularly compelling argument because at the time many elections were held by public voice vote.)

Limited suffrage, by contrast, would implement, not violate republican principles. Morris considered it absurd to think that every person ought to be allowed to influence the course of public events: "Children do not vote. Why? Because they want prudence, because they have no will of their own. The ignorant and the dependent can be as little trusted with the public interest."[70] Property qualifications seemed to Morris a reasonable means of excluding those who ought to be prevented from participating in public affairs. Property not only gave one independence, it gave one a stake in the community. It was, therefore, critical that the men of property have the influence in politics.

> Now it appears to me that the duration of our government must, humanly speaking, depend on the influence which property shall acquire; for it is not to be expected, that men, who have nothing to lose, will feel so well disposed to support existing establishments as those who have a great interest at stake.[71]

Morris did want the first branch of the legislature to be the people's branch. But by the people he meant freeholders, those whose property would allow them to participate meaningfully and responsibly in politics. Restriction of suffrage was the necessary means to make the House of Representatives a true guardian of the people's liberty, an effective barrier against aristocracy.

Morris also thought that property was *due* a certain influence in government, and that this should be a consideration in the design of the House. He did not argue that the political influence of individuals should be proportional to their wealth; but he did think that property should be a measure of the influence due to people taken in the aggregate, that is, to the states.

> Mr. Morris objected to the scale of apportionment [one representative for every 40,000 inhabitants]. He thought property ought to be taken into the estimate as well as the number of inhabitants. Life and liberty were generally said to be of more value, than property. An accurate view of the matter would nevertheless prove that property was the main object of Society. . . . If property then was the main object of Government certainly it ought to be one measure of the influence due to those who were to be affected by Government.*[72]

The striking thing about this argument is that Morris was not arguing that it would be expedient or useful to have property taken into account, but that property deserved influence. To exclude property as a factor in apportionment would not be (or not only be) unwise, but *unjust*. "He could not persuade himself that numbers would be a just rule at any time."[73] He did not, however, argue that property should be the sole measure of influence due: "Property ought to have its weight, but not all the weight."[74]

The structure of the legislature alone was not, in Morris's view, sufficient to protect either property or liberty. The House was not a sufficient guardian of the interests of the people, and the Senate was not a sufficient check on the House. In Morris's scheme the executive and a council of revision were to provide the additional safeguards, largely through their veto power.

Morris's plan for the executive once again points to what he saw as the central danger and the basic weakness of the Constitution: the political power of the wealthy. As the institutions were structured, both the House and the Senate would be composed of the wealthy; and it was in the nature of the wealthy to try to usurp power and oppress.

> The Legislature will continually seek to aggrandize and perpetuate themselves. It is necessary then that the Executive Magistrate should be the guardian of the people, even of the lower classes, against Legislative tyranny, against the Great and the Wealthy who in the course of things will necessarily compose the Legislative body.[75]

The problem posed by this composition was not simply that the House would pass bad laws, but that the legislature as a body would try to usurp power. The Senate, therefore, could not provide a check against this.

> The check provided in the second branch was not meant as a check on Legislative usurpations of power, but on the abuse of lawful powers, on the propensity in the first branch to legislate too much to run into projects of paper money and similar expedients. It is no check on legislative tyranny. On the contrary it [the Senate] may favor it [legislative tyranny], and if the first branch can be seduced may find the means of success.[76]

If the executive were to be the "great protector of the Mass of the people"[77] against legislative usurpation, it was essential that he not be dependent on the legislature either for his appointment or his removal. Morris therefore not only opposed legislative impeachment,[78] but made the radical proposal that the people elect their "guardian." Morris was unconvinced by the argument that the people would be in no position to choose the executive because the candidates would be unknown to them.

> If they [the candidates] be known to the Legislature, they must have such a notoriety and eminence of Character, that they cannot possibly be unknown to the people at large. It cannot be possible that a man shall have sufficiently distinguished himself to merit this high trust without having his character proclaimed by fame throughout the Empire.[79]

Morris was convinced, moreover, that the people would choose such an eminent man: "they will never fail to prefer some man of distinguished character, or services; some man . . . of continental reputation."[80]

The protection of the people was not, however, Morris's only reason for wanting a strong and independent executive. He also held the much more common belief that the executive should check democratic excesses. In arguing for a veto,

> [h]e dwelt on the importance of Public Credit, and the difficulty of supporting it without some strong barrier against the instability of legislative assemblies . . . He recited the history of paper emissions, and the perseverance of the legislative assemblies in repeating them, with all the distressing effects of such measures before their eyes.[81]

Morris also wanted to arm the executive with an absolute veto as a defence against the tendency of the "Legislative Authority to usurp the Executive,"[82] which only an absolute veto could prevent. But in this instance, Morris was not concerned about the oppression and usurpation by the rich as a class. He was concerned about the encroachments of the popular branch as such. "If the Executive be overturned by the popular branch," he warned, "the tyranny of one man will ensue."[83] He was careful to distinguish this from a usurpation of power by the upper classes: "In Rome where the aristocracy overturned the throne, the consequence was different."[84]

Legislative usurpations could then take place in more than one way. Not only could the wealthy members of both branches, in collusion with one another, usurp power in the interest of the aristocracy; the legislators in the popular branch could use the interests and passions of the people to usurp power for their own personal advantage.

> Emissions of paper money, largesses to the people—a remission of debts and similar measures . . . will coincide with the interests of the Legislature themselves, and that

> will be a reason . . . for pushing them. It might be thought that the people will not be deluded and misled, . . . but experience teaches another lesson.[85]

Legislators taking advantage of the misguided passions of the people was one of the dangers Morris was most apprehensive about. This fear explains both his major argument that the real threat came from the rich and his claims that democratic excesses were a danger (all previous checks had proved subservient to the democratic branch). Morris was not in fact worried about the people effectively controlling the House and promoting their interests at the expense of the rich. What he was worried about was designing demagogues, most likely rich ones, using the passions of the people to enhance their own power. In such instances, demagogic legislators furthered the interests of neither the rich nor the poor, but only their own ambition. Without adequate checks, legislators could gain power by pandering to the people and ultimately destroy public liberty.

The weight of the system tended so strongly in the direction of legislative usurpation of one form or the other, that Morris thought the executive alone could not provide an adequate check: "The interest of our Executive is so inconsiderable and so transitory, and his means of defending it so feeble, that there is the justest ground to fear his want of firmness in resisting encroachments."[86] Morris therefore advocated a Council of Revision that would add the power and weight of the national judiciary to the authority of the executive. Together they would veto any unwise or improper laws. Like Madison, Morris saw the Council of Revision as a means of protecting both the executive and the judiciary from direct legislative encroachments, that is, laws intended to deprive them of their power. And Morris, too, thought such a check was so important that he remained completely unconvinced by the argument that such a council would undermine the authority of the judges by involving them directly in the political process. (He apparently could not foresee the powerful check the judiciary would build on their claim to political neutrality.)

IV. Political Liberty in a Commercial Republic

Morris's major contribution was his insight into the relation between economic and political power, his perception that the true danger in a commercial republic was not from the poor, but from the rich. But after considering his proposals for countering this threat, one is struck that the primary means of doing so is limiting the people's access to political power. The obvious question is whether all his talk of the dangers from the rich is subterfuge, attractive rhetoric aimed at consolidating political power in the hands of the few—exactly what he purported to oppose. Just what was the "public liberty" he invoked to justify the restrictions of the people's power?

Public liberty clearly was not the right to direct participation in government. Under Morris's plan, the people were to have very little role *in* the government; they were not, in effect, to govern. They would choose their representatives and have the influence over them that frequent election brought. But Morris did not expect the legislature to be composed of the people.*[87] This was not because property qualifications for office would exclude them. Morris did not advocate such qualifications; they were unnecessary since "in the course of things" the people would elect the great and wealthy as their representatives. Morris wanted the people to elect the president because he was confident that they would chose not one of the people, but a man of continental reputation.*[88] Morris argued that the people's interest would be protected at all levels, but he also wanted to ensure that their will was checked at each level. In Morris's scheme, then, the role of the people would be to give consent and influence government through mediated and controlled institutions. And only freeholders would be able to do even this. Morris expressed neither regret nor hesitation about excluding the propertyless from what in 1779 he had called that "eternal maxim of free government: that no man can be bound by laws to which he does not consent."[89]

The public liberty which the people were in danger of losing to demagogues or to the rich appears then to have been the right to have an indirect, but nonetheless critically important, share of power. Public liberty was the right of all property holders, small as well as large, to have some share of public power. The reason public liberty could be equated with the rights and interests of the people was that it was only in a free, balanced government that the people could expect to have *any* lasting share of governmental power. If the balance that maintained public liberty were destroyed, it was the people who would lose. The rich stood a chance of maintaining control of usurped power; the people did not. Nevertheless, it was the people who were most likely to be duped into destroying the critical balance. Hence, the seemingly paradoxical argument that to protect the public liberty of the people, their power had to be controlled and restricted.*[90]

Morris's discussions of how public power should be structured suggests that he could not envision the people actually running the government. The danger he saw was not that the people would create a system that would promote their interests at the expense of the rich; they would create a violent aristocracy or a violent despotism, which would be to the advantage of no one but those in power. In a complex commercial society, the people were not capable of governing, either in their own best interests or those of society. Democracy was simply not compatible with complexity and sophistication. A society had to choose between the two.

> Arts produce a Change as essential as Population. In order that Government decide properly it must understand the subject. The Objects of Legislation are in a rude Society simple in a more advanced State complex. Of two things therefore one. Either Society must stop in its Progress for the Purpose of preserving political liberty or the latter must be checked that the former may proceed.[91]

Morris also suggested that it is not just the complexity, but the inequality of commercial society which made it incompatible with democracy. As he said in the quote opening this section, "Let the rich mix with the poor and in a Commercial Country, they will establish an Oligarchy. Take away commerce, and the democracy will triumph."[92] The prosperity of commerce brought with it inequality, which made democracy unsafe for ensuring the rights and rules a commercial economy required. Conversely, it seems that without the inequality and complexity of commerce, the people could sustain a democracy. Morris argued that through envy and incompetence the people would, if given the power, destroy the economic system and the foundations of the republic. But he was somewhat disingenuous when he said that the only alternatives were violent despotism and violent aristocracy. He had himself evoked another alternative: democracy built on the equality and simplicity of a rude society which had destroyed commerce. For Morris, that alternative implied a choice between all the advantages of commerce—progress, prosperity, civilization, strength—and what he characterized as the vain pride of political liberty. He seemed to think that the choice should be clear to everyone.

If a commercial society were to be sustained, governing required special qualifications. Political institutions should, then, be designed so that only those with the requisite abilities would get into office. Morris was never very explicit about what those abilities were, but the men he suggested would have them were those who would be likely to understand the requirements of commerce. Men from the "Western Country" were, for example, unlikely prospects. "The busy haunts of men not the remote wilderness, was the proper School of political Talents. . . . The back members are always most averse to the best measures."[93] Morris had no qualms about denying political power to those who would not elect men with the ability to govern: "He mentioned the case of Pennsylvania formerly: The lower part of the State had ye power in the first instance. They kept it in yr own hands [despite a shift in population] and the country was ye better for it."[94]

The idea that government offices should be restricted to those who had the requisite abilities is, of course, elitist, but it is not necessarily antidemocratic. The political elite could, for example, be drawn from all social and economic classes. For Morris, however, wealth was apparently a criterion for, and indicator of, political capability. Property was certainly a prerequisite for selecting the governing elite. The propertyless had neither the independence nor the stake in society to be entrusted with this task. Morris also thought that unless wealth were included as a basis for apportioning representation, undue power was likely to be allocated to areas which would not have enlightened men of political talents.[95] Perhaps the clearest indication of Morris's views is that he always spoke of men in power as men of wealth. Not only did he say that in the course of things the great and wealthy would be chosen to govern; he never suggested that it was misjudgment on the people's part to select such men to govern them.

Morris did want to reserve one branch of the legislature for the "people." But I think it is clear that he did not expect those elected to be literally representative of even the propertied he would have allowed to vote. His intention was not to have the House composed of lower level mechanics and shopkeepers, but of men of "moderate fortune." Even so, he did not seem to have much confidence in their abilities, particularly with respect to the crucial area of economics. The "people's" branch should do what the people were capable of doing: not actually governing, but providing a check on those who were.

If political liberty was only a matter of pride, not right, and the people were not really capable of governing, why did Morris care about public liberty? *Did* he really care whether republican government survived in America? In part the answer is that he was not committed to it in principle, and he later became increasingly convinced that the government needed to be "higher toned." But Morris's first concern was fostering the kind of market society he envisioned—with all of its economic liberties, openness, opportunity, fluidity, and prosperity. All of his attention was devoted to implementing the mutually sustaining political and economic institutions necessary for this society. He wanted to restrict the power of the people because they would undermine the foundations of the market republic he wanted. He wanted the government to be aristocratic in the good sense in which he used that term: characterized by the virtues of the upper class. And he did want members of the upper class to do most of the governing. But he did not want a system in which a fixed upper class held all the power.

Morris seemed to think that an aristocracy would not foster his preferred values. An aristocracy would want only to consolidate its power and privilege. An entrenched elite would not foster the openness necessary for all the advantages of a market economy. Men of middling fortune were much more likely to appreciate the virtues and requirements of such an economy and could prevent the wealthy from subverting it. I think Morris was very serious in his opposition to institutions which he thought would work for a stable aristocracy and against both the market and the republic. I have already mentioned his arguments against economic policies which would encourage tying up capital in land and, ultimately, a landed nobility. He thought such a class would undermine both productivity and the political institutions necessary for an open market to flourish. His arguments against slavery are even more telling. He did think that slavery was morally wrong. But he also stressed that slavery was an aristocratic institution.

> Domestic slavery is the most prominent feature in the aristocratic countenance of the proposed Constitution. The vassalage of the poor has ever been the favorite offspring of aristocracy.[96]

Morris's views on slavery are another instance of the way he saw the interdependence of economic and political institutions. As an economic system, slavery was antithetical to the norms of the market. (He also argued that it was unproductive.)[97] Equally important, the distribution of power slavery produced would be destructive to the republic. Slavery not only set up the gross inequality between master and slave; it maintained a stark inequality between those who had the wealth and power derived from the forced labor of others and those who commanded only their own labor. Slavery made this gap difficult to overcome; it fixed the power of the slaveholding class and reduced the power and numbers of small landholders. Such a class structure would make it difficult for the people to serve as adequate checks against the wealthy and for the middling classes to resist the folly of the poor: "A nation of landholders [i.e. many small landholders] will not easily permit themselves to be ruled by the scum of other countries poured into their large towns to ferment under the influence of designing scoundrels."[98]

V. Property as Boundary

If Morris's reason for restricting political liberty was to protect the values of a market society, his theoretical justification was the absolute priority of property. Having seen what this priority meant for the structure of institutions, we can now see what Morris shows us about the nature and implications of property as the boundary to political liberty.

What is really at issue in the conflict between political liberty and property is the right of the society, the government, or the majority of the people to interfere with rights of property. This raises the question of the origin or status of property rights: are they inviolable natural rights, or are they purely conventional rights subject to the varying determinations of society, or something in between?

Morris's position was clear: he wanted property rights to be treated as inviolable; property should be seen as an individual civil right that limits the power of government. His concept of property—the right to free use—had built into it the idea of freedom from governmental interference. By focusing on use, Morris tied property rights directly to individual freedom. He was thus able to identify government interference not as a rearrangement of socially determined rights, but as a fundamental violation of individual liberty. The right to the free use of property must therefore take clear precedence over any mistaken objects such as equity or "the public good." Once identified with freedom, the case for the inviolability of property was a powerful one.

At the same time, he tacitly recognized that property could not be outside the sphere of governmental power, because it is the very object of government. It is in the nature of property rights that they require government (and hence are the origin of government) in ways that the rights of conscience, for example, do not. Morris implicitly acknowledged that property rights are always defined, determined, and regulated by society. And, of course, he explicitly recognized that a democratic legislature had the *power* to interfere with or alter the laws which define and protect property. His objective, nevertheless, was to invest the rights of property (and contract) with a sanctity that would effectively place them beyond the reach of democratic legislatures.

Morris's position is compelling in its clarity and certainty, but his very certainty reveals a tension fundamental to a conception of property as the boundary to the legitimate scope of governmental authority: the absolute rights of property required redefinition. A great part of Morris's political activities was devoted to persuading his fellows that the rights of property and contract should be understood in the ways a market economy required. He insisted that the failure to properly define, and thus protect, these rights constituted violations of individual freedom. This task of persuasion was necessary because the concept of property and the freedom associated with it were contested at the time; his point of view did not reflect a consensus.

In 1787 government regulation in the name of basic principles of equity was a standard practice. The regulation of the prices of bread and other basic commodities was an old and deeply entrenched practice. The prevailing concept of contract still included a notion of equity that could void "unfair" agreements, contracts which were not based on the "just price." Morris's emphasis on virtue and morality may have been aimed at countering these older notions of equity. In the name of the absolute sanctity of property rights, Morris was trying to foster a redefinition of the nature of property.

This irony was implicit in the dual quality of Morris's arguments about the importance of protecting property rights. He argued both that they were fundamental rights not subject to limitations in the name of the public good and that the test of all economic policy should be productivity. Of course he thought that property rights properly understood and protected *would* promote their productive use. He was, nevertheless, in effect arguing that property should be reconceived in such a way as to make the dominant forms of wealth productive. The fact that he genuinely believed that his conception of property fostered, indeed constituted, individual liberty, does not change the fact that he wanted to reshape traditional notions of property in order to achieve his vision of a market society. His vision required both subtle reconceptions of property and a belief in its absoluteness.

The tension in Morris's stance—the claims for absoluteness and the instrumental arguments for change—reveals a tension that has remained an important part of American constitutionalism. Our tradition of limited government has been founded on a concept whose ambiguity carries within it the irreducible tension between democracy and individual rights, a concept which has been amenable to a complex interplay between natural rights and utilitarian arguments.

Morris's clear subordination of political liberty to property also sheds light on the complex status of liberty in our tradition. Madison, the more representative thinker, never accepted that subordination in principle. But, like Morris, he proclaimed justice not liberty as the end of government.[99] The great focus of the Framers was the security of basic rights, property in particular, not the implementation of political liberty. To a considerable extent they shared Morris's hierarchy between civil and political liberty. His argument that the degree of political liberty appropriate to a given society was that compatible with the security of property expressed a powerful sentiment at the convention. Ultimately, however, the Constitution incorporated a more subtle and ambiguous approach to the relationship between these categories of liberties. The institutions which were accepted gave greater scope to political liberty and incorporated fewer checks to ensure "justice" than either Madison or Morris advocated. Nevertheless, one of the most important legacies of the Framers has been their categories and hierarchies of rights. The distinction between political and civil liberties and the different kinds of equality appropriate in the two spheres have become a deeply embedded part of our tradition.

VI. The Clarity of Single-Mindedness

The insights Morris provides arise from his characteristic strengths, which are also his major weaknesses: the single-mindedness of his concerns and the absoluteness of his priorities. Morris could see and acknowledge implications of the proposed Constitution which were left largely unexamined by those of his fellows who tried to balance a broader range of values. It was as though Morris had no unease about conflicting values to cloud his vision. He was almost alone in his willingness to acknowledge that the poor would have rights they could not exercise, that the inevitable economic inequality of the system would limit the reality of the equality of rights proclaimed in republican rhetoric. He was altogether more candid about the consequences of the new system for the distribution of power and advantage. Morris shared the dominant view that the efforts of the poor to improve their condition—usually by schemes to deprive the wealthy of their property—were wrongheaded and would work to the detriment of the poor in the long run. But he never implied that the interests of the rich and the poor were ultimately the same. He did not invoke a common good to hide the reality of a deep and hostile conflict. Morris's discussions suggest that the interests of the people generally were to have more of the necessities and some of the comforts of life, and the interest of the poor was to escape their poverty. The interests of the rich were to maintain and improve their position of wealth and power. The difference was that the interests of the rich would be automatically furthered if the system as a whole were flourishing. Conversely, there was *no* measure which could satisfy the interests of the poor as a class without threatening the rest of society. Individual poor men could become rich to the advantage of the society, and Morris believed they would. The poor could be better or worse off depending on the state of the economy and the oppression by the rich, and Morris wanted a system in which they would be better off. But there was no means of eliminating the poverty of a whole group in society, or even of distributing the material benefits of society more equally, without infringing on the rights of property and thus undermining both the economy and the republic.

Morris was apparently willing to face these implications because he was confident of his values and his priorities. The scheme of government he proposed would do everything possible for the people: it would protect them from oppression, guarantee them a share of power, and provide the conditions for a thriving economy from which they would benefit along with the rich. The government would not do the impossible, eliminate poverty, or the absurd, give the people the power to destroy their liberty and prosperity.

Morris's focus on the irreducible conflict between the classes seemed also to have sharpened his perception of the power of the wealthy. This was his most important contribution and it seems to have been almost entirely lost on his fellow Federalists. It may be that the reason Morris failed to persuade his colleagues of the danger from the wealthy was that his institutional solution to the problem seemed hopelessly outmoded and unworkable. There seems to have been a consensus among the Framers that the "mixed regime," a balance built on class, was not suitable for the new republic. Their task was to find a new way of creating a stable government with its own internal checks. The Federalists were preoccupied with containing the power of the people, and it may be that Morris did not have a sufficiently compelling institutional design to make them take seriously his different perspective.

It is also true that Morris's understanding of political struggle was crude in its single-mindedness. Unlike Madison, he did not see the multiplicity of conflict likely in a large, diverse republic, nor did he share Madison's vision of the advantages of such multiplicity. On the contrary, he was prepared to stake his entire political system on the hostility between the rich and the poor, and he was distressed when it turned out that the political divisions were not along clear class lines.

> Much will depend [for the future of the republic] on the union of talents and property. There is a considerable mass of genius . . . now at work to overturn our Constitution. If these be not met by a phalanx of property under the guidance of our ablest men, I think there will be a scuffle, and that, in the course of it, many large estates will be put into the melting pot. . . . *It seems, however, probable, that the property in this country will be divided on political questions, and if so, we may expect mischief.*[100]

Morris could not imagine either the security of property or a successful republican government unless the men of property united to form a single, powerful, political force. (At the time of the convention, he was confident that they would, and, accordingly, pointed out the potential danger of their power.) But while Morris saw that "property" was not behaving as he thought it would and should, he did not reconsider his position on the fundamental split in America. He thought the situation dangerous precisely because he still believed his premises to be correct: there was a basic conflict of interest between the rich and the poor, and if the rich failed to see that, they would lose both their property and their government to men "who have nothing to lose."[101]

Morris's political thought is in many ways more simplistic than the Madisonian approach adopted at the convention. The Constitution incorporates a broader range of values and leaves their priority more ambiguous. But Morris had an astuteness about power, a clarity of vision, and a candor of expression which allows us to see more clearly the values and limitations of the Constitution. He explored the relationship between economic and political liberty which was to become a dominant theme in American political thought as the market society he envisioned came into being. And he identified the problem of the interrelation between economic and political power, which the Constitution does not address and which has continued to plague the system.

4 The Democratic Federalist Alternative: James Wilson and the Potential of Participation

James Wilson stands out among his fellow Framers as the only one who declared that property was not the main object of government.[1] Indeed, Wilson gave priority to what was seen by his colleagues as the major threat to property: the political liberty of the people. Both Madison and Morris (along with most of their fellow Federalists) saw a fundamental tension between the security of property and the exercise of political liberty in a republic. And both, in their different ways, gave priority to property in their attempts to resolve that tension within the framework of republican government. Wilson, on the other hand, took the sovereignty of the people as his first and guiding principle. The exercise of political liberty was his chief interest, and he devoted his most creative energies to its theoretical basis and its institutional implementation. In short, he showed none of the hesitations about the political power of the people that a concern for property engendered in his most thoughtful and astute colleagues.

Wilson's attention to the issue of political participation is his chief contribution to political thought and provides an important critical perspective on the Madisonian approach. If Morris reveals that Madison underestimated the danger of the few, Wilson suggests that the dominant Federalist perspective underestimated the political capacity of the many. For Wilson, the solution to the dangers of republican government was not to contain the power of the people, but to foster their political participation. While Morris points to a neglect of the relation between economic and political power, Wilson points to a neglect of the democratic foundations of the republic.

Wilson's distinctive approach to participation and property rests on his conception of the nature of man and the objects of government appropriate to that nature: men have the intellectual abilities to enable them to participate; their highest ends have a social as well as individual component; individual liberty is a means to those ends, but is not itself primary; political theory and government must therefore focus not simply on individual rights, but on man's highest ends and their inherently social nature. Property is only a means to a means (liberty) in this structure, while participation is essential both for the social bonds between men and for the attainment of excellence and happiness, their highest ends.

The difference between Wilson's perspective and those of his Federalist allies reveals the importance of the starting point of political thought, the difference it makes when the object of government is conceived of in terms of the development of man rather than his rights and interests. Wilson also shows us how popular participation in politics can be taken as a goal of institutional design—and the difference between that goal and the general commitment to republican principles that characterizes the Madisonian approach. Finally, Wilson offers a Federalist alternative freed from the preoccupation with protecting property.

I. Philosophical Foundations

A. The Nature of Man

Wilson saw man as an inherently social creature and believed that all men are naturally endowed with the faculties of "common sense" and "moral sense." He drew a distinction between reason, of which only a few are capable, and faculties involving immediate apprehension, which all men possess. Man's "moral sense," perhaps his most important faculty as a social and political being, falls into the latter category.*[2] In Wilson's view, the perception of moral truths, or right and wrong conduct, has the same immediacy and the same reliability as visual perception.[3] Reason is an important aid in some moral decisions, but the first principles of morality, the basis for all decisions about the ends of actions, are discernable only by this moral sense. And most moral questions require only the exercise of the moral faculty.[4] All men also have the general faculty of common sense, by which first principles of all kinds are perceived: "In the greatest part of mankind, no other degree of reason is to be found. It is this degree of reason, and this only, which makes a man capable of managing his own affairs and answerable for his conduct towards others."[5]

Wilson's distinction between faculties allowed him both to acknowledge the obvious differences between men's intellectual abilities and to suggest that all men could be relied on as having these basic and, ultimately, most important faculties. Reason is required to determine the means of achieving ends, including those in politics. But all men have the faculties necessary to determine the ends of politics. This view was the foundation of Wilson's faith in the people and the expectations he had of them.

Man's faculties of moral sense and common sense are important not only because they are the shared grounds for the exercise of all other mental faculties, but because they are man's *social* faculties. They are the basis for the perception of his duties to others; they make him "answerable for his conduct towards others."[6] As such they both constitute and demonstrate his inherent sociability. Man is, therefore, not to be understood primarily as an individual, separate from his fellows. He does have needs, interests, and abilities that are strictly individual, that is, which can be understood as belonging to an individual in isolation. These are, however, inadequate to explain human nature. Man also has needs, affections, and faculties which are fundamentally and irreducibly social. And it is the development and exercise of these which constitute man's excellence. To see man at his best and most interesting, he must be viewed not only in his individuality, but in the social context which alone makes him fully human.

The most obvious aspects of, and evidence for, man's natural sociality are his "passions and affections." Men have "all the emotions, which are necessary in order that society may be formed and maintained."[7] Wilson thought men were endowed not only with the obvious social affections for those near to them, but with a capacity for "moral abstraction." This "moral power," the "principle of benevolence and sociability," gives man the ability to love and be responsible toward not only individuals, but communities, states, and even mankind.[8] Wilson found it regrettable that philosophers had failed to give this power of moral abstraction the same attention they had given to intellectual abstraction.[9] He believed that men have intellectual faculties which "imply necessarily a society with other beings, social as well as intelligent."[10] A purely individualistic conception of man must be inadequate, because it will fail to take account of these faculties. Neither they nor man's social affections are reducible to individual interest or faculties.

> The attempts of some philosophers to reduce the social operations under the common philosophical divisions, resemble very much the attempts of others, to reduce all our social affections to certain modifications of self love. The Author of our existence intended us to be social beings; and has, for that end, given us social intellectual powers. They are original parts of our constitution; and their exertions are not less natural than the exertions of those powers, which are solitary and selfish.[11]

Because man is a social creature, his highest ends have a social quality. It is the will of God that man "pursue his happiness and perfection,"[12] and society is necessary for the latter as well as the former. Man's potential for excellence is based primarily on his social faculties: "In point of dignity, the social operations and emotions of the mind rise to a most respectable height. The excellency of man is chiefly discerned in the great improvements, of which he is susceptible in society."[13]

B. The Social Principles and the Bonds of Society

It is a truism that rights imply duties, at least of restraint. But in Wilson's treatment of rights, the fundamentally reciprocal nature of right and duty goes beyond the obvious. Man's capacity to perceive his natural rights is essentially a capacity to perceive his obligations to others. It is his moral sense. Rights thus take on a social character in Wilson's treatment. For example, two fundamental natural rights, "the right to be free from injury, and to receive fulfillment of engagements,"[14] derive from the two great social principles: the obligation to perform promises and the obligation to "submit to any distress or danger, rather than procure our safety and relief by violence upon an innocent person."[15] Our natural moral sense informs us of these obligations.[16] The social dimension of Wilson's approach to rights creates a kind of inversion of the now familiar claim that rights imply duties: our moral sense reveals our duties, and from them we discern our rights. Wilson's conception of rights thus takes its starting point from the bonds between individuals, rather than from defence against aggression or intrusion.

There is also a social element in Wilson's conception of the right to natural liberty: "The right of natural liberty is suggested to us not only by the selfish parts of our constitution, but by our generous affections; and especially by our moral sense, which intimates to us, that in our voluntary actions consist our dignity and perfection."[17] Wilson suggested that an important part of our natural liberty is the freedom to perform generous actions towards others and that this social element is basic to the relation between human freedom and human dignity. Moreover, Wilson's concept of natural liberty has built into it not only social restraints, but positive social responsibilities: a man has a right to do what he wants "provided he does no injury to others; and *provided more public interests do not demand his labours*. This right is natural liberty."[18] Thus the natural rights and liberty that are ordinarily the basis of an individualistic philosophy of man, are for Wilson part of man's capacity to live as a social being.

We can also see the social quality of his conception of man in Wilson's two accounts of the origin of society. In the first version, he gave a conventional account of the social compact but stressed man's social capacity for mutually binding promises.[19] More importantly, he offered a second version of the emergence of society in which the original unit was not an originally isolated contracting individual, but a family—which is, of course, appropriate since Wilson argued that human beings cannot properly be conceived of in isolation from others. In a family, he suggested, "some room will be afforded for social enjoyments, and for the finer operations of the mind."[20] But there would be strong incentives to form larger social units not for defensive, but for positive purposes.[21] His emphasis was not on the protection of individual rights, but on the advantages of sharing, of pooling skills and labor.

Still more revealing of Wilson's distinctively social approach to politics is his deep interest in the bonds that constitute and sustain society. The argument most important for Wilson's approach to property is his claim that natural inequalities serve to strengthen the social bonds between men. In his view the inequality of men with respect to their "virtues, their talents, their dispositions, or their acquirements" is not to be regretted. It is not the cause of misfortune and strife, but of harmony and social unity.

> It is fit for the great purposes of society that there should be, great inequality among men. In the moral and political as well as the natural world, diversity forms an important part of beauty; and as of beauty, so of utility likewise. That social happiness, which arises from the friendly intercourse of good offices, could not be enjoyed, unless men were so framed and so disposed, as mutually to afford and to stand in need of assistance. Hence the necessity not only of great variety, but even of great inequality in the talents of men, bodily as well as mental. Society supposes mutual dependence; mutual dependence supposes mutual wants.[22]

The mutual dependence of men of different talents who can supply each others needs is, of course, easy to see. It may seem naive, however, to describe the relation between those able to offer and those in need of assistance as *mutual* dependence, or to suggest that the feelings of those in need are of the sort to promote social happiness. But Wilson's focus on the basis of connection among men was different from the usual political perspective of power and domination. He clearly thought that feelings of benevolence and gratitude were bonds of strong attachment. And in stressing mutuality, he may have assumed that those in need of assistance with respect to some things, were able to offer it with respect to others. Perhaps it is only when economic inequality pervades all of our capacities that we imagine some to be capable only of need. In any case, Wilson was certain that in creating inequalities, it was the intention of Providence to foster interdependence and to strengthen the bonds necessary for society.

Wilson's conception of man as a social creature in general minimized the importance of conflict not only among individuals, but between society and individual rights. His emphasis on social obligation did not, for example, imply a priority of society over the individual; no such priorities were necessary because there was no conflict. Individual rights and even interests do not exist in tension with the public good. God created man and society in such a way that the interests of individuals are in perfect harmony with the interests of society.[23] Man's natural state is not that of warring individuals, but of "society and peace."[24] Under good government, this natural harmony extends to civil society: "the industry of every citizen extends beyond himself. A common interest pervades the society. Each gains from all, and all gain from each."[25]

Wilson did not, however, naively believe that this harmony is automatic. Men are naturally inclined toward, and equipped for, harmonious social life, but they must exert a certain responsible effort to achieve it.[26] They must recognize their social obligations. Wilson's lectures and speeches seem designed to teach that lesson, often in dramatic tones: "There is nothing more certain than the excellent maxim of Plato—that we are not intended solely for ourselves; but that our friends and our country claim a portion of our birth."[27] This exhortation was premised, however, on the view that there was no conflict between individual rights and obligations to others. The two are only different expressions of the same moral principles.

The importance of Wilson's concept of man as a social creature is not that it replaces a concern with man's individual rights and interests, but that it denies that this is all there is to man—or that this is all the political thinker need be concerned with. Man can be seen as an interested individual with selfish passions and private rights, but it would be a mistake to base a political theory or a government on the narrow individual view of man. Such a theory or government would fail to recognize man's capacities and to meet his needs.

We can see now the nonlibertarian cast to Wilson's thought. He did value liberty highly; it is a natural right and essential both for man's happiness and his excellence. But it is not sufficient for either, nor in itself, the highest good. Liberty is neither the sole nor the primary object of man's existence, nor, therefore, of society and government.

The relative unimportance of property in Wilson's theory should be understood in this context of Wilson's nonindividualistic, nonlibertarian premises and priorities. Wilson was not primarily interested in man's independence from others; he did not stress the unimpeded exercise of individual liberty; he did not focus on the defence of individual rights and interests against the encroachments of others. Thus property did not derive primary importance as the basis of any of these concerns. Wilson was more interested in the advantages and pleasures of cooperation and social intercourse. The special qualities of man and the potential for excellence which interested Wilson are essentially social and without any direct connection to property.

II. The Objects of Government

A. Society, Character, and Liberty

In Wilson's view, societies, not individuals, founded governments. Government therefore has a responsibility not simply to individuals, but to the society that formed it.[28] Government's obligation to society is, in turn, linked to the goal of excellence. Society is necessary for man's improvement, and government should foster those social institutions that will foster virtuous development. Indeed, "a nation should aim at its perfection. The advantage and improvement of the citizens are the ends proposed by the social union. Whatever will render that union more perfect will promote these ends."[29] Thus government has an obligation to maintain society as such, to strengthen its social bonds.[30]

Man's character (or manners or virtue) was of great political concern not only because his excellence was the highest object of government, but because government must rely on the character of its citizens: "The constitution and our manners must mutually support and be supported."[31] The virtues Wilson considered essential for free government are those standardly claimed as such by his contemporaries: "a warm and uniform attachment to liberty," "frugality and temperance," and industry.[32] In addition to these standard virtues, Wilson stressed a sense of positive obligation to exert oneself politically: "[I]t is the duty of every citizen to use his best and most unremitting endeavors for preserving [a good constitution] pure, healthful and vigorous."[33] Wilson wanted to impress upon the people their own importance, to urge them to recognize their political responsibilities. A willingness as well as ability to accept these responsibilities must be part of the character of a free people. It was therefore essential that the institutions of free government foster such a character. Moreover, government will necessarily have an effect on character, whether it acknowledges character as an object or not. For example, "[G]overnment founded on improper principles, and directed to improper objects has a natural and powerful bias, both upon those who rule, and upon those who are ruled."[34] In sum, the mutual dependency between character and government is inevitable.

The most important way Wilson thought free government affected character was by securing liberty. He thought liberty both ennobled and sustained the aspects of character that liberty itself required.[35] Wilson stressed that the effects of liberty on character were as important as the material advantages of free government.[36] There is, further, a reciprocal relation between virtue, liberty, and the flourishing of the arts and sciences. Taken together, they are part of the great progression towards the perfection of man—the highest good in Wilson's system.

> Where liberty prevails, the arts and sciences . . . flourish. Where the arts and sciences flourish, political and moral improvements will likewise be made . . . mutually supported and assisted all may be carried to a degree of perfection hitherto unknown.[37]

Thus Wilson's nonlibertarian position that man's excellence is a proper object of government included the view that liberty is essential to that excellence.

B. Property and the Security of Rights

When Wilson spoke of the advantages of liberty, he had in mind the security of rights as well. The noble character of the free man is derived in part from the secure protection of the law.*[38] In fact, in some formulations Wilson defined the principal object of government as the protection of rights: "Government, in my humble opinion, should be formed to secure and to enlarge the exercise of the natural rights of its members; and every government, which has not this in view, as its principal object, is not a government of the legitimate kind."[39]

Man's natural rights, Wilson explained, "result from the natural state of man," that is, prior to government, but in society. In this state man exists both as a single individual and as a member of social units. He enjoys rights in both capacities: "[A] man finds himself, in some respects, unrelated to others; in other respects, peculiarly related to some; in still other respects, bearing a general relation to all." From each state a class of rights and corresponding duties arises.

We have already seen man's rights and duties in his relation to others. They are defined by the two great social principles, the right to be free from injury and to receive fulfillment of promises. Wilson also outlined the rights and duties of man in his particular relations as a husband, father, and son. The main significance of these rights for my purposes is that government should refrain from interfering with them. For Wilson, the family seems to have been both a private sphere into which government should not enter and a social institution necessary to sustain the republic.[40]

In his unrelated state, "man has a natural right to his property, to his character, to liberty, and to safety."[41] These rights, of course, look like the familiar objects of government. The distinctive elements lie in Wilson's treatment of property,[42] our main concern here, and the addition of character (meaning reputation) to the conventional list. This addition was indicative of Wilson's great concern with esteem, honor, and public recognition of talent and meritorious services.*[43] Wilson saw "the natural love of reputation and the fear of dishonor" as the crucial motivations for the public participation free government requires.*[44]

Wilson's views on property combined the conventional wisdom of his time with his own distinctive approach. Like many of his contemporaries, Wilson used the historical origin of property as a basis for claims for it as a necessary and natural right. Unlike most of his contemporaries, however, Wilson actually did some research into historical forms of property. He produced an odd mixture of historical examples, theoretical speculations, and recitation of standard maxims of the day. His historical arguments reveal a more complex and contingent view of private property than that underlying the Madisonian approach, but one not fully integrated into his analysis. He concluded from his inquiry that the "establishment of exclusive property may justly be considered as essential to the interests of civilized society."[45] Yet he also had a conception of possible alternatives to private property, which occasionally seemed to illuminate his arguments.[46] Perhaps his sense that private property was not literally the natural order of man subtly shaped his unwillingness to treat property as a limit to political liberty.

Wilson's views on the importance of securing property are clearer than his thoughts on its nature and origin and more directly relevant to his approach to the Constitution. His two basic points about government and the security of property are conventional, yet significantly different from those of his fellow Federalists. First, he compared free government, which respects the rights of property, with tyrannical government, which treats property capriciously.[47] Second, he argued that good government must establish laws which protect the property of its citizens against criminal attack. In neither case did Wilson discuss what was perceived by his contemporaries as the major threat to property: democratic tyranny. His comparison was always between tyrannical and free governments, not between just democracies and tyrannical democracies. Further, the protection of property against criminal attacks is, of course, a concern with protection against individual aggression; it is not a concern with protecting the minority against oppression by the majority. This is not to say that Wilson never addressed himself to the problem of democratic tyranny. He did. But that was not his concern when he discussed the importance of securing property rights.

This divergence from his colleagues may have been related to the ambiguity or ambivalence in his views about the status of property rights. He suggested, in passing, that a society may legitimately make whatever arrangements of property it sees fit; there is nothing inherently wrong even about making all property communal: "It is the power of a nation to establish, among its citizens, a community of goods."[48] Of course, if private property is purely a matter of positive law rather than an embodiment of natural rights, the issue of violations of property rights by a democratic legislature takes on a very different aspect. Wilson never articulated a clear position on this issue. He referred to property as a natural right, yet made implicit references to it as a positive institution.*[49] He recognized the various forms property arrangements have taken, yet made arguments implying that no ordered society was possible without private property. It is clear that Wilson thought that the security of property was essential to liberty and that security entailed protection against public caprice and private aggression. It is not clear what sorts of legislative modifications of the rules of property would have violated Wilson's conception of security.

While there is some ambiguity in Wilson's views on the status of property rights, there is no such uncertainty in his position on the inequality of property. The security government should guarantee was expressly equal protection for unequal property. (Note, however, that his emphasis is not on protecting the property of the rich.)

> By these laws, rights, natural or acquired, are confirmed, in the same manner, to all; to the weak and artless, their small acquisitions, as well as to the strong and artful, their large ones. If much labor employed entitles the active to great possessions, the indolent have a right equally sacred, to the little possessions, which they occupy and improve.[50]

We have already seen that he thought an inequality of talents was divinely ordained and that this inequality was the motivation for private property. The obligation of government is to secure the natural inequality of possession resulting from the competition between the weak and artless and the strong and artful. The secure possession of property was important in large part because of its relation to freedom. While private property was not a necessary basis for individual liberty, Wilson suggested that the use of property was an element of freedom and that property could provide a sphere of freedom from the power of others.[51] But Wilson offered little discussion of this notion of a protected sphere*[52] and neither emphasized nor explicitly discussed the free use and disposition of property.

He did not even make a claim for the right to the free use of property when it would have been rhetorically useful. In his opposition to price controls, for example, he was reported as arguing against their efficacy, but there is no reference to a principled stand on the right to the free use and disposition of property (such as Gouveneur Morris made).[53]

I have tried so far to give a sense of how Wilson understood the rights of property*[54] and the ways in which he thought they were important. But the most significant aspect of Wilson's views on property as a right and an object of government is, of course, the importance he was *not* willing to accord it. Property assumed an important position in his law lectures as an object of study, but never as a right of the highest value. Indeed, Wilson repeatedly made remarks indicating the lesser status of property.*[55]

One of Wilson's most explicit and important statements about the proper importance of property came in his discussion of whether it was appropriate for him, as a judge of the Supreme Court, to be a law professor. His argument was that being a law professor is certainly as dignified as being a judge; a judge protects property, but a law professor does something far more important: he contributes to the education of a free people and the improvement of society. Property, he argued, must never be overvalued: "Property, highly deserving security, is, however, not an end but a means. How miserable, and how contemptible is that man, who inverts the order of nature, and makes his property, not a means but an end!"[56] And security should not be mistaken as the only aim of society: "Society ought to be preserved in peace, most unquestionably. But is this all? Ought it not to be improved as well as protected?"[57] The security of property may be necessary for prosperity and closely tied to liberty (both of which he valued), but Wilson's highest end was both nonmaterial and nonlibertarian. Indeed, all of the rights which it is the object of government to secure may be seen to take their value from their relation to the true end: man's rights as an individual must be protected so that he can thrive and develop; his rights in relation to others must be protected because they are necessary for society; and it is only in society that man can achieve the improvement of which he is capable.

III. The Principles of Government

One of the important characteristics of Wilson as a political thinker and as a Framer is that he was interested in the exercise of political rights involved in the process of self-government. He was concerned with the nature of government itself, with the problems of legitimacy, of sovereignty, of consent; and he devoted his most creative energies to examining these problems. The political principles he arrived at are not in themselves unusual; they were the standard republican maxims: consent is the only legitimate basis of government and sovereignty resides in the people. What is unusual is that Wilson does not treat these principles merely as means of securing individual rights.

A. Consent, the Sovereignty of the People, and Majority Rule

The theoretical problem Wilson addressed was how free and equal men can form a government and submit themselves to it. The basic answer he arrived at was that men are capable of binding themselves: they form societies and governments by entering into mutually binding agreements with one another.[58] In Wilson's view, once it is clear that the essence of government is the mutual consent of free men, all the other principles of free government follow. In particular, the much debated problem of the nature of sovereignty becomes clear: the sovereign power of government resides in the free men who join together, and it is constituted by their aggregate rights and powers.[59]

Wilson took literally and seriously the idea that sovereignty resides in the people. He insisted that it was not merely a theoretical postulate and that Blackstone was completely wrong in treating it as "a political chimera, existing only in the minds of some theorists; but, in practice, inconsistent with the dispensation of any government on earth."[60] On the contrary, Wilson argued, not only does sovereignty reside in the people at the origin of government, it can never be legitimately taken from them. He explicitly rejected the idea that the people confer their sovereignty upon some third party or that the essence of government is a contract between the people and their governors in which the former turn over their sovereignty to the latter. The people may indeed delegate particular powers, but it is always a temporary delegation to be rescinded at will. Moreover, Wilson did not hesitate to stress the full implications of this principle: "In the great article of government, the people have a right to do what they please . . . the fee simple of freedom and government is declared to be in the people."[61] This means that they have the right to alter or abolish their government as they see fit. It is evidence of the depth of Wilson's commitment to this principle that he did not try to obscure it in favor of veneration for the new Constitution. He emphasized that the people are exercising, not relinquishing their sovereignty when they adopt a constitution; they remain the supreme power above the constitution. And Wilson argued that this "revolution principle,"[62] as he straightforwardly called it, should be taught to each new generation.

In Wilson's view it was the great advantage of free governments that "the supreme, absolute, and uncontrollable power *remains* in the people."[63] Indeed, he saw this as a solution for all the ills of government, a "panacea in politics."[64] But it is also the final limitation of a free government.

> There is a remedy, therefore, for every distemper in government, if the people are not wanting to themselves; if they are wanting to themselves there is no remedy. From their power, there is no appeal; of their error there is no superior principle of correction.[65]

Wilson pointed out that in every government the final authority, from which there is no appeal, must reside somewhere. It rightfully belongs with the people and they are the least likely to abuse it. But Wilson had to acknowledge that if the people themselves perpetrate errors, his system could offer no solution; there could, on his principles, be no higher power to control or correct them. Wilson reaffirmed this point in both its positive and negative aspects in his commitment to majority rule.

According to Wilson, the will of the majority must be taken as the will of society. This is the only just way for a society to function, and those who join either society or government bind themselves to accepting the will of the majority. The majority may then be substituted for the people in the discussion of sovereignty: the majority have the absolute supreme power and may make whatever political arrangements they wish. Wilson added only one qualification: if the majority violates or goes beyond the intentions of the original union, the minority is no longer bound to submit to the will of the majority. But even in that event, the right of the majority to do as it pleases is not diminished. The only right reserved to the minority is to withdraw with their effects.[66] What this comes down to is that the people have an absolute right to impose upon themselves whatever form of government they wish. They have, indeed, the right to deprive themselves of political liberty. If they want to exchange a good government for a bad one there is, in principle as well as in fact, no power that can stop them. In short, political liberty posed no limit to majority rule.

Private liberty, however, was a different matter. Citizens' rights stand above the will of the majority, for "right is weighted by principle; it is not estimated by numbers."[67] In a conflict between an individual and the people as a whole—which, practically, means the majority—the people have the power to decide the conflict in their favor at the expense of the rights of the individual. But Wilson stressed that this power is not equivalent to right. In the original compact of association, no individual gave the others the right to deprive him of his personal rights.

The language of rights is confusing here because there are interlocking issues of political right, private right, and moral rightness. These different meanings of right need to be distinguished in order to understand Wilson's position on majority rule.

The people, i.e., the majority, enjoy the supreme power by political right—based on the compact between free and equal men. But the political right conferred upon them by compact does not extend to the violations of the private rights of individuals. Nevertheless, as a *political principle*, the absolute power of the majority remains intact. It can only be limited by a *moral principle*. No human body can have the political right to assume the power to enforce this moral principle against the will of the majority. Thus Wilson argued that injustice is always morally wrong whether committed by legitimate authority or not, and that the consequences of injustice are always harmful to the state; but he never suggested that there should be some higher power to correct and control the will of the people. In short, for the majority to violate the rights of individuals is morally wrong and exceeds the authority the majority enjoy by political right. But the only solution is for the people to understand this. Ultimately, there is no legitimate political alternative to majority rule.*[68]

Wilson thought that there were in principle more limits to the right of the majority with respect to private rights than to public liberty. But in the final analysis, his theory provided for no appeal from the power of the people in either case: "of their error there is no superior principle of correction."[69]

B. Participation

Wilson believed that the people should exercise their sovereignty not only in the last resort as the final authority, but in the ongoing process of government. Free men who enter into political association together have the right not only to consent to, but to participate in their government. Wilson literally and wholeheartedly believed that in a free state the people *are* the sovereign.

In a free state, the citizen is both governor and governed. Wilson approvingly quoted "the great political authority," Aristotle: "A citizen is one partaking equally of power and subordination."[70] Wilson stressed that *all* citizens partake of both; the roles are not divided between different classes. Thus Wilson defined citizenship as the right to elect *and* the right to be elected into office. He made clear that by the latter he did not mean simply absence of formal restrictions;

he repeatedly emphasized that in a free government offices must in fact be open to all men. Every free citizen should therefore be prepared to hold office.

> In a free commonwealth, the path to public service and to public honor is open to all. Should not all, therefore sedulously endeavour to become masters of such qualifications, as will enable them to tread this path with credit to themselves, and with advantage to their country?[71]

As both elector and potential office holder, the free citizen must equip himself for his participation in government. He must know some law, for as the sovereign power, the people are responsible for conducting national affairs in accord with the law of nations. He must understand his rights and duties: "[U]nless in some measure . . . he knows those duties and those rights, he can never act a just and independent part."[72] And, most important, he must make public affairs his affair.

> In a free country, every citizen forms a part of the sovereign power: he possesses a vote, or takes a still more active part in the business of the commonwealth. The right and duty of giving that vote, the right and duty of taking that share, are necessarily attended with the duty of making that business the object of his study and inquiry.[73]

This active interest in public affairs is, in fact, not just preparation for participation, but one of the most important aspects of political participation. To encourage this participation, Wilson argued, suffrage should be extended as widely as possible.

> The correct theory and the true principles of liberty require, that every citizen, whose circumstances do not render him necessarily dependent on the will of another, should possess a vote in electing those, by whose conduct his property, his reputation, his liberty, his life, may all be materially affected.[74]

Widespread suffrage has a number of positive effects. First, it promotes the active engagement with political affairs which Wilson advocated for all citizens: "The man who enjoys the right of suffrage on [an] extensive scale . . . will naturally turn his thought to the contemplation of public men and public measures."[75] He will engage in politics on a daily basis by reading newspapers or political commentaries, by discussing politics with friends and neighbors. This level of engagement is of intrinsic value to the citizen; it is enlightening, it enlarges the scope of his mind. It is also of great benefit to the state: "A habit of conversing and reflecting on these subjects, and of governing his actions by the result of his deliberations, would produce in the mind of the citizen, a uniform, a strong, and a lively sensibility to the interest of his country."[76] In addition, this political engagement cements the bonds between citizens. In sum, the full participation promoted by widespread suffrage has the greatest advantages for both the state and the individual.

> The right of suffrage, properly understood, properly valued, properly cultivated, and properly exercised, is a rich mine of intelligence and patriotism . . . it is an abundant source of the most rational, the most improving, and the most endearing connexion, among the citizens . . . it is a most powerful, and, at the same time, a most pleasing bond of union between the citizens and those whom they select for the different offices and departments of government.[77]

Wilson acknowledged that this understanding of the sovereignty of the people, of the necessity of such participation in government, demands a great deal of the people: "[I]t ought not be concealed, that the public duties and the public rights of every citizen of the United States loudly demand from him all the time, which he can prudently spare, and all the means which he can prudently employ, in order to learn that part, which it is incumbent on him to act."[78] But Wilson did not think this expectation was unreasonable. To achieve this level of participation, however, the people must both have power and feel their own weight and importance. Thus Wilson made a point of trying to communicate to the people the full extent and importance of their responsibility. It was his aim, he said,

> to excite the people to acquire by vigorous and manly exercise, a degree of strength sufficient to support the weighty burden which is laid upon them—with an aim to convince them, that their duties rise in strict proportion to their rights. . . .[79]

It is essential that the people understand that if they fail to exercise their right to participate, free government is in jeopardy: "[F]ew are able to trace or to estimate the great danger, in a free government when the rights of the people are unexercised."[80]

C. Representation

In keeping with his understanding of the sovereignty of the people, Wilson held direct democracy to be the ideal form of government: "All power is originally in the people; and should be exercised by them in person, if that could be done with convenience, or even with little difficulty." In large states, however, this is impractical: "The people cannot assemble together. As they cannot therefore act by themselves, they must act by their representatives."[81] Representation is thus nothing more than a necessary substitute for direct democracy; he never suggested that representation is an improvement on direct democracy. On the contrary, the question he posed was whether representation is inferior to direct self-government. He concluded that representation is not inferior "in point of right," and "in point of utility" there is no disadvantage to "free and adequate representation."[82]

The object of a system of representation is then to make it "the faithful echo of the voice of the people."[83] In his view representatives neither could nor should refine the views of the people. Thus for elected representatives, Wilson preferred direct election. He argued that it was impossible for indirect election (through the medium of electors) to be an improvement on the immediate choice of the people, because the character of all successive appointments or elections is determined by the quality of the people's initial choice: "It is the first concoction in politics; and if an error be committed here, it can never be corrected in any subsequent process."[84] Wilson also thought that the right of immediate representation had important consequences that indirect election would undermine.

> The political connexion between the people and those whom they distinguished by electoral offices, and the reciprocal sensations and engagements resulting from that connexion, I consider as most interesting in their nature, and most momentous in their consequences. This connexion should be as intimate as possible. . . . Confidence—mutual and endearing—between those who impart power and those to whom power is imparted, is the brightest gem in the diadem of a republick.[85]

Wilson also argued that if representation is to be substituted for direct democracy, the people have a right to a system that will reflect their views as accurately as possible.

> To the legitimate energy and weight of true representation, two things are essentially necessary. 1. That the representatives should express the same sentiments, which the represented, if possessed of equal information, would express. 2. That the sentiments of the representatives, thus expressed, should have the same weight and influence, as the sentiments of the constituents would have, if expressed personally.[86]

This means that votes should be "equally, freely, and universally diffused."[87] No factor should allow any group, region, or individual to have more than its proportional weight. In Wilson's view property was no exception to this rule. Since "all electors ought to be equal," property deserved no special weight. Property should, on principle, not be represented.[88]

D. Conclusion

In Wilson's view, popular sovereignty, majority rule, participation, and representation are matters of right. To deny them is to violate the natural freedom and equality from which they derive. Moreover, the exercise of these political rights is as important for man's improvement as is the secure enjoyment of his personal rights: life, liberty, character, property, and the fulfillment of promises. Political rights are not mere means to these ends. Participation in political affairs broadens the mind and ennobles the character. Dignity, independence, courage, and intelligence are all fostered by the active exercise of the right to self-government. The exercise of political rights also affects the quality of society. Participation fosters bonds among citizens, between them and their representatives, and contributes to citizens' attachment to the state.*[89] In short, government based on the full exercise of political rights promotes the excellence of both the individual and the political community.

These basic precepts of Wilson's theory rest on the conception of man with which this chapter began. Wilson's focus on the potential of man and the sometimes striking absence of conflict in his vision of republican government, makes sense in terms of his starting point. The basic figure in this theory is not the interested individual. Wilson did not deny that man is motivated by interest and that clashes may occur. He did deny that self-interest is the only, or even the primary, motivating factor, and he denied that clashes of interest are the most important—or even politically most important—aspect of man's interaction with his fellow men. Wilson did not see government arising out of clashes over competing interests, and he spent relatively little time discussing government as an adjudicator of conflicting interests. In Wilson's theory, the protection or promotion of individual interests is not what is most important to man or most important as an object of government. The promotion of man's interests and even the protection of his rights are insufficient for his happiness or his perfection. Man has social and spiritual-intellectual needs and capacities which are as important as his private rights and material interests. Wilson's theory of government was addressed to man in his full dimensions: it was concerned with the development of his character and his mental capacities; it attended to the nature of human relations which constitute the political community; and it had a direct interest in giving full scope to the dignified exercise of his right and capacity to govern himself. Property plays no more than a minor role in any of these concerns.

IV. The Institutions of Government

Wilson's chief object in designing the new government was to give effective implementation and protection to the people's*[90] political rights. To this end he advocated a uniformly democratic structure with internal checks to prevent those in office from usurping power. He wanted the system to give the government stability and energy, but he wanted the people to give the direction to the government at all levels.

A. The Legislature

The base of the structure was the first branch of the legislature, which should be "the most exact transcript of the whole society."[91] It should therefore be elected directly on the basis of proportional representation.[92] To ensure free and equal representation apportionment should be on the basis of population. To those who argued that wealth ought to be admitted as a factor because property was the object of government, Wilson responded by rejecting the premise.

> [H]e could not agree that property was the sole or the primary object of Government and Society. The cultivation and improvement of the human mind was the most noble object. With respect to this as well as the other *personal* rights, numbers were surely the natural and precise measure of Representation. And with respect to property, they could not vary much from the precise measure.[93]

Wilson wanted a system in which the "legislators may feel the direct authority of the people."[94] To facilitate this connection and encourage faithful and accurate representation, Wilson advocated annual elections.[95] The people would then have close ties to the government and be able to give direction to their representatives.

Wilson did not, however, think that small election districts (or a small ratio of representation) were necessary to establish the desirable connection between the people and their representatives. On the contrary, he believed that small election districts increased the main danger of an elected legislature: the election of dishonest men who would not faithfully carry out their trust: "[T]he smallness of the districts . . . give[s] an opportunity to bad men to intrigue themselves into office."[96] In fact, he offered as a "general maxim" that "the more extensive the district of election is, the choice will be the more wise and enlightened."[97] Despite his emphasis on the intimate connection and confidence which should exist between the people and their representatives, Wilson did not discuss any limits to this general maxim. He does not seem to have given much thought to the effect of the size of election district on this relationship.

Large election districts were also better suited to selecting men of "enlarged" ideas and information.[98] Wilson made it clear that although the representatives should faithfully represent the views of their constituents, the national legislators were not simply to be advocates of local interest. They should be informed of, and sympathetic to, the interests of their constituents, but they should also "possess a general knowledge of the interests of America and a disposition to make use of that knowledge for the advantage and welfare of their country."[99]

Wilson's preference for those with enlarged ideas was not, however, a suggestion that he preferred representatives who would "refine" the views of their constituents. National representatives should perhaps have a broader range of information than most of their constituents, but their task is still not to improve upon the "sense" of their constituents: representatives should "express the same sentiments, which the represented, *if possessed of equal information*, would express."[100]

In advocating large election districts, Wilson did not intend (like some of his colleagues) to establish a system in which only the prominent and wealthy would be elected to office. In his view, one of the chief advantages of democracy was "an opportunity of bringing forward the talents and abilities of citizens without regard to birth or fortune."[101] And, as we have seen, he urged all citizens to prepare themselves for public office, because "in the United States, the doors of public honors and public offices are, on the broad principles of equal liberty thrown open to all."[102] He repeatedly stressed that offices were in fact, as well as on paper, open to all: "Is there any office . . . in this system but is as open to the poor as to the rich? to the inhabitants of the country, as well as to the inhabitants of the city?"[103]

Wilson did not expect the people to choose men exclusively or primarily from the upper class. On the contrary, he thought that a free man would naturally choose as his representative someone who "speaks and acts in the same manner as himself."[104] Wilson was sure that the people would recognize virtue and merit and he did not think that they would see it only in the wealthy. He did not expect men who were equals under the Constitution to bow in political matters to their social and economic superiors.

Finally, Wilson did his best to implement liberal suffrage qualifications for the House. As an alternative to freehold suffrage, he proposed[105] to make the qualifications the same as those for the popular branch in each state and that plan was finally adopted. When he discussed this plan in his law lectures, he made clear that he thought the state provisions for suffrage were, in general, liberal.*[106]

Wilson's rejection of the common view that a freehold was required to make a man a "safe depository of republican liberty,"[107] rested on his faith in the political capacity of the people. He believed that republican government has the virtue of being able to improve itself and its people; confidence in the people will be rewarded by an actual increase in their political abilities and responsibility. If the people are allowed to participate in important elections, they will come to view their right to elect as important and exercise it with due consideration.[108] On the other hand, if they are not allowed significant participation they will not value the right of suffrage or exercise it responsibly. The political intelligence and responsibility of the people is thus not a fixed element; if the people are allowed to exercise their political capacity, it will grow. It is thus a dangerous and self-perpetuating error to design a system aimed at restricting rather than maximizing the power and participation of the people.

Wilson's faith in the people did not mean that elected officials posed no threat. Wilson thought that no government body should be without checks on its power. Even the best designed legislature should be divided as a defense against both rash measures and legislative despotism.[109]

Wilson did not, however, think that in order for the two branches of the legislature to provide a mutual check, each had to have different interests and be based on different principles. The Senate as well as the House ought to be based on proportional representation and direct election. Wilson did not want the second branch to be more removed from the people. He stated his position most clearly when supporting the direct election of the Pennsylvania senate. He argued that in some instances (e.g., the judiciary) there must be a "removal" between the people and their officials. But, he asked, "Is this any reason for multiplying or lengthening them [removals] without necessity?"

> Is it a reason for introducing them into the legislative department, the most powerful, and if ill constituted, the most dangerous of all? No. But it is a strong reason for

> excluding them wherever they can be excluded; and for shortening them as much as possible wherever they necessarily take place. Corruption and putridity are more to be dreaded from the length, than from the strength, of the streams of authority.[110]

At the same time that he clearly acknowledged the danger from the legislature, he equally clearly rejected removal from the people as the answer.

Although Wilson wanted the second branch to be based on the same principles as the first, he did not want the two to be identical. He thought the senators should have longer terms, to promote stability; he supported Madison's proposal of a nine-year term, one third to go out annually. And he wanted the Senate to be smaller, to facilitate deliberation: "It was a maxim that the least numerous body was the fittest for deliberation; the most numerous for decision."[111] The second branch would thus complement the first which had "the most local and recent information of the circumstances of the people."[112] Wilson also expected the Senate, as the smaller, more stable body, to be less susceptible than the House to the various shifts in the "mood" of the people. In outlining the advantages of the Pennsylvania legislature, he argued that "[i]f at any time, the passions or prejudices of the people should be ill directed or too strong; and the house of representatives should meet, too highly charged with the transfusion . . . the senate [would] introduce the requisite . . . mildness and moderation." But this stability was not simply a check on the people's passions: "If a benumbing torpor should appear in the body politic . . . and if the contagious apathy should spread itself over the house of representatives; . . . the senate [would] infuse into the public councils and public measures the proper portion of life, activity, and vigor."[113]

B. The Executive

Wilson also argued that the executive and judiciary should be "purely democratical" in their principles.[114] Wilson advocated the direct election of a single executive for a short term (three years).[115] He should be reeligible and impeachable while in office.[116] He would thus be a "dignified, but accountable magistrate of a free people."[117] Dependent directly on the people (a "tenure of the noblest kind"),[118] he would be a guardian of the interests of the whole and a man of the people. He would also have the independence to serve as the "mediator between the intrigues and sinister views of the Representatives and the general liberties and interests of the people."[119]

Wilson also advocated an absolute executive veto to provide a check on the encroachments and usurpation of the legislature. Although he thought "the restraints on the legislative authority must, from its nature, be chiefly internal,"[120] an external check was necessary to prevent them from destroying the divisions of power essential to free government.[121] Wilson was so convinced of the importance of maintaining a separation and balance of power against encroachments by the legislature, that he maintained his support for an absolute veto throughout the convention. "Without such a self-defence the Legislature can at any moment sink it [the executive] into non-existence."[122] He remained unpersuaded that a qualified veto would serve the purpose (as Madison suggested) or that no one man should be able to overrule the decided and cool opinions of the legislature (as Sherman argued).[123] In Wilson's view, a qualified veto "might go in peaceable time; but there might be tempestuous moments in which animosities might run high between the Executive and Legislative branch, and in which the former ought to be able to defend itself."[124]

Again, it is important not to confuse this strenuous attempt to control the legislature with a desire to restrain the people. On the contrary, Wilson had in mind protecting the people from the sinister designs of the legislatures, from intrigues to usurp tyrannical power. The executive veto was to protect the people's public liberty. In his arguments for an absolute veto, Wilson never referred to the need to provide security against the unsound passions of the people; he made no reference to popular attempts to infringe on property rights or to promote measures which would impair the public credit. It was the representatives, not the people who posed the threat. Wilson's maxim about the trustworthiness of representatives was this: "In acts which were to affect them and their constituents precisely alike confidence was due. In others jealousy was warranted."[125] Clearly anything which involved their own aggrandizement, the increase of their power, fell into the latter category. One might, finally, ask why Wilson seemed to have more confidence in the executive than in the legislators. But that would be to misstate the problem. The principle is one of mutual checking. The emphasis is on checking the legislature, because it was seen to be by far the more powerful and thus more dangerous department. In addition, as a collective body it could intrigue and combine in sinister design. The executive of a republic, on the other hand, would not have the power to pose much of a threat. Wilson's views did not, of course, prevail. The vote to reject an absolute veto was ten states to none.[126]

Throughout the convention Wilson remained unconvinced that the qualified executive veto was best. But by the time of his law lectures in 1791, he seems to have reconsidered.*[127] After discussing the disadvantages of an absolute veto, he argued that a qualified veto would provide an index of "the strength and height of the current of public opinion and public movements." If after all the discussions of a bill, after the president has returned it with his objections, two-thirds of each house "are still of the sentiment that it ought to be passed in law; this would be an evidence, that *the current of public opinion in its favor is so strong, that it ought not to be opposed*. The experiment, though doubtful, ought to be made, when it is called for so long and so loudly."[128]

The underlying difference between this view of the veto and the one Wilson had in the convention is that in the law lectures he spoke of the legislators as reflecting the views of their constituents. In the convention he had focused on protecting the people from attempts by the legislature to usurp power and act in opposition to the interests of the people. Hence his support for the seemingly undemocratic measures of an absolute negative. But when he considered the legislators as acting on behalf of their constituents, his position was true to his principle of majority rule. Wilson did not explain why at one point he saw the legislators primarily as usurpers of power and at another the faithful representatives of the people. But in neither case was his rationale for the executive veto the need to control the popular passion for injustice.

I think Wilson's views on the executive veto point to his basic understanding of the possibilities and the problems of republican government. He did not think that the primary object of checks within the government was to restrain the people, to prevent their passions from carrying them to disaster on the current of public opinion. On the contrary, his fear was that the government might not be sufficiently responsive to, or might even oppose, the people. But as long as the government officials accurately represented the people, he was willing to rest his faith on majority rule. He apparently did not see popularly mandated legislative injustice as a significant problem. In particular, he voiced no concern about the vulnerability of property to popular attack.

C. The Judiciary

Because he did not share his colleagues' concern with preventing the unjust schemes of the people, Wilson's participation in the convention appeared to give very little attention to the protection of private rights (as opposed to public liberty). But he gave a great deal of attention to the branch of government he considered chiefly responsible for this protection, the judiciary. "Personal liberty and private property, depend essentially upon the able and upright determinations of independent judges."[129] Wilson primarily stressed the need for an independent and impartial judiciary. Judges should be removed from political pressure so that they might decide both criminal and civil suits in strict accordance with the standards of justice. The citizens would thus be assured the secure enjoyment of their private rights. If, on the other hand, the judiciary made its decisions not according to justice, but political aims, it could wield arbitrary and tyrannical power of the most dangerous kind.

> Nothing is more to be dreaded than maxims of law and reasons of state blended together by judicial authority. Among all the terrible instruments of arbitrary power, decisions of courts, whetted and impelled by considerations of policy, cut with the keenest edge, and inflict the deepest and most deadly wounds.[130]

His assumption was, of course, that there are standards of justice which exist independently of policy considerations; his plan for the judiciary was designed to give it the independence necessary to protect rights in accordance with those standards.

Wilson proposed that the judges be appointed by the executive, who as a "single responsible person," would be in the best position to make appointments on the proper grounds of virtue and ability. Appointment by the legislature was inappropriate because "intrigue, partiality and concealment were the necessary consequences" of "appointments by numerous bodies."[131] He considered even the Senate too numerous to participate in the appointment.[132] Wilson also urged that neither the salary nor the tenure of the judges should be subject to political pressure. Judges should therefore hold office during good behavior. He opposed the motion for removal of judges by the executive, on application by the Senate and the House, saying, "The judges would be in a bad situation if made to depend on every gust of faction which might prevail in the two branches of government."[133] In the law lectures he made this point in still more general and forceful terms:

> Can dignity and independence be expected from judges, who are liable to be tossed about by every veering gale of politics, and who can be secured from destruction, only by dexterously swimming along with every successive tide of party? Is there no reason to fear, that in such a situation, the decisions of courts would cease to be the voice of law and justice, and would become the echo of faction and violence?[134]

Wilson's discussions of the independence of the judiciary are almost the only points at which he clearly indicated that he expected the government to be subject to the sway of faction. In striking contrast to his fellow Framers, he did not stress faction when he discussed either the structure of the legislature or the need for a veto. He apparently had little fear of faction in the properly political arena of the legislature, but became concerned when it might affect the branch which was entrusted with the task of protecting private rights. The suggestion seems to be that if subject to the factional sway of the legislature, the judges would not have the independence to protect individual rights; but if judges did have the necessary independence, rights could be adequately secured despite the "gusts of faction" which may from time to time prevail in the legislature.*[135]

Like Madison, Wilson was insistent on the participation of the judiciary in the executive veto. It is worth noting one of his arguments at some length because it is an interesting statement of the role of the judiciary that Wilson envisioned:

> The Judiciary ought to have an opportunity of remonstrating against projected encroachments on the people as well as on themselves. It had been said that the Judges, as expositors of the Laws would have an opportunity of defending their constitutional rights. There was weight in this observation; but this power of the Judges did not go far enough. Laws may be unjust, may be unwise, may be dangerous, may be destructive; and yet not be so unconstitutional as to justify the Judges in refusing to give them effect. Let them have a share in the Revisionary power, and they will have an opportunity of taking notice of these characters of a law, and of counteracting, by weight of their opinions the improper views of the Legislature.[136]

Note that the term "rights" in this speech refers to the constitutional rights not of the citizens, but of the judiciary. As with his arguments for the executive veto, it is concern about legislative encroachment and the destruction of the separation of powers that the veto is primarily designed to meet. The judiciary can only secure the rights of citizens if its own constitutional rights, its judicial domain, is secure from legislative usurpation. Wilson also makes the more familiar-sounding reference to unwise and unjust laws, but there is again nothing to suggest that the people themselves would demand such laws. On the contrary, the judicial role in the veto is to protect against "encroachments on the people as well as themselves."

Wilson apparently thought that the judges should be removed from direct pressure from the people. He never suggested that popular election of the judges would be appropriate. The judiciary is the one branch in which independence from all political pressure is not only necessary, but safe.

> [W]e have all the reason in the world to believe, that [the federal judicial power] will be exercised impartially; for it would be improper to infer that the judges would abandon their duty, the rather for being independent. Such a sentiment is contrary to experience, and ought not to be hazarded. If the people of the United States are fairly represented, and the president and Senate are wise enough to choose men of abilities and integrity for judges, there can be no apprehension; because, the government can have no interest in injuring the citizens.[137]

In most of his discussions of the judiciary Wilson emphasized the protection of private rights. But at one point he also made a significant reference to public happiness: "I believe that public happiness, personal liberty and private property, depend essentially upon the able and upright determinations of independent judges."[138] He did not spell out what he meant by public happiness, but I think that what he had in mind was the set of benefits which come from the secure enjoyment of liberty: virtue, confidence, an upright and expansive character, and, in particular, the ability and inclination to participate in public life. Men can only have the confidence, independence, and public spiritedness to turn their attention to public affairs if their private rights are secure from tyrannical and arbitrary oppression. Wilson placed great weight on an impartial and independent judiciary as a source of security from arbitrary power. And he was confident that the Constitution would provide such a judiciary: "I hope no further objection will be taken against this part of the constitution, the consequence of which will be that private property (so far as it comes before the courts) and personal liberty, so far as it is not forfeited by crimes, will be guarded with firmness and watchfulness."*[139]

Property rights, which Wilson gave so little attention to when discussing the legislature and executive, play a prominent role in his discussions of the judiciary. These discussions are also one of the few points at which Wilson directly addressed the related issue of such great concern to his fellow Federalists: public credit. Wilson wanted the federal courts to have the jurisdiction necessary to prevent states from impairing national commerce and credit. He proposed jurisdiction over cases "between citizens of different states, and between a State, or the citizens thereof, and Foreign States, citizens or subjects."[140] He supported the inclusion of a clause prohibiting states from interfering with private contract*[141]—noting, however, that he understood this to refer to retrospective interferences only.*[142] He also moved to add to the prohibitions on the state, "nor emit bills of credit, nor make anything but gold or silver coin a tender in payment of debts," thus "making these prohibitions absolute, instead of making the measures allowable with the consent of the Legislature of the United States."[143] Wilson expected the courts to enforce these prohibitions by declaring void any law which contravened them.[144] Indeed, Wilson was willing to go further in controlling the laws the states could pass: he supported a proposal to give the national legislature the power to veto any state law which interfered, "in the opinion of the legislature with the general interest and harmony of the union." He argued that

> self-defence . . . is . . . necessary for the General Government. The firmness of Judges is not of itself sufficient. Something further is requisite—it will be better to prevent the passage of an improper law, than to declare it void when passed.[145]

Wilson apparently did not see restrictions on state legislatures as restrictions on the will of the people. He tended to treat the state governments not as instruments of the will of the people, but merely as bureaucratic subdivisions necessary because of the size of the country.*[146] He thus treated them with the general suspicion he had of officials—a suspicion that was probably compounded by the fact that state governments operated in a contracted sphere which made corruption and intrigue more likely. Whatever his reasoning, Wilson considered the national government as the true representatives of the people and had no hesitation about preventing the lesser subdivisions from doing anything which might adversely affect the national interest.

Finally, it is important to note that there was an explicitly democratic element in Wilson's conception of the judiciary: juries. Through juries the people were to play a direct role in the administration of justice. Wilson considered this one of the best and most important elements of the judicial system. He argued that it was right that juries determine law as well as fact even though they were less educated in law than the judges.*[147] But because the people were to bear such an important responsibility, he did urge them to prepare themselves by acquiring some knowledge of law.

> Is it not then of immense consequence to both [the public and individuals accused] that jurors should possess the spirit of just discernment, to discriminate between the inno-

> cent and the guilty? This spirit of just discernment requires knowledge of, at least, the general principles of law.[148]

This emphasis on preparation is characteristic of all the democratic elements in Wilson's system. He did not claim that the responsibilities he wanted to vest in the people would require no special skill or effort. Rather, he expressed the confidence that the people were capable of acquiring the knowledge necessary to fulfill their responsibilities—and that they could be expected to do so. And like all forms of responsible participation, the jury system had as one of its chief advantages its beneficial effects on the people.

> To promote an habitual courage, and dignity, and independence of sentiment and of actions in the citizens should be the aim of every wise and good government. How much are these principles promoted, by this beautiful and sublime effect of our judicial system.[149]

This democratic element of the system thus not only provides for the fair and safe dispensation of justice, it fosters the kind of citizenry necessary for a free government. The jury trial is thus "the best guardian of both public and private liberty."[150]

V. Democratic Injustice and Democratic Participation

In the previous section I discussed the institutional structure Wilson advocated for United States. But this discussion is incomplete in two important and related ways: it is incomplete with respect to Wilson's understanding of the most important and most positive aspects of republican government, the participation of the people; and it is incomplete with respect to the guiding concern of this book, the issue of property. The preceding section still leaves unanswered the question of why Wilson did not share his colleagues' pressing concern with protecting property against popular attack or, more generally, with controlling the turbulence and oppression of democracy. In this concluding section I shall look more closely at how Wilson saw the problems of demands for paper money and similar measures. And I shall show that although Wilson, like his colleagues, disapproved of these measures, he understood the general problem of democratic oppression quite differently. Wilson's views on democratic injustice do not appear in the discussion above of institutions because he did not see the solution to the problem in terms of institutional controls. The only hope for this inherent problem of democracy lay not in checks on democracy, but in its own advantage: the effect of participation on the nature of the citizens. The final section examines Wilson's understanding of this solution to the problems of democracy.

A. The Problem: Democratic Injustice

We have already seen that the institutional system Wilson advocated was not designed to control the people or prevent their representatives in the House from implementing the people's wishes. The question is why not. Did Wilson not share his fellow Federalists' belief that the people and their representatives in the most popular branch were likely to advocate unjust and oppressive measures? Did he not think that property in particular was in any danger from the demands of the people? We know that he believed in standards of justice and that property deserved protection; why then did he approach the problems so differently?

Let us start with Wilson's view of the popular demands for paper money and debtor relief which inspired the fears of his colleagues. Although Wilson offered little exposition of his economic views, his stands on the issues of the day are well known. In the discussion of the judiciary, we have already seen his concern with public credit and his disapproval of debtor relief acts. It is clear that he thought the popular measures commonly complained of undermined public credit and that one of the important tasks of the new government would be to restore public credit.[151] In the Continental Congress, Wilson was one of the major opponents of depreciating currency in 1783*[152] and of price controls in 1777.[153] And he continued to oppose demands for the latter in Pennsylvania.[154] He was also one of the leading advocates of the Bank of North America. In terms of economic theory, Wilson identified himself as an admirer of both Adam Smith and Sir James Stewart, a Scottish political economist whom Wilson repeatedly quoted on the importance of public credit. In short, his stands on economic policy were identical with those of Gouverneur Morris, and his economic assessment of the much reviled measures of the day did not differ from those of the most conservative Federalists.

But despite his agreement about the economic evils of these measures, his treatment of them differs significantly from that of either Madison or Morris. He did not invoke the sanctity of property in his arguments.[155] I think it is fairly clear that he thought that depreciating currency and tender laws undermined the security of property. But he did not usually choose to base his arguments on this point; he did not bring forth the violation of property rights as the surest evidence of the iniquity of a measure. He chose rather to focus on the broader issues of public credit, confidence in the government, and general principles of paper money and price controls.*[156] Even more important, he did not offer polemics against these measures in either the constitutional convention or the ratifying debates; unlike his political allies, he rarely cited these measures as evidence of the fundamental problems of the confederation or used them as proof of the need for institutional checks. Although he shared his allies' economic assessment of these measures, he did not share their political appraisal of the problem.

For Madison and his colleagues, popular demands for paper money were so important because they were symptomatic of the fundamental problems of republican government. Wilson, however, saw these demands as unwise and unjust, but not as evidence that class conflict or majority tyranny were the central problems facing the American republic. When Wilson discussed the structure of the legislature and the need for checks on it, he never brought up paper money as an instance of the kind of popular demands which needed to be checked. In fact, he gave no indication that he considered either property or a future propertied minority in any particular danger from republican institutions. The closest Wilson came to identifying democratic excess as one of the chief problems of the confederation was his discussion of the need for a new government in the Pennsylvania ratifying convention. Here he spoke of "contention and poverty at home, discredit and disgrace abroad." He said, "the rock of freedom" has been "undermined by the licentiousness of our own citizens . . . Private calamity and public anarchy have prevailed." He noted in particular that, "devoid of credit, our public securities were melting in the hands of their deluded owners."[157] But he did not refer to popular demands for unjust measures. Moreover, he did not suggest that the solution the new government would provide was a better check on the passions of the people or a better security against the demands of the majority. What he offered was an efficient national government which would have the power to prevent "the weakness and imbecility of the existing confederation." In particular, it would have the power to "prevent excessive importations," to raise revenues and ensure the performance of treaties.[158] The emphasis was on the inefficacy, not the injustice of the confederation, and it was strength and effectiveness Wilson claimed for the new government, not the prevention of popular injustice.

If, as I have suggested, Wilson did not see popular demands for bad economic measures as indicative of either the insecurity of property in a democracy or the still more general problem of majority oppression, it is understandable that he emphasized neither these particular measures nor the general problems. But the real question is, of course, why he did not make that connection. Why did he not share his fellow Federalists' view that these measures are instances of the inherent problem of democracies: the power of the many to threaten the rights of the few? The basic answer seems to be that

Wilson did not see American society as divided into the many and the few. Apparently, he did not expect all the property in America to be concentrated in the hands of the few. He made no references to a future propertyless majority. He never suggested (as Madison did) that in the future only the few would have an interest in property rights, and he had no fears about extending suffrage to those without property (although not to the "hopelessly dependent"). Wilson did not explicitly comment on his view of the future distribution of property in America, but he did comment on the virtually boundless opportunity America offered and her capacity to provide a good life to Europe's excess population.[159]

Wilson did of course expect an unequal distribution of property, but he did not seem to believe that these inevitable inequalities would give rise to significantly different attitudes towards the rights of property. Wilson's biographer comments that "almost alone among his contemporaries Wilson foresaw that America's commercial spirit was not the exclusive possession of a caste, but the most emphatic expression of a national psyche."[160] I think it is also likely that Wilson thought that those not sharing in the commercial spirit could be educated to understand the justice and importance of providing security for the rights of property and for commercial transactions generally.*[161] In any case, it is clear that Wilson did not think that the majority of Americans (present or future) held hostile, threatening attitudes towards property or the propertied.

Not only did Wilson not see a hostile conflict between the rich and the poor, he did not see American society as fundamentally divided over any conflict of interest.*[162] Wilson considered it reasonable to view America as an essentially harmonious whole and stressed the virtue of such an attitude:

> Expanded patriotism is a cardinal virtue in the United States . . . this passion for the commonwealth, superior to contracted motives or views, will preserve inviolate the connexion of interest between the whole and all its parts, and the connexion of affection as well as interest between all the several parts.[163]

I think the clearest expression of Wilson's basic understanding of the different interests in America and their relation to the whole (and, by implication, to each other) is his argument for the direct election of the Pennsylvania senate. He argued that interest would play a role in elections in any case; but if the people (rather than electors) elect, "interests of the individuals added together, will form precisely the aggregate interest of the whole."[164] And again: "If every individual among the people attends to his own advantage; the common advantage, which is the joint result of the whole, will be provided for."[165] This argument must, of course, be premised on the belief that there are no deep and fundamental conflicts between the interests of different groups or classes. The primary object of republican government is then to provide free and equal representation for all, not to protect or balance one group against another.

We have seen then that Wilson did not dwell on the excesses of paper money that so concerned his fellow Framers, that he did not think the majority would inevitably pose a threat to property rights, and that he did not see American society as divided into mutually hostile and threatening classes. Nevertheless, he did see the danger of democratic injustice, but not in terms of class conflict or of the structure of democratic institutions. He offered two important discussions of this problem, neither with reference to the design of the Constitution.

In the more general of these discussions, Wilson set out the basic dimensions of the problem as he saw it. It was cast initially not in terms of a democratic legislature or any other government institution, but in terms of the relation between members of a political society in which all are equal and voluntary members.

> From the necessity of the case . . . if a controversy arises between the parties to the social agreement, the numbers [i.e., the society as a whole], or a selection from the numbers, must be the judges as well as the parties.[166]

This is the fundamental problem inherent in any society based on equal rights and participation: there can, in principle, be no third body above the parties to the controversy to act as a disinterested judge. It is important to see that this formulation does not posit any fundamental division or conflict within the society. The problem is inherent in any body of free and equal citizens because any conflict between an individual or group and the society as a whole must, by right, be decided by the latter—although, as an interested party, it may not be inclined to justice.

Wilson thus did not see the problem in terms of how democratic institutions are designed. The problem will exist in the same form in any truly representative system, that is, whenever there is full and equal representation so that the representative body may be said to stand for the whole society. Wilson did not, therefore, propose institutional solutions, but addressed the fundamental question of justice involved. His objective was to persuade his audience of the nature and importance of this issue.

> But because those of one party must, from the necessity of the peculiar case, be the judges likewise; does it follow,

> that they are absolved from that strict obligation, by which every judge is sacredly bound to administer impartial justice. Does it follow, that they may, with avidity, listen to all the interested suggestions, the advice of which a party would pursue. When the same person is and must be both judge and party; the character of the judges ought not to be sunk in that of the party; but the character of the party should be exalted to that of the judge.[167]

Having set up the general problem and urged a commitment to justice as the answer, Wilson moved on to some specifics: this problem is particularly likely to arise in legislative bodies with respect to "pecuniary questions."

> When [pecuniary] questions are, as they generally must be submitted to the decision of those who are not only parties and judges, but legislators also; the sacred impartiality of the second character, it must be owned, is too frequently lost in the sordid interestedness of the first, and in the arrogant power of the third.[168]

Although Wilson did not explicitly say so, it is quite clear that the pecuniary questions he had in mind here were the same ones of such pressing concern to Madison and Morris.[169] Wilson went on to compare the legislator who refuses payment of an honest demand with a highwayman. Gouverneur Morris made the same analogy, but his point, unlike Wilson's, was that the rights of property are violated in both cases. Wilson made no direct reference to property; his point was that the *character* of the legislator is that of a highwayman: "He who robs as a legislator, *because* he dares, would rob as a highwayman—*if* he dared."*[170] Wilson then extended this point to argue that such corruption is contagious; public injustice can destroy the character of the state itself, both in the sense of reputation and in the sense of nature or quality. If the state allows its "interest" to outweigh justice, it will find that "the paltry gain will be as dust in the balance, when weighed against the loss of character—for as the world becomes more enlightened, and as the principles of justice become better understood, states as well as individuals have a character to lose." These "paltry gains" must be weighed against the "many other pernicious effects which flow from the example of public injustice."[171] They included loss of credit, the contempt of other nations, and the weaknesses these must produce: "Among merchants, credit is wealth, among states and princes good faith is both respectability and power."*[172] In short, the "public must be losers" by the state's injustice because such conduct undermines the principles of good faith and responsibility which the state itself rests on.[173] Promises, after all, are the only possible basis for free government and society. Thus when public injustice undermines the principles of honesty and good faith, and replaces them with "vicious principles and dispositions,"[174] the foundation of the republic is endangered.

Wilson expressed this same basic concern in his argument about the injustice and bad faith of the repeal of the charter of the Bank of North America. He pointed out that not all legislative acts place the legislators in the position of an interested party acting as judge. Wilson distinguished between laws which affect particular individuals or groups—e.g., "a law to vest or confirm an estate in an individual, a law to incorporate a congregation or other society"—and laws "respecting the rights and properties of all the citizens of the state."[175] The rules of justice which govern these two classes of laws are very different. In particular, the right of a state to exercise her power to alter, extend, or repeal laws at pleasure depends upon the kind of law.

> In a law respecting the rights and properties of all the citizens of the state, this power may be safely exercised by the legislature. Why? Because, in this case the interest of those who make the law (the members of the assembly and their constituents)*[176] and the interest of those who are to be affected by the law (the members of the assembly and their constituents) is the same.[177]

On the other hand,

> very different is the case with regard to law, by which the state grants privileges to a congregation or other society. Here two parties are instituted, and two different interests arise. Rules of justice, of faith, and of honour must, therefore, be established between them: for if interest alone is to be viewed, the congregation or society must always be at the mercy of the community.[178]

In the latter case, the community (through the legislature) retains the power to revoke such laws, but as a matter of *right* it is bound to its agreements: "whenever the objects and makers of an instrument, passed under the form of a law are not the same, it is to be considered as a compact, and to be interpreted according to the rules and maxims by which compacts are governed." Wilson offered examples to show that if the legislature does not consider itself bound by its agreements, certain rights will cease to exist as "rights." He cited the case of an estate vested or confirmed in an individual by law and a foreigner naturalized by law. If these laws can be revoked at pleasure, then the rights they confer lose their meaning: "A person seized of an estate in fee simple, under legislative sanction, is, in truth, nothing more than a solemn tenant at will;" the naturalized foreigner is then "a citizen only during pleasure." Similarly, the function of acts of incorporation is to give "the legislative stamp of stability and permanency." But "if these acts may be repealed without notice, without accusation, without hearing, without proof, without forfeiture; where is the stamp of their stability?"[179] If these acts are not seen as binding commitments on the part of the legislature, then they become subject both to the legislators' changing perception of the "interest" of society and to the conflicts within society.

> Those acts of the state which have hitherto been considered as the sure anchors of privilege and property, will become the sport of every varying gust of politics, and will float widely backwards and forwards on the irregular and impetuous tides of party and faction.[180]

This is one of the few points at which Wilson spoke of factions influencing the legislature and threatening rights. It is clear that he thought the tides of faction are sufficiently important and common to pose a major threat to rights, *if* the legislature does not understand and accept that its commitments are binding. Wilson's interest here was different from Madison's concern with factions. Wilson treated the majority as representing the whole society, not a separate faction or interest. The sense of the whole may, however, shift with the varying gusts of politics, and these shifts should not be allowed to affect prior commitments. The focus of Wilson's concern was, therefore, the fundamental importance of honoring commitments. Society and its representatives in the legislature must recognize that the obligation to fulfill promises applied to legislators and limited their legitimate power.

In both Wilson's discussions of democratic injustice, as in his discussions of particular measures such as paper money, it was not the protection of property which primarily concerned him. He did not treat the violation of property rights as itself the most important problem or as indicative of the seriousness of the dangers of democratic injustice. In Wilson's treatment, the security of property is only a particular, insignificant by comparison with the general issue of the obligations which form the basis of democratic society: "rules of justice, of faith, and of honour."*[181]

Of course much of the discussion above sounds very similar to Madison. But there are two important and related differences: Wilson did not treat the potential for injustice as class-based and that potential did not lead him to try to insulate property from democratic control. Wilson did see that a certain degree of stability is essential to the very meaning of rights, including property. But that important recognition did not make him wary in general about democratic legislation affecting property rights: when laws affect all instead of only some, there is no danger.

This distinction between kinds of laws is, of course, problematic. Wilson's argument suggests that if the legislature wanted to abolish, say, *all* fee simple titles, that would be all right because it would affect the legislators in the same way as their constituents. The problem, however, with even general rules of property, tax, or currency is that their impact is not uniform, but highly disparate among the population. Madison's recognition of that necessary disparity was one of the sources of his concern about legislative injustice. (But then Madison relied upon his own, equally problematic, distinction between laws that merely regulate property and those that violate property rights.) Wilson's discussions of legislative injustice reveals a certain lack of depth of inquiry and a failure to fully come to terms with the complexity of property rights. But what is important for his understanding of the problems and potential of republican government is that he believed that the legislature could, in general, be trusted with the laws of property and, in those instances where there was a potential for injustice, his focus was not on controlling the power of the people, but on ensuring that they understood the obligations that form the basis of democratic society.

We see then that Wilson recognized the potential for legislative injustice as a problem in democratic government—although he saw it differently from his colleagues who concentrated on majority threats to property or class conflict more generally. Unlike his fellow Federalists who referred to this problem constantly, Wilson did not address it when discussing the institutions for the new government. Nor, when he did discuss democratic injustice, did he discuss institutional remedies. What, then, did Wilson propose to do about this problem? Was he content to rely on the exhortations he offered in his law lectures and in his address to the Pennsylvania assembly? Why did the problem of democratic (legislative) injustice hold such a different place in his thought from that of his political allies? These questions lead back to Wilson's primary objectives and their connection to his interest in political participation. Participation was the basis for his hope for democratic government, his democratic solution to the inherent problems of democracy.

B. The Solution: Democratic Participation

From Wilson's perspective the solution to the problem of democratic injustice could not be sought in terms of controls on the people.

The problem did not arise out of a conflict between those with and those without property or out of any other deeply-rooted conflict of class or interest. The solution could not, therefore, be found in institutions which balanced such conflicting interests, or which prevented one interest from being in a position to oppress the other. The problem, in Wilson's view, existed in social terms because of controversies which must inevitably arise between individuals and the society at large. In political terms, the problem arose out of the commitment to the principles of the sovereignty of the people and majority rule. In a free government the power of the people's representatives must be sufficiently broad to leave open the possibility of injustice. This is not to say, of course, that there should be no restraints on the legislature, or that there should be no constitutional limits on the government as a whole. Both are necessary to protect the people from the government, and, as we have seen, Wilson advocated a full range of restrictions within the structure of the federal government. But he never suggested either that the purpose of the system of checks is to restrain the people or that he expected the checks to prevent the national legislature from implementing the will of the people—even if it were unwise or unjust. The checks were to prevent legislatures from usurping or abusing power, not from implementing the people's (unjust) wishes. Wilson seemed to accept that, after all the checks consistent with a free and effective government have been instituted, the power to perpetrate injustice would remain.

In Wilson's view the only sure security for justice and civil liberty, and indeed for political liberty, was a vigilant and informed citizenry who would understand the principles of justice and would elect good men to office. This may sound like a platitude without practical significance. But Wilson gave considerable thought to the kind of institutions that would foster such a population and worked in the convention to incorporate such institutions in the Constitution. His institutions were designed to achieve not the careful control of the people, but their full participation. And it was the effects of this participation which he relied on to uphold both civil and political liberty.

I have already noted the two most important aspects of Wilson's understanding of participation: first, political participation has an enlightening effect on the minds of the citizens; second, when the institutions of government are such that the people enjoy a significant responsibility for their own governance, they can be expected to concern themselves actively with public affairs. Here I want to look more closely at Wilson's understanding of the consequences of political participation for the prevention of injustice, beginning with the most basic form of participation, suffrage.*[182]

Most of Wilson's discussions of the significance of suffrage were in the context of the participation required by the institutions of the new Constitution.*[183] He made his points about the importance of responsible participation sometimes by urging its necessity and sometimes by proudly proclaiming its benefits. The urging was necessary because the people could not be expected to understand the significance of their responsibility immediately; the benefits could be proclaimed because the institutions were such that Wilson was completely confident that the people would recognize and fulfill their responsibility.

The participation he expected the new institutions to foster did not consist merely of casting a ballot every few years: suffrage, in Wilson's terms, was not the right to give passive consent, but the right and duty to take an active role in politics.

> [The citizen] should be employed, on every convenient occasion, in making researches after proper persons for filling the different departments of power; in discussing with his neighbors and fellow citizens the qualities that should be possessed by those who fill the several offices; and in acquiring information, with the spirit of manly candor, concerning the names, and history, and characters of those, who are likely to be candidates for the public choice.[184]

The citizen should, and can be expected to, pursue his political concerns in his leisure hours by reading newspapers and engaging in discussions. This active engagement in public affairs had a whole series of important effects. First, thinking about political issues and discussing the requirements of office develops what may be called the political intelligence of the citizens: they become more capable of understanding the issues, of discerning the interests of the country; they are better able to judge both the qualifications and performance of those in office. Such citizens will, of course, be more likely to elect good men to office and to have sound views for these men to reflect. Wilson suggested that the people give the direction to the government, not simply consent to the direction given by those in office. And he spoke not just of the direction, but of the "force" of the people's "original movement."*[185] By force I think he meant the extent of their involvement, that is, the number who vote, the attention they devote to public affairs, the strength of the popular participation in politics. Wilson's point was that the people's participation should give sufficient force to their actions as electors to keep the government under their controlling power. He went on to emphasize that all free governments must rely on the people's responsible and intelligent exercise of this "momentous" right of election: "On the faithful and skillful discharge of this primary duty the public happiness or infelicity, under this and every other constitution, must in a very great measure, depend."[186] A properly designed constitution must, therefore, ensure that this duty is recognized and this right is exercised. Fortunately, truly democratic institutions will do exactly that; they will allow for participation which is sufficiently extensive and significant to develop the responsibility and intelligence required by free institutions.

Wilson not only suggested that an intelligent and involved citizenry would be better equipped to fulfill their responsibilities as electors; he suggested that the best men would be more likely to seek election by an enlightened population. Wilson believed that "the love of honest and well earned fame is deeply rooted in honest and susceptible minds."[187] He considered the laudable ambition to high offices a powerful and positive motivation to public service, "which all wise and free governments had deemed it sound policy to cherish, not to check."[188] But this noble love of fame is not a desire for applause of any kind: "To souls truly ingenuous, indiscriminate praise, misplaced praise, flattering praise, interested praise have no bewitching charms."[189] The best men would have no desire to seek acclaim from an undiscerning multitude. The honor of an intelligent and engaged population, on the other hand, offers the strongest incentive for public service. When "public approbation is the result of public discernment," the best men can be expected to seek it.[190] (One should remember here that, in Wilson's view, neither the best men nor laudable ambition were restricted to the upper class.) Wilson also thought that with an enlightened citizenry, the representative's dependence upon public approbation would have an improving effect on him: "His dependence is not of an irrational or illiberal kind. It is of a kind, which, instead of depressing, will arouse and elevate the temper and character."[191]

Wilson also saw a reciprocal relation between the enlightenment of the citizenry and the excellence of the laws. Wilson urged a *rational* love of the laws. "I mean not to recommend to you an implicit and undistinguishing approbation of the laws of your country. Admire but admire with reason on your side."[192] A people capable of rational love of their laws will be a happy people, indeed. "The rational love of the laws generates the enlightened love of our country. The enlightened love of our country is propitious to every virtue, which can adorn and exalt the citizen and the man."[193] And the virtue of the citizens will "heighten the excellence of the laws" which, in turn, will "improve the virtue of the citizens."[194]

Finally, Wilson thought ongoing engagement in public affairs not only fostered a critical intelligence, but an essential attachment to the country and to one's fellow citizens.

> By these means [making a habit of conversing and reflecting on political questions] pure and genuine patriotism—that kind which consists in liberal investigation and disinterested conduct—is produced, cherished and strengthened in the mind: by these means, and in this manner, the warm and generous emotion glows and is reflected from breast to breast.[195]

This, I suggest, is the essence of Wilson's answer to the problem of democratic injustice. Institutions that are truly democratic, that allow the people significant participation, will foster a citizenry that can be relied on not only to elect good men, but also to act in the spirit of enlightened patriotism in the laws they support and in the direction they give to government generally. They will understand the true interest of their country and be prepared to further it. Participation in democratic politics will not bring conflicts and hostilities to the fore; it will, on the contrary, establish bonds of attachment between the citizens, it will foster the sense of their shared love of their country.

I think one may fairly apply this line of argument to the particular problems of paper money and debtor relief which so concerned his colleagues. A public whose political intelligence has developed in the exercise of their right to participate in politics will be enlightened enough to understand that such measures are not in the true interest of the country, and patriotic enough not to demand them.*[196] Enlightened citizens will not see their interests in opposition to those of the government or their fellow citizens. They will understand the principles of justice and will neither desire unjust measures nor be susceptible to the wiles of designing demagogues. If the broader interest, which they will rightly feel is *their* interest, requires temporary sacrifice, their disinterested conduct can be relied on. I conclude, then, that Wilson did not concern himself in the convention with controls on the people because his emphasis on making the institutions as democratic as possible contained in itself the answers to his colleagues' fears. The solution was not to set the interest of property in opposition to those of the people or to remove the government from the direct control of the people; the solution was to establish institutions so truly democratic that the people's active participation would make them intelligent, patriotic, and reliable citizens.

If participation was indeed Wilson's answer to the problem of democratic injustice, we need to look further at why he thought it would work and some of the questions such a solution raises. It is important to see that Wilson's confidence in the political capacity of the people is based on a particular theory of the nature of man. As I showed in the opening section, Wilson believed that all men possess the ability to perceive first principles, which direct their ends not only in daily life, but in politics. In light of the concern with popular injustice, it is particularly important to remember that all men possess an innate moral sense that commands them to fulfill their promises and makes them feel the injustice of a failure to do so. The requirement of public faith in government is thus in harmony with man's natural sense of justice and obligation. Government thus need only allow this natural sense to prevail; its task is not to control the naturally rapacious instincts of man.

Wilson's views on participation were not, however, simply based on the natural goodness of man. He did not suggest that man's inherent morality and sociability were themselves sufficient to produce political responsibility. He did not argue that any people can be relied on, because of their natural goodness, to act according to enlightened patriotism. On the contrary, he quite clearly argued that the people's political capacity must be developed through the exercise of political responsibility and that the institutions of government must be designed to foster this development. Wilson was not blind to human "frailties and imperfections." Rather, he thought it essential to consider government's effects on human character because he recognized people's weaknesses as well as their capacities. Finally, it is important to remember that Wilson proposed institutions designed not only to maximize participation but to provide checks on each other against the usurpation or abuse of power to which men in office were prone.

Wilson's confidence in the political capacity of the people was not then based on blind faith, nor did the system of institutions he advocated rest solely on this confidence. But Wilson's system did rely on the amount of time and energy he expected the people to devote to politics. He made no effort to hide this and, indeed, brought it out forcefully in his exhortations to the people: democracy requires the citizen's "most unremitting endeavors," his employment "on every convenient occasion" in political pursuits. Citizens should, further, prepare themselves for their responsibilities by learning at least the general principles of law.

One might well ask whether it is reasonable to expect such strenuous and ongoing political exertions from the people at large. Is not a system which relies on such exertions doomed to failure because it is based on unrealistic expectations? Would it not be wiser to place one's reliance on controls on the people, rather than on maximizing their participation and thus the demands on them? Wilson never directly addressed these questions beyond his general arguments that if the people are given responsibility they will exert themselves to fulfill it.

But we have already seen his most basic answer to these questions: republican government *must* rely on the people's political responsibility, which, necessarily, involves a certain amount of exertion. There may be various institutional structures, various checks and controls on the people's power, but, at bottom, the government must rest on some degree of participation by the people. A government which does not do so is not a republican government. And if that participation is not responsible, the government cannot succeed.

Wilson's emphasis on the demands and benefits of democratic institutions was really an explicit recognition of the dependence on the political capacity of the people that is implicit in all republican theories. One can imagine him saying that if this dependence is unreasonable, if the people cannot be expected to be actively interested in the public affairs they have the power to shape, if they cannot be expected to put forth the effort to govern themselves, then the whole idea of free government ought to be abandoned. If it is not to be abandoned, then the reliance on the people should be recognized, the principles made clear, and the consequences attended to. And this is just what Wilson's system did; it tried to effect the political responsibility other systems merely hope for. By focusing on the very basis of republican government, Wilson's theory gives the impression of itself having a fragile foundation: if the people's responsibility fails, everything fails. But in Wilson's view this was always the case. His system did not create the problem, but recognized and responded to it.

The issue of class conflict raises another serious question about the adequacy of Wilson's understanding of democratic participation. Does his view of the benefits to be expected from popular participation stand or fall on the accuracy of his perception of America as a basically harmonious society? If Wilson was wrong about the divisions in America, does his system really mean that the rights of the minority (property rights in particular) are to be placed at the mercy of the "pure and enlightened patriotism" of the majority? Could democratic institutions, as he understood them, accommodate serious conflicts of interest?

I think Wilson's theory offers two answers to the question of conflict of interest. The first is that his system will indeed accommodate a certain level of conflict. He never suggested that there would be unanimity on all issues or that the true common interest would always be apparent to all. He explicitly acknowledged some conflict between regions and economic interests (although not over property rights). But he did posit the existence of a true common interest benefiting all. In this, however, he did not differ from his colleagues who were fearful of majority tyranny. The real difference between Wilson and those fearful of the people lay not in their perception of conflicts of interest, but in their confidence in the people's ability to understand their true interest.

The second answer concerning conflict of interest goes directly to a deep and genuine conflict, such as that Madison and Morris saw between those with and those without property. The answer implicit in Wilson's theory is that if the majority should really be expected to pose an ongoing threat to the rights of the minority, then successful democracy is not possible. Majority rule must, by right, prevail, and if the majority cannot be trusted the prospects for free government are hopeless. Wilson did think that a population enlightened by participation would understand the importance of the rules of justice. But he did not suggest that this would be effective against permanent divisions and hostility based on serious conflicts of interest. Under those circumstances, even from Wilson's perspective, it seems unlikely that the effects of political participation would be pure patriotism and endearing connections among the citizens. Wilson's answer would then be that his theory did rely, as all republican theories must, on a basic harmony of interests in society. It could not accommodate a majority which would always see its interests in direct conflict with those of the minority. In particular, Wilson would presumably have been willing to admit that his system could not offer secure protection of minority property rights against a majority determined to violate these rights. But he would add that no free government could.

There is also a different, perhaps even more important, answer Wilson would make to those who would question his emphasis on the people's responsible participation. Participation and its beneficial effects are not simply means of governing; they are themselves ends. Participation in public affairs fosters social bonds, which are essential to human happiness, and enlarges and enlightens the mind, which is itself the most noble object of government. Wilson also took literally and seriously the proposition that the absolute sovereignty of the people is the first principle of republican government. He believed that participation in one's own government is a fundamental right of free men. Its value cannot, therefore, be judged only on its efficacy as a means of government. If it appears that a system based on popular participation may involve a risk to property, the issue is one of competing rights, not simply the adequacy of means. That is, the crucial issue is not the adequacy of participation as a means of protecting property, but the relative importance of the political right to participate and the civil right to property. I think it is clear where Wilson stood.

The fundamental principles of equality and political liberty, and not a concern for the protection of property, must guide the formation of the new government. Wilson's system, with its emphasis on democratic institutions and the participation they both demand and encourage, was an attempt to implement these principles as fully as possible. His concern with participation shows an attention to the effects of the structure of government not only on private rights and interests, but on the community and on the human mind. His scheme of government was designed to protect civil liberties, to maximize political liberty, and to further the noble objects that went beyond either.

Finally, we must acknowledge that this impressive vision was not the result of a full exploration or, indeed, recognition of the unresolved tensions it encompassed. Wilson's apparent willingness to give priority to political participation over the security of property was not based on a careful inquiry into the nature of property rights and their vulnerability to conflict and change. And although there are ways of understanding Wilson's simultaneous emphasis on majority rule and his advocacy of an absolute executive-judicial veto (as well as his assumption of judicial review), one cannot say that he had worked out the problematic quality of his positions. Nevertheless, Wilson's vision of a republic whose working principle was participation, not control, stands as a model to guide constructive inquiry into the true potential of democratic constitutionalism.

5 The Madisonian Constitution

James Madison had a clear vision of the Constitution. He spelled out the problems he thought the Constitution had to solve and he explained how the institutions he proposed would do so. He presented both the problems and the solutions in terms of a republican theory of limited government. His proposals did not prevail in every instance but his basic vision did. The basic structure of institutions followed his design, and the underlying principles, as they were articulated by those whose views prevailed at the convention and as they have continued to be expressed in our tradition of constitutional thought, reflected his understanding of republican government.

The Constitution can be characterized as Madisonian because of the ways in which Madison articulated the mode of thought that won out at the convention. By understanding the strengths and weaknesses of his thought, we can see the strengths and weaknesses of the foundations of American constitutionalism. The implications and consequences of Madison's vision are clearest when his perspective is contrasted with that of Morris and Wilson. The comparison among these three highlights the limitations of Madison's thought and helps us to understand their sources. We can then see more clearly how Madison's vision was embodied in the Constitution of 1787 and how it has shaped our tradition of constitutional thought.

I. Class, Power, and the Hierarchy of Rights

Morris provides two basic insights into the Madisonian vision that prevailed at the convention: first, his arguments about the power of the rich in a commercial republic make clear that the Madisonian approach neglected the relationship between economic and political power and the problems it would pose in the new republic; second, Morris articulated the crucial distinction between civil and political liberty that lies at the heart of the Madisonian approach.

A. The Rich versus the Poor

Morris's stark approach to the conflict between the rich and the poor and the need to institutionalize that conflict allows us to see the class implications of the Madisonian approach. Morris argued that the rich would do all the ruling in the institutions the convention adopted. With no legislative body reserved for the people, they would never actually accede to office. Morris feared that the wealthy would control the votes of the people, through outright purchase, intimidation, or demagogy. Large election districts combined with the natural prominence of the talented elite and patterns of deference would mean that all government offices would be held by the wealthy.

Madison seems to have aimed at and expected a similar outcome. As we saw earlier, one of the primary objectives of his institutional design was to ensure that the right kind of people would be elected to office, and he consistently associated the requisite abilities for office with men of substantial property. His comments on education, enlarged perspective, and reputation make clear that it was not the common freeholder he intended his institutional structure to draw into government. (And when we look at his views on the role of the propertied in the government we must remember that he expected that, in the future, the vast majority would be propertyless.) In addition, like Morris, he recognized the informal influence that the wealthy would have over their fellow citizens. But, unlike Morris, he did not treat these combined formal and informal powers of the propertied as a problem. It is as though he simply did not see a problem in the fact that one class, the propertied few, would in effect, rule another, the propertyless many. Yet, his own repeatedly stated concern that one group not be left to rely on the disinterestedness of another should have alerted him to the consequences of government offices being in the hands of the propertied. When Madison envisioned the unjust schemes of the majority, he treated the propertied and the propertyless as opposing interests. But when he envisioned a government run by the propertied, he seemed to see only the rationale for such an arrangement: it was in the interest of all that property be protected and that offices be held by those fully competent to do so.

Because his scheme did not formally give "all power to property," the de facto control by the propertied did not seem to trouble him. He did not share Morris's sense that men in power from a single class were likely to use their power to promote their own interests. (Of course, part of the issue is that Madison did not perceive the propertied as a single class.) More importantly, he did not see that their power would be especially dangerous both to republican principles and to the public good, because the economic power wielded outside of the government would support and be supported by the power within. Madison finally recognized this problem when confronted with what he saw as overt corruption in the 1790s: "the stock-jobbers will become the praetorian band of the Government, at once its tool and its tyrant, bribed by its largess and overawing it by its clamours and combinations."[1] From the beginning Morris saw that this problem of reciprocal advantage and influence was inherent in a system of institutions that would routinely return the wealthy to office: men would use their economic power to attain office and would use their office to enhance the value of their economic power both within and without government. In a commercial republic, economic and political power could not be kept separate unless the institutions were specifically designed to do so.

Morris's design was the old-fashioned one of basing government directly on class. Madison moved beyond this to an institutional design that recognized the multiplicity of differences that cut across class. The success or failure of Morris's system would have depended entirely on the correctness of his perception of the class differences in America and the capacity of the institutions to exactly balance those differences. Madison's approach has, of course, become rightly famous for the insight that differences arise from every human faculty, reason as well as passion, values as well as interest. Wherever there is liberty, diversity—and thus conflict—will prevail. Madison's understanding of the problems of governing a free people is subtler and more profound than Morris's. But Morris's insights into the nature of power in a commercial republic point up Madison's failure to recognize that the power his system would accord to property would threaten the republican values the system was to embody. The rights and interests of the propertyless would be left to the impartiality of the propertied in power. And republican liberty would be undermined by the interpenetration of economic and political power. The capacity to shape government policy, to protect one's rights, to serve the public good in public office, and, principally, to participate in one's own governance would be distributed unevenly between the rich and the poor.

Madison did not focus on the potential danger from the rich in part because he was designing a constitution to solve a problem peculiar to republican government: majority tyranny. The basic principles of republican government created the problem of majority oppression, and minimized the threat from minorities.[2] A serious threat from any minority thus did not fit easily into Madison's framework. And in particular, it would have been hard to see the group whose rights were most vulnerable in a republic—the propertied—as the major threat.

The danger of majority tyranny was inherent in a republic because it could arise in the ordinary course of governing. No formal usurpation was necessary for a majority to perpetrate injustice. Both Madison and Morris had expended a great deal of energy trying to get the public to see that debtor relief laws were unjust, even though a duly elected legislature had passed them. But Morris saw that the propertied few, if they held all the offices, would also be able to perpetrate injustice while acting within their designated powers. And he recognized that this threat too was likely to go unheeded: the wealthy would be able to pursue their own unjust interests in ways that would simply seem a normal part of governing. In short, Morris saw the wealthy few as the main threat in a commercial republic for the same kinds of reasons that Madison focused on the propertyless many: the institutions would generate a threat that, unless countered by an appropriate structure, would go unrecognized precisely because it was inherent in the normal operations of government. Madison was blind to this parallel.

The failure of Madison and his fellow Federalists to see past their preoccupation with the threat of the many was compounded by the institutions they designed to deal with that threat. Large election districts were aimed at minimizing the effectiveness of local demagogues and ensuring that only men of property and standing could gain the recognition necessary to win. The system of electors for the president was designed to select men of national prominence with similar expectations of the class from which such men would be drawn.

Madison, as we have seen, would have provided additional protection: possible property qualifications for suffrage in House elections, representation of property in the Senate, and qualifications for suffrage in presidential elections, if they were to be direct. (Remember that he opposed property qualifications for the candidates as unnecessary; in large districts, the people could be relied upon to discriminate on the basis of property holding more effectively than any stated qualification.) And his national veto on state legislation would have concentrated still more power in a government designed to be more effectively removed from the control of the people than those of the state governments. Madison did not, of course, succeed in getting any of these additions adopted. But that does not mitigate the force of Morris's arguments. His criticisms and warnings were directed at the design adopted by the convention. Moreover, the probable class composition of the new institutions was something on which almost everybody agreed.

In short, the Constitution of 1787 embodied Madison's neglect of the problem of the relation between economic and political power.

And having rejected Morris's proposals for protecting the people by reserving a branch of the legislature for them, there was little discussion of how the institutions should be designed to counterbalance the political power of the wealthy. There were, of course, charges of aristocracy[3] within the convention itself (as well as later by the Anti-Federalists), but they did not generate serious concern among the Federalists. The idea that the solution to majority tyranny generated its own threats by concentrating power in the hands of the wealthy was, apparently, unable to penetrate the general preoccupation with the folly and injustice of the people.

Morris also reveals the implicit consequences of the Madisonian system for the respective interests of the rich and the poor. He treated the two groups as in genuine and irreducible conflict. The rich want to maintain their power, privilege, and property; the poor want to take at least some of these for themselves. Morris agreed with Madison that the particular measures the poor were likely to demand would ultimately do them no good. And, like Madison, he thought that the benefits of stability and the security of property would filter down to the poor. But the inevitability of the plight of the poor did not lead Morris to obscure the genuineness of the conflict or the fact that it was a conflict the rich had to win. Morris was explicit that the interests of the rich had to be protected, and, to the extent that the government succeeded in doing so, the interests of the poor could never be satisfied. Although Madison confronted the same problem as Morris, he could not bring himself to be as forthright about the consequences of his solutions. Morris's bluntness brings into focus the hard edges of Madison's subtle and ambivalent approach. A basic "fact" for Madison was that the future majority would "labor under all the hardships of life and secretly sigh for a more equal share of its blessings;" the problem was how to prevent that majority from using their numerical power to translate those sighs into public policy. Madison's entire structure of government was designed to provide solutions to that problem. (That was not, of course, the sole purpose of Madison's plan, but every institution was designed with that problem in mind.) If the institutions worked as he hoped they would, the propertied few could use them to get what they wanted, but the propertyless many could not.

I do not, of course, mean that all of the propertied could get everything they wanted all of the time. Indeed, they would not always want the same thing. Part of the virtue of the "extended republic" was that the conflicting interests of those with different kinds of property would prevent "the propertied" from acting as a monolithic group (as Morris, by contrast, hoped and expected that they would).

Men of property could use the institutions to pursue their interests, which would generally be particular, and thus conflicting, interests. Mediating among these interests would be the chief task of the government. But it would also be a central task of the government to ensure that the foundations of these particular interests, the rights of property and contract, were secure. Thus the people, who would want to disrupt those foundations, must be prevented from doing so.

The form of prevention was not, however, prohibition. Madison's plan and the Constitution of 1787 formally limited the people's use of federal institutions in very few ways. Article I, Section 9, lists the specific limitations on the power of Congress. Most of those limitations can be understood as efforts to prevent the abuse of congressional power.[4] In that category were the basic protections from suspension of the writ of habeas corpus, from bills of attainder and ex post facto laws, the protections against corruption, and the requirements of accountability in the stipulation that no money be drawn from the treasury but "in consequence of appropriations" and with regular accounting of the expenditure of public monies. But these abuses were not those that Madison and his fellow Federalists associated with the threat of the majority. They were abuses likely to be generated by regional conflict (e.g., no preference to the ports of one state over another) or by tyrannous officials acting for their own power or advantage. (Of course, the Bill of Rights, specifying the now famous list of prohibitions, was added later. And these prohibitions, reflecting Anti-Federalist rather than Federalist concerns, were also aimed at the tyranny of faithless legislators.)

Madison's objective, embodied in the 1787 document, was not formally to preclude the people from using the federal government for unjust and destructive purposes, but to make it extremely difficult for them to do so. And difficult in ways that were not the same for the propertied and the propertyless. It is worth reiterating how the Constitution (as it was adopted, not just Madison's preferred plan) structured these difficulties, because they reveal a choice to contain the democratic foundations of the system rather than to limit its outcomes.

It would be difficult for the propertyless to get elected. It would be difficult for them to communicate across the distances of the federal republic and thus difficult to coordinate their plans. In the large scale republic, they would have less influence than the propertied with their fellow voters (most of whom they would not know or be known to) and with their representatives (who would also be strangers to them.) It would be difficult for them to persuade their representatives to implement plans that shifted the rules and expectations of entitlement in their favor (i.e., plans that "violated" existing property rights and expectations), because the propertied representatives would be the sort of men who understood the dire consequences of such violations. To be fair, the representatives' same broad vision and enlightened perspective might make it difficult for some of the propertied to get particular legislation they thought would be in their interest. But unlike the longings of the propertyless, the demands of the propertied could be expected to shift and vary. The legislators would have to choose among competing interests and demands and everyone would probably lose some of the time. But in the long run, the basic interests of the propertied were requirements for the economic and political health of the republic. The propertied would, therefore, have their basic objectives met. And in the long run, Madison hoped, the propertyless would not.

These relative difficulties are those widely agreed upon by Madison and his fellow Federalists as well as by the opponents of the new Constitution. The picture that emerges is not that of a specified set of limits to what the people could do through their federal government, but rather a careful structure of institutions whose geographical scope and levels of remove from the people combined to place distance between them and their government. The people's influence and access (to office and to office holders) were constrained by the indirect mechanism of large election districts. The Senate and the executive veto provided additional layers of insulation between the will of the people and public policy.*[5] The structure of the institutions was such that it would be very difficult, though not impossible, for the people either to actually run the government or to implement policies for which they could mount a sustained, widespread demand.

The Constitution provided yet another set of barriers to the people through its restrictions on state governments, which remained threatening instruments of popular will and folly. It could not, of course, restructure those governments to contain the checks and controls of the federal government. The threats posed by the people at the state level, therefore, had to be either contained by the scope of the federal government or met by direct limits. Madison was certain that only the sweeping power of the federal government to veto any state legislation could provide an adequate check. In the end, the Constitution limited the checks to specified areas that had proved to be most vulnerable to popular abuse in addition to those that were essential to the federal government's status as a national government in international affairs. Thus along with the limitations with respect to treaties, "Letters of Marque and Reprisal," import duties, troops, and war, Article I, Section 10, denied the states the power to "coin Money; emit Bills of Credit; make any Thing but gold and silver Coin a Tender in Payment of Debts; pass any Bill of Attainder, ex post facto Law or

Law impairing the Obligation of Contracts, or grant any Title of Nobility." In these crucial areas, the rights vulnerable to popular attack were protected by direct limits on what the people could use their political power to achieve. These were, of course, limitations on state *governments* and thus would also prevent state legislatures from tyrannically acting in opposition to the will of the people. But the concern consistently voiced about paper money and debtor relief—to which some of these prohibitions so clearly responded—was of legislators implementing, not overriding, the will of their constituents.

In sum, at the federal level, the Constitution handled the problem of the threat of the propertyless majority through a careful structure that made it difficult, although not impossible, for them to implement their unjust designs. At the state level explicit limits were necessary. The underlying assumption was that it was preferable to limit the participation, influence, and access of those with unreliable political judgment (the future majority), rather than rely on specified prohibitions, which were both more fragile and more limited than controlling the danger at its source.

In fact, with the addition of the Bill of Rights and the development of judicial review we ended up with a Constitution that constrains democracy both through structure and through specific prohibitions. Although the Bill of Rights was aimed at Anti-Federalist fears of abuse by those in power,*[6] it took on the significance it now has because it was ultimately implemented by a system of judicial review profoundly shaped by Federalist fears of the people. Thus the feature of the Constitution that is most widely and positively associated with the protection of minority rights resulted from a combination of Federalist and Anti-Federalist concerns. The popular identification of the protection of minority rights with specific Constitutional prohibitions misses the Federalists' basic reliance on the structure of the institutions to contain popular injustice and, more broadly, to confine the political efficacy of the people.*[7] This dark side to the justly lauded virtues of the American tradition of rights-protection is also part of the system of judicial review that implements the Bill of Rights. Toward the end of this chapter, I will return to the Bill of Rights and argue that judicial review was the culmination of the Federalist conception of politics, formally institutionalizing the hierarchy of civil over political rights, and further limiting the democratic foundations of the republic.

Let me pause here to avoid a possible misunderstanding. My argument about the undemocratic quality of the constitutional structure does not claim that there are no virtues to the Constitution's subtle combination of separation of powers and checks and balances. We have many reasons to believe that complex systems can do a better job of implementing democracy than the simple majoritarianism of a unicameral legislature. In a large society, democracy is probably best actualized under a complex structure that divides the legislative, executive, and judicial functions (and federal and state powers).*[8] But that claim presumes that the basic purpose of the structure is to give voice to and implement the considered will of the people. Claims for the democracy-enhancing qualities of the separation of powers must be qualified if the structure is designed to return to office an economic elite who will at each level be further removed from the people in the sense of responsiveness and similarity of background and interests. The Madisonian framework created a complex system in which the people do not govern themselves, even though they are governed with their consent. The challenge is to identify the genuine advantages of the Madisonian system (such as Bruce Ackerman's important insight that no one branch of the government can authoritatively claim to speak for "the people"),[9] and to determine if those advantages can be separated from the problem of drawing the economic elite into office. Systems of separation of powers and checks and balances *can* help accomplish the difficult task of translating the views, interests, and desires of thousands of citizens into governmental policy and action. But it is an independent question whether the purpose and effect of a particular system of checks is to limit the capacity of ordinary people to participate in their own governance—as I have argued is the case in the Madisonian Constitution.

Finally, a critical stance towards the undemocratic character of our institutions does not require a naive image of the innate virtue of "the people." We need not abandon Madison's insight that not only perfidious men in office but the people themselves can be the source of unwise and unjust measures. But that insight should make us no less critical of a system that controls the danger of the people by relying on the superior capacities of the economic elite.

B. Civil versus Political Liberty

The discussion so far has been about the ways that Morris reveals the judgments and choices implicit in the Madisonian Constitution. More importantly, Morris helps us see the conceptual framework that made these choices seem inevitable. The Constitution was Madisonian not simply in the structure of its institutions, but in the understanding of republican government that gave meaning and legitimacy to those institutions. The comparison with Morris helps us grasp the contours of that understanding. His most direct contribution is that he makes explicit what is left implicit by Madison and most of his fellow Federalists: the distinction between civil and political liberty.

The Framers had to struggle with the inadequacy of the political language that had served American statesmen through the revolution. The language of rights and liberty was vague and ambiguous, leading to confusion about the relation between the rights that are the object of government, what the people could do by right, and what the nature of the right to participation was. Everyone agreed that no man should be bound by laws to which he did not consent. Everyone knew that a man's rights could not otherwise be secure. And no one questioned that the purpose of government was to secure rights. But when the laws to which the people had consented violated rights, the terms to describe the problem were elusive.

The nature and scope of the people's right to consent was uncertain. Did it flow from the natural equality of all, that is, directly from the nature of man? Or was it derivative from the need to secure rights? Madison somewhat uneasily skirted the issue of the status of the right to consent, even as he succinctly captured the problem in his persons-property-political rights formulation. This formulation placed the security of rights in the foreground—the task is to equally protect both the rights of persons and property—while posing equal political participation as the problem. Morris's clear distinction removes the confusion of language: it is the protection of *civil* rights that is the task of government. And his hierarchy provides the conceptual framework for solving the problem: political rights are merely the means to the end, the protection of civil rights. Once the relation of means to ends is clear, necessary limitations on political rights follow as a matter of logic.

Madison never explicitly or comfortably accepted the idea that there was no intrinsic right to political participation. But he framed the problem in the terms Morris made explicit. The rights of persons and property were Morris's civil rights, which were rendered unequally secure by political rights. Civil rights were the objective, political rights were the problem. Madison not only used the distinction between civil and political rights, he tacitly accepted the hierarchy Morris boldly announced.

It was in large part the special importance of property that made clear the need for this hierarchy. We have already seen that Morris and Madison each had a set of arguments about why it was essential that the new Constitution ensure the security of property. When we look at their arguments together, we get yet one more perspective on the status of property in their thinking about the Constitution.

One of the most telling indications of this status is the peculiar way they used the word. Like most of their fellow Federalists, Madison and Morris rarely spelled out what they meant by "property;" the meaning varied according to context. Sometimes the word referred to the rights of property (as in the modern sense of a bundle of rights): the right to secure possession, to free use, to acquisition. Sometimes the word meant literally concrete property: land, money, chattels. Sometimes it meant men of property, the propertied class. But very often the word carried all these meanings, as when the "influence due to property" was discussed. When property was used in this sense, it connoted the intrinsic significance of the fundamental rights of man and of his basic needs, the importance of security, of independence, and of superior power and influence. Used in this broad sense, the word indicated the central and pervasive importance of property. It was not simply a right, an interest, or a class; it was a basic element of politics which took its overwhelming importance from all of its meanings.*[10]

Morris also provides a much more direct statement of the importance of property, which both reveals the rationale for the status he accorded property and helps us see the important similarities and differences between his approach and Madison's.

> Relying on long experience and mature reflection, I hesitate not to assert, that plenty, power, numbers, wealth and felicity will ever be in proportion to the security of property, and thence is deduced the corollary, that a legislator, who omits securing property, neglects his duty.[11]

Morris's position is clear: property is the keystone which, if not protected, will bring down with it all the advantages of government. A legislator, statesman, or theorist who does not give adequate attention to property necessarily risks all other objects of government. No government could survive without the support of the most powerful group in society, the wealthy, and their support was contingent on the secure protection of property rights. This protection was necessary not only for their individual security, but for an economy in which their various enterprises could thrive. Moreover, it was essential in a republic to deprive demagogues of the opportunity of rising to power by means of attacks on property. In short, the security of property was essential for the objects and the very existence of republican government.

Madison was less interested than Morris in plenty, power, numbers, and wealth, but he shared Morris's assessment of the pivotal role of property. If a republican government failed to protect property rights, it would fail to provide justice and thus would threaten its own foundations. This was, in essence, Madison's somewhat pragmatic justification for the hierarchy between civil and political liberty. The purpose of political liberty was to achieve justice, and liberty would only survive to the extent that it succeeded in that purpose. And since it was property that political rights put at risk, Madison ultimately agreed with Morris's stark claim that there was a trade-off between property and political rights, and property must prevail.

Madison's approach was, however, more subtle and more ambiguous than Morris's, as was the institutional solution adopted by the convention. It is important both to reveal the priorities underlying the subtlety and to recognize the ambiguities in the institutional design. This will help us see the choices implicitly made in the institutional structure and the choices left open or unresolved.

Driven in large part by pragmatic concerns (doubts about the popular acceptability of a freehold franchise and the dangers of excluding large numbers of the population), Madison came to see that formal restrictions on political rights were neither necessary nor optimal to contain the political power of the people. The indirect mechanisms could structure the whole relation of the people to the federal government, shape the patterns of participation, and limit the effectiveness of the poor. The necessary control of popular injustice would thus be embedded in the very foundations of the political system, in its daily practices, rather than being accomplished by explicit exclusions of the people from office or franchise or by the designation of vulnerable rights as beyond the reach of the legislature. This more pervasive form of control did not proclaim a subordination of political to civil rights. But the principled justification for containing the capacity of the people to implement their will came from the hierarchy of civil over political rights.

The pervasive constraints on the people may have had a deeper effect on the quality of democracy fostered by the Constitution than direct limits would have had. It is nevertheless equally important that by avoiding such limits, the Constitution of 1787 stated no formal preference for civil rights (even property) over political rights.

One might think that all these points are glosses on the obvious foundation for the priority of property, namely, that it is a natural right. While that is true at one level, it entirely misses the complexity of the problem the Federalists faced. For the Framers, property was both a natural and a positive right, and it was a right that could not simply be declared to be beyond the reach of government because it required government (and was therefore the origin of government). We have seen that both Morris and Madison tried to invest the social (or positive) rights of property with the sanctity of natural rights without actually claiming natural rights status for them. Both used the connection between property and freedom to suggest that government interference with property was a fundamental violation of individual liberty. But even this claim could not completely resolve the underlying problem. If the specific rights of property were a matter of positive law, then pointing to the existence of an underlying natural right or connection to freedom would not be sufficient to protect any given property right because the general claim could not define which particular rights were a matter of societal choice and which were fundamental.

I think there was a reason why none of the Framers resorted to a simple, crude claim that the existing rights of property deserved protection because they were natural rights. The presence of slavery meant that the distinction between natural and positive rights of property could not be cavalierly ignored. No one in 1787 defended the ownership of slaves as included among the natural rights of property. And yet most of the Framers believed that since slavery existed as a matter of positive law, slave owners could claim the right to have their property secure. This painful reminder that not all positive rights of property were natural rights, or perhaps even consistent with natural rights, meant that the arguments for the security of property could not simply rely on claims of natural right.*[12] And this was not merely a matter of rhetoric. Property rights had to be conceived and institutionalized in ways that reflected both the sense that natural rights were the foundation of existing property rights and the (less conscious) recognition that the two were not identical.

The inherent ambiguity of the status of property rights is especially apparent and problematic in the basic issue confronting the Framers: determining the proper role of government with respect to property. As the Framers conceived property (and as we conceive it today), it would not make sense to have a constitutional provision stipulating that Congress shall make no law respecting property. In ways very different from, say, freedom of religion, property requires positive governmental action.*[13] The rights of property must be defined and enforced by law in order to be fully enjoyed. The obvious problem then is to distinguish between governmental action which is necessary to define and protect property (including, inevitably, laws regulating conflicting property rights) and laws which are "interferences" with, or violations of, property rights. As the Framers thought of property, there were no simple categories that could accomplish this crucial task. As we have seen, Madison simply spoke as if the difference were clear, at least to him: "The regulation of these various and interfering interests forms the principal task of modern legislation,"[14] but popularly demanded depreciating currency was clearly a violation of vested rights. The inherent ambiguity in the status of property is linked to the dual requirement of government action and limitations on that action to secure property rights. Thus, the focal point of Madison's system—property as symbol of the vulnerability of rights in a republic—carried with it the unresolved question of how to define those rights. Madison left that problem unexamined and the Constitution of 1787 left its solution open.

II. The Neglect of Self-Governance

Morris helps us see the importance of property in Madison's thought and the corresponding role of the elite and subordination of political liberty. Wilson makes the significance of these issues clearer still by helping us see how the preoccupation with property skewed the Federalist perception of the problems and possibilities of republican government. His perspective suggests that Madison underestimated the people's political capacities and gave little attention to the institutional arrangements that might develop those capacities. Wilson's images of the people's direct engagement with public affairs contrast sharply with Madison's view of the limited scope of the people's political competence: "There can be no doubt that there are subjects to which the capacities of the bulk of mankind are unequal, and on which they must and will be governed by those with whom they happen to have acquaintance and confidence."[15]

For Madison the republican objective was not therefore that the people take an active interest in public issues, in which they were incompetent, but that they choose leaders who were competent. Madison's version of Wilson's picture of neighbors getting together to discuss politics would not have them engaged in thoughtful dialogue, but repeating the leading opinions of the day.

Even within the legislature, Madison assumed deference to an elite. Because only a few were actually capable of governing, he warned that "in all legislative assemblies the greater the number composing them may be, the fewer will be the men who in fact direct their proceedings."[16] The object then is to get a body of representatives sufficiently small and superior to the bulk of the people to minimize the dominance of the few—by being composed of the few. This Madisonian objective is, of course, a far cry from Wilson's image of the House as an exact mirror of its constituents.

Wilson's emphasis on the importance of participation helps us to see its absence in the Madisonian vision. The new republic was not to be government *by* the people. Indeed, part of Madison's message was that Americans should avoid the fatal democratic error of thinking that the people are literally capable of governing themselves. For Madison republican government was an *improvement* on democracy[17] because the system of representation, especially in large districts, allowed for a government for the people, but composed of leaders superior to the people.

Madison showed no hesitance in constructing a system in which the common people would not hold office. The issue for Madison was exclusively instrumental: which institutional arrangements could best achieve the ends of government (in ways compatible with republican principles). Even when Morris joined the debate with the argument that the Madisonian system gave dangerous power to the rich, the subject at issue was the threat to rights and interests, and the potential subversion of republican government. Neither Morris nor Madison ever suggested that if the system effectively (although not formally) excluded people from office, they would be deprived of something of value or something to which they had a right.

Morris did actually talk about the importance of being able to serve in public office and the importance of ensuring that such service could be the path to "Glory" for those driven by the love of fame. This love is "one of the strongest passions in the human breast" and could be a boon to society because it is "the great spring to noble and illustrious actions."[18] Morris warned of the danger of not providing proper outlets for this passion and spoke with his own passionate anger of the pain and frustration of those unable to satisfy their desire for distinction and recognition through public office.[19] These were, however, concerns that applied only to the elite. The glowing love of fame was an aristocratic virtue not to be looked for among the common folk.*[20] Pride was the great principle that actuated the poor as well as the rich; but in the poor it was manifested in resistance to authority[21] and not, presumably, in the desire to exercise authority. The purpose of reserving one branch of the legislature for the people was not so they too would have scope for their love of fame, but to provide protection for them against the machinations of the rich who would otherwise dominate the government.

Morris's concern with the opportunity for the elite*[22] to win recognition and distinction by serving in public office was an important strain in Federalist thinking. A less aristocratic version of Morris's concern underlies Madison's more typical expectations about who would hold public office and why. But in the views that prevailed at the convention, none of the various forms of attention to public office as meeting a need for public recognition led to a concern about the role ordinary people would play in their government. Wilson alone among the Federalists treated political participation as an essential element of the highest ends of government: human happiness and improvement. As such, it was not reserved for any one class, but was a basic part of the liberty republican government was intended to achieve.

Through Wilson we see that, in the Madisonian framework, self-governance is not intrinsically valuable as an exercise of autonomy. People should be able to protect themselves from the abuse of their rights, and only government by consent can ensure such protection. But the Madisonian approach does not include the idea that people have a right or need to directly shape the decisions that will affect them, to partake in, rather than cede to others, the process of governing.*[23]

The contrast between the meaning of participation for Wilson and the subordinate status of political rights in the Madisonian framework raises the question of whether Madison and his fellow Federalists were committed to republican government at all, and if so why. Were they trying to design a republican government simply because that was what prevailing popular opinion required? Was republican government just the best, or most acceptable, means available at the time? Or, put more precisely, if republican liberty was purely instrumental to the achievement of extrinsic ends—the protection of rights which do not themselves entail or include political rights—then would republican government lose all claims to legitimacy if one could show that some other form of government were better at protecting those rights? For Morris the answer was clearly yes. He provides a contrast at the opposite end of the spectrum from Wilson, and reveals the Madisonian, and characteristically Federalist, position. For Morris republican liberty was almost exclusively instrumental. He had little attachment to republican government as such. If a "higher toned," more aristocratic government would do the job better (as he came to think it would), there would be no loss.

Madison was more ambivalent in part because of his pride in Americans designing their own government. Government in America would not be imposed by force or conquest but by the choice of its people. It is clear that Madison accorded great value to this foundational act of self-governance, as well as to America's capacity to prove that republican government could work. So it would be wrong to say that for Madison there was no intrinsic value in self-governance, and wrong and misleading to say that there was no right to self-governance. Madison clearly thought republican government was the best, indeed the noblest, form of government.[24] His effort at the convention and in all his writing was to figure out how to make republican government work, to find republican solutions to republican problems. So we are back to the question, why the commitment to republican government?

Ironically, the first answer itself entails the subordinate status of political participation that has raised the question. For Madison, the security of civil rights for *all* can only be achieved under republican government. Despite tacit and unacknowledged compromises, Madison was genuinely committed to the protection of the rights of all and to the republican government such protection required. Taking the equal protection of civil rights as the object of government entailed the subordination of political rights as means to this end, on the one hand and on the other, required republican government with its claims for the rights of self-governance.

Madison also seemed to believe that the same natural equality of man that requires the equal protection of civil rights commands a right to be governed only with one's consent. Political liberty therefore follows from this basic equality, although Madison never inquired very closely into the nature of the connection or into the kinds of political rights required by the equality of man.

The difference between Madison and Wilson is thus not that Madison accorded *no* value to political liberty: the difference lies in the literalness of their conception of self-government. Wilson actually envisioned the people doing the governing. For Madison, republican government meant essentially government by the elite with the consent of the people. Moreover, Madison paid virtually no attention to the importance of the ongoing participation in public affairs of a politically active and engaged citizenry. By contrast, participation for Wilson meant not just the genuine opportunity to hold public office, or even the right to vote, but the daily interest in politics and the informed oversight of governmental action such engagement made possible. In short, the value Madison accorded to political liberty was largely unconsidered and never led to a sense that the people's participation in politics was important either for them or for republican government.

Wilson's democratic solutions to republican problems raise the question of just what the Madisonian scheme relied upon for good government. Wilson wanted to render the people capable of literal self-government. Madison thought that was impossible and tried to circumvent the problem their incapacities posed.

Of course the first Madisonian solution to the dangers of popular government was the mitigation of faction made possible by the extended republic. But Wilson's perspective suggests that with all the advantages of the extended republic outlined in *The Federalist*, No. 10, Madison still ultimately had to rely on the virtue and understanding of the people. Madison said that he did not want to rely on enlightened statesmen alone, but his solution is not adequate to the problem. Consider the example he posed, taxes and paper money. He said an extended republic would make it unlikely and difficult for those of unjust designs to combine. But where is the implausibility or difficulty for the representatives of the landed interests from all over the country combining in the legislature to push through a tax system which favors their interest? Madison himself suggested that ties of economic interest were stronger than regional differences.[25] He said the rage for paper money or other attacks on property might take over a state, but were unlikely to spread throughout the whole country. But if the majority were to be propertyless and without the hope of acquiring property, what "interests" could they have which would be strong enough to prevent them from combining against those with property?*[26]

The multiplicity of interests might mitigate the effects of some conflict; but it must have a limited impact on the most common and durable source of factions: the various and unequal distributions of property. Madison must finally rely to a great extent on enlightened statesmen. And what would make a factious and unjust people elect wise and just representatives? Large election districts might help (as Wilson would agree) but surely this is not a sufficient answer. Ultimately, the people must have the virtue and understanding to elect men of wisdom and justice. Wilson tried to envision the institutional means of developing these characteristics; Madison did not. Madison placed his faith in a system designed to get a government better than its people. Wilson suggested that was impossible.

In all fairness to Madison, I should say that Wilson's position relies on his different perception of American society. If he had also believed that America would be divided into the mutually hostile rich and poor, he could not have been so confident about the people's understanding of the rules of justice. Perhaps what is really remarkable is not Wilson's faith in the people, but Madison's faith in republican government.

Nevertheless, it is important to see the foundation of Madison's faith. He had to assume that there would be an elite with the capacity to govern, and whose prominence would be sufficiently commanding to ensure election in large districts—requiring, of course, the people's capacity to recognize and choose this prominent elite. Morris also expected to rely on the elite to govern, but he designed an institution exclusively for that purpose. He expected the wise and faithful guardianship of a Senate elected for life, not the vigilance or good judgment of the people, to secure both public and private liberties.

Madison's system, however, did not rely on the pure disinterestedness of those in office. The institutions were designed so that it would be difficult for the legislators to use their position to promote their private interests. Madison, like Morris, assumed that if the legislators' private interests were frustrated, they would turn their attention to the public good. His system required vision and wisdom from the elite, but not a constant ability to rise above self-interest. The institutions would check self-interest rather than assume its absence.

The interlocking roles of self-interest, conflict, and the public good are complicated in the Madisonian Constitution. On the one hand,

Madison had a particularly deep understanding of the nature of conflict among free men. We saw that in the contrast with Morris and see it again in comparison with Wilson. Wilson's strength was that he considered the problem of cohesiveness and the effect of government on the nature of the community. But his vision of a harmonious society was not the result of having come to terms with the implication of the actual conflicts that flourished in the new states, or those (as Madison would remind him) that have characterized all societies. On the other hand, for all Madison's sophistication about the sources of conflict, he had little more to offer as a solution than the neutralization of that conflict. He explained how his system of government would allow cross-cutting interests to cancel out each other's political efficacy at the federal level. But he offered little about what the public good actually consisted of and how his system would ensure that it was "discerned" and pursued. And he had little to say about what would promote sufficient harmony among the conflicting groups to develop some sense of common purpose. Madison's system had to rely on a certain level of public spiritedness, at least among those in office. He wanted the lasting interests of the nation to override local and partial interests. But the institutions were not designed to foster a population out of which at least some would rise above the conflict of interests and which would select such men for their representatives.

Wilson alerts us to Madison's limited conception of democracy and to the problems that emerge from a system of republican government designed to contain the threat of the people rather than to enhance their participation and their political competence. Three questions remain about the critique Wilson implies: First, is there significant depth to his perspective, or is his theory essentially a naive vision of the virtues of democracy that fails to take seriously its inherent problems? Second, is the implied critique really a criticism of the Constitution, since Wilson enthusiastically endorsed the Constitution the convention produced and many of his most stirring commentaries on the virtues of participation are made in praise of the Constitution? And third, if there are important differences in Madison's and Wilson's political theories, but they accepted much the same institutions to implement those theories, do the differences matter? The discussion of all three questions converges on the answer to this last: the differences matter to the conceptual framework that underpins the Madisonian Constitution, a framework that became dramatically more important and institutionally crystallized in the next stage of the formation of the Constitution, the establishment of judicial review.

In answer to the first question, the strength of Wilson's thought is his insight that political participation can enhance political competence. His suggestion that the ongoing exercise of political responsibility would generate bonds between citizens and mutual commitment to shared ends is persuasive. Far less persuasive is his vision of natural harmony and the tacit suggestion that the commitment and connection among the citizens would be sufficient to overcome all perceptions of conflicting interests. Wilson was not as profound a thinker as Madison in part because he did not recognize tensions between his values or the problems that the very success of political liberty might generate. It was Madison's genius to see the multiple ways that liberty itself generates conflict and to recognize that the rights he thought derived from the natural equality of man were in tension with one another. But Wilson's message is nevertheless substantive and important: when envisioning good government, we must bear in mind all the dimensions of the people who are to be governed, their highest potential as well as their most destructive inclinations; we must recognize their social capacities as well as the capacity for conflict; we can no more afford to ignore what fosters the bonds of community and the capacity to discern and deliberate about the public good, than we can afford to ignore conflict. Wilson did neglect conflict. But he offers us a framework for thinking about republican government which provides an important alternative to the Madisonian conception. Wilson invites us to think about conflict in a broader context and thus to develop a more complete and compelling alternative. And, perhaps most importantly, he reminds us of the questions we must ask, even if we are not always fully satisfied by his answers.

There is still the problem of Wilson's enthusiastic endorsement of the Constitution, which raises doubts about his understanding of democracy. If he wanted as close an approximation to direct democracy as possible, why did he show so little sympathy for the smaller scale state governments? The Anti-Federalists, who shared Wilson's concern with the role of the people in the government, opposed the new Constitution because its scope and structure would ensure that it was dominated by the elite, leaving no room for the "middling sort" of men in office.

Wilson is an interesting mixture of views and perspective. He shared the Federalists' objectives: a central government capable of promoting the conditions for an expanding, prosperous economy with the necessary strength at home and abroad to protect the nation's interests. And he shared the Federalists' sense of the impediments to these objectives: the complete inadequacy of the central government under the Articles of Confederation and the foolish and dangerous policies, such as paper money, pursued by state governments. But Wilson's perception of the problems of republican government was far closer to the Anti-Federalists' than to Madison's focus on majority tyranny. When Wilson talked of the need to provide checks on the different branches of government, he treated government officials as the potential enemies of the people, not their instruments of injustice. Such an approach was, of course, consistent with his confidence in the people, but has an oddly anachronistic character to it compared to Madison. Wilson seems preoccupied with the "old" political question of the rulers versus the ruled, rather than the problems posed when the people become their own rulers. Part of the reason for this preoccupation may have been that Wilson thought participatory institutions would make the people good rulers of themselves, leaving only the "old" problem of preventing perfidious usurpation by those in office.

The question remains, however, why Wilson thought the new Constitution would foster the kind of participation he thought desirable, when the Anti-Federalists so vigorously disagreed, and his allies hoped otherwise. Unfortunately Wilson did not have much to say directly on this point. He simply argued that the dangers of abuse of power were best controlled in large districts. Although the nature of the abuse he foresaw was different from what Madison was primarily concerned about, he made the standard Federalist claims that people of true merit would stand out in large districts and that it was easier for designing demagogues to prevail in small districts. He offered the conventional example of corruption in small districts in England. He seems never to have taken seriously the Anti-Federalist arguments that only the merit of the *economic* elite will have a chance of standing out in a large district, or that the close ties he hoped for between citizens and their representatives would best be fostered in small districts. Wilson wanted the people to feel that the governing of their country was their business, but he never even tried to counter the argument that the scale of the new government would create a distance between it and the ordinary citizen.

We can see another slant on this puzzle of how Wilson could be committed both to popular participation in politics and to the Madisonian Constitution in his disparagement of state governments. He was as eager as any for constraints on state power to prevent the abuses that Madison and the rest of his allies were concerned about. We can make sense of Wilson's position if he based it on the judgment that these unwise and unjust policies proved that the state governments did not truly reflect the will of the people. At first glance this interpretation seems hard to swallow. It was virtually uncontested that there was a popular demand for these same wicked policies. However, Wilson may have thought that the fact that the people sought foolish solutions to legitimate problems showed that the government was not working as it should. In the comparatively small districts of state governments, the people were being misled by designing demagogues to think, for example, that paper money rather than the notes of a well-established bank was the solution to the lack of capital and a circulating currency. The state governments were obviously not returning the right sort of people to office or fostering the intelligent and responsible citizenry that a properly designed republic could. Wilson's principles did not imply that every group of people was entitled to have its wishes fulfilled, but that government institutions should make it possible for the people as a whole to implement their will through active and responsible participation. Wilson's faith in the people and his view that the institutions of government have an effect on the character of the people could have led to the conclusion that the state governments were hardly the optimal form of republican government. Constraining their power was not constraining the democratically expressed will of the people, but the abuses a bad structure of government had spawned. And designing a federal system with a significantly different structure was an appropriate solution to problems the state governments were generating.

If Wilson's position is sufficiently thoughtful to serve as a critique, is it in fact a critique of the Constitution of 1787? To see why the answer is yes, we must first recognize that Wilson was wrong about the capacity of the new institutions to implement the ideals he so eloquently articulated. His fellow Federalists and the Anti-Federalists were right about the economic elite dominating the national government. But even though his institutional judgments were wrong, the questions he tells us to ask about institutional structures and their consequences remain crucial and stand as the foundation of an important critique of the Constitution.

It is not an accident that Wilson, the only one of the Federalists to turn his attention to the potential of participatory democracy, was also the only one who denied a primacy to property as an end of government. For Wilson, property was only a third order value; he did not foresee a majority interested in attacking property, and he placed far less weight on stability than Madison did. Stability was one of Madison's highest priorities; he always invoked it when arguing for the necessity of checks on the people. Wilson treated stability as desirable but not of such paramount importance. He was willing to acknowledge that republican government cannot solve the problem of instability. It was the price one had to pay for political freedom. Wilson could focus on enhancing the people's role in government because he was willing to tolerate instability and, implicitly, a certain insecurity of property.*[27] Wilson's stance toward democracy, and the relation between his views of property and democracy, reveal a basic difference between his approach to republican government and the Madisonian focus on majority tyranny as the inherent problem of republican government. Wilson agreed with Madison that the new Constitution would achieve the ends and solve the problems of republican government. But Wilson conceived both the ends and the problems differently. As we shall see more fully in the final chapter, Wilson's most important contribution to our understanding of the Constitution is the insight he indirectly provides into the basic conceptual underpinning of the Constitution.

III. The Limitations Confirmed: The Anti-Federalist Perspective

I have focused so far on the implicit critiques of Morris and Wilson because they offer the most nuanced insights into the weaknesses of the Madisonian Constitution. Their shared interest in the problems of making republican government compatible with justice, security, and liberty makes their "internal" critique a better source for critical reflection than the hostile attacks of the Constitution's opponents, the Anti-Federalists. Wilson and Morris also have more to tell us about the problems of constructing a *national* republic than do the Anti-Federalists, who did not really share that goal. But the Anti-Federalists serve to reinforce the implicit critique of Morris and Wilson by making it explicit. And, most importantly, their attacks were directed to the Constitution the convention actually produced. Their arguments show that the weaknesses Morris and Wilson indirectly reveal were in fact incorporated into the Constitution.

One of the Anti-Federalists' basic objections to the structure of the new Constitution was that only the few would hold the offices it created. Their objection embraced Morris's insight that in a commercial republic—or rather, in the sort of commercial republic the new Constitution would establish—the rich would hold all the power and abuse it to their own advantage. But unlike Morris, the Anti-Federalists' objections were not based on the protection of rights and interests alone. Like Wilson, they cared about the role the people would play in government and the consequent effects on the character of the republic and its people.

At the core of the Anti-Federalists' politics was a close and active relation between the citizen and his government. The Anti-Federalists acknowledged that direct democracy was not practicable, but they wanted representation to approximate it as closely as possible. The citizen should feel a direct responsibility for, and attachment to, the government. If the people as a whole could not directly participate in the councils of government, they should at least be represented by men they knew and understood. The kind of knowledge necessary would not be possible in the larger election districts the new Constitution set out.

> Opinion founded on the knowledge of those who govern, procures obedience without force. But remove the opinion, which must fall with a knowledge of characters in so widely extended a country and force then becomes necessary to secure the purpose of civil government . . . [28]

Only representatives like themselves, known and observed by them, could give citizens the necessary confidence in their government.

> In a republic of the extent of this continent, the people in general would be acquainted with very few of their rulers: the people at large would know little of their proceedings. . . . [They] could not possibly be made acquainted with the conduct of their representatives, nor be informed of the reasons upon which measures were founded. The consequence will be, they will have no confidence in their legislature, suspect them of ambitious views, be jealous of every measure they adopt, and will not support the laws they pass.[29]

It was thus not the formal right to vote, but the ability of the citizens to make considered judgments that would sustain their confidence in government.

The approximation of direct democracy required that the representative body closely resemble the people at large: "A full and equal representation is that which possesses the same interests, feelings, opinions, and views the people themselves would [possess] were they all assembled."[30] Although the Anti-Federalists realized that this goal could not be fully attained, they wanted at least a "representation large enough to secure a substantial (if not proportionate) representation of the middling classes, in particular the sturdy yeomanry."[31] The middle class was felt to be more trustworthy and reliable than either the rich or the poor. But representatives from the middle class, the Anti-Federalists believed, could be elected only in a system that relied on real knowledge of the character of candidates, rather than on reputation across a large district.

> [W]hen we call on thirty or forty thousand inhabitants to unite in giving their votes for one man, it will be uniformly impracticable for them to unite in any men, except those who have became [sic] eminent for their civil or military rank, or their popular legal abilities: it will be found totally impracticable for men in the private walks of life, except in the profession of the law, to become conspicuous enough

> to attract the notice of so many electors and have their suffrages.[32]

The Anti-Federalists wanted a government in which the people would take an active, responsible part. This scheme required equality among the citizens and a general capacity for public virtue, both inconsistent with the Federalist vision of a large, commercial republic.[33] The Anti-Federalists sought to foster a reciprocal relation between the character of government and the character of the citizens under it: "Government operates upon the spirit of the people, as well as the spirit of the people operates upon it . . . Our duty is to frame a government friendly to liberty and the rights of mankind, which will tend to cherish and cultivate a love of liberty among our citizens."[34] Thus, a republican citizenry must not only be free and independent; it must also be interested in and devoted to public good.

The Anti-Federalists also saw that one could not expect a citizen to be devoted to the public good, if some groups clearly benefited far more from that public good than others. As Herbert Storing put it, the Anti-Federalists wanted "a society in which there are no extremes of wealth, influence, education, or anything else—the homogeneity of a moderate, simple, sturdy, and virtuous people."[35] The Anti-Federalists tacitly agreed with Madison that if there were a large group in society who "secretly sigh for a more equal share of life's blessings," they were likely to pose a threat both to the common good and to the rights of others. But the Anti-Federalists did not treat the existence of such a group as inevitable. They thought some forms of government would foster this sort of dangerous inequality, and others would not. The Federalists' Constitution clearly would.

> If there are advantages in the equal division of our lands, and the strong and manly habits of our people, we ought to establish governments calculated to give duration to them, and not governments which never can work naturally, till that equality of property, and those free and manly habits shall be destroyed . . . [36]

The Anti-Federalists believed that differences in a society should not so divide the community that they render the pursuit of the collective good impossible. Nor should private interests divert attention from the civic virtue a republic requires. Prosperity great enough to sustain luxury was thus not the object of, but a threat to, a republic.

The protection of private rights and interests should not be the sole concern of the citizens, nor should it be the sole concern in designing the republic. Like Wilson, the Anti-Federalists placed a high value on the citizens' active participation in the affairs of state*[37] and understood that government had to be designed to facilitate such participation. They did not want a citizenry that looked only to its private interests and left the public good in the hands of distant representatives. Beyond basic prudence lay a strong Anti-Federalist belief that truly free men control their own destiny and govern their own affairs, both public and private.[38] The Anti-Federalists were committed to the protection of rights, but they were also interested in the potential of genuine self-government.[39]

For the Anti-Federalists, the proposed Constitution did not meet these objectives. Because the political values discussed above could be realized only in a relatively small community, the Constitution made a fundamental mistake in shifting the locus of power from the states, where genuine republican government was possible, to a central government, where it was not.*[40] The Federalists claimed that the central government, required extensive powers[41] and that the great advantage of the new Constitution was that it would structure the necessary power to make it safe. The Anti-Federalists were unconvinced: not only was the power assigned to the federal government dangerously misplaced, but the proposed structure itself was a threat to republican liberty.

Although the new Constitution was based formally on the consent of the people, the Anti-Federalists predicted that real access to power would be limited to the elite.[42] The large election districts for the federal legislature would not give the common people a chance for effective representation, but instead would "commit the many to the mercy, prudence, and moderation of the few."[43] The inclination of those in power to serve their own ends was well known, and the Anti-Federalists had no confidence that the "few" would serve the interests of all.[44] The Anti-Federalists feared that the Constitution's "tendency is to collect the powers of the government, now in the body of the people in reality, and to place them in the higher orders and fewer hands. . . . [N]otwithstanding the parade of words and forms, the government must possess the soul of aristocracy."[45] Thus, in the Anti-Federalists' view, the Constitution was designed to destroy any existing equality and to make true republican government impossible.

Despite the great differences in perspectives, values, and allegiances, the Anti-Federalists' critique reinforces Morris's and Wilson's (indirect) insights into the weakness of the Madisonian Constitution. There is a remarkable confluence among the basic insights and objections. This is in part because there was a striking degree of agreement among all—Federalists and Anti-Federalists—about how the new system would work: for the people as a whole, the Constitution would foster and rely on private interest, not public virtue; the talented few would run the government; the large republic would create a great distance between the people and their representatives.

While the Anti-Federalists attacked each of these features, the Federalists were confident that they provided the proper foundation for successful republican government. The Federalists offered in place of active political involvement a distant but smoothly functioning state that would ensure the conditions necessary for the effective pursuit of private gain.*[46] The people as a whole would be relegated to the margins of politics, but guaranteed the freedom and security to pursue their private interests—which was the real purpose of government. The reliance on private gain would generate an inequality that the new Constitution would encourage and entrench by concentrating both wealth and power in the hands of the few; but that inequality was the natural result of liberty and needed to be protected in the interests of the weak as well as the strong. The Federalist Constitution would simply put those competent to do so in power.

Prosperity and security born of effective government would provide an attachment to government that would substitute not only for the confidence that would have developed from a close relationship between citizen and representative, but also for the attachment based on civic virtue that the Anti-Federalists advocated. Yet the Federalists did not simply resign themselves to a society without public virtue. They did believe in the public good, but they had faith only in the elite's capacity to discern and pursue it. This position is entirely consistent with the Federalist assumptions that inequality of wealth is inevitable and that one of the essential conditions of prosperity is preventing the poor from ruining the economy and undermining the republic by trying to gain a greater share of the wealth.[47] The Federalists considered the poor prone to misunderstanding their own best interest, particularly the importance of securing private property. The rich, on the other hand, could be relied upon both to discern the public good and to pursue it. In the Federalists' proposed system, the elite could genuinely devote their attention to the public good with the confidence that the common interest they were promoting was in no conflict with their own.

In dismissing the viability of a generally shared civic virtue, the Federalists seem indirectly to have acknowledged that the public as well as the private benefits of their system would be unequally distributed. The Federalists saw that, under their system, industry and its attendant inequality would make impracticable the Anti-Federalist reliance on civic virtue as the foundation of society.[48] Economic inequality would make the people dangerous and require that their role be limited.*[49] For this reason, the Federalists designed a structure that would render the experiences that foster, sustain, and reward civic virtue and public interest inaccessible to the great body of the people.

The Anti-Federalists echo the connections we have already seen between inequality and the Madisonian inattention to participation. The Federalists may well have been correct that a government based on public-spirited participation is impossible when the economy fosters inequality. To sustain such an economy, inequality may indeed have to be reproduced in the political process. Although the Federalists genuinely believed that their system would serve the best interests of the poor, they were justifiably uncertain about relying on a popular commitment to the Federalists' conception of the public good. Citizens can be expected to act in the common interest only when they perceive their interests to be common.[50] If fundamental conflicts of interest prevent a system from working genuinely for the benefit of all, civic virtue can be at best the prerogative of the advantaged.

This last argument invites us to confront directly the Federalist claim that the Madisonian framework of elite rule would in fact promote the public good of all and the corollary claim that fuller or more direct participation by the people would only make them worse off. These claims are really the moral foundation of the Madisonian Constitution, and if they were really true most of the criticisms I have outlined would fall or at least pale before them. But the claims are subject to two kinds of objections.

The first we have already discussed with respect to Madison: just as in his thought the picture of the elite in office promoting the public good was never fully consistent with the image of politics as a matter of competing interests, so the Constitution and its best defense reflect this same unresolved tension. One need not embrace the notion of politics as nothing more than the jockeying and negotiation among conflicting interests to heed Madison's own warning that no group should have to rely on the disinterestedness of another to protect its interests. Whatever the skills of the propertied elite in discerning the public good, we should still worry about their taking advantage of their virtual monopoly of public office at the expense of the poor and even the middling classes. Since the Constitution is not designed to meet that threat, we cannot share the Madisonian confidence in elite rule.

The second objection goes directly to the substantive issue of property and redistribution. To accept the Madisonian claims for elite rule we must accept the substantive vision of the public good that defines redistribution as a central threat. We must accept *both* the claim that attempts at redistribution will make those at the bottom worse off *and* the claim that they will not be capable of seeing this "truth" for themselves. If either claim fails, the moral foundation for Madisonian elite rule crumbles.

Of course, one need not reject the notion of politics as the pursuit of the public good in order to reject the Federalist claim for elite rule. The links the Federalists claimed rested on a vision of the public good which is only possible under elite rule. It was the Federalists' unwillingness to submit their vision of the economy to democratic evaluation and control that required and justified a system designed to be run by men of wealth.

The Anti-Federalists, by contrast, were by and large willing to entrust economic matters to popular control.*[51] I think this willingness must have entailed a substantively different judgement about what constituted a violation of property rights, as well as a general faith in the people and commitment to democratic control. The consequence of the Federalist victory was therefore not only a less democratic government, but a kind of freezing of the Federalist certainties about the truth and justice of their understanding of the requirements of the economy.[52] Their success in insulating that understanding from democratic revision meant that very early in American history we cut off a range of experimentation with the different forms of economy compatible with republican government.

The notion of the public good and elite rule is related to the Federalists' faith in centralization and the Anti-Federalists faith in decentralization. Part of the explanation of the Federalists' stance is the basic Madisonian insight into the virtues of cross-cutting interests in a large republic.

> In the extended republic of the United States, and among the great variety of interests, parties and sects which it embraces, a coalition of a majority of the whole society could seldom take place on any other principles than those of justice and the general good.[53]

Madison seems to be saying that the people themselves will be less of a threat at the Federal level: "the larger the society, . . . the more duly capable it will be of self government."[54] But I think the Madisonian faith in the centralized government of a an extended republic is only fully comprehensible when combined with a confidence that the propertied would run that level of government (the same reason the Anti-Federalists distrusted centralization). Cross-cutting interests neutralizing each other will only promote the public good if the right sort of people are in office to implement it. And only a (properly designed) federal government could be relied on to put them there. The Anti-Federalists placed their faith in what was virtually the opposite strategy: the closeness of the connection between the people and the government, which was only possible in reasonably small scale units. And they were able to rest their faith in the people in part because their conception of the public good did not require insulation from popular redefinition and control.

Finally, it is important to emphasize that the Anti-Federalists were no less interested in the protection of rights than the Federalists, although they placed far less emphasis on property in particular. It was, after all, the Anti-Federalists who insisted on the addition of the Bill of Rights. (It seems, however, that it was Madison who added the specific protection for property in the "takings" clause: "nor shall private property be taken for public use, without just compensation."[55] This provision was the only one in the Bill of Rights that had *not* been among any of the recommendations from the states.[56]) The Anti-Federalist rhetoric is full of warnings about threats to rights, but their understanding of that threat was fundamentally different from the Federalists'. The basic threat was not from the people themselves, but from arbitrary and tyrannical governors. And that threat was exacerbated by the distant, powerful, central government the new Constitution would put in place. The Anti-Federalists' fear was that no rights, presumably including property, would be secure under such a government.

Their faith in decentralized government did rest on a faith in the people and a willingness to submit economic matters to democratic control. But that faith in turn rested not on an indifference to the security of property and other rights, but a different judgment about the nature of the threat and therefore the nature of protection required.[57]

IV. The Madisonian Constitution: Republican or Liberal?

One of the most important contemporary debates about the American constitutional tradition is whether it is essentially "liberal" or "republican."[58] Although most of the scholarship is about the Jeffersonians, this debate is particularly useful in understanding the Madisonian framework because it allows us to see the ways the Federalists drew on and transformed elements of both liberalism and republicanism to create a new form of political thought. The debate is also centrally concerned with many of the issues I have focused on here: popular participation, civic virtue and elite rule, the role of private interest and the public good, and the protection of rights as the defining problem of republican government. The thoughtful discussions of these issues in the republicanism debate offer points of contrast which illuminate the content of the Madisonian vision.

Lance Banning provides a helpful starting point with his characterizations of liberalism and classical republicanism as distinct philosophies.

> *Liberalism* is a label most would use for a political philosophy that regards man as possessed of inherent individual rights and the state as existing to protect those rights, deriving its authority from consent. *Classical republicanism* is a term that scholars have employed to identify a mode of thinking about citizenship and the polity that may be traced from Aristotle through Machiavelli and Harrington to eighteenth-century Britain and her colonies. . . . A full blown, modern liberalism, as [Joyce] Appleby and [Isaac] Kramnick appear to use the term, posits a society of equal individuals who are motivated principally if not exclusively by their passion or self-interest; it identified a proper government as one existing to protect these individuals' inherent rights and private pursuits. A fully classical republicanism, as [J. G. A.] Pocock may best explain, reasons from the diverse capacities and characteristics of different social groups, whose members are political by nature. No republicanism will still be "classical" if it is not concerned with the individual's participation with others in civic decisions, where the needs and powers of others must be taken into account. Liberalism, thus defined, is comfortable with economic man, with the individual who is intent on maximizing private satisfactions and who needs to do no more in order to serve the public good. Classical republicanism regards this merely economic man as less than fully human.[59]

After offering this helpful clarification of terms, Banning goes on to say that it would be a mistake to think that "the analytical distinctions we detect were evident to those we study" or to believe that "in America, one of two separate and competing modes of thinking displaced the other in the years before 1815."[60]

I am sympathetic to the view that liberal ideas were only part of our inheritance, and, as will become clear, I think that Madisonian federalism provided a new synthesis of competing ideas. This sythesis has continued to stir up (with ebbs and flows of intensity) the conflicts out of which it was framed. Had there been simply one monolithic tradition in America, it is hard to imagine the constitutional debates of the 1780s or the fierce partisan conflict of the 1790s or the debates in the 1980s over the meaning of the Constitution and its tradition. Nevertheless, it is important to recognize, first, that the Federalists' synthesis rested on distinctions Banning says they did not see,*[61] and, second, that in 1787 one perspective did triumph, and the other (or others) became submerged. Indeed, were it not for the extraordinary, long-term effectiveness of the triumph, it would not have been necessary for historians to work so hard to resurrect the defeated alternative. With the acceptance of the Madisonian Constitution, choices were made and those choices have remained with us in powerful and complicated ways.

A. The Status of Political Liberty

Let me begin with the status of participation or political liberty in our founding tradition. This issue is central to the republicanism debate[62] and will lead us to the related (and disputed) questions of the role of the elite, of civic virtue, self-interest, and commerce. My understanding of political liberty in the Madisonian vision stands in contrast to Banning's picture of the Jeffersonians: "American Revolutionaries and Jeffersonian Republicans attempted to combine (and probably confused) concepts of liberty deriving from a classical tradition—freedom *to*—with more modern or liberal concepts that associated liberty more exclusively with the private, pre-governmental realm—freedom *from*."[63] But it is just this distinction that was so crucial to Madisonian constitutionalism. By distinguishing political liberty (freedom to participate in and shape public affairs) from civil liberty (freedom from interference with one's private rights), the Madisonian approach provided the basis for moving beyond the inadequacies of traditional political thought.

Classical republicanism is characterized by the distrust of government as a threat to liberty.[64] The Madisonian approach transformed this suspicion by redefining liberty and relocating the threat. The Federalists are sometimes treated as lacking in this classic distrust because they defended the power and scope of the new government against the more traditional-sounding attacks of the Anti-Federalists. But what is important is that the Federalists transformed both the problem and the solution so that the structure of the new government became the means of protecting liberty. They were as concerned as any about the threats government might pose to citizens' liberties. Indeed, I think it was their primary concern. But they relocated the focus of their distrust; in a republic it was the people themselves who posed the threat through their numerical power in government. One could comprehend and contain that threat by distinguishing between kinds of liberty: the political liberty of a republic threatened the civil liberty that was its ultimate purpose. This is the conceptual move that is most clearly "liberal" and that is the foundation of the Madisonian approach to republican government. This approach provided a reformulation of the traditional identification of the people with the liberty that needed protection, and government with the sphere of power and threat. Once that problem was redefined as a threat by political liberty to civil liberty, the Federalists could convincingly argue that a properly structured, and sufficiently powerful, federal government could actually protect (civil) liberty from the threats the people would pose and, at the same time, invoke the tradition of defending liberty against invasions by government.

But as the Anti-Federalists saw, the Federalist conception inverted the role of the people from potential victim and vigilant guardian to threat. The guardians of liberty in the Federalist scheme would be the elite the new Constitution would put in office. Despite this inversion, there is an interesting confluence with the civic virtue of the elite in classical republicanism. Most scholars agree that in the republican vision, civic virtue was required for good government. Politics was not simply about the pursuit of private interests and trade-offs or arbitration among them. The object of government was the public good, which should stand above private interest. What is more ambiguous is who had the capacity, the civic virtue necessary, to promote that objective. On the one hand, a characteristic of republicanism is the concern with the moral character of all citizens. On the other, there is the hierarchical dimension of classical republicanism.

Joyce Appleby associates civic virtue with the need to control the "power lusts" of human beings, which made civil society fragile. The classical solution to this fragility was "the existence of two social groups available for checking each other." The political roles of the two groups were distinct: "Achieving stability by balancing the superior talents of the few against the numerical strength of the many meant, of course, that the few acted as the statesmen, judges, and generals who ran the government whereas ordinary people acted solely to check any undue augmentation of elite power."[65] This form of balance is very close to what the Federalists hoped to achieve with the new constitution. The people would play an important checking function, but they would not actually do the governing. The fact that the elite in government would be the propertied elite is also in keeping with classical republicanism: property "rooted men in their society and was supposed to liberate them for the practice of politics;"[66] "property [Harrington stressed] gave men the independence to place the common weal above their private concerns."[67] This property-based rationale for the role of the elite in government raises, in turn, the interlocking issues of hierarchy, natural rights, self-interest, and the public good. In each case, we see both links to republicanism and its transformation into a distinct alternative.

The reliance on a traditional hierarchy was problematic for the Federalists in several ways. Appleby notes that in late eighteenth-century America social reality was conforming less and less to the classical model of hierarchy. Geographical and economic mobility were undermining the traditional role of property: "Property rooted men in their society [only] until they decided to move."[68] And deriving an income from property did not permit the lofty removal from mundane affairs of business assumed in the republican model, but required a constant attention to the demands of the market. Moreover, property no longer conferred the privileges assumed in republicanism: "Deference—the acquiesence to the authority of one's social superiors—was disappearing with remarkable rapidity."[69] These changes were disturbing, and for many of the elite, classical republicanism gave them a language to express their anxiety and disapproval—even as that language became less and less capable of explaining the changes.

At the same time, there was a language of natural rights, the language we associate with liberalism. Appleby suggests that this language, with its implicit equality, did not fit comfortably with the older notions of hierarchy. I think one of the best ways of understanding the Madisonian Federalists is to see how they succeeded in blending these discourses, to create what has become our dominant tradition. Once again, I think the distinction between civil and political rights was crucial. The Federalists could comfortably proclaim the protection of the equal rights of all as the objective of government—as long as it was clear that those rights were civil rights. It was the very primacy of those rights that justified direct or indirect limits on the political power of the people. It was the need to protect those rights from folly and injustice that made it essential that the right kind of people hold office in the new government. The Madisonian Federalists could thus consistently both invoke the natural rights of all and design a government to ensure the rule of the elite—who were the only ones who could be relied upon to secure the rights of all. This comfortable mix of hierarchy and natural rights is made possible by distinguishing and subordinating political liberty as a mere means to achieving civil liberty.

Just what was expected of the elite in their role as office holders is one of the most contested issues in the debate over republicanism. Briefly put, the question is whether the Constitution aimed at men whose civic virtue would place them above the pull of private interests, or whether the new system dispensed with civic virtue and relied solely on the pursuit of private interest, properly structured by the new Constitution. Isaac Kramnick's view is that in late eighteenth-century America classical republicanism had been rejected. A new notion of virtue had emerged, "one that dramatically rejects the assumptions of civic humanism. Citizenship and the public quest for the common good were replaced by economic productivity and hard work as the criteria of virtue. . . . It is a mistake, however, to see this simply as a withdrawal from public activity to a private, self-centered realm."[70] The nature of public behaviour and contribution to the public good had changed; it had become economic. Joyce Appleby concurs. She rightly points out that the new Constitution relied on "the self-interest of individual officeholders to preserve the boundaries among the legislature, the executive, and the judiciary." She concludes, somewhat starkly, that "self-interest was accepted as a functional equivalent to civic virtue."[71] Gordon Wood takes an opposite view. He argues that it was the Federalists, not the Anti-Federalists as commonly argued, who were true to traditional republicanism.

> The Federalists' plans for the Constitution . . . rested on their belief that there were some disinterested gentlemen left in America to act as neutral umpires. In this sense the Constitution became a grand—and perhaps in retrospect a final desperate—effort to realize the great hope of the Revolution: the possibility of virtuous politics. . . . Despite the Federalists' youthful energy, originality, and vision, they still clung to the classical tradition of civic humanism and its patrician code of disinterested public leadership. They stood for a moral and social order that was radically different from the popular, individualistic, and acquisitive world they saw emerging in the 1780s.[72]

In general, I am sympathetic to Appleby's and Kramnick's arguments. Most of what is most important about the 1787 Constitution seems to me to be liberal rather than republican. But on the question of civic virtue and disinterestedness, I think Appleby and Kramnick, as well as Wood, overstate their points. The questions I think we must start with are why the Federalists wanted the propertied elite to rule and why they thought it was legitimate for them to do so. If the public good consisted in nothing other than the outcome of the give and take among competing interests, why would it be preferable (or indeed, permissible) for one group rather than another to participate in the exchange? Even if we recognize that the propertied included different interests—merchant, financial, landed—it is clear that other "interests"—the propertyless, the "middling sort"—would not be represented in the same way as the interests of property. If the common good is what emerges from a fair fight among all the interests (the interest group model of politics Wood is rejecting), then surely it is essential that all the interests be represented. Indeed, Madison sometimes spoke in just those terms: no group should be at the mercy of the disinterestedness of another. But in fact, that was not the model for the Constitution.[73]

However inconsistent Madison may have been, the choice in 1787 was for rule by the competent elite. What it was hoped they would be competent at was discerning the public good. And the further requirement was that they have the virtue to pursue it.[74] Wood rightly invokes Madison's description of the sort of men he wanted the new Constitution to put in office: "Men whose enlightened views and virtuous sentiments render them superior to local prejudices, and to the schemes of injustice."[75] I have already argued that one of the problems with the Madisonian Constitution is that it was not designed to foster the public virtue it depended on. Nevertheless, Wood overstates the system's reliance on disinterestedness in its public officials. As he notes, Madison hoped that the competing interests in a large republic would "neutralize" themselves, allowing the enlightened elite to promote the public good. The question is how this neutralization was to take place. Part of the Madisonian scheme was that the institutions of government would be so designed that it would make it difficult for those in power to promote their own interests. This is where Appleby's reference to interest combating interest, ambition counteracting ambition, comes in. There would be sufficient checks within the government, relying on interest (both personal and institutional) to drive them, that office holders would rarely be called upon to literally rise above self-interest. Those in office would have neutralized each other's private interests, leaving them free from temptation and able to use their talents as the elite to promote the public good. Thus the Madisonian system does rely on interests canceling each other out, but that cancellation does not itself yield the public good. It enables those who have the requisite abilities to undertake the difficult task of discerning it—without having to suppress their self-interest at the same time.

Wood's rejection of the "interest group politics" approach remains important, even though the Madisonian public official need not be quite the paragon of virtue he suggests classical republicanism called for. The public good is not itself the outcome of the clash of interests. It has a content that requires discernment, of which only those with the proper education, broad perspective, and understanding of justice are capable. Thus the Madisonian system did not aim at a legislature that was an exact replica of the population, encompassing all competing interests. On the contrary, the new Constitution was to draw out not a cross-section but the propertied elite, who could undertake the substantively demanding task of governing.

There is an irony to this Madisonian mix of interest and civic virtue. On the one hand, I have argued that the Federalists focused on governing as the protection of rights and interests, virtually ignoring any intrinsic value in self-governance. (Hence the ordinary folk were not deprived of anything valuable as long they were provided with competent representatives.) On the other hand, I think Madison and his fellow Federalists cared more about preserving their prerogative to rule than about protecting their economic interests. It is difficult to tell, of course, since their system was also designed to protect the basic values of property and contract that were the foundation of their economic interests. But their debates and private correspondence are full of concern about getting the right sort of people into the government, without comparable discussion of their economic interests as such. And of course they well knew that their particular private interests might compete with one another. I think it is hard to immerse oneself in the arguments of the Federalists and come away seeing them as a group of men bent on promoting the interests of their class in any simple, material way. They do appear as a group very anxious to retain control of political power,[76] and unself-consciously confident that their conception of the public good would in the long run promote not only their interests but the interests of all.

B. Politics and the Market

I turn now to the role of the market in the Madisonian Constitution. I use as a starting point Joyce Appleby's compelling picture of the Jeffersonians' enthusiastic embrace of the freedom and equality of the market place.[77] It does not matter for my purposes whether she is correct in her description of the Jeffersonians.[78] She offers an exceptionally interesting statement of the links between the conception of freedom, the role of the market, and the distinction between the private and the public, or the proper domain of politics. These links have been so important in American constitutionalism that it is worth looking closely at her picture of Jeffersonian republicanism and comparing it to the Madisonian vision.

According to Appleby, by the end of the eighteenth century men were abandoning the conceptual framework of republicanism in part because it did not provide a language for understanding, rather than lamenting, commerce. New models emerged: "The individual with wide-ranging needs and abstract rights appeared to challenge the citizen with concrete obligations and prescribed privileges."[79] The Jeffersonians embraced and helped develop these new models.

> In the 1790s when the Jeffersonian Republicans and Federalists confronted each other, the battle lines had been drawn around opposing conceptions of civil society. The passions mobilized by this contest over national leadership reflected this fact. . . . For the Jeffersonians the economy offered an escape from the predicaments implicit in traditional ways of looking at social order. Here was a system operating independently of politics and, like the physi-

> cal universe, taking its cues from nature. Where politics achieved stability by imposing its structure of power, the economy appeared to elicit voluntary participation as it wove ever more extensive networks of free exchange. It also discovered a rationality in the humblest person whose capacity to take care of himself could be used as an argument for freedom.[80]

Appleby is talking about the contests between the Jeffersonians and the Federalists at the turn of the eighteenth century, and our discussion will soon follow her into this later time period. But for the moment I want to compare her vision of the Jeffersonians with the constitutional thought that triumphed in 1787.

Appleby portrays the Jeffersonian embrace of the market as a "retreat from politics."[81]

> In their depiction of America's future, freedom was expanded by drastically limiting the scope of government so that individual citizens would be empowered to act on their own behalf. Democratic values were invoked not to enlarge the people's power in government but rather to justify the abandonment of the authority traditionally exercised over them. In espousing limited government the Jeffersonians endorsed a redrawing of the lines between the public and private spheres, and this meant reordering their significance for the whole human enterprise.[82]

The freedom made possible by this limitation of the scope of government was a new conception of freedom, "wherein men—and, of course, it was a white male vision—were free to define and pursue their own goals." And the market was a sphere basic to this freedom: "The importance of the free market to this development cannot be reduced to economics. Nor can Jeffersonians be distinguished from Federalists on the basis of the enthusiasm for economic development. It was the economy's ordering of society with minimal compulsion that stirred the Jeffersonian imagination, not its capacity to produce wealth."[83]

There are both important similarities and important differences between this striking picture and the Madisonian vision of 1787. The Madisonian approach to property has obvious resonances with the connections between the market and freedom. Property derived much of its value from its relation to freedom, and a freedom that was, at least in significant part, economic freedom. That connection is clearest in Morris but present in Madison and most of the Federalists. Most of the Madisonian language, however, emphasizes not freedom, but security, stability, and justice with their overtones of social order. In this sense the Madisonian vision was a kind of amalgam of the classical concern with order and structure and the new liberal vision of freedom in the market place. One of the ways the amalgam was constructed seems to involve a sort of class-based division of labor that parallels, but transforms, that of classical republicanism.

The distinct role of the elite in the Madisonian Constitution presumes that they have different tasks and different preoccupations from those of the citizens at large. While the elite in office must understand the public good, a focus on private interest is sufficient for the people in general. The Madisonian Constitution is not designed to foster public virtue. The Madisonian Federalists did not direct their attention to the character of the people that their institutions would promote. They tended to invoke character in the context of the destructive consequences of a government's failure to honor public commitments and enforce private ones. But they did not emphasize the affirmative effects of their proposed structure on the character of the citizens because they did not treat character as a basic object of government. The appropriate scope of government was thus not that of the classical republicans, but of modern liberals. The task of government was to provide security, justice, prosperity, and liberty. It was the private concern of the individual citizens what they did within this framework.

Thus with respect to most of the population, the goals of the Madisonian Constitution were similar to the freedom for private pursuits Appleby says the Jeffersonians wanted. But there is one crucial difference. Madison and his fellow Federalists understood that providing this liberal framework was a matter of the most basic *political* importance. Their attention to the economy was not a retreat from politics. One of the basic tasks of the new Constitution was to ensure that the federal government could maintain the proper framework for the economy, i.e., the rules of property and contract. They understood that these rules were the source of intense political conflict. Even if they believed, as Appleby says the Jeffersonians did, that the right rules for the market were given by nature, they knew that not everyone saw it that way. The propertied needed to run the government because they were the only ones who could be relied upon to keep the structure of the market intact. The prohibitions against paper money and impairment of the obligation of contract were efforts to ensure that state governments (not reliably run by the propertied) did not change the rules that made the market function.

The difference between the Madisonian approach and Appleby's picture of the Jeffersonians is not a matter of the degree to which they thought the economy needed to be regulated. It is something more fundamental; it is a recognition that the rules that constitute the market are not given by nature (or at least not given effect by nature), but are the subject of political contests. The battles in the state legislatures over paper money and various forms of debtor relief had taught the Federalists that. They tried to insulate these crucial and contested rules by removing them from the power of the states and ensuring that federal offices would be held by those who would take as given the importance of the security of property and contract. This was a strategy to withdraw the rules of the market from political debate. But this strategy recognized that controlling those rules is one of the most important issues in a political system. Had the Madisonian Federalists believed that the market was truly outside of politics (as subsequent liberal ideology has taught us) they could have been far more sanguine about popular access to public office and far less worried about controlling the power of state governments. To be sure, even believers in a natural, apolitical market could fear that those in government might interfere by "regulating" what should be left to the natural functions of the market. But that was not the focus of the Federalists' concern. The threats they feared amounted to changing the rules of the market and thus entailed at least a tacit recognition that the rules themselves were matters of political choice. Of course, like twentieth-century advocates of "the market," the Federalists were confident that there was only one right choice.

The Madisonian Federalists envisioned a market economy and valued it for its freedom as well as the prosperity and national strength they thought it would bring. But they understood that a market economy is not an absence of a social order. It is a particular kind of social order. And they wanted a government that would protect the foundation of that order: the freedom and security to acquire and exchange property.[84] The Madisonian preoccupation with protecting property is only fully understandable in this context. As the Federalists saw it, the role of the elite was necessary not to protect class interests in a narrow sense, but to ensure the foundation of a market-republic—with the freedom, justice, prosperity, and strength they thought it promised.

The question of class interest brings me to another, related distinction between Appleby's picture of the Jeffersonians and my understanding of the Madisonian Federalists of 1787. Appleby stresses the enthusiastic optimism of the Jeffersonians and offers a compelling picture of how the market economy held out a promise of equality and freedom unparalleled in traditional political thought. She helps us to understand the attraction of this image and urges us not to confuse it with a late twentieth-century understanding of the suffering and inequality of capitalism. But if the Jeffersonians were as optimistic as she says, the Federalists were not. They embraced the market, but at least the most thoughtful of them knew the cost. Appleby offers as an example of twentieth-century insight that the social consequence of a market economy is "a permanent division between dependent laborers and independent employers."[85] But it was just that inevitable division that Madison anticipated (and tried to point out to Jefferson). The problem of the rights of persons, property, and participation was critical because that division was inevitable. The Constitution was designed to make republican government work and the market secure *given* that division. Madison's task would have been far simpler if he had not foreseen the inequality that would be the consequence of the system he hoped to put in place. And here I should qualify my earlier remark that the distinction between political and civil liberty had made possible the combination of natural rights language with a traditional hierarchy for public office. The distinction made it possible for thoughtful men like Madison to both invoke the language of natural rights and design a system to put the elite in office. But as I have already argued, it did not make it possible for him to actually solve his problem of equally protecting the rights of persons and property while providing equal political rights to all. The propertied would do the ruling, and only if one completely abandons the idea that no group should be at the mercy of the disinterestedness of another (as Madison did not) could one believe that the rights and interests of the propertyless were not at comparative risk.*[86]

Madison's vision works as a whole because of the (sometimes wavering) synthesis it achieves of elements of classical republicanism and modern liberalism. The role of the elite is justified because there is a substantive public good to be achieved, and it requires both vision to discern it and virtue to pursue it. The security of acquisition and exchange is an essential element of this public good, and it can be legitimately secured against the threats of the majority because it will truly be in their best interests. Madison's system is simultaneously designed to accommodate the conflict of interests as the daily stuff of politics and to rely on the rationale of the ultimate harmony of interests in his vision of the public good. Madison needed the faith in this harmony and the certainty that the basic rules of the market would foster it to justify a system composed not of a representation of all the competing interests, but of the elite who could see beyond them. The system thus requires knowledge, understanding, and civic virtue from the elite, but not from the people as a whole.

This system clearly draws on elements of classical republicanism, but with a crucial difference: the *purpose* of the Madisonian structure is to protect rights. The substantive vision of this quasi-republican system is itself essentially liberal; it is a market republic based on the rights of property and contract. Although the conception of the market economy was not fully worked out, there was a clear commitment to the basic ingredients of private property and contract, and to the freedom and security they promised.*[87] The only "character" necessary for the general population of the market republic was, therefore, the respect for property and contract the market required. And even this respect was not necessary or expected of all, for the system was designed to contain the inevitable threats from those who wanted a more equal share of the inevitably unequal benefits of the market. The Madisonian system could effectively contain these threats because it could simultaneously neutralize conflict and put the kind of men in office who understood that the just protection of the rights of property and contract was the purpose and foundation of the republic.

By claiming that the Madisonian system was designed to implement a liberal vision, I want to simultaneously insist on the substance of that vision and to recognize the ways in which it was deliberately more limited, less substantive, than that of classical republicanism. There are those, who have argued that the U.S. Constitution was not designed to implement a "regime," in the sense of a set of higher ends and values.[88] That is correct in a partial, but important way, and captures something crucial about the liberal vision of the Constitution.

Wilson provides a helpful contrast here. For him, the highest object for men, their excellence, was the highest object of government. The Madisonian aspiration was different. He never suggested that the objects of government he was so concerned about, property in particular, were intrinsically the highest of men's values. Government had certain basic tasks, such as providing justice and security. But these tasks were tacitly treated as the preconditions for individuals' capacities to lead the good life, not as *constituting* the good life. The scope of government is thus narrower, in the (now) classic liberal sense Appleby refers to.[89] Government is to provide the conditions for the freedom to define and pursue one's own goals.

But as the Federalists knew, the conditions for this freedom were not an empty set, not a mere absence of impediments. In opting for this liberal vision, the Framers did not simply make a choice for choice. They chose a set of values and subordinated others, and they chose institutions that would promote and protect some values and not others. They rejected some ways of seeing the problems and possibilities of republican government and embraced and developed others. All of these choices matter to the lives and "character" of citizens as profoundly as does the pursuit of specified higher ends.

At some level the Federalists knew that, but they did not resolve the tensions in their thought. On the one hand, they treated the character of citizens as beyond the new narrow scope of government. On the other, they retained a sense that governmental institutions influenced the character of a people. They certainly thought, as I noted above, that institutions that failed to honor public and private obligations would generate a downward spiral of character and behaviour. The Federalists and the Anti-Federalists debated about the effects on character the new system would have. But in the end, the Federalists treated character as outside the scope of governmental responsibility without reconciling this division with their residual understanding of the effects of government (or the demands of their own system) and without trying to demarcate clearly just where the line was to be drawn that would define the proper scope of this more limited, liberal government.*[90]

V. The Conceptual Framework

The Framers set in place not only an institutional, but a conceptual framework for government. Together they have defined American constitutionalism. In the contests over the creation of the Constitution the purposes, problems, and principles of government were debated. In the process, competing ideas were crystallized and refined. In the end, it was very largely the Madisonian vision that prevailed at this conceptual, as well as institutional, level. It is obvious that we live (with some important changes) with the institutions the convention of 1787 designed for us. It is less obvious, but no less important, that we also live (with some important changes) with the conceptual framework that shaped and gave meaning and legitimacy to the Constitution of 1787. We need to see how that framework has shaped our understanding of politics, of republicanism, of constitutional government. We need to recognize the presuppositions of this framework, the questions it teaches us to ask and those it suggests we ignore, its insights and its limitations as a foundation for constitutional democracy.

The Madisonian vision we have inherited defined what counted as a problem to be solved—such as democratic excess—and what was to be taken as a fact of life—such as the future poverty of the majority. It defined the choices to be made, such as the security of property versus equal political power for all, and the grounds for making them: the hierarchy of civil over political rights. The result has been a language in which to analyze politics that provided sophisticated tools for understanding some problems, and virtually none for dealing with others.

The most basic strength of the Madisonian framework is the subtle analysis of the problem of majority tyranny. Madison not only taught us to see the potential for oppression as inherent in liberty, he showed that (in a large republic) the diversity born of liberty can itself mitigate the dangers of oppression. This approach insists that the causes of conflict, and thus of the incentive for oppression, cannot be eradicated (without destroying liberty itself). We should not try. We should turn our attention elsewhere for solutions: to institutions that make it difficult for people to give effect to their inclination to oppress, without destroying the liberty that fuels the inclination in the first place. This insight into the connection between liberty and conflict is profound. But it also tells us to accept as given particular conflicts, such as those arising from the vast inequality of property. The Madisonian approach constructively directs us toward what it defines as a soluble problem, and away from what it treats as a fact of life.

Madison's analysis of the problems and solutions to republican government is premised on the distinction between civil and political liberty. *The Federalist*, No. 10, tells us that civil liberties of all kinds—freedom of speech, of religion, of the right to acquire and exchange property—breed conflict. But it is the form *political* liberty takes that determines the nature of the threat this inevitable conflict will pose to the civil liberty that spawns it. The value of civil liberty is treated as a given; it is the purpose of government. Political liberty is the problem. The question is how to structure it so that liberty (of both kinds) does not destroy itself.

The distinction between civil and political liberty is probably the most important legacy of Federalist thought. It is the foundation of American constitutionalism. As we have seen, the hierarchy which defines civil liberty as the end of government justifies the limitation of political liberty as the mere means to that end. This hierarchy is the basis for our contemporary notion of rights as limits to democracy. This conception of rights did not take its current form until the rise of judicial review. But the conceptual foundation for judicial review was laid in the Madisonian framework which defined civil, not political, rights as the bedrock of legitimate government. Government by consent was a necessary, but not sufficient condition of legitimacy. The legitimate scope of government by consent was defined by its purpose: the protection of civil rights.

One of the important aspects of this approach is that it took the meaning of civil rights, and property in particular, as unproblematic. For all the importance of property, its meaning was not the subject of inquiry. The focus on containing the threat to property could have the clarity it did because the meaning of property was presumed, and its security treated as a matter of obvious justice. The problem becomes muddier if one sees property as a set of social choices which will be the (proper) subject of debate and change. If property is seen in those terms, one cannot avoid the problem of what distinguishes an illegitimate violation of property rights from necessary regulation or appropriate redefinition. Madison and his fellow Federalists did not address this question. They could focus clearly on how to contain the threat of the people because they did not also have to figure out how the meaning of property was to be determined over time. One of the great virtues of the Madisonian framework is that it identifies a tension between justice and democracy, between civil and political liberty. But it is a framework that takes the meaning of justice and civil liberty as obvious, and political rights as subordinate.

Madison's approach helps us think about how to protect rights from democratic threat, but it does not help us with the problem of how rights that define limits to legitimate democratic power can themselves be democratically defined. If (civil) rights are to be treated as the ends to which political participation is merely the means, it is difficult to imagine the meaning of rights as the product of a democratic process. Madison's confident focus on protecting rights requires a source for the meaning of rights outside the democratic process, a source which has no place for collective decision making. In short, the Madisonian approach requires some notion of natural, uncontested rights. If we can no longer accept such a notion, and if we are to retain Madison's basic insight into the tension between individual freedom and democracy, we will have to confront the meaning of rights in some new way, for which our inherited framework is of limited help.

The uninquiring stance toward civil rights also has implications for how we think about property in particular. Although, as I noted earlier, it is important that Madison did not actually posit property as an end in itself, he did not in fact treat it as a means. For Madison, property is an end of government, and it is that status that mattered, not some underlying relation between property and liberty. We have seen the difference between Madison's treatment of property and Wilson's, in which property truly stands as a third order value. Similarly, we saw in the comparison with Jefferson that Madison did not treat property, or its distribution, as contingent on its fulfillment of the higher ends from which it derived its value. The Federalist mode of thought we have inherited does not invite an inquiry into the purposes of property as a basis for assessing the extent to which a given conception of property serves those purposes. Neither the value nor the meaning of property was treated as an open question. On the contrary, part of the Federalist task was to see to it that property was not reevaluated or redefined by democratic legislatures. The tacit message is that the true ends of government are best served if property is treated as a sacred value that requires protection, not evaluation.

The focus on property also reveals something about the conception of liberty underlying the Madisonian framework: its relation to security. Security is necessary for liberty. But liberty is also in tension with security. Security fixes things, guarantees expectations in ways that must ultimately limit the scope of liberty. Any theory of freedom or conception of free government must make some judgment about the degree of security that is optimal for the ultimate ends of government.

Madison's focus on property is in effect a focus on security. We have already seen the high value Madison placed on stability, which is particularly clear in contrast with Wilson. For Madison, the main issue of liberty is the way it can be threatened. He has far more to tell us about how to contain the dangers of political liberty than how to promote the flourishing of either political or civil liberty. Fear is a basic element of Madison's approach, and it casts its weight heavily on the side of security. In this context, it is important to remember that Madison posited not liberty but justice as the end of government, and that justice was very largely securing to each his own.

Finally, the conceptual framework of the Constitution offers little to help us understand the problems of the relation between economic and political power or the potential of participatory democracy. Our tradition gives us a powerful set of concepts for understanding majority tyranny. It provides nothing comparable on the ways in which economic power may also threaten rights, the public interest, and the basic principles of republican government. Morris provided a framework for thinking about this problem, but it had no impact on the dominant mode of thought at the convention. A recognition of the threats the majority may pose has been an integral part of our understanding of republican government since 1787. The problem of the relation between economic and political power has never achieved that kind of integration despite periodic surges of concern such as that the Progressives were famous for and contemporary efforts such as campaign finance laws.[91] Similarly Wilson offered a way of thinking about popular participation in government that focused not on its dangers, but on the ways participation was essential to the highest ends of government and on the possibilities of participation itself mitigating the dangers inherent in collective action. But on that score, he had no influence. The Madisonian framework does not help us figure out how to foster participation or how to think about its value. No such inquiry has been a central part of our tradition.

These limitations are not incidental, but integral to the Madisonian framework. They derive, as do their corresponding institutional limitations, from the preoccupation with protecting property from the threat of the people. We have seen the ways in which this preoccupation was a central part of the Madisonian approach to republican government. And from Madison's own perspective, what I call limitations follow almost as a matter of logic: if the chief task is to contain the threat the people will inevitably pose, it hardly makes sense to concentrate on enhancing their participation; and if the propertyless will have the power a republic accords to the majority, one need hardly focus on the dangers posed by the propertied, inherently vulnerable, minority.

Madison was right that majority tyranny is an inherent problem of republican government, and his insights have made American constitutionalism the powerful force that it is. But both the institutions and the conceptual framework are distorted by the focus on the threat to property as the paradigmatic instance of majority tyranny. The institutions were not designed to cope with the problems of economic power nor to foster an actively engaged citizenry. And our most powerful tradition of political thought is equally ill-equipped for helping us think constructively about these issues—which, contrary to the Madisonian formulation, are as basic to the challenge of republican government as majority tyranny.

VI. Judicial Review: The Consolidation and Transformation of the Madisonian Framework

When the Constitution was ratified in 1788, its basic framework was in place. But there were two important pieces yet to be added: the Bill of Rights, the chief contribution of the Anti-Federalists, and the establishment of judicial review, the ultimate triumph of the Federalists.*[92]

The Anti-Federalists had never been persuaded that the structure of the new federal government was not a threat to rights. And the failure of the document to guarantee basic rights was their best ammunition against this powerful new government. Although the Federalists held firm in their insistence that the Constitution be ratified without amendment, they informally promised to add the sorts of guarantees the Anti-Federalists demanded. The Federalists correctly judged that by doing so they would destroy the basis for any further effective opposition. And although Madison (who introduced the amendments in Congress) had little faith in paper barriers, he thought they might have the salutary effect of instilling basic values in the population.[93]

The Bill of Rights had a purpose and rationale different from the rest of the Constitution. It was aimed at the Anti-Federalists' fear of tyrannical rulers, not the Federalists' fear of the people. Nevertheless, it fit quite comfortably within the Federalist conceptual framework: it defined rights as limits to the legitimate authority of government. One might say that the additional prohibitions helped correct the imbalance between protections for the rights of persons and the rights of property. But the Bill of Rights did nothing to change the structure that created the imbalance of power and vulnerability between the propertied and the propertyless.*[94] The irony is that the Bill of Rights has taken on the significance it has in our system because of the establishment of judicial review, the final consolidation of the Federalist conception of constitutional government.

The establishment of judicial review as a basic part of the American constitutional system provided a sort of institutional solution to a set of issues left open or unresolved in the Madisonian Constitution of 1787. In the Madisonian conception rights limited the scope of legitimate governmental power, but there was no clear sense of how these rights were to be defined. Neither the institutional structure nor the thought behind it offered much on this subject. We are left with the impression that the Federalists took the content of rights to be self-evident, or at least that it would be to the sort of enlightened men who were to govern. Property is a clear instance of the unresolved problems built into this conception. Madison never explained what distinguished necessary regulation from illegitimate infringement, or who was to draw the distinction. The Constitution of 1787 reflects both Madison's sense of the importance of the problem and his vagueness about the solution.

It was, of course, the judges, exercising the power of judicial review, who would come to handle these problems. They would define the rights that limited legislative power; they would struggle with the question of when laws affecting property rights were regulations and when they were violations. And they would enforce the limits on the states. They would determine what constituted a violation of the obligation of contracts. In short, the courts would handle the line-drawing implicit in the Madisonian conception of the Constitution. The Madisonian conception of rights divided the world into public and private spheres bounded by those rights. The courts would define the boundaries to the realms government could not legitimately enter.

The Madisonian Constitution had stopped short of directly institutionalizing the conceptual hierarchy between civil and political rights. The Constitution of 1787 sustained a tension between democracy and individual rights. Judicial review transformed that tension by institutionalizing the supremacy of individual rights. It consolidated the Federalist structure of power and carried its conceptual underpinning to its logical, institutional conclusion. But the consolidation was also a subtle transformation. In answering questions left unresolved, it closed down some of the possibilities left open in 1787. When judicial review hardened the conceptual hierarchy into an institutional one, yet one more weight was cast into the already skewed balance between property and democracy.

The establishment of judicial review added the law-politics distinction to the conceptual foundation of American constitutionalism. This distinction was the justification for the courts' authority to define the limits to government. As it was formulated in the first several decades of the new republic, the distinction entailed the claim that law and politics were wholly separate spheres; that it was for the courts to determine the line between them and that some of the most important elements of republican government counted as law.

The power of the Supreme Court to draw the line between individual rights and legitimate governmental authority, between different branches of government, and between the state and federal governments was not clearly established until the first decades of the nineteenth century.*[95] This does not mean that judicial review was first conceived or practiced then, but that the institution was not yet established as a central part of the structure of government. In the early years, the Court was seen as so unimportant that Washington had trouble finding men to accept positions on it. The transformation of the Court into the powerful institution we know today took place in the context of the emergence of the first political parties.

During the late eighteenth century, basic disagreements raged over the shape the new republic should take. These disagreements were not perceived as minor policy differences but as disputes over the nature of government and of the good society. It turned out to the horror of all that neither the legacy of the Revolution nor the new Constitution had a single, accepted meaning. Within the broad confines of consensus about government by consent, the existence of basic rights, and even commitment to the Constitution, there remained differences that seemed fundamental and thus heretical. As George Haskins put it, "The factional strife of the late 1790s had pitted Republican against Federalist to the point that each group believed that the other was bent on total destruction of the Union."[96] The Federalists accused the Republicans of scheming to "introduce a new order of things as it respects *morals* and *politics, social* and *civil duties*."[97] The Republicans accused the Federalists of trying to transform the republic into a monied aristocracy. These conflicts were played out in the battle between the emerging parties—a battle the Republicans appeared to have won in the election of 1800. Jefferson's victory was hailed as a "Republican Revolution" that ended the Federalists' control of the executive and Congress.

The federal judiciary became a center of controversy both because of substantive disagreements over its proper nature and structure and because it was, after 1800, a Federalist stronghold in a government dominated by Republicans. The Republicans feared that the "Federalist Supreme Court might paralyze the government for partisan purposes"[98] and the Federalists feared a systematic attempt to destroy the independence of the judiciary. The response of the Federalist judiciary was brilliant and subtle. The Jeffersonian victory had taught the Federalists that they could not control elected offices and that the victory of 1787 had not secured the foundations of the republic from democratic threat. The courts would now have to do so.[99]

The Federalist strategy was to try to remove the most fundamental and most threatened issues from the contested political realm by designating them "law." Law would include the rights, rules of exchange, and structures of government necessary for the market republic the Federalists envisioned. That is, the basics of politics would be called law, placed securely in the hands of the (Federalist) judiciary and insulated from the shifting passions of democratic legislatures. Over the course of the first decades of the nineteenth century the Marshall Court succeeded in claiming the power to do so and giving a meaning to the categories of law and politics that made that power seem inevitable.

This achievement involved both straightforward shifts in judicial behaviour and subtle shaping of language and argument. At the most basic level, the judges backed away from overt partisanship in ways that both protected them from attack and reinforced their effort to stake out the territory they would define as law. For example, the explicit political rhetoric that had been common on the Bench became unacceptable. As Haskins tells us, "The delivery of political speeches in the course of charges to grand juries was common, especially after the Revolution. Such charges were regarded as an appropriate means of popular education. . . . [But] by the last decade of the eighteenth century . . . when the strife between Federalist and Republican factions was becoming rampant, these preambles frequently became vehicles for harangues, in the course of which the presiding judge gave full vent to his personal party feelings."[100]

The presumption of consensus, upon which the eighteenth-century model of the judiciary may have rested, was no longer tenable.[101] An absence of consensus poses a theoretical problem: what should the role of the judiciary be in a divided society? How can judges *neutrally* arbitrate conflicts when there is not a consensus on the norms to be applied? When the relevant norms are contested, a decision either way can be seen as weighing in on one side of a societal conflict rather than neutral adjudication. The notion of neutral adjudication presumes either consensus or some form of natural rights which can supply an independent standard. This theoretical problem posed a concrete threat to the Federalists: if the Federalist judges could not distinguish their role from partisan politics, they would lose their positions and any hope of providing a bulwark against the excesses of democracy. Thus when Justice Chase was unsuccessfully impeached for, among other things, an improperly political jury charge, the Federalists responded even though the impeachment failed. They assailed the impeachment as an attack on the independence of the judiciary, but Chase subsequently moderated his statements from the Bench and a general change in "judicial style" followed.[102]

Another form of the effort to present law as distinct from politics was the trial of Aaron Burr. Marshall's interpretation of the law of treason was a deliberate and convincing effort to show that the law could not be used to prosecute personal or partisan vendettas. More obviously, in the Embargo Act cases, the Court demonstrated that it was willing to uphold legislative and executive acts even when they were part of a policy of which the Federalists vehemently disapproved.[103] More subtly, the Court also used the nonconstitutional and private law cases that were the bulk of its work to establish its "legal" authority. It not only navigated around volatile political issues, it developed convincing and useful legal doctrine. For example, the Court demonstrated its legal competence and acumen in the complex technicalities of maritime law, of prize insurance, and salvage cases.[104] The Court thus succeeded in establishing a claim to special legal expertise, which supported the claim to special competence in defining what counts as law. Not surprisingly, the often celebrated "prudence" of the Marshall Court can be understood in the same context. *Marbury v. Madison* is, of course, the classic instance of avoiding confrontation in the course of claiming to draw a line between law and politics.

> The province of the Court is, solely, to decide on the rights of individuals. . . . Questions in their nature political, or which are, by the constitution and laws, submitted to the executive, can never be made in this court. . . . Certainly all those who have framed written constitutions contemplate them as forming the fundamental and paramount law of the nation, and consequently, the theory of every such government must be, that an act of the legislature, repugnant to the constitution is void. . . . It is emphatically the province and the duty of the judicial department to say what the law is.[105]

A less familiar example is *Stuart v. Laird,*[106] in which the Court backed down from a head-on clash with the Republican legislature over the Judiciary Act of 1802. The Act repealed the Federalists' Judiciary Act of 1801, which would have restructured, strengthened, and expanded the jurisdiction of the federal judiciary. Both acts were highly charged in part because of the controversy aroused by President Adams' last-minute appointment of sixteen new Federalist judges to the offices created by the 1801 Act. The Court upheld the repeal despite plausible arguments about jurisdiction[107] and the importance of the 1801 Act for the Federalist program.

In other cases, the Court found ways of avoiding contentious issues by selecting the basis for their decisions. For example, the politically charged issues of British impressment of American seamen gave rise to suits challenging the English common law rule "once a citizen, always a citizen." This rule, used to justify the British practice, was opposed by Jefferson's administration at the executive level. When the Court faced a case raising the expatriation issue, it sidestepped the common law rule by deciding the case on statutory grounds.[108] More importantly, in *United States v. Hudson and Goodwin,* the Court held that it was not within the implied power of the federal courts to exercise criminal jurisdiction in common law cases. The decision to interpret their power as excluding this jurisdiction[109] seems to have been an astute judgment based on the general political consensus.[110]

The famed prudence that these cases reveal should be seen as part of the Court's skill in creating a convincing case for the categories it was trying to establish. The cases show that the Court had important political judgments to make both as to substantive policy (e.g., the meaning of treason) and who should set that policy (e.g., the legislature should define crimes), and that it made the judgments with sufficient skill and good sense that they were accepted, and accepted as "law." The definition of the boundaries between law and politics is a crucially important political decision, and it is a decision that the Supreme Court successfully laid claim to—in part by having the skill and judgment to avoid being drawn into overtly political conflict.

The judicial techniques discussed above are merely the elementary aspects of the Court's effort to carve out a distinct sphere of law. It was no accident that the Supreme Court undertook this effort at a time of deep political division. By the early 1800s, the Federalist solution to the problem of serious differences was to determine the areas in which conflict was tolerable and should be accepted as part of the normal course of events, and those which needed to be insulated from conflict. The former would be defined as politics and the latter as law, and the Court's claim to establish such categories would be sustained by its deference and tolerance with respect to the political realm. This distinction implied another set of categories that have continued to be part of our political language: the Marshall Court succeeded in tacitly defining some political issues, values, and goods as "rights" and others as mere "interests." Rights belonged in the realm of law and were entitled to the protection of the courts, while interests were the proper subject of the shifts and clashes of politics.

One might think from these descriptions that the Court defined as "political" those issues that were contested and as "law" those that rested on deep consensus. In fact, the insulation of the "law" was necessary for those issues that were both fundamental to the new republic (as the Federalists saw it) and likely to be threatened. The problem that judicial review and its law-politics distinction had to solve was that in the absence of consensus on fundamental issues, the very foundation of the republic could be shaken by the political process. As John Marshall put it, "the wild and enthusiastic democracy . . . of that [earlier] day . . . brought annually into doubt principles which I thought most sound . . . [and] proved that everything was afloat, and that we had no safe anchorage ground."[111]

The threat to basic principles came, as both Marshall and the Framers had seen, not primarily from faithless legislators,*[112] but from "enthusiastic democracy," from legislative programs reflecting an alternative (and to the Federalists, dangerously misguided) vision of society and politics, or at least, alternative policies that threatened the foundations of the system. The rise of the party divisions suggested that the multiplicity of clashing interests could not be relied on to neutralize each other sufficiently to insulate the fundamentals from attack. On the contrary, the political system seemed to be dividing along lines which both sides perceived to be fundamental. The only safe anchorage from such divisions was an institution that could define itself and its sphere of competence as apolitical. If the people and their representatives could not be relied upon to recognize and respect the foundations of a commercial republic, then those foundations should be removed from the realm of political conflict and change.

The Court could not have succeeded in such an undertaking in the absence of some *general* consensus on the values, structures, and rules it wanted to define as fundamental and inviolable. Everyone agreed that property was a fundamental right, although there were serious differences over what constituted violations of property rights. Property was thus a perfect issue around which to build judicial review: it was a widely shared value; its meaning was contested; and the Federalists thought the correct meaning was essential for the republic. The definition and protection of property therefore became a central part of the Court's efforts to establish a "rule of law" protected from the vagaries of politics.

Property and contract disputes directly raised questions concerning the basic terms of entitlement and exchange. The cases of the early years show that the Marshall Court successfully claimed authority to set those terms and set them in accordance with the Federalist vision. The most important assertion of the Court's authority to define property at the constitutional level was of course *Fletcher v. Peck*,[113] in which the Court denied the power of the Georgia legislature to revoke state land grants. *Fletcher* involved extensive bribery of the legislature and presented a clear case of faithless legislators. The Court, however, avoided consideration of the motives of the legislature and the accompanying political controversy. Instead, the Chief Justice raised the spectre of legislative injustice by popular mandate.

> [T]he framers of the constitution viewed, with some apprehension, the violent acts which might grow out of the feelings of the moment; and . . . the people of the United States, in adopting that instrument, have manifested a determination to shield themselves and their property from the effects of those sudden and strong passions to which men are exposed. The restrictions on the legislative power of the states are obviously founded in this sentiment . . .[114]

Marshall asserted the power of the Court to limit legislative interference with vested rights on the basis of the contract clause, while Justice Johnson did so in reliance on "the reason and nature of things."[115]

The Court used the power of judicial review in this case and others like it in order to define and assert the fixed principles it hoped to set as limits to legislative action. In doing so, the Court built upon the general acceptance of the sanctity of property, but gave that general sense the particular meaning the Federalists considered necessary to a stable market economy and to a free and secure society.

The judicial foundation of the commercial republic lay not only in constitutional cases. Herbert Johnson shows this in his useful survey of the cases, from commercial law to public lands policy, through which the Court defined basic terms of exchange, of property rights, and of the boundaries to the legislatures' authority to interfere with either.[116] One remarkable case is *Huidekoper's Lessee v. Douglas*, which involved land distributions of the Pennsylvania legislature that were subject to ambiguous settlement requirements. Invoking the private law of contract against Pennsylvania, Chief Justice Marshall found that the common law principle of equitable estoppel barred legislative action that called into question the preexisting title of a large land company. Thus, Johnson points out, in both private law and constitutional cases the Court pursued a common object—denying the states the power to define property.

> *Fletcher* thus shares with *Huidekoper* the common theme that the American States, when dealing with property rights, were bound by an internal law—a common constitutional limitation—that was independent of any federal jurisdiction or the operation of the supremacy clause of the federal Constitution. There was, as the Chief Justice mentioned in *Fletcher*, a commonality of property rule which, at the very least, prevented legislative takings without compensation. . . . [Marshall] referred not to *federal law* but to a *common American law* of property and constitutional limitations.[117]

By building on the idea of a common law of property, the Court not only expanded the scope of its power to control legislatures, it justified this power by a convincing claim to special competence. Property rights, though clearly an important political issue, were also entitlements long defined by the common law. If determinations had to be made about what constituted infringements of such rights, who could better make them than the traditional expositors of the common law, the courts? With property as one of the chief subjects of judicial review, the Court could call upon the traditions of the common law to support their assertion that the issues at hand were fundamentally legal, not political. The definition of property rights in both private and constitutional cases thus served the double purpose of securing the foundations for a commercial republic and justifying the claim that those foundations were neutral, apolitical, and properly entrusted to the courts.

The unstated question of who was to define rights and otherwise draw the boundaries entailed in the Madisonian vision was thus answered without admitting it as an open question. But it would be misleading to suggest that judicial review actually resolved the problem of how to draw those lines. The problem of the status of property rights continued to be played out in Supreme Court cases. *Calder v. Bull*, for example, is famous for Chase's ringing assertion of natural rights as limits.

> There are certain vital principles in our free republican governments which will determine and overrule an apparent and flagrant abuse of legislative power. . . . [For instance,] a law that takes property from A, and gives it to B. It is against all reason and justice for a people to intrust

> a legislature with such powers; and, therefore, it cannot be presumed that they have done it.[118]

These lines have been quoted for almost two hundred years whenever the Court, or anyone else, wanted to demonstrate that property rights-as-limits is an integral part of our constitutional system. But Chase's opinion also includes a less well-known statement of the positive nature of property law (virtually every text book that reprints *Calder* edits out this section).

> It seems to me, that the *right of property*, in its origin, could only arise from *compact express*, or *implied*, and I think it the better opinion, that the *right*, as well as the *mode*, or *manner*, or acquiring property, and of alienating or transferring, inheriting, or transmitting it, is conferred by society . . . and is always subject to the rules prescribed by *positive* law . . . [119]

Chase did not try to integrate these two points. Are we to infer that no legislature can take property from A and give it to B, but the legislature can determine what counts as property? Can it also *change* what counts as property? We know that what counts as "taking" property has been the subject of jurisprudential debate from the start. The courts have claimed this as their prerogative, but in the twentieth century have come, in practice, to defer to the legislatures. The "takings" issue is, of course, just the most obvious form of the unresolved question of when governmental action is part of the necessary regulation of property and when it is a violation of property rights. The answers have varied, but no clear, principled basis for the solutions has emerged despite almost two centuries of effort. What the rise of judicial review did resolve was that these line-drawing problems, which lie at the heart of the Constitutional framework, will be decided by the courts—with the illusion of certain answers decided by fixed principles—rather than by the more public forums of debate, with overt fluctuations, uncertainty, and clashing interests.

By 1800 the Federalists had reason to be worried about the republic they thought they had established in 1787. The rules of justice, the foundations of the commercial republic, and the structures necessary to secure them, were all under attack. Something more was needed if the basic Federalist vision was to take hold. Judicial review and the law-politics distinction provided the answer. This paired idea and institution constituted the culmination of the Federalist understanding of politics—an understanding based on the priority of civil rights and shaped by a distrust of the people. Judicial review was also, as I indicated at the outset, the consolidation of the Federalist solution outlined in the Constitution. The Court successfully placed the very structure of government in the category of law and thus in the domain of the Court. In a brilliant sleight of hand, Marshall argued that since the Constitution was fundamental law, and courts interpreted law, the interpretation of the Constitution belonged to the Court. Marshall used an accepted image of law as simple rule application to buttress the Court's claim to the power of judicial review and to suggest that judicial review was itself radically distinct from politics. He suggested that in overturning laws, the Court would be engaged in a process that bore no resemblence to the choices and conflicts of politics. The Courts would not be weighing in on one side of a conflict, they would simply be giving effect to the true will of the people, as it is clearly and unequivocally expressed in the Constitution. In the context of the heated and fundamental conflicts of the early Marshall years, I think this characterization of constitutional interpretation as a straightforward application of law must be seen as disingenuous.*[120] And certainly from the perspective of the late twentieth century it is implausible.

This subtle confusion of categories of law sustained the claim that the political structure itself—the boundaries to the powers of government among departments, between States and the Federal government, and between government and the people—should be thought of as law. The structure was the Federalists' solution to the problem of democratic excess. The categories of law and politics would now insulate the structure itself from the realm of democratic politics and, in so doing, would subtly change that structure. Judicial review added one more level of protection between the fundamentals of the system and the popular political process. Moreover, by identifying those fundamentals as law, it gave them an enforceable primacy over the political process.

Again, to avoid confusion, I do not intend this critique of Marshall's argument (and thus of Hamilton's similar argument in *The Federalist*, No. 78) as an attack on separation of powers or of constitutional limits more generally. It is not that there is something inherently troubling about a constitutional structure that places limits on the powers of different branches and expects the judiciary to play an important role in interpreting and enforcing those limits. The problem lies in the disengenuous characterization of the Constitution as "law" (not politics) and the concomitant implication that it is the exclusive province of the judiciary to interpret the Constitution since it is law.[121]

The exercise of judicial review also provided an authoritative statement of the categories and hierarchies of values underlying the constitutional structure. The Court's opinions gave an official articulation and justification of the nonmajoritarian values on which the system was based, of the existence of rights and substantive values that set limits to the democratic process. The Court defined those limits, both by its actions and its rhetoric, in terms that accorded to courts, the least democratic branch, the power to define the scope of politics. In doing so, it dramatically narrowed that scope. The very issues that had been the subject of intense and productive political debate since the Revolution—basic rights, the structure of government, and the rules of property necessary for justice and for economic freedom and prosperity—were now to be removed from the realm of politics.

One need not be dedicated to simple majoritarianism to be concerned by the implications of the law-politics distinction. When an issue is designated as law, it is insulated not only from the clashes of politics, but from the attention of public debate. First, the language of the law is inaccessible in its technicality. More importantly, it is the language of individual rights, of neutral, immutable principles. It hides the assumptions, values, and judgments about the nature of the good society which underlie the conception of rights. It obscures the decision to designate some issues as rights and others as mere interests. The language of law takes these assumptions as given and replaces debate on them with the fine points of rule application.

The nature of contractual obligation was, for example, to be defined by the courts, not publicly debated in terms of the kind of society or economy the people would like their legal rules to foster. The definition of the obligation of contract or of the rights of property in fact reflects judgments about the nature of freedom and justice, about the good society, and about what sorts of values a government can and should foster. But the language of law in which these issues are cast suggests that our system is preoccupied with individual rights and makes few pretensions to the public good beyond the security of those rights. In fact, the establishment of judicial review transferred*[122] to the courts the basic political judgments inherent in competing conceptions of rights.

The development of the categories of law and politics shows the ways in which the Federalist judiciary succeeded in transforming one side of a serious ideological debate into "the rule of law." The place of commercial values in the society, the scope of the power of democratic legislatures, the form of the development of public lands, the importance of local control versus national power, and the definition of the basic terms of exchange and entitlement were all claimed to be in the domain of the Court. And they were all resolved according to the Federalist vision of the commercial republic. The political judgments underlying these contested issues were submerged in the neutral language of the law. In short, the division between law and politics not only secures the foundations of the system from majoritarian disruption, it insulates basic political issues from public debate and analysis.

Finally, the designation of an issue as law obscures questions of class or social conflict. In the debates over the Constitution, the language of class was clear and explicit: fears of aristocracy on the one hand and the unjust designs of the propertyless on the other. Again, in the conflict between the Federalists and Republicans, accusations of aristocracy and Jacobinism were hurled with all the vigor of the orthodox charging heresy. It may be that it was especially important to redefine as law those issues over which class antagonism was seen as particularly threatening. Thus, for example, the protection of property rights was cast in the language of the nature of free government and universal rights rather than conflicting class interests. The successful transformation of contested issues into the terms of law, and the narrowing of the sphere of politics that transformation entailed, may be part of the reason the language of class dropped out of mainstream political debate.

I am not suggesting that the development of the categories of law and politics was arbitrary, cynical, or self-serving in any narrow way. On the contrary, my point is that this development was a logical (though contested and not inevitable) extension of the Federalist conception of politics. It was based on a deep belief in the existence of basic rights, on a serious commitment to a particular vision of the new republic, and on rational fears that unconstrained democracy would threaten both. While this conception of politics contains important insights into the problems of democracy, it is also narrow and in some ways pernicious and misleading. It led at the outset to a structure of institutions that would undermine participatory democracy, and it culminated in categories of law and politics designed to remove basic issues from popular understanding, debate, and control. The consequences have not merely been an undemocratic allocation of decision-making power, but a limitation in our tradition of political thought.

VII. Afterword

I close this chapter with some clarifications about the meaning of its basic claims. The claim that the Federalists won does not mean that their Constitution completely or immediately determined the system of government in America, and the claim that the Constitution was Madisonian does not mean that the political system implemented under the Constitution is exactly what Madison wanted.

The Federalist vision was embodied in the Constitution and proclaimed and enforced through judicial review, but those achievements did not suppress all competing visions or foreclose all avenues of conflict. In the early years of the republic there continued to be active debate over the appropriate forums for political deliberation and conflict. Some of the contested forums have been submerged and others have become lasting parts of our political system. For example, the issue of the proper role of the people in politics became a heated subject of debate in the 1790s in the opposition to Jay's treaty with Great Britain. That treaty had crystallized the conflict over the reaction to the French Revolution and the problem of the relations the new nation should have with two great powers in conflict with one another, France and England. When town meetings passed resolutions on the Jay treaty and societies formed to "associate, in order to compare and consolidate their opinion on those subjects and . . . convince their public agents, that the minds of the people were not with them,"[123] the Federalists opposed those forms of public deliberation as tending to "popularize" American politics. Their argument was that the true representatives of the American people were the elected representatives, not self-selected minorities purporting to speak for the people.[124] The Federalists seem finally to have prevailed on the subordination of local, popular forums of deliberation, but this subordination was not the immediate consequence of the implementation of the Constitution. (And one can still hear this argument in the context of "interest groups" and administrative agencies.)

More importantly, the conflicting visions of the republic continued to be played out in competing political parties. The emergence of a party system was unanticipated by the Framers. Indeed it was virtually unanimously considered anathema to a good republic because parties were equated with faction. The institutionalization of political conflict in parties became a basic part of our political system that was not part of the Federalists' design.

The Federalist Constitution also did not immediately determine the nature of the government established under its framework. "To the extent that the Federalists favored genuine centralization, they won a major battle in 1787–88 only to lose the war by 1801."[125] The actual practice of nineteenth-century government reflected more localist than centralist sentiment.[126] By the twentieth century the power of the federal government had the scope the Federalists had envisioned, but of course the Civil War had intervened with its ensuing constitutional amendments. The Federalists won a victory that was, in the end, lasting because our political system developed around the structure provided by the Constitution, both institutionally and conceptually. But that structure was not magically self-implementing nor was it the only force operating in American politics.

Although our Constitutional framework is Madisonian, I think Madison wanted a better republic than we got. He wanted the rights of persons as well as property to be respected; he did not want the wealthy to be able to use the government to pursue their own self-interest at the expense of others. He wanted a better balance among the competing rights of participation, persons, and property than the Constitution produced. His own solutions, however, generated the imbalance that he was dismayed by in the 1790s and that has remained a problem of American politics ever since.

The Constitution did succeed in achieving Madison's goals, largely by the means he advocated, but not in ways consistent with his highest aspirations—because his own solutions were not capable of meeting those aspirations. The Constitution did not just rely on the multiplicity of factions of an extended republic. It relied on the elite in office and the constraint of the political power of the people. Even as Madison had envisioned it, the conception of the public good of the elite in office would have their self-interest built into it. And (as he had not envisioned) his institutions would also give them the power simply to pursue their self-interest. The unresolved relation of the public good and private interest worked in the interest of the few. The capacity of ordinary people to protect their interests or develop alternative conceptions of the public good was limited by their lack of access to public office. The Supreme Court's official proclamation of a property-centered vision of justice and the public good made it more difficult for the people to imagine redefinitions of property, justice, or the public good. And finally a system whose presupposition is that ordinary people are not really competent in public affairs generates a political culture that does not encourage people's capacity to act in their own interest or to try to develop their own conception of the public good.

Some of these means of protecting property and securing a Madisonian conception of justice and the public good were consistent with Madison's highest values; but the government they added up to was not. It could not equally secure the rights and interests of the propertyless or their capacity to have their voices heard in public affairs. Madison had been blind to the weaknesses of his system, but when they bore fruit in the Washington administration, he parted company with the Federalists. For example, in the debate over the redemption of depreciated government securities, he took the side of "equity and humanity" against those who emphasized the rights of property. He thought Hamilton's plan to pay the full value to the current holders would benefit wealthy speculators and ignore the interests of the original holders who had been forced by the government to take them in payment and then forced by need to sell them at depreciated values. Madison found it hard to articulate why the arguments about property rights and security of transactions were inadequate, but he knew that the least advantaged would bear the greatest burden. He ended up arguing that in questions of great and unusual morality "the heart was a better judge than the head."[127] The sort of protection of the propertied Hamilton had in mind was not the equal protection of the rights of persons and property Madison had aspired to. While he never dissociated himself from the Constitution that had given rise to these problems, he dissociated himself from the Federalists who gave effect to the advantages the Constitution accorded to the propertied. He allied himself with Jefferson whose commitment to the interests and the participation of the people was far stronger than that embodied in the Constitution.

The Jeffersonians won in 1800, but the Federalists' Constitution endured and brought with it not Madison's highest aspirations, but the weaknesses (as well as strengths) of his design. The Constitution generated a government that worked not as Madison had hoped, but very largely as he ought to have expected, if he had been able to acknowledge the consequences of his own conceptual framework and the institutions designed to implement it.

Finally, Wilson gives us another angle on understanding why the Constitution is properly described as Madisonian even though it was not all Madison hoped for. As we shall see more fully in the following chapter, the Constitution not only embodied Madison's institutional solutions, it was designed to solve his, not Wilson's, conception of the problem of republican government. When we look at Wilson's vision of republican government, we can imagine the difference it would have made if he had been able to persuade the convention to turn their collective talents to creating a constitution that would embody his vision of a participatory republic. But that was not their project. Madison literally set the agenda for the Convention,[128] as well as effectively formulating its dominant concerns. The Framers' objectives and their product were very largely Madisonian in conception, and Wilson helps us see the importance of that conceptual framework. He makes us ask the right questions, and lets us see how those questions are generated by one framework and virtually precluded by another.

The Constitution of 1787 did not instantly implement its vision, nor fix it in stone. Institutions change, but those changes are shaped and channeled by the underlying conceptual framework. Ideas change, but our collective capacity to envision alternative frameworks is constrained by the institutions we live with. The Federalists' victories set in place a form of constitutionalism whose institutions and conception were largely Madisonian.

6 The Legacy of the Formation and the Limits of American Constitutionalism

The enduring legacy of the property-centered formation of the Constitution is reflected in three basic issues confronting America today: the weaknesses of the democratic tradition; the unsolved problems of the interpenetration of economic and political power; and the conception of limited government and its institutionalization in judicial review, which have become increasingly hard to comprehend and justify in the modern welfare state. In recent years these problems have been gathering attention in both scholarship and public debate. In this concluding chapter I place these contemporary problems in the context of the basic structure of our constitutional system. This context does not resolve the problems nor provide a full explanation of them; it offers a framework for other more detailed inquiries. From the perspective of the formation of the Constitution it becomes clear that problems of participation and economic power are not aberrations, but consequences of the system. They are not failures to put ideals into practice, but failures of a whole structure of ideas and institutions of which our ideals are a part. The primary focus of the conclusion is, therefore, the conception of limited government that is the essence of American constitutionalism. I begin with some of the basic distortions of our conceptual legacy and then turn to the problems of public liberty and economic power which our institutional and conceptual framework have generated.

I. The Madisonian Conceptual Legacy: Private Property, Inequality, and the Distortion of the Republican Problem

A. The People as the Problem

Madison gave shape to the concerns that animated the Federalists by effectively articulating the insight that government by the people breeds its own form of tyranny: majority oppression. This now trite observation did not fit easily with the rhetoric of the Revolution and needed to be formulated in comprehensible and persuasive terms. Madison did so, and he offered brilliant solutions to the problem. But by taking property as the central instance of the inherent vulnerability of rights, Madison provided a distorted picture of the enduring problem of collective oppression. That distortion is the real significance of property in the Constitution of 1787.

The republic that Madison wanted required security for a right which the majority would inevitably threaten. Defence against such a threat posed a problem quite different from that arising from the general insight that in a republic majorities may oppress minorities. It is one thing to say that everyone's rights are vulnerable to the possibility of majority oppression. It is another to say that an essential ingredient of the republic is the protection of rights that the majority will never fully enjoy, will always want more of, and will therefore always want to encroach upon. Seeing the majority as a permanent threat to property is not the same thing as recognizing that everyone has rights which, at some point, some coalition might think it had an interest in violating. Although Madison spoke of this broader problem of protecting minority rights, the problem he focused on was not that of the shifting possibilities of oppression—which one would expect from the extended republic argument. Madison's problem was a certain, enduring threat to a basic value, property. With property as the paradigmatic problem, the locus of the threat shifts from society at large to a particular class. The protection of property requires controlling not possible majorities, but a particular majority: the propertyless. The focus on the vulnerability of property necessarily bred a fear and, perhaps, contempt of the propertyless, who were to be the vast bulk of the people. The "people" as such—not in the sense of the society as a whole, but in the sense of the ordinary people, those not members of the propertied elite—were the threat that had to be contained. While Madison struggled to find a solution true to republican principles, an approach that identified the "people" as the problem could hardly be expected to foster the popular participation that, at one level, is the essence of republican government.

We can now see more clearly why Wilson's solution could not solve Madison's conception of the problem. Wilson argued that participation would develop the people's political intelligence and commitment to the common good. But such development could only work if there were not deep, irresolvable conflicts of interest. Often Madison spoke as if there were not. In particular, he argued that the unjust schemes he opposed would, in the long run, benefit no one, whereas the protection of property would be to the lasting benefit of all (an assessment Wilson agreed with). But, in fact, under Madison's plan, the propertyless were not, in the long run, going to get what they wanted. They were only going to get the best Madison thought they could hope for. Madison, probably wisely, did not expect that the experience of participation in public affairs could be relied upon to get the "people" to scale back their hopes to what Madison thought was reasonable. It is one thing to believe, like Wilson, that the people would come to recognize better solutions to their problems, it is another to hope to satisfy a majority permanently condemned to "secretly sigh for a more equal distribution of [life's] blessings."[1] Madison did not hope to satisfy them; he hoped to render them politically ineffective.

The Constitution of 1787 was a solution to Madison's not Wilson's conception of the problem of majority tyranny. Madison's preferred plan did not prevail in every instance, but the basic structure did. And it was the structure he relied upon. The structure of the extended republic, with large election districts and institutions providing successive layers of distance between the people and those in office, would contain the ever present threat of the "people" by rendering not just public office, but public affairs relatively inaccessible to them. The message would be that ordinary people were not the sort to understand the issues of politics. They were competent only to grant or withhold their consent, approve or reject the actions of an elite. And indeed, the Constitution hardly suggested a high level of confidence even about that level of competence. The people were to be given the minimum scope for consent that would still be thought compatible with republican government: direct election of the first branch only. In short, the Federalists succeeded in putting in place a structure of institutions with little to invite ordinary people to participate and a conception of government that treated them formally as the foundation and, in practice, as a problem.

B. The Problem of Inequality

The problem of property arose for the Framers because their conception of property was inseparably tied to inequality. The link to inequality was liberty. Property was important for the exercise of liberty and liberty required the free exercise of property rights. And this free exercise would inevitably lead to an unequal distribution of property. Property arose as a problem for government because this inequality required protection; those with property had to be protected from those who had less or none. Without security, property lost its value. And the threat to security was inevitable, for (the Federalists presumed) it was in the very nature of a productive system of private property that many, perhaps most, would have none.[2]

The fact that it is not the protection of property as such, but the inequality of property that is the central problem for republican government is clear in the Madisonian formulation we saw earlier. The equal protection of persons and property is only a problem if political rights are granted equally. And political equality is only a problem because the distribution of property will be so starkly unequal: the majority will have none.

We can now see why it was impossible for the Constitution to meet the challenge Madison had defined. Given a conception of property that entailed stark inequality, no political arrangement could ensure equal protection of the rights of persons, property, and participation. If a minority's vested rights were to be protected against democratically determined choices to redefine those entitlements, the political power of the propertyless majority would have to be controlled. And to reduce their political power relative to the propertied had to put them at a comparative disadvantage with respect to protecting their rights and interests from the potential threat of the few. The Constitution did both.

But it did so indirectly and, in a sense, not definitively. The balance among the competing rights was not an even one, and could not be, given the conception of both property and the "people." But the Constitution of 1787 reflected a recognition of all of these rights and sustained a tension among them. Despite the tacit priority of property, the rights of participation were only subordinated, not denied, and the propertyless and poor were left vulnerable, but not powerless. The Constitution left room for the conflicting rights to continue to clash, with the potential for constant, subtle realignment of pressure, power, and advantage. Sustaining this tension was an important achievement, for it is a response to a basic and enduring problem of politics: the potential conflict between the individual and the society of which he or she is a part. The Federalists saw this conflict in terms of individual rights—with property as their symbol—and the potential threat of the majority, given effect through democratic decision-making. They responded to the problem by trying to protect property without destroying the democracy required by republican principles.

There are, however, two ironies to this important, if partial success. The first is that the democratic side of the tension was maintained at the cost of undermining it at its foundations. Madison preferred to rely on the indirect effects of his structure of institutions, rather than on mechanisms such as judicial review that straightforwardly announced the subordination of democratic decision-making to the security of certain rights. He argued against judicial review on the principle that the judiciary should never have the final word. But this argument presumes a democratic process controlled at its source, returning only the right sort of people to office. Madison made clear his opinion of the efficacy of paper barriers in his initial response to the idea of a Bill of Rights. He thought it was safer to control the power of the "people" at the foundations of the government, rather than try to undo undesirable outcomes after the fact.[3] Madison's very commitment to republican principles moved him to make sure that the participation of the people was rendered as safe—which meant as ineffective—as possible.

The second irony is that by directing his vision beyond the narrow boundaries of protecting property to the broader problem of majority tyranny, Madison distorted our perception of this fundamental problem. As a result, the Federalists' preoccupation with protecting property had a far greater impact than it could have had if they or their most thoughtful spokesmen had been merely self-interested representatives of their class. The Constitution could not have endured as it has if it were devoted merely to the protection of the property of the few. And Madison's brilliant formulation of the problems of republican government would not have continued to shape our perception of those problems if he had merely articulated a need to protect property.

C. The Distorted Lens of Property

Both the Federalists' focus on property and their insistence that property stood for broader issues and deeper values make a good deal of sense. The Federalists were not crass materialists of either the self-interested or philosophical variety. They were not devoted to property for its own sake. Their preoccupation with property had its origins in the connections they presumed between property and other basic human goods, in particular, liberty, and security. In some ways property is an excellent symbol for individual liberty. First, it is an effective symbol because it is not merely a symbol, but a concrete means of having control over one's life, of expressing oneself, and of protecting oneself from the power of others, individual or collective. The need for the security of property in order for it to serve these purposes expresses the important link between security and liberty: although the two values are not the same and can be in tension with one another, some level of security is necessary for liberty to have meaning.

Property is a powerful symbol of this link for it literally loses its meaning without security. We mean by property that which is recognized to be ours and cannot be easily taken from us. Hence the connection between property, law, and government. Property is a right that requires collective recognition and enforcement. And, in part for that reason, property becomes a compelling, yet complex, symbol of the potential conflict between the rights of the individual and the power of the collective. Property requires the involvement of the collective for definition and defense, and thus is peculiarly vulnerable to collective power—at the same time that one of the basic purposes of property is to provide a shield for the individual against the intrusions of the collective. Property defines what the society, or its representative, the state, cannot touch (in the ordinary course of things). It defines a sphere in which we can act largely unconstrained by collective preferences. But the definition and protection of that sphere must reside with the collective itself. Property thus captures the essence of the problem of self-limiting government. But property also distorts it.

Property (at least as the Framers understood it) must distort because it makes inequality rather than liberty, or individual autonomy, the central problem. (Note that what follows is not an argument that there must be equality of property. It is an argument about what happens when property, conceived of as inherently unequal, becomes the central symbol for protecting individual rights.) The Federalists' approach presumed that the threat inequality posed to property captured the inevitable threat democracy posed to individual freedom and security. But in fact, not all rights, all means to or components of liberty, must be enjoyed unequally. Indeed, perhaps property need not, but the Framers' conception of property had inequality—and thus fear, anger, and resentment—built into it. The problem of protecting the rights of the propertied few against the demands of the many is not the same as protecting individuals from the ever-present possibility of collective oppression. The cost of Madison's depth of vision and insight is that he cast the general problem in the terms of the particular—and we have continued to think about the problem in his terms.

Madison saw that the potential for conflict and oppression is part of human nature, and that for all the virtues of society, when people join together, their combination actually exacerbates these tendencies. People are more likely to be carried away by unjust passions and behave badly towards others, in groups, than on their own. When they join together, the power of numbers is likely to overwhelm beliefs about rights, virtue, and obligation. The great democratic values of the Revolution—the fundamental equality of all, government by consent, the right of people to form their own government and reject an oppressive one—were genuine values, but they provided no solution to the problem of collective oppression. They were not sufficient for good or just or even legitimate government.

At some level, Madison recognized the basic problem of finding a way for public institutions both to implement the right of each member of society to an equal say in collective choices and, at the same time, to protect the equal right of each person to some measure of inviolability and respect. He saw that this task is difficult because the collective choice determined by the equal voices of all may be to violate the rights of some. Madison was right that any good government must find a solution to this problem. And his arguments continue to sound a warning to anyone who claims that democratic values alone can be an adequate foundation for government. But the warning was not made in those terms.

It took the form of a general distrust of democracy, and of the "people" in particular. It closed off the capacity to see the Wilsonian argument that the forms of participation may themselves mitigate the threat democracy poses to other, distinct values. The Madisonian formulation suggests that once we recognize that there are rights distinct from, and potentially threatened by, democracy, the solution must be to contain democracy, to have less of it, or to limit the efficacy of the democratic dimension of government. Madison's approach became a justification for government by a class-based elite. The inequality of property had to be reflected in political inequality: the protection of property *required* disproportionate power for the few with property since they needed to be able to defend themselves against the many without.

The tension between the individual and the collective is not inevitably about inequality and domination. The protection of unequal property is. In accepting vast economic inequality as a given and the contours of property rights as obvious, Madison was in fact focusing on protecting the rich from the poor, not individuals or minorities from the collective of which they are a part. Madison's formulation turned attention away from the real problem: fostering the ongoing collective formulation of rights in a political culture that respects both democratic decision making and individual freedom and recognizes the need to sustain the inevitable tension between them. Madison recognized the tension, but he was too focused on the rights-protection side of it. He was preoccupied with insulating property from democratic decision making. As a result, he saw the ongoing reformulation of property rights as a danger to avoid, not as a basic social process in which the values of both democracy and individual rights must be integrated. Madison transformed a widespread fear about threats to property into a sophisticated analysis of the inherent problem of majority oppression. But in doing so, he also transformed this general problem into a question of how to contain the power of the people.

He gave us a language, a conceptual framework for understanding the problems of democracy in which the values and potential of democracy became submerged.

D. Rights as Limits

There is one final point I should make to dispel a possible misunderstanding of my claims about the importance of property for the Madisonian conception of republican government. The Federalists' concern with property profoundly shaped their understanding of limited government, but property was not the origin of their belief in rights as limits to legitimate government. Property could assume the role it did because of the widely shared starting point that the protection of rights was (at least) part of the purpose of government and thus a measure of its legitimacy. The Declaration of Independence had proclaimed this belief. The focus on property shaped the Madisonian conception of constitutional government, but we can only understand that conception if we see it as premised on the notion that rights limited the legitimate authority of government. Indeed, some of Madison's most striking early statements about limited government referred not to property, but to freedom of religion. In a widely circulated "Remonstrance" against a "Bill establishing a provision for Teachers of the Christian Religion," Madison wrote that

> the preservation of a free government requires not merely that the metes and bounds which separate each department of power may be invariably maintained, but more especially that neither of them be suffered to overlap the great Barrier which defends the rights of the people. . . . Either then, we must say, that the will of the Legislature is the only measure of their authority; and that in the plentitude of this authority, they may sweep away all our fundamental rights . . . or we must say that they have no authority to enact into law the Bill under consideration.[4]

And, of course, threats to freedom of religion, not property, were the form of government tyranny originally most familiar to Americans. Religious persecution had brought many to the colonies in the first place, and conflicts over religious freedom continued to arise in the new land.[5] It may well be that some of the most important early American formulations of limited government developed around the issue of religious freedom.

What matters for my argument here is that religion, despite the earlier concern with it, was not a central issue at the constitutional convention. In the Framers' discussions of the use of governmental power to violate rights, property was the prime example. And it mattered that property, not religion, was the focal point for the design of the Constitution. Indeed the contrast between the problems posed by the two rights helps make clear the significance of property as the focus, but not the origin, of the Federalists' concern with the vulnerability of rights to governmental power.

First, property poses the problem of inequality in ways that religion does not. Although there may be a majority of believers in one religion, there is nothing inherent in the exercise of religious freedom that means that some will more fully enjoy it than others. Religious freedom need not generate deep divisions in society as the exercise of the right to acquire property inevitably would (although differences in religious beliefs were among the many potential sources of conflict that liberty would bring). Despite the world's long history of religious intolerance, the Framers did not seem to think that the new republic would regularly face a religious majority determined to use its numerical power to pass legislation threatening the religious rights of others. Part of the reason for this apparent lack of concern goes to the second difference between the problems posed by protecting freedom of conscience and protecting property.

Religion was not a matter that would routinely and inevitably engage the attention of the federal legislature. It was not just that religion was a matter properly within the states' jurisdiction, and thus best left to them to protect or regulate as they saw fit. After all, if freedom of religion had seemed to be at the center of the problems facing the new republic, the Constitution could have tried to protect it from state interference as it did the security of contract. The point is that it seemed possible for a government, the federal government in particular, simply to have nothing to do with religion. Whereas the regulation of the conflicting interests of property was a basic part of the ongoing business of government.

In short, religion does not pose the central problem of a right that is both the subject of governmental action and the limit to it; and religion does not pose the problem of rights as limits in a way that inevitably raises the problem of inequality. In both these respects, the focus on property transformed the basic notion of the protection of rights as the object and requirement of legitimate government into a sophisticated but skewed conception of limited government.

II. The Failure of Public Liberty

Hannah Arendt is perhaps the most eloquent critic of the kind of democracy the American Constitution established: "the Revolution, while it had given freedom to the people, had failed to provide a space where this freedom could be exercised. Only the representatives of the people, not the people themselves, had an opportunity to engage in those activities of 'expressing, discussing and deciding' which in a positive sense are the activities of freedom."[6] This failure is both institutional and conceptual: the institutions do not provide this opportunity and the reigning conception of democracy cannot comprehend the problem. These are the Madisonian weaknesses which have endured despite the vast expansion of suffrage, the direct election of the Senate, and the ascendancy of democratic rhetoric.

Arendt thinks that the germs of insight into the true nature of political freedom were present during the founding of the new republic but were lost "when the spirit of revolution . . . failed to find its appropriate institution."[7] She is surely right that the insights could not have become an established part of the American tradition without institutions that embodied and thus sustained them. But we have also seen that the institutional failure sprang from the conceptual failure of treating political participation only as a means to an end. The Federalists' instrumental conception of politics triumphed over Wilson's insights and the Anti-Federalists' aspirations. Arendt's point helps us understand the lasting impact of the Federalists' success in 1787. Although the Jeffersonians won the elections in 1800, leaving the Federalists permanently eclipsed in electoral politics, Jefferson's vision of democracy never became the dominant conception in American political thought. The institutions of the Constitution together with the establishment of judicial review entrenched the Federalist vision of politics. Not only did the institutions provide no "space" (to use Arendt's language) for a notion of the intrinsic value of participation to flourish,[8] but judicial review provided an official organ for the articulation of basic American values, and the vision the Court expounded was that of the Federalists.

The failure of the democratic tradition that Arendt points to is the virtual exclusion of the ordinary citizen from the actual practice of politics. The role of the citizen is reduced to withholding or granting consent and perhaps putting demands to those who govern. The deep hold of this limited vision of democracy is reflected in the language of leading scholars. For example, Robert Dahl describes democratic theory as "concerned with processes by which ordinary citizens exert a relatively high degree of control over leaders." Verba and Nie define political participation as "those activities by private citizens that are more or less directly aimed at influencing the selection of governmental personnel and/or the actions they take."[9] Both presume the exclusion of ordinary citizens that Arendt laments.

This exclusion is not simply the inevitable result of a system of representation rather than direct democracy. The focus of Wilson's concern and that of the Anti-Federalists was the scope and structure of representative institutions that would foster an ongoing sense of interest in politics and connection to those carrying out the duties of representation. Of course, the problem of fostering truly participatory democracy in a large country is an extremely difficult one. It was already difficult with the size of the population in 1787. But Wilson, the Anti-Federalists, and Jefferson were interested in it, and we have political scientists and even politicians addressing it today.[10] The Federalists were not interested in this problem. The institutions outlined in the Constitution were not designed to foster active political involvement by ordinary citizens. One might argue that the institutions succeeded in doing what they *were* designed to do: to prevent the sort of majority oppression the Federalists feared and the tyrannous abuse of faithless officials (the latter largely, as intended, through the system of checks and balances). It should be no surprise that the Federalists' "machinery of government . . . could not save the people from lethargy and inattention to public business."[11]

If the exclusion of the people from politics is not the inevitable consequence of representation but of the particular forms it takes, it *is* inevitably connected to the instrumental conception of political participation that treats it as a mere means to an end. We have seen that the hierarchy between civil and political rights justified both the subordination of participation and the rule by the elite (who were competent to protect the true ends of government). Arendt reveals that once institutions exclude the people from genuine participation in public affairs, politics *must* become instrumental: "The most the citizen can hope for is to be 'represented,' whereby it is obvious that the only thing which can be represented and delegated is interest, or the welfare of the constituents, but neither their actions nor their opinions. In this system the opinions of the people are indeed unascertainable for the simple reason that they are non-existent. Opinions are formed in a process of open discussion and public debate, and where no opportunity for the forming of opinions exists, there may be moods . . . but no opinion."[12] We are left then with a kind of self-fulfilling Federalist vision of politics: They were afraid the people would use their political power to pursue their private interests at the expense of the rights of others and of the public good; they created a system in which the only possible relation between citizen and representative was that of advocate and arbitrator of interests.[13] The institutions did not foster the ongoing engagement with public affairs that could have transformed raw private interest into considered political opinion. That was the Wilsonian solution to the democratic threat that his fellow Federalists could not comprehend. They were right that unmeditated private interest backed by political power was dangerous,[14] but they focused on containing rather than transforming the threat. Citizens' limited perspectives were not to be enlarged, but contained or refined by representatives capable of an approach to politics which "the people" were not.

The Federalists' limited vision of citizens' relation to politics has become the dominant view of politics as a whole. It is taken as a given that politics is about the pursuit and juggling of conflicting private interests. This pervasive assumption is reflected in both academic and popular discussions of politics. Even thoughtful reformers trying to think through the meaning of modern American democracy, such as Bruce Ackerman, accept the vision of politics (or at least "normal politics") as private interest. He even recognizes and accepts its consequences: "If this means that liberal politics will often suffer from apathy, ignorance, and selfishness, we all have to learn to grin and bear it."[15] He is concerned with more than the standard reform of trying to make sure that everyone has an equal shot at getting representatives to promote his or her interests. But he still reflects the basic presuppositions of the tradition of thought we have inherited from the Federalists: the nature of public involvement in politics is taken as a given, rather than the product of institutional design. There is no suggestion that involvement might change under different institutional conditions. In time-honored fashion, contemporary commentators juxtapose the public good and private interest. In this vision it is only in the rare person or the rare time when the public good may be expected to be the central concern.

There is, of course, some basis for this traditional approach. There are the obvious conflicts of time, attention, and interest; and the demands of public involvement must be taken seriously. But the American tradition obscures the possibility that the sharp split between public and private interests may be reshaped when citizens routinely engage in collective self-determination. The Federalists succeeded in getting two centuries of Americans to accept their assumptions about the characteristics of people and politics, rather than seeing those characteristics as (at least in part) consequences of the institutions the Federalists put in place.

When we see the American practice and conception of the politics of private interest as a limited form of democracy, rather than a self-evident truth of politics, we can understand why the expansion of the franchise did not itself transform the nature of American democracy. When women and Blacks were finally permitted to vote, they too could use the political system to try to protect and advance their interests. Even allowing for the extra-legal impediments to their effective use of this power, it was not a trivial advancement of equality. With everyone else contending for their own interests, exclusion can be costly and dangerous. But while the formal political inclusion of

Blacks and women may have changed society in important ways, simply expanding the range of contending forces in politics does not itself change the nature of participation.

In an interesting essay on different conceptions of the nature of American "constitutional aspirations," Hendrik Hartog notes that "a more republican vision" of our Constitutional system would treat "participation in public life [as] . . . the primary good to be secured by rights." But then he notes, that, to a large extent "the right to vote was for both white women and freedmen a means to an autonomous life, rather than the other way around."[16] Of course, it makes sense to treat the right to vote as a means, when that is what it is. The form of participation women and Blacks were admitted to was not one that could itself be a primary aspiration. Their "constitutional aspirations" recognized the instrumental quality of the participation available to them under the U.S. Constitution.

I have argued that the Federalists' institutions were not designed to foster popular engagement with public affairs and that they not only reflected a judgement about who was politically competent, but made that judgement part of the political culture. Their success is reflected in the dismal, class-based, participation rates of American voters. In recent years, only about half of those eligible have voted in presidential elections, and the higher figures (above 80%) of the nineteenth century reflected a narrower class composition of voters.

> [T]hat was the vote of an elite, determined by restriction of the suffrage to male, largely white, non-transient, often tax-paying, literate members of established societies or machines. Today, among an equivalent elite, those making over $50,000 a year, the voting rate is 79%. Among college graduates it is 79%. The more privileged in our society still vote in significant majorities. But of those making less than $5,000, only 38% vote. And of those with only a grade school education, only 43%. Comparative studies show that, in other governments, non-voting is not a necessary concomitant of lower income. Why is it in America?[17]

The answer to that question does not lie solely in the structure laid out in the Constitution. But we can easily see the relevance of the arguments of the Anti-Federalists about the consequences of a government run by a distant elite. The barriers to participation that various levels of government may erect[18] work far more easily when the poor already see government as distant, incomprehensible, and inaccessible to people like themselves. When we try to understand why Americans, and particularly poor Americans, don't vote, we should remember that the basic structure of our institutions was not designed to encourage their participation.[19]

It is not the case that the institutions and vision the Framers set in place made no contribution to democratic government.[20] Part of their plan for the Senate was to make it a place where genuine deliberation could take place. Arendt admires it as "a lasting institution for the formation of public views [built] into the very structure of the republic."[21] Although the Federalists never quite sorted out the relation between private interest and the public good (a confusion which persists), their vision of the role of the representative remains an impressive one and we have reason to believe that many in federal public office have had honorable, even noble, public careers. The problem is not that the vision or practice of deliberating on public affairs is itself deplorable, but that the process of "expressing, discussing, deciding" is reserved for the few. The exclusion of the people encourages a politics of private interest because representation can then only *represent* interest; but the elite Madisonian statesman would do more than represent. To invoke Arendt once again, she claims that, the U.S. government "can be called oligarchic in the sense that public happiness and public freedom have again become the privilege of the few."[22]

III. Economic and Political Power

The problem of exclusion is exacerbated because "the few" are largely an economic elite. The Federalists designed their institutions well. We have almost exactly what they hoped for: considerable economic mobility, but access to public office primarily for those who have already succeeded in becoming part of the economic elite. It is of course difficult to define and document an elite. But it seems clear that members of Congress "are better-educated, possess higher status occupations and have more privileged backgrounds than the people they 'represent.'"[23] It also seems well documented that "many key occupations are, and always have been, drastically underrepresented. Low status occupations—including farm labor, services, trades, manual and skilled labor, and domestic services—are all almost unknown on Capital Hill."[24] And the expected difference between the House and Senate also appears, the Senate being even more elite. It is clear that Congress is hardly the mirror of the population that Wilson and the Anti-Federalists hoped for, and that the lowest economic and status groups are virtually excluded. It is harder to tell whether the Anti-Federalists' fear of the exclusion of the "middling sort" has proven justified. Part of the problem lies in the large number of lawyers in Congress. The "ordinary town lawyer" may be reasonably classified as part of the middle class,[25] but lawyers are also an elite occupation in many ways. In any case, the Anti-Federalists did not seem reassured by their expectation that lawyers would have particularly easy access to public office.[26] In general, it seems that while some Congressmen were born into a middling background, most have risen above it by the time they are elected to office.

The predominance of the elite in both ordinary participation and in Congress raises the issue not only of participation but of economic power in politics. If representatives represent private interests, whose interests do they know and serve? If they are enlightened and public-spirited statesmen, whose vision of the public good do they share and how inclusive is it? How able are they to assess the "real welfare of the great body of the people?"[27]

I will not even try to canvass the issue of whether federal policies have equally served the interests of all. I merely note that, given the level of economic inequality with all its implications for access to goods and services (including such basics as education and health care), true even-handedness seems hard to credit.[28] To the extent that public officials have tried to serve the "welfare of the great body of the people," they have acted on the Madisonian vision of politics that took the public good and impartiality seriously but reserved them for the elite. Madison's vision of elite rule had nobility, and Americans have probably reaped some benefits from it. Our institutions were designed on the basis of imperfectly integrated notions of private interest and the public good, and it seems likely that the latter has never been completely subsumed in the former. Elite rule has meant a loss of "public liberty" for all, and it has surely served the interests of the elite, but the original failure to try to insulate political from economic power has not resulted in simple oppression by the rich.

The forms of oppression are complicated and obscured both by the institutions and the political thought we have inherited. One of the most useful ways of looking at the interpenetration of economic and political power is to remember Madison's fears: the majority would use its political power to achieve a "more equal share of the blessings of life." Reformers have tried to figure out ever since why the majority has not succeeded, or succeeded more fully.[29] I have tried to show the ways in which the Constitution was designed to make it difficult. My argument directs our attention to the most basic structure of the system in trying to find the answers. Madison counted on the whole structure to secure the rule of the elite without resorting to disenfranchisement. Roughly speaking, he succeeded. At their best, the elite in office have protected the foundations of an economic and political system certain to produce inequality but, within that framework, have tried to serve the interests of all. At their worst, they have served their own interests and those of their class at the direct expense of others.

The failure to examine the relation between economic and political power runs deep in the American tradition. Even the countless attacks on the power of big business during the progressive era failed to make the political power of wealth or "business" a basic issue in mainstream American politics. The periodic concern with "corruption" has treated the influence of wealth as an aberration; it has not suggested or invited an inquiry into the way political and economic power are intertwined in the structure of our institutions.[30] In recent years, talk about money and politics has become commonplace, that is, frequent and generally without much depth. There have, however, been some efforts to understand and control the political power wielded by the economic elite. These efforts do more to reveal the depth of the problem than to solve it.

The clearest instance is the effort to control campaign finance, the most direct or obvious form of the interpenetration of economic and political power. But even here, the efforts meet the resistance of a system of thought and institutions ill-equipped to deal with the problem. Preventing "corruption" or vote buying seems to be the most straightforward form of the problem. When it can be shown that people give money to politicians who, in return, promote their donor's interests, that exchange violates American norms. But the relationship is rarely so simple. It appears that campaign contributions affect legislators' voting only at the margins.[31] We need a more sophisticated conception of the proper relation between representatives and the public good and of the ways all of their connections with particular interests may distort that relation. But as soon as we inquire deeply into that issue, we will run up against the more basic problems of the elite composition of Congress and class-based patterns of participation. The concepts of "corruption" or even "influence" do not capture the depth of those problems. The efforts to equalize access to office and influence by controlling expenditure, while salutary, are inevitably limited—and have been even more limited by judicial interpretation (as we shall see in a moment). The prevailing conceptions of political equality are too shallow and limited to provide an adequate basis for significant reform.[32] And truly adequate conceptions would direct our attention past campaign contributions to the structure of our institutions.

Perhaps the most striking instance of the prevailing inability to comprehend the problem of political equality and economic power is the opinion for the Court in *Buckley v. Valeo*.[33] The case involved challenges to several key provisions of the Federal Election Campaign Act of 1971. The provisions relevant to my discussion here were: (a) individual political contributions were limited to $1,000 to any single candidate per election with an overall annual limitation of $25,000 by any contributor; (b) independent expenditures by individuals and groups "relative to a clearly identified candidate" (as opposed to directly to the candidate) were limited to $1,000 a year; and (c) campaign spending by the candidates themselves was limited. According to the Court, even the Act's supporters cast its primary purpose in terms of the prevention of corruption and the appearance of corruption. Two "ancillary" interests were claimed: first, the limits would serve "to mute the voices of affluent persons and groups in the election process and thereby to equalize the relative ability of all citizens to affect the outcome of elections; and second, it is argued, the ceilings may to some extent act as a brake on the skyrocketing cost of political campaigns and thereby serve to open the political system more widely to candidates without access to sources of large amounts of money."[34] The Court found the primary purpose sufficient to justify limit (a) on campaign contributions, but not to justify the expenditure ceilings, (b). The limits on expenditures covered advocacy of candidates "made totally independently of the candidate and his campaign." The Court found that this absence of prearrangement "alleviates the danger that expenditures will be given as a quid pro quo for improper commitments from the candidate."

Once the Court moved beyond this narrow focus on corruption to the ancillary interest in "equalizing the relative ability of individuals and groups to influence the outcome of elections," it flatly asserted that "the concept that government may restrict the speech of some elements of our society in order to enhance the relative voice of others is wholly foreign to the First Amendment." With respect to limits on candidates' expenditures from personal or family resources, the Court similarly announced that "the First Amendment simply cannot tolerate S.608(a)'s restriction upon the freedom of a candidate to speak without legislative limit on behalf of his own candidacy." In invalidating overall campaign expenditure ceilings, the Court rejected the "skyrocketing costs" argument with the rather astonishing pronouncement that "[i]n the free society ordained by our Constitution it is not the government but the people—individually as citizens and candidates and collectively as associations and political committees—who must retain control over the quantity and range of debate on public issues in a political campaign."[35] The Court seemed to sense no tension between their image of "the people" controlling the nature of debate and the power of money in shaping that debate. I leave to later in this chapter a fuller discussion of the unstated presuppositions about the nature and entitlements of property in this decision. Here I just want to offer it as an example of the reigning limitations in our capacity to deal with the relationship between economic and political power,*[36] and to note that in this instance the links between those limitations and the (unacknowledged) privileged status of property seem particularly clear.

Within academic circles, at least, there is now another deeper form of concern with the relation between political and economic power that does focus on structure. Its most important exponent is Charles E. Lindblom. In *Politics and Markets*[37] he argues that major economic interests must have a disproportionate influence on government because of the range of vital functions allocated to private business. Roughly speaking, governments in market economies must accommodate the demands of business. This insight into economic control of political power and the limits of political control over economic power is a way of describing the interrelation between economic and political power in capitalist democracies, or polyarchies, as Lindblom calls them. (A similar, if cruder, conception of this relation is captured in Gouverneur Morris's claim that for republican government to succeed in America, it would have to satisfy the demands of the rich.) Of course, Lindblom's argument extends beyond the institutions of the United States. But it also directs us to the particular ways our system has fostered the limited capacity of political institutions to exert democratic control over economic matters. One of the most important has been the prohibitions of Article I, Section 10, particularly the contract clause, which (as interpreted by the courts) greatly restricted the state legislatures' power to define the foundations of their economic systems.

Remember that one of the Federalists' objectives was to prevent the people from tampering with the rules of exchange and entitlement. The fear of democratic excess was not that the people would expropriate the property of the rich, but that they would change the rules of the game through debtor relief laws or undermine the security of transactions through depreciating paper currency. In other words, the Federalists' fear was not that the people would redistribute the "outcomes" of the market economy, but that they would reshape the very structure and rules of the economy. They did not want this structure to be subject to democratic politics or, to use their language, subject to the people's shifting and ill-conceived perception of their interest. The most important source of this democratic threat was the state governments, which, as we have seen, the Constitution restrained with direct prohibitions.

As implemented by the Marshall Court, Article I, Section 10, confined the scope of democratic politics and designated the foundations of the economy as a matter of law rather than democratic politics. For Joyce Appleby the lasting consequences of this constitutional constraint have been both an undermining of the impetus for democracy and an economy insulated from democratic control.

> Had the states been left with the economic powers they had before the ratification of the Constitution, the momentum of popular politics would not have been checked. Never having lost the normal scope of legislative power, the states could more easily have maintained the traditional connection between the government and the economy. . . . Moreover, without constitutional protection, it seems unlikely that private property rights would ever have achieved their rhetorical status as sacred. This is not to suggest that the majority of Americans disliked the market economy or that commercial expansion would not have taken place. It is to say that the people acting in their capacity as citizens with the power of the state at their collective disposal could have had a larger part in making decisions. The social and the economic would not have been constitutionally divided, and ordinary men in America could have shaped the course of commerce as part of government and not simply as individual buyers and sellers.[38]

Lindblom points to the constraints of capitalism, but in the absence of constitutional limitations, the states might have developed different forms of capitalism with greater scope for democratic control. The problem here, as always with the Constitution, is a matter of both ideas and institutions. It is not just that for about 150 years judicial review was exercised to limit democratic control of the economy, but that we have come to think of the basic contours of the market as something outside the realm of political choice. Even egalitarian reformers tend to take "the market" as a given and focus on redistributing its outcomes or trying to contain its impact.[39] There is too little attention to the possibility of restructuring the market itself or of restructuring the political system so that the legal rules that constitute the market would become the subject of democratic debate and control.[40] Americans have largely accepted the Federalists' distinction between law and politics and the idea that the foundations of the market economy fall into the category "law." That notion gives credence to the "neutral rules of the game" image of the market and further insulates it from effective democratic control. This institutional and conceptual insulation of the basic terms of the economy has been one of the most important impediments to controlling the political power exerted by those with economic power. When the very sources of economic power are treated as outside the bounds of political contest and change, the mechanisms of control become peripheral. When "the forces that dominate social structure"[41] are taken as a given, reformers are forced into a rearguard action, trying to set up barriers between those forces and institutions of government that were designed to be controlled by those forces. Our constitutional system has fostered too little experimentation with democratic control of the economy and democratic restructuring of the sources of economic power. We have largely accepted the Federalists' conception of the choices facing a commercial republic, and we have lived too unquestioningly with their formulations of the problems and their institutional solutions.

Of course, since 1937 the judicial constraints on legislative control of the economy have been loosened virtually to the point of disappearing. I will turn shortly to the significance of this shift. Here I just want to note that 150 years of constraint have left their mark. The most elemental components of the market economy, the "private law" rules of property, contract and, tort were firmly in place by 1937, as was the distribution of wealth and power the market economy generated. And the notion has endured that this basic structure is a matter of law and neutral rules, not a set of choices about the nature of economy and society that should be the subject of ongoing political debate. (Later in this chapter, I will comment on the ways this notion has endured in popular discourse, political rhetoric, public policy, judicial opinions, and law school texts *even though* most legal scholars purport to have adopted a sophisticated post-Realist understanding of law as social construct.)

The failure of American institutions and political thought to deal adequately with the possibilities of a fully participatory democracy or the problems of the relation between economic and political power is probably the most important legacy of Madisonian federalism. And I have done little more than sketch the argument for the relation between these failures and the constitutional framework of institutions and ideas the Federalists set in place. To do more would require empirical studies beyond the scope of my project here. I leave my claims as directions for further inquiry. I turn now to the conception of limited government that is the intellectual and moral foundation of American constitutionalism, and to judicial review which both embodies and articulates that conception.

IV. The Puzzle of Property

Today the meaning of limited government in America is anxiously contested. Both the anxiety and the disagreement have their origins in the role of property in the formation of the Constitution and its underlying conception of limited government. The following sections of the conclusion focus on understanding our contemporary dilemmas of constitutionalism by unraveling the puzzle posed by the role of property in our constitutional tradition.

A. The Paradox of Property's Status

Property poses a paradox in the American constitutional system. Private property was for at least 150 years the quintessential instance of individual rights as limits to governmental power. Property set bounds between a protected sphere of individual freedom and the legitimate scope of governmental authority. But the rhetorical power and absoluteness of these bounds has been matched by their shifting permeability in practice. The legal concept of property—a symbol of stability and security—has undergone changes that amount to disintegration, even though property seems to retain its symbolic force as the foundation of American freedoms. It is still a central American value and an integral part of our system. Our conception of property still defines appropriate "private" power and our notion of when something, like government regulation, constitutes "interference" with that power. But property has lost its traditional constitutional status. For decades, property has ceased to serve as a significant formal boundary between individual rights and governmental power.[42]

The paradox appears in theoretical treatments of property as well. It remains a subject of avid legal commentary, but commentators display a perception of property far different from its traditional meaning as boundary and a comfortable ignorance or disregard of the difference. And at the very time that property has lost its traditional status, it is the focus for the hopes of conservatives, liberals, and radicals alike.

A striking number of different advocates of reform have proposed property as the vehicle for change. They want to reconstitute the constitutional meaning of property by tying it to the (related) values they want to promote, such as political participation, privacy, and autonomy. The concept of property would be the means (by incorporation) of extending protection to these values, and the values would be the basis for defining and limiting the constitutional protection available to property. This focus on property reflects a faith in the possibility of using the tradition itself to effect radical change. The object seems to be to make property mean what the reformers want and thus to turn the enormous rhetorical power of property to the ends of reform: "What is the point of treating the right to a quality of life as a property right? . . . Why not just put it forward as a human right? . . . If it is asserted as a human right separate from the property rights, the whole prestige of property will work against it rather than for it. We have made property so central to our society that anything and any rights that are not property are very apt to take second place."[43]

At the same time, conservatives use the tradition to resist egalitarian redefinitions of property rights and to oppose the changes that have already taken place. They urge a return to the good old days when the courts protected property rights and economic liberties in keeping with "the intent of the Framers" and the basic values of the American constitutional system. In their view, property was, and should be, not only the symbol, but the source and guarantee of individual liberty. They argue that if we properly understood our constitutional system and the values underlying it, we would see that since 1937 the Court has betrayed that tradition, putting our liberties, our prosperity, and the very essence of our constitutional system at risk. The resurrection of what they see as the traditional importance of property stands at the center of their program for reclaiming the tradition.

The conservatives are right in at least this respect: the key to understanding the changes in property and their implications for our system lies in the tradition. But the message of the tradition is itself a puzzle. On the one hand, it is characterized by the enduring importance of property, which is the central claim of this book. My argument suggests an integrity and continuity of the Constitution and of the central importance of property in the structure of its institutions and ideas.

On the other hand, the history of property also seems to point in the opposite direction: our constitutional system has had an extraordinary capacity to absorb changes which, from a theoretical perspective, ought to be revolutionary—and which conservatives have decried as the portents of doom in 1787, in the 1820s, the 1890s through the 1930s, and again in the present. The dreaded changes have in many cases come to pass, and the system has endured, as has the image of property as sacred. This immense flexibility points to one of the most interesting and puzzling aspects of property: the enduring and consistent rhetorical power of the sanctity of property in American political thought—despite radical shifts in meaning and incursions on that sanctity in legal practice.[44]

How can "the tradition" be characterized by both coherence and endurance *and* by an apparently unlimited mutability in the purported core of the structure? The paradox itself suggests the answers: it is the *myth* of property—its rhetorical power combined with the illusory nature of the image of property—that has been crucial to our system. And it is this mythic quality that current changes in the concept may threaten. The complex, paradoxical, and mythical dimensions of property's importance in American constitutionalism emerge from an examination of the changing and contradictory status of property in the history of American law. I turn therefore to the puzzle posed by the history of property, and to what that puzzle reveals.

B. The Dual History of Property

The most striking form of the puzzle is the contrast between the central importance of property in the formation of the Constitution and its current minimal role in constitutional law. For the Marshall Court, as for the Madisonian Federalists, the rights of property and contract formed basic limits to the legitimate scope of government. Today it is the rare case in which any governmental action (short of physical invasion) is found to violate the rights of property or any economic regulation is held to be an impairment of the obligation of contract.[45] Since 1937, the Supreme Court has virtually abandoned the means it had established for preventing legislative interference with property rights.[46] Making sense of this current stance in light of my claims about the enduring importance of property is the central piece of the puzzle. But we need to see it against the background of the shifting and contradictory status of property in the nineteenth century.

One part of the story is the continuation of the Marshall Court's protection of property. The most famous version of Marshall's approach as the lasting foundation of constitutional law is Edwin S. Corwin's: the underlying doctrine of American constitutional law is the "Doctrine of Vested Rights," without which "it is inconceivable that there would have been any Constitutional law."[47] The Court under Chief Justice Taney (1836–1864) continued to use the contract clause to protect property from legislative incursion,[48] as did the Waite Court (1874–1888).[49] Perhaps the most famous and dramatic judicial protection of vested rights in this period was the *Dred Scott* case (1857), in which the long-simmering tension around property and slavery culminated in the ruling that Congress had no power to outlaw slavery in the territories because nothing in the Constitution "gives Congress a greater power over slave property, or . . . entitles property of that kind to less protection than property of any other description."[50] After the Civil War, the Court initially refused to use the new amendments to expand their power to protect property from state legislation, but Justice Field's dissenting articulations of substantive due process had won out by the close of the century. From this perspective the laissez-faire era, from roughly 1890 to 1937, is part of a strong and continuous tradition of judicial protection of property rights.

Also part of this picture is the role of the state courts in protecting property though various forms of substantive due process,[51] and the constant rhetoric of the sanctity of property as a foundation of the American republic. Some of the greatest spokesmen—Joseph Story, Daniel Webster, James Kent—come from the close of the Marshall years, carrying the message on into the following decades.[52] The rhetoric continued, if not always as eloquently, and took its modern laissez-faire form in Thomas Cooley's *Constitutional Limitations* (1868) and Christopher G. Teideman's *Limitations of Police Power* (1886). In the 1870s and 1880s the dire warnings of those who feared the Court would not exert sufficient control over new economic regulation sounded like precise echoes of the fears of democratic threats expressed by the Federalists in 1787 and those fighting the expansion of the suffrage in the state constitutional conventions of the 1820s.[53] And, of course, by the end of the century, the Supreme Court had heeded the warnings and was providing impassioned expositions of the laissez-faire vision.

We have then a consistent picture of property conceived of as a basic right limiting the scope of government, with the courts articulating and enforcing this conception against democratic incursions. In other words, the Federalist vision enacted for 150 years, from 1787 to 1937.

But there is another story of property and the courts in the nineteenth century that looks very different. Morton Horwitz has convincingly shown that in the decades before the Civil War, the courts were actively engaged in reshaping the rules of the common law. (Some of Horwitz's arguments are disputed, but generally not those about the extent—as opposed to the dates and purpose—of the transformations in the common law.)*[54] Changing the rules of property, tort and contract involved destroying vested rights. Judges undertook these changes in the name of progress, economic development, and the common good. Their reasoning was "instrumental,"[55] invoking utilitarian sorts of arguments. Instead of extolling the sanctity of property, these opinions tell us that individuals cannot stand on their rights in ways that impede the needs of society. These common law cases provide a startling contrast to the picture of constitutional law I have just outlined. But even constitutional law turns out to have sanctioned serious incursions on vested rights. The courts, usually state courts, permitted virtually unchecked use of eminent domain to foster economic development, even when legislatures delegated the power to private companies. And this pattern was most prominent just when the sanctity of property was increasingly loudly trumpeted as the foundation of the republic: "the heyday of expropriation as an instrument of public policy designed to subsidize private enterprise" was from the 1870 to 1910.[56] Indeed, one of the things that is most striking about this other side of the story is that these judicial incursions, or sanctions of incursions, did not generate an alternative to the basic image of the sanctity of property. The courts invoked the common good and condemned selfish insistence on private rights, but they did not argue that property was essentially a matter of social convention and shifting priorities, a right contingent on collective judgments about the common good. They did not try to articulate an alternative conception of property or its place in constitutionalism.*[57] Judicial practices with respect to property were in sharp contrast with one another. But there were not two competing ideologies or rhetorics of property. The dominant image prevailed of private property as a fundamental American value, a basic individual right secure against encroachment, even by the powers of government.

Of course, the incursions on private property rights designed or sanctioned by the courts were not instances of the propertyless majority seeking to claim some of the benefits of the wealthy few. My stories of property in the nineteenth century have deliberately avoided the difficult issue of whether these changes in the rules of property favored those already in positions of economic advantage. By the end of the century there was an unprecedented concentration of wealth in the hands of the few, and it seems likely that this development was related to the legal framework of the economy. But it is extremely difficult to prove that any given shift in common law or even any legislatively conferred advantage, such as the power of eminent domain, systematically favored a given class.[58] But although many argue that nineteenth-century law served the economic interests of all, no one suggests that the pattern reveals a failure of the courts to thwart the unjust designs of the poor trying to get a greater share from the rich.[59] The instrumental side of the judicial treatment of property is not a reversal of the Federalist vision in that regard. But it does point to a stark gap between the rhetoric and reality of the sanctity of property.

A closer look at even the picture of continuous constitutional protection of property reveals a kind of blurring of the clear conceptual image of rights as limits to legitimate power. For example, in the contract cases following Marshall's reign, his eloquent arguments seem to dissolve into the endless complexity and uncertainty of deciding when a legislative change in remedy "acted directly upon the contract itself"[60] or what exactly was included in the irrevocable status of state grants[61] proclaimed in *Fletcher v. Peck*.[62] Over the course of the nineteenth century it became increasing clear that the "rules of justice" did not have the self-evident and certain quality to them that Madison had assumed and Marshall had asserted. And the continuous conflict between redefining property in ways that seemed demanded by the public good and the image of the enduring inviolability of individual rights must at some level have shaken the confidence in the judicial capacity to defend rights as limits in the neutral fashion required by the Federalist vision.*[63] The works of Cooley and Teideman can be seen as efforts to prove that the line-drawing required by the judicial protection of property could in fact be done on the basis of the sort of principles that underlay the Madisonian vision.*[64] And one can see the rise of laissez faire as an increasingly confident claim to know what those principles were and where to draw the lines around legitimate state power.

The standard textbook discussion of the laissez-faire, or *Lochner*, era argues or implies the evil of the Supreme Court's invalidation of legislation designed to cope with the problems of industrialization and the concentrated power of big business. The favorite quote from the period is Holmes's dissenting pronouncement in *Lochner* that "the Fourteenth Amendment does not enact Mr. Herbert Spencer's Social Statics."[65] In fact, however, the *Lochner* era opinions show more than an endorsement of Herbert Spencer and his fellow Social Darwinists; they show an impressive continuity with the Federalists' vision of constitutionalism, complete with the rights of property as the central boundary to state power, a suspicion of popular efforts to use democratic power to threaten those rights, and contract as a focus for protecting them. Of course, in important ways the offending legislation of the early twentieth century was different from the laws Marshall struck down in the early nineteenth century and those Madison feared in 1787. The twentieth-century legislation could broadly be described as an effort to set limits on the power of private property ("big business") and to provide legal protection against this power for groups such as labor unions and employees who would otherwise be subject to the unmitigated power of large-scale property in a market economy. Madison, not having faced the concentrated economic power of the twentieth century, thought the democratic threat would be directed at redistribution, not controlling or realigning power in the market. But the notion that property and contract were essential ingredients of the liberty the Constitution was to protect, was common to Madison, Marshall, and the twentieth-century advocates of laissez-faire. And the idea that property and contract could define the legitimate scope of governmental power was a basic component of constitutionalism from 1787 to 1937.

Of course, this conception of constitutionalism did not take account of the other side of the story of property in the nineteenth century. It did not account for transformative judicial redefinition of property nor take up the underlying problem that the rights that were to provide boundaries would always have to be defined and redefined by judges enforcing those boundaries. If the invocation of the common law[66] once seemed to solve the problem of definition, it could hardly do so in an unproblematic way at the end of the nineteenth century. Property rights had indeed been consistently invoked as the principled basis for limiting government, but they had not in fact been able to provide boundaries that were clear and consistent or principled in the sense of being based on a unitary conception of individual liberty. The dividing lines turned out to be amorphous concepts like "acting directly on the contract itself." And individual liberty was never in practice the only relevant value in defining property, for the law was constantly balancing not only competing interests but conceptions of the public good. We need to understand the 1937 rejection of property and contract as basic boundaries in light of both of these aspects of the preceding history.

There was a consistent vision of constitutionalism throughout the nineteenth century. It was essentially Marshall's version of Madisonian Federalism, and thus identified property as a central, limiting value. This conception of constitutionalism remained virtually untouched by actual judicial practices with respect to property, and it remained unchallenged as the dominant articulation of the purpose and meaning of constitutional government in America. But it never actually delivered what it promised. Property never did provide boundaries to the power of the state. The purported boundaries were neither respected in practice, nor clear in law, nor pure in theory.

C. The Coherence and Illusion of Property-Based Constitutionalism

After decades of aggressive use of "liberty of contract" and the rights of property to strike down social and economic regulation, the Supreme Court made its famous switch in *West Coast Hotel v. Parrish* (1937), when it upheld minimum wage legislation and repudiated its *Lochner* doctrine. It has been very important for defenders of the New Deal and the welfare-regulatory state it spawned to prove that *West Coast Hotel* represented a return to the light of reason and that the Court had been *wrong* to strike down regulatory legislation. Of course, case by case, one can make cogent arguments that the judges need not have interpreted "liberty of contract" to prohibit the legislation in question. One can easily point to inconsistencies and dubious distinctions (such as that between regulation of wages and hours). And there are compelling arguments that the regulatory legislation was important, beneficial, and in keeping with the deepest American values of freedom and justice. Nevertheless, it distorts both the history and the contemporary problems of American constitutionalism to insist that the *Lochner* era was some sort of horrible aberration. The distinctions drawn by Field, Peckham, Sutherland et al were no more dubious than those used by their predecessors—although the consequences may have been more pernicious. In every era it is easy to find sloppy reasoning, persuasive arguments for the opposite decision, and a reliance on legal concepts that seem incapable of bearing the weight assigned to them. But, of course, it is not really the legal reasoning of the *Lochner* era its opponents care about. It is the fundamental challenge that our regulatory-welfare state constitutes a break with our constitutional tradition, a break that the Court tried, but failed, to prevent. That is the challenge the opponents have tried to dismiss, and that I think we should take seriously.

For 150 years property served as a focal point for American constitutional thought. Property was in 1787, in the 1820s, in the disputes over what to do about slavery, and again in the laissez-faire era, a way of defining basic values and identifying and countering the threats to them. As we have increasingly come to see in the late twentieth century, it is extremely difficult to define the contours of individual liberty and to provide a consistent, principled basis on which to determine when state action has overstepped the bounds of legitimacy. For a century and a half, the concept of property made that task seem easier. It provided a focus for organizing the vast range of issues involved. It provided a compelling symbol of both individual rights and of a boundary that the state could not cross. More particularly, it seemed to offer a foundation for the constellation of values that go by the name of "the market," and a rationale for defining the rules of the market as outside the ordinary scope of political debate and choice. And, as I argued earlier, the focus on property made it easy to define as "law" the central political problem of determining the legitimate scope of the state. The common law tradition of property provided a rationale for turning this problem over to the courts and gave them familiar tools with which to handle it.

We need to understand three things about this property-centered conception of constitutionalism. First, it has a logic to it, although not the airtight consistency the term sometimes implies. It offers the coherent Madisonian vision of the purpose and limits of government and of the central problems that make those limits necessary. Second, there are unresolved problems at its core, and those problems have now emerged. Third, largely because of these problems, the vision was never quite what it purported to be. It defined the limits to the legitimate scope of government, but as we have seen, those limits were always more problematic than Madison recognized or Marshall implied.

In short, we had a property-based tradition of constitutionalism that was both coherent and misleading about the nature of its coherence. People have been able to organize their thinking around property as a limit (as Madison did), however flawed that foundation proved to be on closer examination. The protection of property as a symbol of justice, security, liberty, stability, and prosperity provided a way of crystallizing a vision of what government was for, what it could and could not legitimately do. This conception of constitutional government "worked" even if in an illusory fashion. It was illusory in the sense that its foundation was not in fact capable of determining boundaries, in part because the meaning of property and the values it symbolized have always been contested—and should be, since they represent such basic political choices. The Madisonian conception of constitutionalism "worked" in the sense that despite these problems, it gave its adherents an understanding of government they could articulate and use as a basis for reasoning about the legitimacy of governmental action. Like most conceptual systems that order our thinking, its flaws and inconsistencies do not prevent it from providing a sense of order without which we cannot comprehend and analyze our world.

The property-centered framework lasted a long time, and there are those who are trying hard to resurrect it. But property has largely lost its persuasive power to define the constitutional limits to the state. And we do not yet have a clear replacement. In *West Coast Hotel* the Court offered a clear rejection of the property-based *Lochner* approach, but it did not offer an alternative basis for determining the bounds to the legitimate scope of government. Judges and legal scholars have been working on that task ever since. The following sections explore the nature and significance of property's displacement, and the ways it illuminates the dilemmas of constitutionalism before us.

V. The Disintegration of Property as Limit

It is now widely accepted that property is not a limit to legitimate governmental action, but a primary subject of it. The states' "police power," which the *Lochner* era Court limited in the name of property and contract, is now uniformly recognized to include both economic regulation and redistributive welfare laws.[67] The presuppositions of constitutional jurisprudence have been reversed.[68] To determine whether economic regulation complies with the due process clause, the courts apply a standard of "rationality." This standard is essentially a statement of the presumption of the constitutionality of the legislation—and a very strong presumption, such that almost all such legislation is found to have a rational basis.[69] In addition, statutes are hardly ever overturned as violations of the contract clause.[70] And the most obvious and direct protection of property, the prohibition against takings for public use without just compensation (found in the Fifth Amendment in the Federal Constitution and in similar terms in most state constitutions) has been in practice almost unrecognizable as a barrier to governmental power.

The dimensions of the shift in property's constitutional status may be most obvious in the law of takings and the academic comment it has generated.[71] There are two issues in cases arising under the Fifth Amendment prohibition (or comparable state constitutional prohibitions): "nor shall private property be taken for public use, without just compensation." The first issue is the strictly limiting part of the prohibition: the "public use" requirement. The courts have interpreted the "takings" clauses to mean that governments may take private property *only* for public use. If the intended use is not public, then a government has no authority to take private property even if it provides compensation. Thus when a government invokes its power of eminent domain (and offers compensation), the property owner may challenge the expropriation as illegitimate because the property is being taken for private rather than public use. This is the clearest, most explicit, instance of property as a boundary to what the government can do. But in practice "public use" has long been defined so broadly that it is almost no barrier at all. The determination of what constitutes a public use is left largely to the legislature: "[T]he role of the judiciary in determining whether [the] power [of eminent domain] is being exercised for a public purpose is an extremely narrow one."[72]

The Michigan Supreme Court's decision in the *Poletown* case provides a particularly dramatic example of how broadly public use can be defined.[73] (Most of the "takings" cases are state cases, and while there are variations among the states, the broad patterns I am discussing apply generally.) The court upheld the expropriation of an entire neighborhood, which was to be razed and sold to General Motors so that it could build its new plant in Detroit. The entire plan was carried out according to General Motors' specifications at an estimated cost of 200 million dollars for the public and eight million for General Motors. The objective was to keep General Motors and its jobs in Detroit, and the rationale was that doing so would constitute a "public benefit." As the dissent vigorously argued, this broad interpretation of "public use" allowed the legislature to take property from one private party and give it to another—the very act repeatedly used to exemplify the limits of legislative power (although in fact a common practice in the nineteenth century).[74]

The Supreme Court has now provided an equally dramatic affirmation of the Michigan court's position. In *Hawaii Housing Authority v. Midkiff* the Court upheld legislation that permitted the state to condemn large tracts of land so that it could be resold to those leasing the land who wished to own the property they lived on.[75] The condemnation would take place at the request of those who wished to purchase the land. The rationale for the legislation was that 90% of the privately owned land in Hawaii was owned by 72 persons (including some large charitable trusts), and that this concentration of ownership inflated real estate prices and contributed to public unrest. The Court of Appeals for the ninth circuit found the legislation to be a "naked attempt on the part of the State of Hawaii to take the private property of A and transfer it to B solely for B's private use and benefit."[76] The opinion provided a long list of ringing quotes from the formation of the Constitution (most of which have appeared earlier in this book) to show that such action violated the foundation of our constitutional system. Justice O'Connor for the Supreme Court, however, found that "regulating oligopoly and the evils associated with it is a classic exercise of a State's police powers."[77] The transfer of ownership was thus a legitimate "public use."

Public use has for so long ceased to be an effective barrier that almost none of the extensive commentaries on the takings clause deal with it at all. The commentators are concerned with the issue of compensation, which arises when legislation—limiting land use for example—that purports to be merely an exercise of the police power to regulate is challenged as amounting to a taking. Any interference with property rights which constitutes a taking must (by definition) be compensated; losses resulting from mere regulation are not compensable, presumably because they are treated as part of the inevitable cost of social order which all citizens must bear. The commentaries are devoted to sorting out these categories, to drawing the line between takings and regulation. This sorting generally amounts to a discussion of when government has to (or should have to) pay for its interferences with private property.

Reading this commentary from the perspective of the formation of the Constitution, one is struck by the implicit transformation of property's place in our constitutional system. The literature is concerned not with limits to governmental power, but with the calculation and rationale for compensation. The basic question seems presumed to be "whether those who lose as a result of the redistribution of property bundles ought to be compensated."[78] This is a radically different question from whether or when a government has exceeded its legitimate authority. The question "What is such a serious interference with property rights that it constitutes a taking?" (and thus requires compensation) becomes converted to "What sort of thing do we think should be compensated and hence called a taking?" This inversion reflects the fact that the sole issue has become compensation, not limits on governmental power.

It is true that the requirement of compensation can serve as a practical limit if the costs are seen as prohibitive. Governments will not impose certain kinds of regulation if they are too costly. In Italy, for example, the requirement of compensation for losses in property values resulting from zoning threatened to bring city planning to a virtual halt. But the choice among competing claims on financial resources is very different from the focus on whether government has interfered severely or unduly with a private right. In both the distributional calculus approach and the focus on property as a limiting value, the practical question may in many instances be the same: when is compensation required? But the difference in focus and conceptual framework is extremely important for the role of property in American constitutionalism.

In article after article on one of the clearest constitutional protections of property, the authors are not concerned with limits to governmental power. The language of boundaries has been replaced by the language of distribution. And the authors seem largely unaware of the transformation or its significance. If the essence of the takings clause has (or should) become distributional calculation, then there has been an important shift away from property as the conceptual boundary to governmental power.

One can argue that property is in fact no longer suited to that role, that the original justification for its privileged position is now gone: property in its traditional meaning is no longer the source of autonomy for most people, and property cannot be conceived of as a boundary to state authority in a regulatory state. But while the Court's abandonment of most constitutional protections for property may reflect some such judgement, it seems as yet not entirely willing to replace a more traditional conception of property with the distributional calculation most commentators see as the rational approach.

There are various ways of characterizing these approaches. For example, Bruce Ackerman describes a contrast between the approach to property of the "scientific policy-maker" and that of the "ordinary observer."[79] The rational calculation of the commentators, based on an understanding of property as a bundle of rights, and, generally, on utilitarian and economic models, are examples (though sometimes imperfect) of the "scientific policy-maker." The ordinary observer starts from the premise of the layman's understanding of property as "things." Ackerman thinks that what accounts for the seemingly unsystematic approach of the courts to the problem of takings is that they are essentially using the approach of the ordinary observer. This view is supported by the argument that although the Supreme Court has said that it follows a balancing test of calculation of loss and benefit (as laid out by Holmes in *Pennsylvania Coal v. Mahon*, 1922,[80] and premised on a bundle of rights theory), it has really followed a straightforward approach of saying that a governmental action constitutes a taking when there is a physical invasion of property.[81] This is clearly in keeping with the layman's understanding of property as "things."*[82]

Since the appointment of Warren Burger as Chief Justice, the composition of the Supreme Court has so changed that commentators have increasingly expressed hopes and fears that the Court would do more than resist the distributive approach to takings, that it would actually begin to use property rights as a significant barrier to legislation. If that is in fact to come, it has by no means happened yet. The Court under Burger and Rehnquist has given weight to property rights when they compete with other constitutional rights,[83] and it can be argued that they have protected the interests and power of the propertied at the expense of values of equality[84] and procedural protections for the vulnerable. But they have not tried to return property to its former status as a central boundary to the power of the state (or at least they have not yet succeeded). Chief Justice Rehnquist sometimes uses "rational calculator" rather than boundary-like language to discuss property rights[85] and the decision in *Hawaii v. Midkiff*, to which I referred earlier, was written by Sandra Day O'Connor (one of President Reagan's three appointments).*[86] There have, however, been some interesting new developments. In 1987 (as if to celebrate the bicentennial) the Court handed down four new takings cases. These cases have generated a new round of debate about whether they constitute a significant shift toward heightened constitutional protection for property.[87] In *Keystone Bituminous Coal Association v. DeBenedictus*[88] the Court divided over whether the justices saw the property affected as a "thing." The case is interesting in large part because the facts are so similar to *Mahon*, which had struck down legislation requiring coal companies to leave enough coal to prevent subsidence of the structures above the mines (despite deeds that had given title to the coal to the companies). The 1966 Act at issue in *DeBenedictus* was enforced by requiring that 50% of the coal beneath structures be kept in place in order to provide surface support. (Again there were covenants, most dating back 70 years, as the majority emphasized, which vested title to the coal in the companies.) Not surprisingly, the Coal Association claimed that the Act was unconstitutional under "a straightforward application of [*Mahon*]."[89] But a five-justice majority, through Justice Stevens, disagreed. Stevens distinguished the "public interest" at issue in the 1966 Act from the mere "balancing of private economic interests" in *Mahon*, and argued that "petitioners have not shown any deprivation significant enough to satisfy the heavy burden placed upon one alleging a regulatory taking."[90] Justice Stevens focused on the percentage of the companies' total resources that the affected coal constituted—which was only about 2%. It was thus only a strand in the total bundle of rights, not a "separate segment of property for takings law purposes."[91] In dissent, Chief Justice Rehnquist (joined by Justices Powell, O'Connor, and Scalia) argued that clearly identifiable, discreet units of property—in other words "things," not just strands in a bundle of rights—had been taken. The issue was therefore clear: "[T]here is no need for further analysis where the government by regulation extinguishes the whole bundle of rights in an identifiable segment of property, for the effect of this action on the holder of the property is indistinguishable from the effect of a physical taking."[92] Rehnquist seems to be trying to assert the thing-like quality of property as against the majority's willingness to act on the implications of the bundle-of-rights conception of property. But he accepts the now dominant language of property as bundles of rights and interests, and tries to reconcile it with the image of property as thing.

This seems like a difficult task, but in fact the Court has managed it for years by focusing on physical invasion. The task of the judicial defenders of property is to make regulation appear like invasion. (Or perhaps I am being unfair. Perhaps it really looks like physical invasion to those who see it as unconstitutional.) An effective mechanism for simultaneously treating property as a bundle of rights and as a "thing" that is taken is what Margaret Jane Radin calls "conceptual severance:" one "severs" the dimension of property affected by the legislation so that that dimension stands apart as a separate thing, which can then be said to have been taken in its entirety. Thus conceptual severance allows one to claim that coal companies' rights to the *supporting coal* has been taken in its entirety, as opposed to the view that the coal companies had to forego 2% of their coal. The Court seems to have succeeded in using conceptual severance in *Nollan v. California Coastal Commission*[93] to construe a "public access easement as a complete thing taken, separate from the parcel as a whole."[94] By doing so, the Court managed to analogize a condition in a building permit to the most concrete form of boundary crossing, physical invasion.*[95] (The practical issue here as in all these cases is compensation, and thus how costly land use regulation will be.)

Radin makes clear the political significance of conceptual severance. It is "an easy slippery slope" to the radical position that

> every regulation of any portion of an owner's "bundle of sticks" is a taking of the whole of that particular portion

> considered separately. Price regulations "take" that particular servitude curtailing free alienability, building restrictions "take" a particular negative easement curtailing control over development, and so on.[96]

Conceptual severance could thus mean that virtually all economic regulation would require compensation.[97]

In the third case, *First English Evangelical Lutheran Church v. County of Los Angeles*,[98] the church was prevented from using its campground after it was damaged in a flood. The challenged ordinance prohibited construction or reconstruction pending the outcome of a study of permanent flood control measures. This case can also be seen as employing conceptual severance, in this instance by "time shares": prohibiting the use of property for a particular time "takes" all property rights for that slice of time, as opposed to the view that there has been an interference with a small percentage of the owner's total rights over time. The Court said that "'temporary' takings which, as here, deny a landowner all use of his property, are not different in kind from permanent takings, for which the Constitution clearly requires compensation."[99] But Frank Michelman argues that given "the presence among the majority of Justices White, Marshall, possibly Blackmun, and most notably Brennan,"[100] we have good reason *not* to interpret *First English* as an endorsement of conceptual severance. And, in fact, it is easy to avoid this interpretation because the prohibition on land use at issue was not actually temporary, but indefinite.

As Michelman sees it, the other potentially significant and disturbing development in these cases is the "heightened judicial scrutiny of the instrumental merit of land-use regulation"[101] present in *Nollan*. This scrutiny looks like a departure from the "rationality" standard of economic regulation in general. But here too, he concluded that "there appears to be less than first meets the eye."[102]

> The decision seems most satisfactorily understood as a further manifestation, albeit in somewhat surprising form, of the talismanic force of "permanent physical occupation" in takings adjudication. *Loretto v. Teleprompter Manhatten CATV Corp.*[103] held that a regulation which directly and unconditionally imposes a permanent physical occupation [a cable attached to a building] on an unwilling owner is a taking per se. *Nollan* holds that when state regulatory action imposes permanent physical occupation conditionally rather than unconditionally, the aggrieved owner can challenge state regulatory action "as" a "taking," and thereby obtain a certain form of intensified judicial scrutiny of the condition's instrumental merit or urgency. There is no clear basis to be found in the opinion for concluding that the

> Court in *Nollan* decided or meant to decide anything beyond just that.[104]

Michelman also offers a particularly interesting analysis of the fourth case, *Hodel v. Irving*. The case involved section 207 of the Indian Land Consolidation Act, which attempted to relieve the problem of parcels of native lands that had been splintered into dozens or hundreds of undivided share interests. The section provided that when the owner of such a share died, the interest "shall not pass to the decedent's devisees or intestate successors, but instead shall 'escheat'—title shall pass—to the tribe whose land it was prior to allotment.[105] Michelman notes the Court's emphasis on its view that "'the right to pass on property' lies at or near the core of the ordinary notion of ownership"[106] and the explicit parallel it drew to "the right to exclude others." According to the Court, both are among "the most essential sticks in the bundle of rights that are commonly characterized as property."[107]

Michelman thinks the second factor determining the Court's decision to overturn the statute was "totality." The Court repeatedly emphasized the "*total* abrogation" of the right to pass on property. The importance of this emphasis for Michelman's analysis is that "totality is a categorical predicate," in form at least, it is a "matter of either-or—it is or it isn't—not a matter of more or less." He sees this as part of the "reformalization of takings jurisprudence"[108] that is emerging.

Taken together these cases could be the beginning of a major and ominous shift.[109] But Michelman offers an account that fits with (and draws on) my arguments about property.

> Permanent physical occupation, total abrogation of the right to pass on property, denial of economic viability—all of these may be regarded as judicial devices for putting some kind of stop to the denaturalization and disintegration of property. They are formulas having both the feel of legality and the feel of resonance with common understanding of what property at the core is all about. . . . I suggest that doctrines like these, which at the most obvious level are instrumentally and even logically vulnerable, can still make sense ideologically as tokens of the limitation of government by law.[110]

The Court thus now seems to be using the means of the "policy maker," but guided by the ends of the layman: they are using the bundle of rights language and the analytic exercises it makes possible (like conceptual severance) to bring their practices more in line with what they see as the ordinary understanding of property. And they are enhancing the "law-like" (as opposed to policy-making) image of their decisions at the same time.

What then does takings law and its commentary mean for the position property holds in the American constitutional system? First, it may be that we should see the Court's approach (including the 1987 additions) as an effort to stop short of destroying the myth of property, of making it impossible for property to maintain its place in American political thought. If property is not a "thing," not a special entity, not a sacred right, but a bundle of legal entitlements subject, like any other, to rational manipulation and distribution in accordance with some vision of public policy,[111] then it can serve neither a real nor a symbolic function as boundary between individual rights and governmental authority. Property must have a special nature to serve as a limit to the democratic claims of legislative power.

The Court's past inclination to retain a thing-like approach to takings cases may reflect a tacit understanding of property's traditional constitutional status and an unwillingness to destroy it. The most recent cases suggest that some of the justices are deliberately trying to emphasize the thing-like quality of property so that they can use it as a barrier, while others seem to accept that when property is seen as a bundle of rights, it is not a boundary, but a basis for calculation.*[112] It may be that despite the efforts of some, the myth of property as thing, as sacred boundary,*[113] may not be able to hold out much longer. Ackerman makes a persuasive case that the layman's concept of property as thing is breaking down. Too many people have to integrate into their daily experience legal technicalities of property which cannot be absorbed into the understanding of property as thing. Soon, he suggests, there will be no simple layman's concept for the Court to apply.[114]

Similarly, Thomas Grey makes a sophisticated and compelling argument that the concept of property has disintegrated.[115] Beginning with the concept of property as a bundle of rights (which he suggests was intended to have a disintegrating, demoralizing effect) and leading to a set of conflicting theories of property, the once compelling idea of private property has broken down. Unlike most legal commentators he sees the political consequences of this breakdown: the disintegrated concept loses its specific moral force, and as it does so, its special place in legal and political thought.

This brings me back to the puzzle I posed at the outset. The idea of private property as a basic individual right and a fundamental value in the American political system has withstood 150 years of alternating judicial redefinition, neglect, and highly contested use. Despite the Court's most recent efforts, should the past 50 years of "takings" law and its commentary make us think that the concept and people's experience have finally been so transformed that property can no longer serve its traditional role?

It seems to me at least possible that the cumulative changes have finally gone to what really matters to the importance of property for political thought—its rhetorical power, its mythic quality as a sacred barrier to incursions on freedom. If property is finally perceived to be merely a legal entitlement, indistinguishable in nature from any other, if it loses its moral force both among the populace and the judiciary, then the consequences are likely to be far-reaching. Either some other concept or value will have to replace it as a symbol of limited government, as the core of constitutionalism, or we may be facing a change in constitutionalism itself.

While the conservatives are fighting such a development—in judicial opinion, scholarly argument, and popular rhetoric calling upon the traditional values of property as a limit to government—there is another set of theorists who seem interested in taking advantage of the disintegration of property to reshape it to new ends. These efforts raise, from a different angle, the question of the consequences of redefinition.

VI. Reform through Redefinition

A wide range of writers has argued that fundamental egalitarian and democratic reform requires a restructuring of the system of property. The authors of proposals for new conceptions of property rights range from those who clearly intend the redefinition to be the basis for a radical transformation of the society, to those who are making an explicitly constitutional argument about the meaning of property. I am interested here in the arguments for using property as a vehicle for providing greater protection for certain values within the basic structure of the American constitutional system. This holds all the appeal of radical reform without revolution, of taking the best of the system and making it better by removing its inequities and strengthening its most attractive values. The appeal is particularly powerful because the arguments suggest the possibility of taking a concept which has traditionally been the basis for inequality and limits on democracy and turning it around to be the basis for equality and democracy. If it could work, this sort of reform by redefinition, transformation through constitutional interpretation, would have a great deal to recommend it. But I wonder about it for a number of reasons.

All of these arguments for redefinition are characterized not only by a recognition of a need to reconceive property rights, but also by a choice to make the concept of property the vehicle for implementing the values they want to protect. A limited instance of such a choice (although one with potentially far-reaching consequences) is the suggestion by a federal district court judge that "the law can recognize the property right of the community to the extent that U.S. Steel cannot leave . . . the Youngstown area in a state of waste, that it cannot completely abandon its obligation to the community, because certain vested rights have arisen out of this long relationship and institution."[116] In 1964 Charles Reich made the now famous argument that various forms of government largess should be treated as "the new property" and thus provided with appropriate legal protections.[117] Frank Michelman has argued that property should be regarded as "an essential component of individual competence in social and political life," particularly stressing property as the basis for effective participation.[118] Steven Munzer suggests that traditional private property is especially well suited for securing the values of control, privacy, and individuality, and, when reconceived, can foster the equitable distribution of these goods.[119] There is, finally, a set of arguments not calling for redefinition of property rights, but a reinvigoration of their judicial protection. One version of this argument belongs among these other approaches because it suggests that greater judicial protection of property, properly understood, would provide greater protection for equality.[120]

What are we to make of this intriguing constellation of arguments? The first thing that is striking about the choice of property as the concept through which we can usher in a new era of greater equality is that it takes place in the context of the disintegration of the concept. In some ways this makes sense. If the meaning of property is disputed, if it is in effect fluid, what better time to try to restructure it in the direction of one's preferred values? On the other hand, there is something peculiarly anachronistic about making property the vehicle for change at the very time that it seems to be losing its place in the constitutional structure.

Despite the hints at a possible shift in the Supreme Court's approach, property does not serve as an important limit to the scope of governmental authority.[121] Although the Court has not formally abandoned property as a barrier to governmental action (and one can still easily imagine some governmental takings or regulations, even short of physical invasion, which would be held to be illegitimate invasions of property rights), neither property nor its sister concept of contract have in fact been effective means of challenging legislation since 1937. But the recognition that the concept of property is losing its place in the constitutional structure (if not in the popular imagination) could lead in more than one direction.

One could, for example, focus on the ways in which property has become divorced from the values of autonomy, which originally lent it its importance. One could focus on how property has been tied to inequality in our tradition and on the consequences of that inequality for our political system and for the distribution of goods associated with property. From this perspective one might watch the further disintegration and decline of the concept with some satisfaction, hoping to give the values once associated with property a primacy now unencumbered by the inegalitarian tradition. This would lead one to consider alternatives to property and replacements for it, which could both foster preferred values and sustain constitutionalism. (A difficult combination, to which I will return shortly.)

But this is not the direction taken by those whose arguments I have referred to. They seem to have chosen to build on the long-standing tradition of property and its continued importance in popular rhetoric and understanding of politics. In each case, the author has correctly identified values that have traditionally been associated with property in legal and political thought and has then argued that these values should become the defining features of property. Thus if the central value underlying property is autonomy or the capacity for effective participation, then the determination of what constitutes constitutionally-protected property could be made on the basis of whether it promotes those values.

As a strategy for change, this is compelling in many ways. A successful redefinition of property could call upon both continued popular support for "property" and a well-established legal tradition of protection. There are, however, serious strategic problems with this approach. One danger is that it may underestimate the power of the concept reformers plan to manipulate. The concept of property has a long tradition, one which may not be easily severed, and which runs counter to the equalitarian and democratic thrust of most of the arguments of the reformers.

I think we can see one indication of this danger in the history of the "new property." Charles Reich argued that private property has traditionally provided a sphere of privacy and independence necessary for individuality and liberty. Now that people are increasingly dependent upon government largess for their material well-being, this largess should be treated as "property" so that it can provide, rather than undermine, the security and independence for which property was traditionally the source. He argued that this security should be ensured by providing procedural protections against withdrawal of government largess. The Supreme Court accepted this argument in *Goldberg v. Kelly*,[122] adopting Reich's phrase "the new property," and holding that a welfare recipient was entitled to a hearing before his benefits were cut off.

This case was the beginning of a "revolution" in procedural due process. But this revolution has been curtailed, and one vehicle for its curtailment has been the very concept of property with which it began.*[123] Having accepted the argument that the rights in question were entitled to protection because they were *property* rights, the Court then argued that only those rights which really involved property-like entitlements required the procedural protections in question. And state benefits, the Court said, constituted property-like entitlements only when the state chose to grant them in terms that looked like property.[124]

There is a certain logic to this apparently circular and highly restrictive, "positivistic" approach: What makes something which doesn't at all resemble traditional property "property-like?" Why, the state's deliberately granting it with property-like entitlements. But there was nothing necessary about this line of reasoning. (Indeed, its positivism runs counter to the tradition.) The Court could surely have proceeded with the reconception of property it started in *Goldberg*. The use of the term "property," however, gave the Court a convenient handle for retrenchment. The conventional, limited conception of property provided a rhetorically consistent basis for pulling back from advances made in the name of property.

The very strength of the tradition of property makes it in some ways a precarious base for innovation. When one chooses to use property, redefined, to provide new kinds of constitutional protection for rights of autonomy, participation, or material well-being, one runs the risk that temporary advances will fall back before a long and much narrower tradition.

There are similar strategic problems with trying to use property as a basis for egalitarian reform by arguing that if property is the foundation of basic values such as liberty, then we have to ensure that everyone has enough property to secure that foundation. An optimistic version of this argument by Richard Funston reveals its characteristic problems. He urges that returning to greater judicial protection for property rights would generate a greater attention to the need for a material, economic base for the enjoyment of rights.[125] Both egalitarian reformers and hard-line conservatives agree that liberty requires an economic base. But they draw very different conclusions from this premise, and part of the difference lies in their understanding of the relation between property, liberty, and inequality.

Funston argues that judicial neglect of property rights arises from a "double standard"[126] of judicial review based on a division between personal rights and property rights. He maintains that this division is at odds with a legal and philosophical tradition which insisted upon the "equality of the values of property and liberty."[127] More importantly, the double standard fails to recognize the integral connection between property and liberty which is, in his view, both part of our tradition and an important political reality. (He is right in the general sense about the tradition, except that, as I have argued above, the Framers did see a tension between property rights, personal rights, and political liberty, and ranked them in that order.)

Funston sees two promising indications that the Court may be moving away from this double standard toward greater protection for property. He cites Justice Stewart's argument in *Lynch v. Household Finance* that "the dichotomy between personal liberties and property rights is a false one. . . . a fundamental interdependence exists between the personal right to liberty and the personal right to property. Neither could have meaning without the other."[128] Funston also finds "a heightened sensitivity to property claims" in the Court's willingness to uphold "property interests against First Amendment and equal protection claims."[129] He sees all this as promising not only because it may redress an unjustifiable imbalance in contemporary jurisprudence, but because appropriate protections for property will provide a basis for fuller, and more egalitarian, protection for liberty.

Funston is not simply talking about protection for the "new property." He also suggests that a renewed recognition of the relation between property and liberty, of the necessary economic basis of liberty, would generate a greater judicial scrutiny of laws that seem to discriminate on the basis of wealth. He argues that a court that was willing to make real inquiries into "the rationality of legislation affecting property-related interests" (as opposed to accepting whatever the state claims to be the purpose and effect of the law) might have come to different conclusions in cases where discrimination against the poor was alleged: the *Rodriguez* case, where the Court rejected a challenge to the local property tax system of financing public education on the (equal protection) grounds that it disadvantaged children from poor districts; and in the *Valtierra* case, where the Court upheld a special requirement for submitting low-income housing proposals to prior referenda.[130] He seems to think that a court used to scrutinizing legislation interfering with property and sensitive to the interrelation between property and liberty would be sympathetic to the dangers of discrimination against the (powerless) poor and perhaps even to arguments that some kind of material equality is necessary for the exercise of the rights the Constitution guarantees.

Without going into it here, I simply note that the argument that civil or political rights require, and therefore entitle one to, economic equality implies a radical leap from our traditional liberal conceptions of rights.*[131] This is the leap which conservatives fear lurks behind arguments like plaintiffs' in *Rodriguez*, and the emphatic conservative rejection of that leap indicates why we should not be sanguine that a renewed judicial interest in property would lead to an egalitarian approach to the need for an economic basis for liberty.

Inequality has been at the center of the traditional American understanding of the relationship between property and liberty. Liberty, according to the tradition, generates unequal property through the free exercise of unequal faculties. The protection of liberty thus requires a protection of inequality with all its political consequences (consequences whose threatening aspects the Constitution was designed to mitigate). C. B. Macpherson also regards this inequality as inevitable, given our prevailing definition of property. "Property as an exclusive right of a natural or artificial person to use and dispose of material things . . . leads necessarily, in any kind of market society . . . to an inequality of wealth and power that denies a lot of people the possibility of a reasonably human life. The narrow institution of property is bound to result in such inequality, in any society short of a genetically engineered one that would have ironed out all differences in skill and energy."[132] His solution is a radically nonmaterial definition of property which is not premised on exclusivity.

I note these arguments to indicate that the conservatives rest on solid ground when they argue that their understanding of proper protection for property and liberty militates against what they see as a dangerous drive toward equality. It is clear that Bernard Siegan, for example, does not think increased security from legislative interferences with property would or should lead to a different outcome in *Rodriguez*. He *wants* property to stand in the way of, to take priority over, affirmative egalitarian measures.

> Had *Rodriguez* and *Maher* [another case on discrimination on the basis of wealth, which held that the Constitution does not prohibit the exclusion of abortions from Medicaid] been decided differently, any societal structure with serious wealth inequalities would have been threatened. At some point the Court would have had to decide that a person does not have a fundamental right to food, clothing, medicine, housing, legal assistance, or other "just wants." If it did not in time so hold, the Court would have imposed a guaranteed annual income that would have been supplied from the pockets of people not represented in the making of these decisions.[133]

From the conservative perspective, the purpose of a return to judicial protection of property and economic liberties is to prevent such ill-conceived egalitarianism. In the eyes of conservatives, claims to substantive equality imply not only redistribution but major shifts from negative to affirmative concepts of rights, from allocation by the market to allocation by political process, and from a limited state to an all-encompassing bureaucracy. Egalitarianism threatens property and liberty. Conversely, property protected by the judiciary can serve as a barrier to such undermining of our tradition.

The conservatives have cogent (though limited) arguments and the weight of history on their side. They do not always take adequate account of the ways property has changed over the years; their conception of property as the source of autonomy and boundary to the legitimate scope of state authority is often anachronistic. Nevertheless it seems more likely that a renewed interest in property rights would follow along a deeply laid groove of inequality rather than serve as a path toward an egalitarian conception of the material base for liberty.

The meaning of property and its proper place in our constitutional structure is contested domain. The fact that conservatives as well as radicals and reformers are urging greater attention to property suggests that one ought to be wary about using property as a vehicle for egalitarian conceptions of rights. It is certainly the case that property has traditionally been associated with the values of independence, privacy, autonomy, and participation. But in our tradition that association has always been shaped by premises of inequality. Even today, when the rhetoric of egalitarianism is commonplace, the inequality of property still seems to be widely accepted. The old categories still prevail, in modified form. The distinction between economic and political rights remains strong. And while political equality is now accepted, it has never interfered with the basic acceptance of (sometimes commitment to) economic inequality.[134] The effort to build on the concept of property in order to foster an equal distribution of its associated values may turn out to work against one of the most powerful elements in the tradition: the link between inequality, property, and liberty.

VII. The Mythic Power of Property

A. Property, Myth, and the Problem of Self-Limiting Government

So far I have been using the tradition to make arguments about strategy, suggesting that efforts to use property as a vehicle for egalitarian reform may be dangerously ineffective: they may backfire by reinforcing the inequality that has been tied to property in our tradition.*[135] If they should succeed, however, they seem likely to do far more than their proponents advocate. These radical redefinitions are potential threats to the mythic quality of property that has sustained the central tension between democracy and limiting values in American constitutionalism. This mythic quality is best revealed by the paradoxical nature of property in our tradition, and so it is to that dimension of the tradition that I now return.

The American conception and practice of constitutionalism developed together with private property—in our categories of rights, in our conception of limited government, and in the institutionalization of rights as limits in judicial review. As we have seen, however, the picture is not a simple one. After the Court had successfully established the power of judicial review and the sanctity of property and contract, there followed a period of some fifty or sixty years in which the courts fostered and allowed the redefinition of the basic rules of exchange and entitlement which it had so carefully claimed as its domain in the first decades of the nineteenth century. Property was, in effect, neither stable, nor sacred, nor a barrier to governmental authority. The *Lochner* era's aggressive use of property and contract to limit governmental power was followed by a virtual abandonment of property as a constitutional barrier and the current state of disintegration of the concept. If property still serves as some kind of outer limit to what legislatures would try to do, or courts would tolerate, it is not a boundary against which government routinely pushes (or when it does, the boundary has been routinely pushed back).[136] Property is not the basis on which the Court tries to draw the line between individual rights and governmental power.

Yet the rhetoric of property rights has continued. Neither the complex history of property in the nineteenth century nor post-1937 judicial practice seems to have shaken the popular force of the idea of property as a limit to the legitimate power of government. However much the "layman's understanding" of property as things is being blurred by increasing contact with legal abstractions, the popularly held idea that "government can't take what's mine" seems to be holding fast.*[137] This belief may in fact be one of the last vestiges of a popular understanding of constitutionalism.*[138] In an era when the language of democracy dominates political rhetoric, there does not seem to be widespread appreciation of the nuances of constitutionalism. "The government can't take what's mine" may, however, still serve, as it originally did, as a basic limit on the idea that "the majority rules." (And, at the popular level, this limit may seem self-evident and uncontroversial, as compared with the limits involved in abortion or school prayer cases). Perhaps the Court's virtual abandonment of property as a barrier has not brought with it a public crisis of constitutionalism because the *idea* of property as a limit endures in popular belief. And the enduring power of this idea may be the single most compelling reason for building upon property to establish new values as the foundations of constitutionalism.

In some ways property is the ideal symbol for the limits to governmental authority because of its concrete character. Physical invasion of private property is a particularly obvious kind of public violation of private rights; one's property can form a literal material boundary to the legitimate scope of state power. But this represents only part of property's paradoxical nature. Property is held out as a symbol of rights which are independent limits to the scope of governmental authority. At the same time, property is, of all the basic rights, perhaps most obviously the creation of the state. If a purpose of government is to protect property, that is in part because property could not exist without the mechanism of government.

Property takes its very meaning from the definition given to it by the state. Remember that even classic American invocations of natural rights and limits to legislative power have been coupled with acknowledgements that property is a matter of positive law.[139] Property is thus the boundary to governmental power, but it is a boundary government itself draws. Through property and its definition by the judiciary, the state creates, and shifts, and recreates its own limits. This is the American form of the essential problem of self-limiting government.

Self (state)-defined limits only work to sustain constitutionalism as we know it if the reality of self-definition is obscured by the mythic quality of those limits. Rights can only be effective as a boundary if the belief in their independent, constitutional status is maintained, that is if people see rights as something radically distinct from the ordinary subjects of political contest and disagreement. At least within legal circles, property's claim to this status has been seriously shaken.

Another mythic element of property is perhaps even more important. The claim that the institution of private property is the only sound basis for individual liberty rests on the belief that the legal entitlement to property is somehow qualitatively different from any other form of legal entitlement. Consider, for example, the argument that freedom of the press can be truly secure only under a regime of private property. This translates into a claim that the protections the state provides for property (protections which enable one to be secure in the ownership of a press and thus independent of government pressure) are more reliable than the protections a state could provide directly against censorship or interference from other public or private sources. The tacit claim for the special security the state can provide property (as opposed to other rights) underlies all forms of the claim that "the only dependable foundation of personal liberty is the economic security of private property."[140] The claim is repeated so often, and in such surprising contexts (Reich, for instance, refers to "the need for a property base in civil liberties"[141] despite the fact that he has a clear understanding of the ways property is the creation of the state) that one can only assume that it has enormous intuitive appeal.

There is, however, nothing obvious about why legal entitlements to property should be intrinsically more secure than legal entitlements to other rights. There is almost certainly no intrinsic difference in the nature of the legal entitlements themselves to justify the claim that protections of property rights are more reliable and provide greater security. The reason for property's special status seems to be the sense that property secured by the power of the state provides a greater *experience* of security, independence, and autonomy than, say, guarantees of noninterference with editorial decisions or income provided by the state. Although the legal protections could be comparable, people feel, or think they would feel, more confident in the security of a relationship defined as ownership than in the security of direct legal entitlements or guarantees. Certainly the role of the state is more obvious in such entitlements or guarantees than in ownership. And direct state action will be invoked less frequently in securing property than dispensing income. But these differences also seem to be matters of psychological experience rather than differences intrinsic to the vulnerability of the entitlements or to the power they confer. If, for example, it is a question of how many steps government would have to go to to deprive one of one's property as opposed to one's income, or what kinds of institutions (legislatures, courts, or administrative bodies) would make the decision, then there seems no reason why the institutional procedures in both cases could not be virtually identical.

We can see another mythic dimension of property in the argument that private property is a foundation for liberty because it entails a decentralization or dispersal of power. In this view private ownership means that citizens are not at the mercy of one central power for their employment, their news, their opportunity to publish, etc. This argument points to something real, but distorts that reality by relying on the mythic image of property as entirely distinct from the state. It is true that the state allocates power through property, and in market economies it generally allocates that power to a wide variety of people.[142] The result is that people are subject to the power of diverse others, rather than directly to the agents or representatives of the state. Leaving aside the question of whether the objective of decentralization might be equally well-achieved through political structures significantly different from ours, what matters for my argument here is the dimension of mystification in the decentralization argument. The argument has the force it does because the role of the state is obscured. Power allocated through property appears to have an independent, nonstate-like quality. It is "private" power. The notion of "privateness" hides the role the state plays in allocating that power through its legal rules of property and contract and in supporting that power by punishing anyone who refuses to obey those rules. Thus however distressing the power one's employer wields, it is not experienced as having anything to do with the state. And conversely the pleasures of owning one's own home or business are not experienced as granted by the state through legal rules structuring the market and the entitlements of property. Once the role of the state has disappeared behind claims of private property, that property can not only support assertions that it secures liberty, it can actually provide the experience of comparative freedom to do what one wants. (And the experience is of course not wholly illusory, for in our system owning property makes one less subject to the power of other owners.) The experience of the power, security, and independence of property seems immediate and concrete compared to elusive arguments (if one ever encounters them) about the role of the state in providing security and allocating power.

If I am right that a psychological experience lies at the heart of why people believe property rights bear a special relation to liberty,[143] that does not mean that we can simply dismiss the belief. On the contrary, the impressive and enduring power of this experience is not to be underestimated. This leads me to ask whether any conception of rights which is not rooted in, or symbolically associated with, something concrete such as material goods can ever have the hold on people's imagination which property has had for centuries. With this question in mind, I return to the implications of changes in the conception of property for American constitutionalism.

B. Undermining the Myth and the Problem of Replacement

If property has been central to the basic tension between democracy and limiting values on which American constitutionalism rests, what happens to the tension and to the system when the pivotal concept of property changes? Implicit in this question is the much larger problem of how flexible the American constitutional system is; whether, for example, the tension can be realigned without undermining its basic structure. The issue of property points in the direction of answers. Part of the answer lies in the legal issues to which the Court has turned its attention since the demise of property. This is itself a large subject which I can only touch on here. In short, however, I think that the Court has increasingly been interested in matters of procedure and that the substantive rights, such as privacy, which it has protected have neither the material base nor the intuitive clarity of property rights. It seems possible that while this shift is in many ways entirely appropriate, it may transform constitutionalism as we have known it.

There may now be less emphasis on limiting values and more on democracy, not because the Court no longer overturns legislation, but because of the kind of legislation it overturns and the grounds on which it does so. This trend may suggest that property has lost its original place because the idea of sharp boundaries between the sphere of individual rights and legitimate governmental authority is not tenable in a regulatory welfare state. The question we must ask is whether a new balance can be struck, whether the new rights being protected can sustain the tension of traditional constitutionalism, or whether we shall have to rethink our notion of limited government altogether.

These questions become clearer when examined in light of proposals for change. Michelman's proposal provides an illuminating focus since his arguments are made in an explicitly constitutional context. He sees a "puzzle" of property similar to the one I have outlined above.

> [I]t is both an implicit premise of the constitutional system that individual holdings are always subject to the risk of occasional redistribution of values through the popularly ordained operations of government, both active and regulatory, and an explicit premise of the system that people can have property, be owners, not only as among themselves but also vis-à-vis the people as a whole organized as the state.[144]

He seems to see this puzzle as reflective of the necessary tension of constitutionalism or what he refers to as "the deeper contradiction in our best attitudes towards popular rule and individual worth, infinitely valuing them both." He suggests that he respects this tension and seeks only a partial resolution, one "that allows us to experience the contradiction as generative tension rather than a dead end."[145]

The premise for his resolution is that "rights under a political constitution, including property rights, are first of all to be regarded as political rights."[146] This premise provides a basis for assigning a meaning to the property rights which the Constitution promises to protect, but does not define: "[W]hat one primarily has a right to is the maintenance of the conditions of one's fair and effective participation in the constituted order. . . . Loss—even great loss—of the economic value of one's [holdings may] not as such violate those conditions. . . . What does, perhaps, violate them is exposure to sudden changes in the major elements and crucial determinants of one's established position in the world, as one has come to understand that position."[147] Michelman suggests that the determination of what constitutes a constitutionally impermissible encroachment on individual "property" rights may be made on this basis.

Assuming the practicality of such a standard, what are its implications? Michelman's proposal purports not to eliminate the tension of constitutionalism, since it offers a standard against which to measure the action of a democratic legislature. He does not simply say that property means whatever the state says it does. But the premise on which the proposal rests seems to eliminate the distinction between political rights and civil rights which was once fundamental to our system. While the justification for all the checks and restraints on democracy was once that political rights are only means to the end of protecting the rights of persons and property (and these restraints are particularly necessary to protect property), we are now told that all our constitutional rights, including property, should be seen primarily as political rights. Even though the right to effective participation is to serve as an independent, judicially enforceable, standard for legislative action, the collapsing of categories of rights seems to threaten the tension of constitutionalism as it has existed in our tradition. At the very least, Michelman turns the original hierarchy upside down: political rights are primary and the rights of property are to be defined in terms of what will safeguard and promote those political rights.

A departure from the original tradition may be appropriate. A political theory which is more democratic than that of the Framers may require a shift in emphasis on political rights. It may be necessary to abandon genuinely substantive limits on the legislature (as opposed to those aimed at protecting the political process) in an era when there is faith neither in natural rights nor in the existence of a unitary common good, certain to be best for all. (Interestingly, the conservatives who advocate a return to traditional protections of property rights seem to have faith that there is a clear common good. They seem confident that their preferred system of economic liberties and free enterprise is genuinely in the best interest of all.) It is important for us to consider, however, that the redefinition of property rights Michelman proposes would reshape the structure of our system by giving a very different meaning to constitutionalism than it has had, and than the system was designed to implement. This brings me, finally, to the question of whether the proposed redefinitions of property could sustain constitutionalism in light of my argument about the psychological basis for the rhetorical power of property.

The idea of constitutionalism need not be based on natural rights, but it does require a commitment to the limiting values which is deep and strong enough to resist the force of majority rule. The values which are to serve as enforceable limits on the will of the majority must command such commitment or either they or the system of constitutionalism built on them will, in the long run, fall before the compelling and legitimate power of democracy. This is surely even more true today than when the Constitution was formed.

In 1787 property was a perfect candidate for such a value. It had an impressive philosophical tradition behind it: both Locke and the Republican thinkers such as Harrington stressed the importance and value of property. The protection of property had been an important issue in the rhetoric of the revolution, "no taxation without representation" being the most famous instance. It was a right with which most Americans had some immediate, personal connection, and it had a concrete quality which made it an ideal symbol for the barrier between individual rights and legitimate governmental power.

This is the tradition upon which those who want to redefine property hope to draw. But will the proposed redefinitions be able to sustain the link with tradition or have sufficient force of their own to serve as effective limiting values? One of the potential problems is that the new definitions remove property from the concrete, material quality the concept has traditionally had. It is certainly not the case that the traditional conceptions of property—either constitutional or common law—have been simple or exclusively material.*[148] But they have had a clear material base which is the core of both the legal and popular conceptions. The problem is that the effectiveness of the new conceptions may depend on the extent to which they are rooted in the material quality which has given property its special, enduring power. It may be that only such rootedness could give them the force, the hold on people's imaginations, to serve as a basis for constitutionalism. Not just the population at large, but judges require a concept, a value with at least some of the mythic, rhetorical power which property has had. And this may prove problematic for the new conceptions.

The new definitions depart from the material base of property precisely because of their egalitarianism. As I noted earlier, Macpherson suggests that this departure is inevitable. As long as property is essentially material and exclusive it will generate inequality. Those who want to redefine property to make it the basis of equitably distributed goods of autonomy, privacy, or effective participation may have to give up the link to property's most compelling aspect. And to the extent that they do so, they may create a concept so abstract that it will not have adequate force as a limiting value. Egalitarian reconceptions thus not only fly in the face of a major part of the tradition, they undermine the most compelling part of the concept of property.

The efforts at egalitarian redefinition raise questions about whether any abstraction, such as autonomy, could serve as an effective limiting value and whether there is something about egalitarianism itself (perhaps its necessary abstractness) which threatens constitutionalism as we have known it. My point is not that there is any theoretical or intrinsic reason why a concept like autonomy (or property redefined in terms of autonomy) could not be the limiting value—as opposed to participation which by its democratic, process-oriented nature threatens to collapse the tension between democracy and limiting values upon which American constitutionalism has rested. My suggestion is rather that property seems to have held its place in American constitutionalism for as long as it has because of its rhetorical, mythical power. If it is to be replaced or redefined, the alternative may have to have the same intuitive appeal, evoke a comparably powerful response, command the same kind of allegiance which property has traditionally been able to. If property redefined loses this force, it may lose as well its effectiveness as the symbolic limit to governmental power.

C. The Subterranean Power of Property

In this last section on the myth of property, I want to specify more clearly the illusory nature of the myth and note some of the ways Americans deny they believe the illusions, yet embrace a structure of thought that is built on those illusions. Part of this clarification requires distinguishing between popular beliefs and the beliefs of judges and academics, and then sketching the schizophrenic quality of the whole picture. My goal is to show how contemporary legal and political discourse simultaneously accepts the Realist view of the law as social construct and yet routinely encompasses arguments that are irreconcilable with that view.

The term myth is appropriate for property not only because there is an illusory quality to Americans' beliefs about property, but because of the power and significance of those beliefs in their understanding of politics and, indeed, of the world. In a way this entire book is about the significance of property, and this chapter tries to capture a sense of the tenacity of the traditional image of property. I have already noted some of the illusory dimensions to this image: that property actually has provided a clear boundary limiting the scope of state power; that property has a nonstate-like quality, which gives it special links to security and freedom; and, a related element; that the meaning of property is not a matter of collective choice. In this section

I will look briefly at some of the ways these illusions are central to American legal and political thought.

The legal Realists did an impressive job of demonstrating that property rights take their meaning from the fact that they are backed by the power of the state, that property rights allocate power to some at the expense of others, and that there are inevitable choices in the definition of property (and tort and contract) that will affect the distribution of power and benefits just as other collective choices do (such as systems of taxation or welfare). In sum, there is something illusory about thinking of rights as distinct from collective power (which makes very complicated their capacity to serve as protection from collective power). Legal rights involve the same sorts of choices backed by the power of the state as other measures, such as regulations, which are recognized as exercises of state power (usually mediating between conflicting interests) and thus as "political."

In some ways this Realist vision of law as politics has taken hold.[149] Virtually everyone pays lip service to the political nature of the law. And virtually no one from the elite law schools would describe law as natural, neutral, essentially prepolitical rules of the game. And yet mainstream legal scholarship (by political scientists as well as lawyers) both presumes a law-politics distinction and is preoccupied with it. And the tacit denial that property is a social construct is the foundation for everything from the public/private distinction to the ongoing market versus regulation debate and the debates over redistribution.

As this list of topics suggests, the illusory image of property affects popular political discourse, judicial opinions, and legal scholarship. Let me begin with legal scholarship. It may be the most overtly schizophrenic because of the pervasiveness of the ostensible recognition of law as a social construct and of the "interest balancing" that makes law a matter of collective choice and public policy. But in ways that remain somewhat mysterious to me, mainstream legal scholarship manages to hold those views and proceed comfortably ahead with doctrinal analysis and presumptions such as the sharp split between the public and the private that are only fully intelligible if law, and property in particular, is something other than a set of policy choices backed by the power of the state. G. Edward White offers an extremely interesting example of this combination in his analysis of the influential torts texts of William Prosser. White shows how "Prosser's abstract endorsement of Realism . . . did not prevent him from making assumptions that ran counter to its thrust."[150] He offers as an example Prosser's concern with the mechanics of deriving general and predictable rules despite his assertion that tort law was an exercise in interest-balancing.[151] White concludes that Prosser's influence came not from his "perfunctory and unrevealing" comments on jurisprudence, but his exceptional capacity to classify the elements of tort law—"classifications that then took on a doctrinal function."[152] Perhaps Prosser was particularly masterful at what Robert Gordon succinctly describes as "the *simultaneous* embrace of the doctrinal and Realist perspectives that had over and over demonstrated one another's incoherence,"[153] but it is my sense that many contemporary case books have this same basic characteristic. They have preambles and periodic pronouncements designed to show their sophisticated post-Realist understanding of law, but then the text itself is organized around a very different vision of law. One of the results of this partial acceptance but fundamental lack of integration of the Realist perspective, has been that the work of the Realists is now being done over again by scholars associated with the Conference on Critical Legal Studies.*[154]

Legal scholars are not as naive as the general public about the boundary setting quality of property, and perhaps they are altogether a little more careful in their use of language. But legal scholarship shares many of the basic illusion-based presuppositions of both judicial and popular political discourse. We can see the nature of the illusions (as well their pervasiveness) more clearly if we look at some examples from these other two spheres.

Cass Sunstein offers an excellent analysis of important Supreme Court opinions that rely on an image of the neutrality of the common law that would seem to have been repudiated with *Lochner*. He begins by providing a particularly clear statement of the ostensibly rejected foundations of *Lochner*.

> We may thus understand *Lochner* as a case that failed because it selected, as the baseline for constitutional analysis, a system that was state-created, hardly neutral, and without prepolitical status. Once the Court's baseline shifted, its analysis became impossible to sustain. As every student of the law of torts is aware, one cannot treat as a "taking" from A to B a decision to transfer resources to which A had no entitlement in the first place. The whole notion of "taking" depends on a belief in an antecedent right to the property in question. *Once the common law itself was seen to allocate entitlements and wealth, and the allocation seemed controversial, a decision to generate a new pattern of distribution could not be for that reason impermissible.*[155]

Sunstein describes this understanding of *Lochner* as "hardly uncontroversial,"[156] but it is quite similar to that offered in one of the standard texts of constitutional law, Laurence Tribe's *American Constitutional Law*.

> Thus the basic justification for judicial intervention under *Lochner*—that the courts were restoring the natural order which had been upset by the legislature—was increasingly perceived as fundamentally flawed. There *was* no "natural" economic order to upset or restore, and legislative or judicial decision in any direction could neither be restrained nor justified on any such basis. . . . the belief that there just *was* no transcendent body of binding general common law . . . ultimately devastated *Lochner's* due process doctrine that legislatures may not upset the "natural" conditions of contract and property enshrined in common law categories and their logical entailments.[157]

It certainly seems that the demise of *Lochner* should have entailed the demise of the vision of the common law—and perhaps of property in particular—as neutral and prepolitical or apolitical. But in fact the endurance of this vision, or at least of arguments that presuppose it, is one of the central puzzles of American legal and political discourse. It is one of the ways in which Americans—Supreme Court justices as well as legal academics and the public in general—have accepted the New Deal, but not its presuppositions or logical implications.

Sunstein begins his discussion of Supreme Court cases that rely on the *Lochner* vision of the common law with *Buckley v. Valeo*,[158] the campaign finance case. He shows that the Court's assertion that the effort to equalize the effective political speech of American citizens was not within the permissible ends of government ("wholly foreign to the First Amendment"),[159] makes *Buckley* "a direct heir to *Lochner*."

> In both cases, the existing distribution of wealth is seen as natural, and failure to act is treated as no decision at all. Neutrality is inaction, reflected in a refusal to intervene in markets or to alter the existing distribution of wealth. *Buckley*, like *Lochner*, grew out of an understanding that for constitutional purposes, the existing distribution of wealth must be taken as simply "there," and that efforts to change that distribution are impermissible.*[160]

Sunstein then turns to the question of which statutory benefits are entitled to the due process protection accorded to "liberty" and "property," issues I noted earlier in the rise and fall of the "New Property." He concludes that "the Court's failure to put benefits said to be created by the government [such as the right to freedom from discrimination, the right to government employment, the right to welfare][161] on the same footing with benefits said to be 'natural' is a clear holdover from the *Lochner* period. The distinction treats the common law as unchosen and statutory benefits as a form of 'intervention.' "[162] He continues on to show (focusing on the shopping center trespass v. free speech cases) that "in state action doctrine, as in the *Lochner* period, the common law provides the benchmark from which to measure intervention."[163]

Sunstein also helps us to see the presence of *Lochner* presumptions in the important debate over the existence of affirmative rights against the government. He uses *Harris v. McRae,* in which the plaintiffs challenged the government's failure to fund abortions needed by poor women. "The Court held that government had no duty to remove barriers 'not of its own creation.' The idea is that poverty is simply 'there'; it is not a product of government action."[164] Once again the Court assumed that the distributional outcomes of the market, of the legal rules of property and contract, were neutral and simply entailed the "inaction" of the state. When we see the image of the law that underlies such decision we can see that

> The Constitution protects some rights and not others. Whether rights are treated as "negative" or "positive" turns out to depend on antecedent assumptions about baselines—the natural or desirable functions of government. State protection of private property and contract appears to be a "negative" guarantee because it is so usual, indeed built into the very concepts of property and contract. Provision of welfare is treated differently because it is in some respects new and in any event hedged with limitations and reservations. Here *Lochner*'s premises, having to do with neutrality and inaction, account critically for current constitutional doctrine with respect to "affirmative" rights.[165]

I won't continue further with Sunstein's catalogue. Suffice it to say that he makes clear that a *Lochner*-like image of the law is crucial to many important areas of current constitutional law. And, as the reader may already have noticed, these legal doctrines are just highly technical forms of basic issues in popular political discourse. Consider, for example, the "market" versus regulation debate. That debate almost always begins with the question of when "interference" with private transactions and decision making is justified. The debate is framed around the assumption that the state has no role in according the power to engage in those transactions or in what counts as a legitimate or enforceable transaction. The "market" is treated as a natural phenomenon, not the product of legal rules of property, contract, and tort (defining liability for injury). To the extent that the role of the law is recognized at all, it is treated as radically distinct from the "regulation" at issue. In most popular forms of the debate, the law and the state are associated exclusively with the "intervention" of regulation. The rights of property owners are simply a given. And it is surprising how many sophisticated commentators (academic and other) adopt the language of "interference" with a presumptively natural market.

The debate over the acceptability of redistribution is another example. The virtually uniform usage treats the distribution arising from market transactions as a given and asks whether reallocating that distribution is justified. Yet the very notion that the market allocates resources efficiently assumes that it constantly redistributes resources towards those best able to use them. But that distribution is never designated as *re*distribution. Even egalitarian liberals adopt the language that implies that it is rearranging the distribution of the "market" that requires justification. This discourse makes sense only if the rules of the market are not themselves the product of collective choices, but neutral and apolitical.

And finally, as I noted earlier, I think Americans have a strong sense of the naturalness of the entitlements of property and of the "privateness" of the power those entitlements provide. The prerogatives of ownership—whether of home, business, or car—are not experienced as made possible by the state (except in the loosest sense of the advantages of living in "a free country"). Virtually everyone talks about welfare as involving a dependence on the state and about property ownership as free-standing, as a source of independence *from* the state, not a condition requiring the power of the state to give it its meaning.

There are several things to note about this picture. First, there seem to be somewhat different forms of belief about property in different segments of the population. For example, elite legal academics are likely to be more precise in their discussions of the nature of ownership than the population in general. They are capable of reproducing the essence of the Realist critique, which makes them cautious in their jurisprudential statements. But they, like the highest level of the American judiciary, engage in arguments that presume an apolitical image of property. Indeed, as I hope this brief sketch shows, that image is central to some of the most important political and legal debates of our day. The image defines the terms of the debate, which proves to be an immense, and totally unjustified, disadvantage to egalitarians and those interested in alternatives to the "market."

This pervasiveness of the image of property as natural, neutral, and apolitical or "nonstate-like," means that property does tacitly define the limits of legitimate state power. This image defines what counts as governmental "interference" which must be justified, at least politically. It defines which system of distribution of power and goods is natural and what must be justified as a deviation. This image of property continues to define who will get constitutional protection for what, despite the demise of property as a formal constitutional limit.

This pervasiveness also gives a sense of the enormous consequences of finally abandoning this mythic image of property: our entire legal and political discourse would have to change. Perhaps that in itself accounts for the tenacity of the myth. It also raises questions to which I do not have the answers, but which are worth posing. Why has the judiciary virtually abandoned property in some forms, but not others? Why give up the overt formal limits with respect to economic regulation and social assistance, and enforce the power and privilege of property against the egalitarian measures of campaign finance laws? Perhaps the answers lie in what is actually a serious threat to that power and privilege. There have certainly been arguments that the emergence of the administrative state had the endorsement of those it would ostensibly regulate.[166] Perhaps control of the expertise of regulatory agencies seemed a safer way to work out the ongoing conflicts between the propertied and the demands of the majority, once judicial prohibitions had become highly conflictive and publicized. Judicial review as it had been exercised in the *Lochner* era may have come to be seen as a crude and heavy-handed tool, not easily controlled or fine-tuned. Capitalism turned out to do just fine without that particular form of protection for property.

Perhaps the tacit limits the Court now imposes seem to go to the heart of a system that uses a particular image of property to allocate power and goods. (Of course what judges and others think goes to the heart of the system changes over time; it is not the same now as it was in 1787 or 1887.) That system remains constitutionalized not through direct protection of property, but through enforcement of the underlying image of property and its link to liberty and security.

Finally, it may be that every society rests on illusory and contradictory beliefs. And it may be, as I have suggested, that there is something compelling about property and its links to liberty and security that cannot be revealed (or shaken) by an analysis of the ways the rules of property are collective choices imposed by the power of the state. I do not reject the role of myth in a well-functioning society. But the myth of property is pernicious because it hides a structure of power and insulates it from democratic debate.*[167]

VIII The Egalitarian Challenge

There are really two dimensions to the vast transformations of property in our system, both of which are related to the deep implications for our conception of limited government, for the meaning of constitutionalism. The first is the extent of economic regulation and the second the provision of welfare in various forms. In both cases spheres once defined as off limits by the concept of private property are now the subject of routine governmental action. Madison thought he could distinguish between the regulation of economic interests, which was the ordinary business of government, and the violation of private rights entailed by such wicked projects as paper money. And he thought that the rights of private property provided the line between them. For 150 years the courts continued to try to draw that line. Now "physical invasion" is practically all that is left of this vision. But that is not to say that judges or academics, much less other Americans, think that there should be no limits to what government can tell them to do or not to do with their homes or their businesses. The point is that if we are to draw such lines, we a need a new conceptual framework for doing so. We need a new way of articulating why it could be legitimate, say, for a government to specify how much rent I can charge, but not to whom I rent my spare room. In other words, the transformation of property requires nothing less than a new conception of the scope of the state. The demands of that task are even clearer and more daunting when viewed in light of the egalitarianism that increasingly pushes to expand the scope of the state.

The premise of the founders that there can be liberty and justice for all while there is property only for some is increasingly questioned in contemporary political theory and jurisprudence. Many of those loyal to the liberal tradition now argue that economic inequality is a barrier to political equality and to the equal entitlement to liberty and justice our system has long proclaimed. This is an attractive and persuasive argument. But our tradition suggests that the inequality originally built into the American concept of private property cannot simply be exorcised from the political system without consequences that extend to its strengths as well as its weaknesses. Private property and inequality are not marginal features of the system which can easily be rearranged. However separable in theory, inequality is linked in our constitutional tradition not only to property, but to our conceptions of liberty, of justice, and of the very nature and scope of government. To transform property and inequality requires a rethinking of all of these.

In the conception crystallized and articulated during the formation of the Constitution, the relationship between inequality, property, liberty, and limited government was as follows: The acquisition and use of property were essential elements of liberty. Given free rein, "men's different and unequal faculties of acquiring property"[168] would result in unequal possessions. Justice required the protection of these acquisitions from the predatory claims of the less successful. The object of government was to provide both this liberty and this justice. The protection of property not only by, but from, government was essential for a government's success in meeting these objectives, and thus for its legitimacy. For a government to cross the boundary of property rights was to trespass on both liberty and justice, and thus to step beyond the scope of legitimate power.

The egalitarian vision is practically a reversal of this founding conception: whether the inequality of property is the result of liberty or not, it stands in the way of liberty and justice for all.[169] The freedom to use and acquire property and the security of one's acquisitions are no longer defining elements of liberty and justice, but the potential objects of regulation and redistribution—aimed at assuring justice and liberty. In the stronger versions of egalitarianism, this objective entails a governmental responsibility either to assure that the ability to exercise one's rights is not contingent on wealth or to provide the resources necessary to make that exercise possible. Far from requiring respect for the boundaries defined by property, the egalitarian conception of liberty and justice requires incursions on traditional property rights. What once defined the limits to governmental power becomes the prime subject of affirmative governmental action.

The problem egalitarianism poses for American constitutionalism is not merely that the egalitarian vision entails conceptions of liberty and justice fundamentally different from those on which our tradition was built, but that this vision is incompatible with the property-based conception of limited government. Egalitarianism does not simply involve infringements on property rights. (American constitutionalism has, after all, survived a long history of incursions on vested rights.) Egalitarianism defines the inequality of property itself as the *source* of the problems to be remedied. Redistribution is not incidental, it is the objective.

The status of redistribution, like property, is thus being reversed. Instead of a prohibition defining the limits of legitimacy, it is increasingly claimed as an acceptable public purpose not only by scholars, but by politicians (among whom it is also increasingly contested). It is true that even in 1787 poor relief was widely accepted as a legitimate object of government, and tax-based donations to the poor always involve some form of redistribution. But the obligation to provide for the poor was charity, which was perceived as something quite different from the redistribution of wealth as a suitable object of government.[170] And I think some (analytically tenuous) distinction of this sort still underlies the acceptance of the welfare state. The conceptual problem arises—or becomes more obvious—as the expansion of welfare programs (supported by an allegedly progressive system of taxation) begins to look more and more like deliberate redistribution. Once redistribution can be held out as a public purpose, it is difficult to see how lines can be drawn defining some redistribution as, in principle, too much or the wrong kind. The problem is in part one of symbols. It is easier to think of boundaries to state action in the pithy terms of the sanctity of property (the legislature cannot take property from A to give it to B). It is not that it is impossible to try to generate principled arguments about the degree and kind of redistribution that is required or permitted, but that it is a difficult philosophic enterprise not easily encapsulated in compelling symbols. In the absence of compelling symbolic boundaries, it seems as though there is nothing to prevent a gradual expansion of the welfare state and its redistributive possibilities[171]—nothing, that is, but political argument and power. For those interested in principle and in effective symbolism, it seems easier to try to return to the original sanctity of property, but the return requires rejecting the welfare state. And that has become not merely unpopular, but implausible.

The loss of boundaries that egalitarianism threatens is particularly apparent in the issue of equal protection on the basis of wealth, which I referred to above. The one boundary the Court has firmly held onto is the view that the Constitution defines only prohibitions, things the government may not do to interfere with liberty; it does not prescribe affirmative obligations to make the exercise of constitutional rights possible. This old and revered distinction between negative and positive liberty still provides an important part of our conception of constitutionalism. But, as I noted above, it is difficult to sustain when claims of equal protection are combined with the provision of basic services. If education is the foundation of democracy, why are the states not obliged to ensure that the system of financing is such that the rich and the poor receive the same quality of education?[172] If the right to choose to carry a pregnancy to term is constitutionally protected, how can the receipt of medicare be conditioned on making the choice the state wants? The majority of the Supreme Court saw that once we acknowledge that some basic rights can only be enjoyed with state economic support, we have left the boundary of negative liberty behind[173] (and, of course, further redistributive incursions on property are likely to follow).*[174] Once this boundary is crossed, we will face another major philosophical challenge in defining the scope of the state—and once again it is not easy to see what will serve as new symbolic limits. And let me emphasize that the issue is very largely one of symbols. The distinction between negative and positive liberty becomes blurred once one takes seriously the active role of the state in defining and protecting property. When we see property as the creature of the state, the private sphere no longer looks so private and the state no longer merely passive in protecting it. But if we can continue to imagine property as a boundary, the traditional lines dividing public and private, positive and negative liberty seem to fall into place.

These issues are central to constitutional debate because the Civil War Amendments transformed the Constitution. What I have been discussing is the problem of superimposing a jurisprudence of equality on a structure and conception of constitutionalism based on the inequality of property. I have been focusing on economic equality, but the foundations of equality jurisprudence were, of course, laid in racial equality. Those foundations contained the problems now more starkly revealed. Enforcing desegregation required a rethinking of the meaning of property, for it entailed a major incursion on previously protected private spheres of property.[175] And it shook up another boundary, the line between the public and private defined by state action, which, in turn, involved a rethinking of the privateness of private property.[176]

We now have an elaborate equality jurisprudence, but it is becoming increasingly clear that it does not have the foundation it needs. Government carries out new tasks, violates old rights and protects new ones, but it does so without an adequate justifying theory. And the problem of producing one is not just the inherent challenge of redefining the purpose, scope, and limits to government. The problem is compounded by the fact that egalitarian liberals are caught in a bind (which is not to say it is inescapable). They want to equalize access to goods such as education, medical care, or effective political speech—generally through the regulation of the use of property or through redistributive mechanisms. They want to change the conception of the appropriate tasks and scope of government and, in so doing, to interfere with traditional property rights. They do not, however, want to give up the idea of individual rights as limits to the scope and power of government. They nevertheless find themselves in the position of undermining property, the traditional symbol of rights as limits. They are, in effect, saying that property rights are contingent on other collective values such as equality, and that the state may—indeed should—tamper with the oldest limiting value in order to foster new ones.

IX. Foundations of Constitutionalism

There have, of course, been many efforts to get around these problems and, more broadly, to provide a conception of constitutionalism suitable for our regulatory-welfare state. Indeed, the sense that we need such a new conception is so widespread that constitutional theory is proliferating at an incredible rate. And the meaning of our Constitution is not only a scholarly preoccupation. It is an important political issue, as the reaction to the nomination of Robert Bork to the Supreme Court made clear. In this final section, I want to sketch what a new conception of constitutionalism must accomplish.

The erosion of the foundation of our traditional conception of constitutionalism, property, has revealed its inherent limitations and provided us with an opportunity to transcend them. Many of the current constitutional theories are in fact moving in the right direction, but they are often doing so in spite of themselves. They claim a continuity with tradition, but in fact are undermining it—sometimes in productive ways. I think we are more likely to develop a better alternative if we candidly recognize the problems we are facing and the limitations of solutions cast in a Madisonian framework. We are in a kind of prolonged moment of transition. Some say go back. Most say we can go forward on the same path if we just smooth it out a bit. I say we have already taken a good many steps off the path of tradition and we should continue in a new direction.

To go back offers the reassurance of a compelling tradition, but a tradition both deeply flawed and unsuitable without major transformations in the nature of the modern state. Trying to patch up the holes in the tradition offers an appearance of continuity, but misjudges the depth of the flaws. Charting a new direction is a daunting task when its full dimensions are recognized. But it is by far the most fruitful path, and one which we seem to be stumbling down already. Acknowledging and defining the task may make the path clearer if not less demanding.

In all my arguments here it is important not to forget that voices for a return to the property-centered tradition are growing louder and stronger and may be amplified further by additional positions on the Supreme Court. And, of course, the debates over the Constitution are part of broader political divisions and uncertainties: has the welfare state gone too far or not far enough? should we accept vast inequality as the price for economic freedom and prosperity? what, if any, are our obligations toward those at the bottom? is "the market" better in principle and practice than "regulation?" The vision of constitutionalism must be tied to a vision of the purpose, responsibility, and limits of government. They are all contested. There is no clear vision on which there is a consensus. I think it is fair to say that the only ones with a fully elaborated vision are those committed to the property-centered vision of the past and prepared to roll back the regulatory-welfare state. But they are a minority. From their perspective (and that of the Madisonian tradition) they have lost: property as boundary has fallen before the demands of the majority, including demands for a greater share of the blessings of life. Most Americans seem to accept extensive economic regulation and some form of welfare. But the legitimacy of economic inequality is still quite firm.[177] There is, I think, no consensus on whether redistribution of wealth is itself an appropriate public goal, despite the fact that it is widely accepted as a means of ameliorating the conditions of the worst off. As I think the rhetoric of recent election campaigns reveals, those committed to the welfare state (most clearly the Democrats) do not have a clear vision of its purpose, of the nature and limits of its objectives. The status of property remains central to the unresolved and contested issues: the power of wealth, the entitlements of private property, the privileged status of private enterprise, the meaning of equality, or even of equal opportunity, and the means of achieving it. Those who advocate a return to the image of property as barrier and a vast limitation on the scope of the state have the advantage of a well-articulated tradition to draw on. But they must (and generally do) accept the inequality that has always been at the heart of this tradition. Those who support something like the alternative that has emerged, or even further departures from the tradition, have not yet developed a comparable articulation of the underlying vision.

In short, the American conception of the purpose of government, of limited government, of constitutionalism is unsettled and contested. This uncertainty provides an opportunity to use my assessment of the strengths and weaknesses of the Madisonian vision to consider where we should go from here, and whether current constitutional theories are likely to get us there.

The greatest strength of the Madisonian conception of constitutionalism was its capacity to sustain a tension between democracy and individual rights. Rights set a limit to the legitimacy of democratic outcomes, but consent was the foundation of the system. Despite the priority accorded to civil over political rights and the correspondingly shallow conception of democracy, both democracy and individual rights have remained banners of the American political system. Both are still part of the rhetoric of American politics. But it is getting harder to account for the status of rights as limits to democracy. In the absence of belief in natural rights or even faith in a common good, the source, content, and enforcement of limiting rights has become deeply problematic.

One important response to this problem is the claim that constitutional rights do not in fact impose substantive limits on the outcomes of the democratic process, they only insure the integrity of the process. The best known of these "process" theories are elaborations of the famous Footnote Four of *Carolene Products*.[178] Following shortly after the Court announced its new deference to legislative decisions in *West Coast Hotel*, the footnote sketched the exceptions to the presumption of constitutionality.*[179] In keeping with this heritage, these theories offer the further attraction of accounting for why the Court's shift with respect to property was in fact no shift at all in the foundations of constitutionalism. In these accounts, truly substantive values, such as property, have never been legitimate bases on which to claim that a legislature has overstepped its bounds. Courts may, for example, overturn voter registration laws on grounds that they exclude minorities from the democratic process; they may *not* strike down properly enacted economic regulation because it is seen as a violation of property rights. Dramatic shifts in the treatment of property, or in any collective preferences about substantive values, would thus pose no threat to the idea of limited government.

These theories purport to provide an interpretation of limited government in America and a philosophical basis for judicial review which rest solely on democratic values. The meaning of democratic values can be stretched to the point that they come to encompass anything the theorist values enough to stipulate as a limit on government (with arguments that the ancillary values are necessary to make democracy effective or meaningful). If the meaning is so stretched, of course, the theory does not avoid the original problem of justifying substantive restrictions on democratic action (or of dealing with the implications of major shifts in the content of these restrictions). But to the extent that these theories are true to their stated aims, they constitute a vast departure from our tradition.

It is the independent status of substantive, civil rights as limits on the legitimate outcome of democratic processes which is the essence of our tradition of limited government. Not only do "process" theories provide an unpersuasive account of our tradition; the exclusive reliance on democratic values undermines that tradition. The "process" theories would collapse the very tension between democratic values and private rights as limits, which has been the strength of constitutionalism in America. Even if these theories aimed to establish a new, democratic, foundation for limited government, they would face the problem of relying on the shallow set of democratic values bequeathed to us by our tradition. Such theories should at least recognize their departure from our tradition and the need to enhance its democratic component if democracy alone is to replace the historic tension with private rights.

There are related theories that focus on the nature of the democratic decision-making that generates a challenged outcome. They suggest that, at least in some circumstances, the quality of the process can determine legitimacy,*[180] and that judges should apply different levels of scrutiny to challenged legislation depending on whether there is reason to suspect that the decision was based not on a deliberative judgment about the public good, but on the raw exercise of numerical power to promote private interests.[181] These approaches have the virtue of fostering an inquiry into the nature of democracy. But the source and status of substantive values remain a problem. Defining legitimacy in terms of public values rather than private interests may be an indirect way of describing the role of substantive values in setting limits. For example, part of the purpose of private property for Madison was to make clear that redistribution could never be an acceptable public objective; it could never be part of a coherent vision of the public good. The rights of property defined redistribution as an illegitimate exercise of political power to promote private interests.[182] Today, the rights of property do not preclude many forms of redistribution, but it is not yet clear whether redistribution as such is a legitimate public purpose.[183] To many, I think it still looks like promoting the interests of some at the expense of others. The substantive limits property once provided defined what counted as a public purpose and what counted as mere private interest. Today there is an ongoing contest over what gets to claim the status of public purpose, and that contest is the flipside of the contest over what counts as a substantively limiting value.

These more sophisticated process theories are characteristic of the best of modern constitutional theory in that they imply a fluidity in the meaning of the basic terms of constitutionalism. The same is true of the efforts to maintain our structure of constitutionalism by finding a replacement for property as its center. I have already noted that those who propose to retain property, but redefine it end up with definitions which have lost the very characteristics that made property an effective limiting value. Concepts like dignity and human flourishing hold out the promise of being able to sustain the original tension of constitutionalism by providing a new focal point for the individual rights that are to define the limits to democracy. But these terms, too, are so broad, vague, and abstract that they shout the fluidity of their meaning. And it is increasingly obvious that the grounds on which the Court has been striking down legislation, such as privacy and equality, have shifting and contested meanings. Some of the most interesting constitutional theory takes this fluid quality as one of the chief characteristics of constitutional (indeed all legal) discourse,[184] but then finds it very difficult to articulate how this endlessly promising rhetoric provides any limits at all.

A vision of constitutionalism that acknowledges the essential fluidity of its terms is a step in the right direction, but it is a step away from the vision we have inherited from Madison and Marshall. It is not easily superimposed on Madisonian constitutionalism. That conception, as we have seen, relied on self-evident rules of justice to define the bounds of legitimacy. The whole relation between democracy and individual rights was premised on the unproblematic nature of those rights. Madison never paused to consider how those rights should be interpreted, or by whom, or how conflicting and changing interpretations were to be handled. That hole in the argument makes sense if the content of rights was to be taken as a given. Marshall, of course, asserted that it was the courts' business to determine when legislation violated constitutional provisions, including protected rights. The rationale that the decisions of "the people" expressed in the Constitution should take precedence over the decisions of the legislature presumed that the people had spoken in clear and permanent terms.

The history of property, once the focal point for the tension between democracy and individual rights, makes it clear that we must now think about the problem differently. We can no longer believe that "property" has a single, fixed meaning. The concept of property reflects collective choices about what sorts of goods should be given the status of secure entitlement, and what sort of security and what sort of entitlement—and those choices change. The institutions that define property—largely the courts in our system—also reflect decisions about how those choices should be made.

In a sense, this perception of the contingent and contested rather than inherent and immutable quality of the meaning of property is not just hindsight. The meaning of property was contested during the formation of the Constitution. The Federalists thought they knew the right or true meaning and wanted to protect it from those who did not know or care. They seem to have truly believed that the problem of paper money and debtor relief was not one of competing conceptions of property rights, but of blind, ignorant, or selfish willingness to violate what really were the rights of property. Their confidence was the necessary foundation for their vision of constitutionalism. We can no longer indulge in such an unselfconscious confidence in the justice of our judgments or the timelessness of our values.

Once we acknowledge the mutability of basic values, the problem of protecting them from democratic abuse is transformed. We do not have to abandon Madison's basic insight that democracy can threaten individual rights but we need to reconsider all of its terms: democracy, individual rights, and the nature of the tension between them. First we must see that the problem of defending individual rights is inseparable from the problem of defining them. Even if there are deep, immutable truths underlying the shifting perceptions of the terms that capture those truths, the ongoing problem of defining those terms remains. And then the relation to democracy becomes more complex, for the definition of rights, as well as the potentially threatening legislation, is the product of shifting collective choice.

That recognition does not mean that we cannot distinguish between those choices, but it does mean that we cannot use a Madisonian conceptual framework to do so. It would be a mistake to posit democracy as the sole criterion for the legitimacy of governmental action, but we need a new way of understanding the source and content of the values against which we are to measure democratic outcomes.

The "counter-majoritarian" problem remains, but now the problem is not just why it is legitimate to prevent the majority from violating certain values, but also what is an appropriate process for the continuous redefinition of those values. One form of restatement of the problem is to say that the task of constitutional government is to insulate some values from ordinary political processes. But our model of insulation must account for ongoing change in the meaning of the insulated values. We cannot ascribe to "normal politics" shifting conflicts over private interests and reserve changes in basic values for constitutional amendment or exceptional times of concerted, extended political activity.[185] First of all, what counts as mere private interest or higher public values is itself part of the terms of constitutional discourse. And these terms are constantly shifting, not static until moments of focused attention on constitutional debate. Of course, the rates of change vary, and change can crystallize into identifiable moments such as *West Coast Hotel* in 1937 and *Brown v. Board of Education*[186] in 1954. But the process is continuous. Judicial review has, in fact, provided a means of insulation from ordinary politics which has proven capable of this ongoing change. But the justification for judicial review—or any other means of insulating basic values—must now ask not only whether it can adequately or legitimately defend basic rights, but whether it can adequately and legitimately define and redefine them. The federalist conception of constitutional government did not try to answer that question.

The transformation entailed in recognizing the fluid quality of the meaning of rights is only the first step. The Madisonian image of rules of justice capable of generating clear boundaries is tied to a deeper problem in our tradition of constitutionalism: the understanding of the need for boundaries in the first place. The core of Madison's insight into the tension between democracy and individual rights may be stated as the recognition that individual autonomy can be threatened by collective power. But the Madisonian understanding of this important truth of human nature was distorted by his focus on property. We have already seen the distortions caused by casting this general problem into the particular terms of the threat "the people" will pose to property, that is the problem of protecting rights enjoyed by the few from the decisions of the many. Inequality was so central to the Madisonian conception of the essential problem of popular government that it is not surprising that egalitarianism has been such a disruptive force in constitutional thought. Now that it has unsettled our understandings of rights and of the purpose and scope of government, it invites us to reconceive the basic problem.

The vulnerability of individual rights is an enduring dilemma of democracy; its particular manifestation in inequality need not be. The American solution of confining democratic politics may be necessary when the system both presupposes and fosters an unequal distribution of basic goods, but such systemic inequality is not inevitable. There will, of course, always be a wide range of unequal skills and abilities. But the relation between these various forms of inequality and the distribution of basic goods can be worked out in various ways. To borrow Madisonian imagery, there need not be one basic division between the rich and the poor which is an inevitable source of faction, that is, a danger to both individual liberties and the public good. There could instead be multiple differences and inequalities which were the source of interdependence rather than a single dominant structure of power and hierarchy. If inequality were transformed, the problem of protecting individual rights would be transformed as well.*[187]

I am not suggesting that the problem of individual rights in a democracy would disappear in a more egalitarian society. On the contrary, I think the tension between the autonomy of the individual and the power of the collective is an inherent part of the human condition. The tension reflects the dual character of human nature as both essentially individual and irreducibly social. The problem of individual rights takes on a different form, however, if systemic inequality is not a premise.[188] There is no reason to see the majority as a constant threat to a cherished value unless they are excluded from it. In any democratic society, there is always the potential that some group will use their collective power to infringe on the rights of an individual. The recognition of that potential is, however, very different from the need to guard against the ever-present threat from the disadvantaged. When inequality does not define the divisions in society, expansion rather than confinement of democratic participation may best protect (and foster) individual autonomy.

The dissociation between the inequality of property and the inherent vulnerability of the individual to the collective makes it possible to try to uncover the essence of that vulnerability—which may or may not involve the issue of inequality.

While egalitarianism threatens the framework of limited government built around property, the claims of equality also open up the possibility of a new approach to the tension between the individual and the collective, free of the constraints of making democracy safe for property. The perspective from the formation warns of the difficulty of simply trying to replace property with some other limiting value. It warns also that to abandon the idea of individual rights as limits in favor of democratic values alone is to dramatically change the notion of limited government that has sustained American constitutionalism for two hundred years. But the possibility of disassociating the founding connection between property and limited government also invites a new way of conceiving and implementing the competing values of democracy and individual rights, of collectivity and individuality, so that both are fostered. The real lesson of the American tradition can be taken to be that democratic values alone cannot be the foundation for good government. They must be counterpoised to the values of individual freedom or autonomy. We need not, however, conceive of democratic values in terms of the shallow, unexamined concept of democracy which has characterized our tradition for so long. Nor need we conceive of the tension between the collective and the individual in terms of the hostile dichotomy which the link between property and autonomy implies.

This brings me finally to the deepest failure of Madisonian constitutionalism and to a challenge whose dimensions I can only sketch here. The entire vision of constitutionalism—the tension between democracy and individual rights, the distinction and hierarchy between civil and political rights, the notion of rights as boundaries—rests on a flawed conception of individual autonomy, a conception captured, amplified, and entrenched by its association with property.

The primary content of this conception of autonomy was protection from the intrusion and oppression of the collective. The autonomy the Madisonian system sought to protect could be achieved by erecting a wall of rights between the individual and those around him. Property was the ideal symbol for this vision of autonomy, for it could both literally and figuratively provide the necessary walls. The perverse quality of this conception is clearest when taken to its extreme: the most perfectly autonomous man is the most perfectly isolated. This vision of the autonomous individual as one securely isolated from his threatening fellows is, of course, not unique to American constitutionalism.[189] It is the core of the liberal tradition. American constitutionalism has, however, institutionalized this vision in a particularly compelling way: judicial review in America has become a kind of paradigm of securing individual autonomy by rights which limit the power of the collective.

The notion of protecting autonomy by erecting barriers of rights that can ward off the dangerous power of the collective makes sense of the focus on clear and fixed boundaries. When the understanding of autonomy changes, the relation between the individual and society looks different, and the conceptual structure of constitutionalism must shift.

A proper conception of autonomy must begin with the recognition that relationship, not separation makes autonomy possible.[190] This recognition shifts the focus from protection against others to structuring relationships so that they foster autonomy. Some of the most basic presuppositions about autonomy shift: dependence is no longer the antithesis of autonomy, but a precondition in the relationships—between parent and child, student and teacher, state and citizen—which provide the security, education, nurturing, and support that make the development of autonomy possible. Interdependence becomes the central fact of political life, not an issue to be shunted to the periphery in the basic question of how to ensure individual autonomy in the inevitable face of collective power. The human interactions to be governed are seen not primarily in terms of the clashing of rights and interests, but in terms of the way patterns of relationship can develop and sustain both an enriching collective life and the scope for genuine individual autonomy. The whole conception of the relation between the individual and the collective shifts: the collective is a source of autonomy as well as a threat to it.

This conception of autonomy resonates with other visions that have emerged in American history,[191] but none that have been successful in defining the basic terms of constitutional discourse. To accept it would be to reshape constitutionalism. The constitutional project would then become not to carve out a sphere into which the collective cannot intrude, e.g., property, but to structure the relations between individuals and the sources of collective power so that autonomy is fostered rather than undermined. In this project participation, or political liberty, stands in a more complex relation to the individual rights that promote autonomy than the Madisonian hierarchy of civil and political rights can accommodate. Political liberty is a dimension of autonomy as well as a potential threat to it. From this perspective constitutionalism must concentrate not on containing political liberty, but ensuring that it enhances autonomy, including individual rights.

The problem of the relation between the individual and the collective power of democracy remains the central question of constitutionalism, but it is transformed. The focus cannot be the boundaries which have been so important to American constitutionalism and which property so effectively symbolized. But the focus on relation rather than opposition does not mean that we should simply invert the hierarchy and place participation in the collective or democracy as the highest value. The Madisonian insight into the danger of the collective was distorted, but it was a distorted version of a basic truth. The collective power of democracy is always a potential threat to individuals, but it is not only that. The problem with American constitutionalism is that the opposition between the individual and the collective is too stark, the focus on the threat is too single-minded. The tension between individual autonomy and democracy should remain the central objective of constitutionalism, but it must be reconceived.[192] And that reconception must rest on a new understanding of autonomy.

After we acknowledge that the collective is a source and democracy a dimension of autonomy, we must still contrast autonomy with democracy in the following related ways: democracy is not itself sufficient to ensure autonomy; autonomy is a substantive value which can be threatened by democratic outcomes, even though the democratic process is itself a necessary component of autonomy; the outcomes of democratic processes should respect the autonomy of all people and should be held accountable for doing so. But the means of "holding accountable" cannot be rights as hard and fixed boundaries. This vision of autonomy fits with the notion of rights as the ever shifting product of collective decision-making. The focus becomes the process by which the terms of autonomy (including rights) are articulated, and the institutions, language, and habits of inquiry through which citizens and representatives (including judges) would check whether laws fostered or undermined autonomy. This long description must replace the pithy claim that rights are limits to democratic outcomes. The more complex vision of the relation and the tension between the individual and the collective requires a more complex expression of the means of sustaining the tension. The concepts of civil and political rights may remain useful language for discussing the tension, but the relation between the two cannot be simply oppositional—just as the relation between the individual and the collective is not simply oppositional. We must have both a process of articulating basic values which is consistent with democracy and a means of measuring the outcomes of ordinary political processes against the basic values.*[193] And as we try to develop these means, we must remember that the basic task is not to generate new boundaries, or even new procedures for defining boundaries, but to work out a conception of the tension between the individual and the collective for which boundary is not an apt metaphor. And once the setting of boundaries is rejected as the ruling metaphor, we will need a new understanding of the nature of law. Not only will the task of law cease to be drawing boundaries of rights between the individual and the collective, but the boundary between law and politics will blur.[194] As the definition of rights comes to be formally recognized as an exercise of collective choice and power, the norms of what count as lawlike forms of argument and decision making must change as well.[195] When we give up property and the conception of autonomy it has symbolized, we will need to develop a whole new conceptual framework for constitutionalism.[196]

This project is consistent with most contemporary constitutional theory and even judicial practice (e.g., the explicit invocation of balancing rather than the application of clear principles capable of determining outcomes). As I said above, the appropriate changes seem to be underway. But they usually are not generated by nor directed at the sort of basic reconceptualization I have argued is necessary. That is in part because the theories are not self-conscious departures from the tradition. On the contrary, virtually all theorists insist that their vision is based on the true tradition. It is only a slight exaggeration to say that whatever the theorists' preferred values are, they find them in the Constitution.

Given my own insistence on the shifting collective determination of basic values, why should I not simply adopt this approach? Why not, for example, say that the core of our tradition is republicanism, with its focus on participation, so that we can invoke the legitimacy of those values when we try to give them greater force and efficacy? Why persist (perversely as some suggest) in presenting my understanding of the tradition for the apparent purpose of identifying its flaws? The answer (in addition to my attachment to the truth of our history as I see it) is that we cannot fully understand the failings of our system or how to remedy them if we do not see that the Constitution was designed to solve a distorted version of the basic problem of constitutionalism.

First, we must take seriously the ways the distortions I have identified are embedded in the institutional as well as the conceptual structure of the American Constitution. What can it mean to say that republican citizenship (or dignity or human flourishing) is the basic value underlying our Constitution if the institutions outlined in the Constitution do not actually promote these values? The proponents of these optimistic interpretations of the Constitution are generally constitutional lawyers who envision generating desirable reforms through judicial review (or at least want to be sure that no such reforms could be precluded). But the expansive optimism of interpretive reform often seems to obscure the question of the sorts of institutional changes that would be required to implement the vision guiding the reform. A failure to acknowledge basic problems built into the Constitution turns our attention away from institutions to the apparently more malleable realm of ideas.

And an understanding of the failures of our tradition is, of course, no less important in that realm. As I have argued, the demands of reconceiving constitutionalism are formidable. We can confront them most creatively and constructively if we see clearly how deep the original conceptual failures go. It is not simply that there are weaknesses in the vision of constitutionalism that developed around property as the paradigmatic instance of the vulnerability of individual rights in a democracy. The greatest strength of this vision, the insight into the enduring tension between individual rights and democracy, is itself a distorted version of the underlying problem of the relation between individual autonomy and collective power. It is distorted at its root, in the image of autonomy it protects; it is distorted in its focus on the danger posed by inequality; it is distorted in its conceptualization of a means-ends hierarchy between civil and political rights; and it is distorted in its institutionalization in a system of representation that neither fosters democratic participation nor prevents the power of wealth from undermining both equality and democracy.

The American constitutional system is an impressive effort at solving a deep and difficult problem. Compared to most of the world, it has done quite well at advancing equality and sustaining both democracy and individual rights. It is this impressive base that now makes it possible to see beyond the limitations of the tradition. Admiration for partial successes should not blind us to failures. The superficial security of remaining within the tradition that has brought us these successes should not make us unwilling to face the need to transform some of its most basic elements. And those transformations are, in any case, underway. We need to recognize them for what they are. The original links to property are eroding in some places, broken in others, and everywhere undermined by a modern welfare state which is incompatible with those links. These shifts permit and require us to return to the basic problem of constitutionalism free from the distortions captured and generated by the original focus on property.

Works Frequently Cited

Cranch	Cranch's United States Supreme Court Reports, 1801–15
Dall.	Dallas' Pennsylvania and United States Reports, 1790–1800
Elliot	*The Debates in the Several State Conventions on the Adoption of the Federal Constitution*, ed. Jonathon Elliot, 5 vols., Burt Franklin Research and Source Work Series 109, reprinted from 1888 edition (New York: Burt Franklin Reprints, 1974)
Farrand	*The Records of the Federal Convention of 1787*, ed. Max Farrand, 4 vols. (New Haven: Yale University Press, 1911–37)
The Federalist	*The Federalist*, ed. Jacob E. Cooke (Middletown, Conn., 1961)
GMC	Gouverneur Morris Collection, Columbia University Special Collections, New York, N.Y.
Haskins, Johnson	*The Oliver Wendell Holmes Devise, History of the Supreme Court of the United States*, volume 2, *Foundations of Power: John Marshall, 1801–15*, George Lee Haskins and Herbert A. Johnson (New York: Macmillan Publishing Co., 1981)
JHL *Works*	*The Works of James Wilson*, ed. Robert Green McCloskey, 2 vols., The John Harvard Library (Cambridge, Mass.: Harvard University Press, Belknap Press, 1967)
McMaster and Stone	*Pennsylvania and the Federal Constitution, 1787–1788*, ed. John Bach McMaster and Frederick D. Stone (Lancaster, Pa.: Historical Society of Pennsylvania, 1888)
Meyers	*The Mind of the Founder: Sources of the Political Thought of James Madison*, ed. Marvin Meyers, The American Heritage Series (Indianapolis: Bobbs-Merrill, 1973)

WORKS FREQUENTLY CITED

Papers	*The Papers of James Madison*, ed. William T. Hutchinson and William M. E. Rachal et al., vols. 1–10 (Chicago: University of Chicago Press, 1972–77)
Sparks	*The Life and Correspondence of Gouverneur Morris*, ed. Jared Sparks, 3 vols. (Boston: Gray and Bowen, 1832)
Storing	*The Complete Anti-Federalist*, ed. Herbert Storing, 7 vols. (Chicago: University of Chicago Press, 1981)
Writings	*The Writings of James Madison*, ed. Gaillard Hunt, 9 vols. (New York: G. P. Putnam's Sons, 1900–1910)

Notes

An asterisk indicates a note of substance.

Chapter 1

1. Max Lerner, "Constitution and Court as Symbols," *Yale Law Journal* 46 (1937): 1290–1319, p. 1300 n. 32.

*2. Of course, I am nevertheless indebted to Charles Beard and the Progressive historians who have given us a large and thoughtful literature on the importance of property in American constitutional government. Read today, their arguments sometimes sound crude or simplistic. I think the core problem lies in inadequate attention to the meaning of property beyond simple economic self-interest.

*3. The Federalists had, as we shall see, important differences among themselves. Nevertheless, most shared a set of basic ideas which can reasonably be referred to as the Federalist mode of thought.

*4. There are, of course, antecedents, particularly in the political thought of the English, Scots, and Puritans. Understanding the sources of American ideas, beliefs, and institutions can greatly enrich our understanding of them. Tracing those sources is not, however, my objective. It is rather to show the development of the American conception of limited government as part of the formation of the Constitution. The project looks forward to the contemporary significance of the formation, rather than back to its antecedents.

*5. I do not use the word man (or men) to stand for all human beings. The Framers were all men, so the use of pronouns in referring to them is straightforward (although one important Anti-Federalist writer, Mercy Warren, was a woman). I think it is clear that when the Framers used the term men, they had males (in fact, white males) in mind. They expected only men to participate in government as voters, office holders, or even members of juries. At some level, they probably thought that in protecting the rights of men, they were protecting those of women as well. But of course, the rights women enjoyed were different from those of men, with respect to "private" rights, such as property and contract, as well as the rights to political participation. James Wilson actually discussed the role of women in the republic, but most simply ignored the subject. However all-inclusive they might have thought they were, I think it is fair to say that they were literally concerned with the rights of *men* and the role of *men* in government. I thus adopt their exclusive use of the male pronoun when discussing their ideas, not because I think it is a suitable referent to all human beings, but because all human beings were not being referred to.

*6. Of course, this general principle had important qualifications. It only covered those considered to be politically competent. While there was disagreement about whether the propertyless fit within this category, there was clear agreement that slaves, women, and children did not.

*7. There were also more subtle conflicts which may have contributed to the pervasive anxiety about protecting property. A variety of legal disputes exposed the difficult problem of the ultimate authority or justification for title to land. The traditional sovereignty of the king had come into conflict with the widely held view that actual settlement was the true basis for claims to land. Title through settlement, in turn, proved to threaten all formal legal claims to undeveloped land—not just those resting on the authority of the Crown. The broader tensions between stability and security on the one hand, and open opportunity and popular will on the other, had bubbled beneath the surface of law-suits for years before the convention. See Elizabeth V. Mensch, "The Colonial Origins of Liberal Property Rights," *Buffalo Law Review* 31 (1982): 635–735. These deep and subtle issues of legitimacy were further compounded by the pressure on land (at least in New England) caused by an expanding population. The relations between fathers and sons and their land were transformed when sons could no longer assume that they would come into a share of the family farm. Property, which had provided stability and security for both individuals and communities, was in a state of transition in the latter half of the eighteenth century. In short, by the time of the convention, the very meaning of property was in flux. The immediate threats of state legislation thus took place in a context of still more profound uncertainty about the meaning, role, and legitimacy of property in the new republic. See Robert A. Gross, *The Minutemen and Their World* (New York: Hill and Wang, 1976), and "Culture and Cultivation: Agriculture and Society in Thoreau's Concord," *Journal of American History* 69 (1982): 42–61 and James Henretta, *The Evolution of American Society* (Lexington, Mass.: Heath, 1973).

8. The meaning of these terms is discussed in ch. 2, n. 3.

*9. Note that these are the sorts of threats the contract clause (Article I, Section 10) was designed to deal with. The eminent domain clause, (in the Fifth Amendment) was only added afterward in the Bill of Rights.

*10. See ch. 5. The Constitution specified limits on the state governments in Article I, Section 10, and on the Federal government in Article I, Section 9. The limits on the Federal government in the first ten amendments were, of course, added after the adoption of the Constitution.

11. Madison, *The Federalist* No. 10.

12. As we shall see, James Wilson, an important Federalist, also had a very democratic vision of republican government.

*13. The Constitution did specify answers to some versions of this conflict: state governments, but not the federal government, were prohibited from impairing the obligation of contracts or issuing paper money, which were the most feared forms of infringements on property rights. The contract clause proved to be an extremely important form of protection for property.

*14. The addition of the first ten amendments, to which I will refer later, in some ways deviates importantly from the implementation of an essentially Federalist conception of limited government. These amendments were the Anti-Federalists' major contribution to the Constitution. They had a fundamentally different thrust from that of the Federalists' concerns: they were aimed at the federal, not the state governments; and they were designed to protect citizens against the perfidy and usurpation of those in office, not against the dangers of the majority. They were introduced to thwart the Anti-Federalist opposition to the new Constitution, and, ironically, ultimately became important because the Federalists were so successful in establishing judicial review, the ultimate anti-majoritarian institution.

15. See "Remarks on Mr. Jefferson's Draught of a Constitution," sent to John Brown, [12] October 1788, *Writings* 5:284–94, reprinted in *The Mind of the Founder: Sources of the Political Thought of James Madison*, ed. Marvin Meyers, The American Heritage Series (Indianapolis, 1973), p. see p. 65–66. (Hereafter cited as Meyers.)

*16. The Federalists of the judicial review era were not exactly the same group as the Federalists of 1787. James Madison, for example, was a staunch Federalist in 1787, but a Jeffersonian in 1800. There were, nevertheless, important continuities of both personnel and ideas.

*17. I want to reemphasize that this is a story of contests at every stage. The Federalists largely succeeded in shaping the new institutions according to their vision of the republic. It was not, however, a total victory. The Constitution bears the marks of compromise and cooperation. The Federalist mode of thought has become the dominant strain in our tradition. But the competing ideas and values of their opponents were not obliterated, only submerged. The tensions and contests of the past continue. In addition, I am not claiming that the Framers' focus on property *determined* their choice of institutions or hierarchy of values. Rather the story of the formation reveals a constellation of ideas and institutional arrangements in which property held a central place—a constellation still with us today.

18. On the importance of understanding the constitutive nature of institutions see Stephen L. Elkin, "Constitutionalism's Successor," a paper presented at a conference organized by the Committee on the Foundations of Democratic Government, University of Pennsylvania, September 1987. See also his references to Phillip Selznick, *Law, Society and Industrial Justice* (New Brunswick, N.J.: Transaction Books, 1969); James Boyd White, *When Words Lose Their Meaning*, (Chicago: University of Chicago Press, 1984); and Robert F. Lane, "Market and Politics: The Human Product," *British Journal of Political Science* 11 (1981): 1–16.

19. Among the best known are: Irving Brant, *Storm Over the Constitution* (Indianapolis: Bobbs-Merrill, 1963); Forrest McDonald, *The Formation of the American Republic 1776–1790* (Baltimore: Penguin Books, 1965); Forrest McDonald, *We The People: The Economic Origins of the Constitution* (Chicago: University of Chicago Press, 1965); Andrew C. McLaughlin, *The Confederation and the Constitution 1783–1789* (New York: Collier Books, 1971); Clinton Rossiter, *1787 The Grand Convention* (New York: New American Library, 1968); and

Gordon S. Wood, *The Creation of the American Republic: 1776–1787* (Chapel Hill: The University of North Carolina Press, 1969), which focuses on political thought.

*20. Madison's ideas are, of course, particularly important because they are reflected in the Constitution. I do not, however, present Madison as an authoritative source for some notion of the binding "intent of the Framers." The (probably insurmountable) problems of establishing their collective intent and its legal authority are not the problems of this enterprise. Madison is important as much as an interpreter as a creator of the Constitution.

Judges often unreflectively claim that the "intent of the Framers" compels a particular interpretation of the Constitution. Of course, in interpreting the Constitution it is helpful, perhaps essential, to understand its structure. The Framers' contributions to that understanding are, however, quite a different matter from reliance on "the intent of the Framers" as binding authority. For an example of the argument that the Constitution must be understood and interpreted as a coherent structure, see Charles Black, *Structure and Relationship in Constitutional Law* (Baton Rouge: Louisiana State University Press, 1969).

21. The phrase "property is the object of government" may strike the reader as somewhat odd or awkward. It is the phrase generally used by the Framers, and I shall comment later, in chapter 5, on their recurrent use of the word property rather than "the protection of property," "property rights," or "interests of property."

22. The critiques or challenges I refer to are those implicit in the strengths of Wilson's and Morris's views, not those they actually leveled against their fellows.

Chapter 2

1. Speech in the House of Representatives, 8 June 1789, Meyers, p. 215.

2. *The Federalist*, No. 10, p. 58.

*3. "Remarks on Mr. Jeffersons's Draught of a Constitution [for Virginia]," October 1788, Meyers, p. 58.

Madison did not define "rights of persons" or "rights of property." I think what he cared about was not precision of categories, but the conditions under which some rights were likely to be well protected and others to be particularly vulnerable. He thought the broad categories of rights of persons and rights of property captured the tension he was concerned about (which this section of the text explores): if all power lies in the hands of the propertyless, the rights of property will be threatened; if the propertied have all the power, they are likely to violate the rights of the propertyless, that is, their rights of persons. Madison consistently used these broad categories, without trying to specify which rights of the propertyless would be particularly vulnerable. The most notable exception to this lack of specificity is his famous, but (as I will argue in this section) uncharacteristic, essay on "Property" (*National Gazette*, 29 March 1792, Meyers, pp. 243–46). Here he argued that "as a man is said to have a right to his property, he may be equally said to have a property in his rights" (p.244). In listing those rights, he treats "opinions and the free communication of them" as well as "religious opinions, and . . . the profession and practice dictated by them" as distinct from "the safety and liberty of [one's] person." Similarly, he tacitly distinguished "land, merchandise, or money" from "the free use of [one's] faculties, and free choice of the objects on which to employ them"(p. 243). While the notion of free use of faculties is important in Madison's arguments at the time of the convention, the other distinctions appear not to be. It is, as I said, the vulnerability of the rights of those with and those without property that Madison was concerned about, not whether, say, the rights of conscience stand in a different relation to this problem than the safety and liberty of one's person.

4. Note to 7 August 1787 Speech, Farrand 2:204.

5. Ibid.

6. Ibid.

7. Ibid., 2:203–4.

8. Ibid., 1:422.

*9. "Remarks on Mr. Jefferson's Draught of a Constitution," sent to John Brown, October 1788, Meyers, p. 58. A later statement makes explicit that the rights which would be violated were, respectively, those of persons and property: "Allow the right [of suffrage] exclusively to property, and the rights of persons may be oppressed. . . . Extend it equally to all, and the rights of property or the claims of justice may be overruled by a majority without property. . . . " Note on 7 August 1787 Speech, 1821, ibid., p. 503.

10. "Remarks on Mr. Jefferson's Draught of a Constitution," ibid., p. 59.

11. Ibid. See also note on 7 August 1787 Speech, 1821, pp. 501–9.

12. Ibid., p. 503.

13. Note to 7 August 1787 Speech, Farrand 2:204.

14. "Remarks on Mr. Jefferson's Draught of a Constitution," Meyers, p. 59.

15. Note on 7 August 1787 Speech, 1821, ibid., p. 503.

16. Farrand 2:204.

*17. It is important here that Madison was not using the shorthand phrases "property" or even "rights of property," but the carefully worded phrase "the faculties for acquiring property." I shall return later to this choice of terms.

18. Speech in the Virginia Constitutional Convention, 2 December 1829, Meyers, pp. 512–19. See also Meyers's prefatory note p. 511 in which he says that "Madison circulated a memorandum on voting rights that helped to win support for the extension of suffrage from freeholders to renters and taxpaying householders."

19. Observations on the "Draught of a Constitution for Virginia," 1788, *The Writings of James Madison*, ed. Gaillard Hunt, 9 vols. (New York, 1900–1910), 5:287 (hereafter cited as *Writings*).

20. To Caleb Wallace, 23 August 1785, Meyers, p. 49.

21. Irving Brant, *James Madison*, 5 vols. (New York: Bobbs-Merrill, 1950), "Speculators vs. Veterans," 3:290–305.

22. To Thomas Jefferson, 8 August 1791, *Writings* 6:58–59, and 10 July 1791, ibid. 6:55.

23. "Property," *National Gazette*, 29 March 1792, Meyers, p. 244.

24. Notes for Speech in the Virginia House of Assembly, November 1786, *Writings* 2:280.

25. Farrand 1:134.

26. Ibid., 135–36.

27. "Vices of the Political System of the United States," April 1787, Meyers, p. 88.

*28. His 1792 reference to property in rights is an isolated example. As noted earlier, Madison used it only for rhetorical purposes to make a particular point.

29. To Jefferson, 19 March 1787, in *The Papers of Thomas Jefferson*, eds. Julian P. Boyd, et al., 19 vols. (Princeton University Press, 1950–1986), 11:219.

30. Farrand 1:134.

31. Ibid., 1:424.

32. *The Federalist*, No. 10, pp. 56–57.

33. Farrand 1:218.

34. Ibid. 1:219.

*35. *The Federalist*, No. 37, p. 234, see also No. 26. It is interesting to compare Madison's and Jefferson's response to the turbulence of the times. Jefferson wrote to Madison that the principal evil of republican governments was the turbulence to which they were subject. However, "even this evil is productive of good. It prevents the degeneracy of government, and nourishes a general attention to the public affairs. I hold that a little rebellion now and then is a good thing" (30 January 1787, Boyd, *Papers of Thomas Jefferson* 11:92). About the same time Madison wrote to Edmund Pendleton: "[T]he late turbulent scenes in Massachusetts and infamous ones in Rhode Island, have done inexpressible injury to the republican character in that part of the U. States" (24 February 1787, *Writings* 2:319). Of course Jefferson wrote from the distant perspective of Paris, while Madison saw the effects at home, among them that "a propensity towards Monarchy is said to have been produced in some leading minds." Ibid.

36. 19 March 1787, *Writings* 2:327.

37. 8 April 1787, ibid. 2:339.

38. 16 April 1787, ibid. 2:346.

39. *The Federalist* No. 44, p. 301.

*40. It is important to remember that these ideas were not merely theoretical deductions on Madison's part. The instability from the state laws interfering with the rights of property was there for all to see—as Madison repeatedly pointed out.

*41. *The Federalist*, No. 44, pp. 301–2. A more extreme example of the connection Madison saw between the disruption of property rights and the stability of society is his response to Jefferson's suggestion that each generation should have an opportunity to enact an entirely new set of laws. Madison objected that each time this would occasion "the most violent struggle between the parties interested in reviving and those interested in reforming the antecedent state of property," and the resulting instability must make such a plan impracticable (To Thomas Jefferson, 4 February 1790, Meyers, p. 232).

42. "Remarks on Mr. Jefferson's Draught of a Constitution," October 1788, Meyers, p. 59.

43. "Property," *National Gazette*, 29 March 1792, Meyers, p. 245.

44. *The Federalist*, No. 10, p. 58.

*45. Note to 7 August 1787 Speech, 1821, Meyers, p. 505. In this casual reference to the Lockean argument, Madison gave no indication that he had thought through the problems it raised—problems that might have been particularly difficult for an owner of slaves.

*46. Speech in the Virginia Constitutional Convention, 2 December 1829, Meyers, p. 512. While I have not found this precise formulation in his writing at the time of the 1787 convention, the statement seems to be a concise version of the view implicit in his arguments at that time.

47. *The Federalist*, No. 10, p. 65.

48. To James Madison, Sr., 1 November 1786, *Writings* 2:278.

49. See my discussion below in "Government in the divided society."

50. 28 October 1785, *The Papers of James Madison*, eds. William T. Hutchinson and William M. E. Rachal, et al., 10 vols. (Chicago: The University of Chicago Press, 1962–77), 8:386–87 (hereafter cited as *Papers*).

*51. This is itself an indication of disagreement. Madison usually made detailed responses to Jefferson's ideas. When he disagreed, however, Madison generally passed over the idea in silence or with a vague or general response.

52. 19 June 1786, *Papers* 9:76–77.

*53. There is no suggestion in Madison's thought that all systems of property are just. It was widely accepted at the time that the feudal system was unwise and unjust. And Madison apparently favored the abolition of entail in Virginia. Brant, *James Madison*, 1:300–301.

*54. It was only in the 1790s, when faced with the perversion of republican government, that Madison addressed the problem of reducing indigence. His brief discussion of this issue in an essay on Parties is one of the most frequently quoted of Madison's writings. It is, however, (like the other favorite on a "property in one's rights") extremely uncharacteristic of his concerns in 1787. See "Parties," *National Gazette*, 23 January 1792, *Writings* 6:86 and my discussion in the section below on "Government in the divided society."

55. "Memorial and Remonstrance Against Religious Assessments," 1785, Meyers, pp. 9–10.

56. "Remarks on Mr. Jefferson's Draught of a Constitution," October 1788, Meyers, p. 59.

57. *The Federalist*, No. 43, p. 293.

58. The phrase is from *The Federalist* No. 10, p. 57.

59. To Jefferson, 4 February 1790, *Writings* 5:440.

60. *The Federalist*, No. 43.

*61. To James Monroe, 5 October 1786, *Writings* 2:273. The context of the quote was the possibility that Congress would allow the right to navigate the Mississippi to be given up to Spain.

62. P. 352.

*63. As we will see later, Madison was troubled by giving the judiciary the power to enforce limits against the will of the majority.

64. Farrand 1:135.

65. *The Federalist*, No. 10, p. 58.

66. Ibid.

67. Ibid., p. 59.

68. To William Barry, 4 August 1822, Meyers, p. 439.

69. The terms in quotation marks are from *The Federalist*, No. 10, p. 59.

70. Farrand 2:10.

71. To Robert Walsh, 27 November 1819, Meyers, p. 414.

72. *The Federalist*, No. 10, p. 59.
73. Farrand 1:135.
74. To George Washington, 9 December 1785, *Papers* 8:439.
75. Note to 7 August 1787 Speech, 1821, Meyers, pp. 503–4.
*76. Speech in the Virginia Ratifying Convention, June 1788, *Writings* 5: 225. There was no simple identity between debtors and the poor or between creditors and the rich. J. R. Pole makes the point that the rich were often in debt and that many people of very modest means lent out whatever extra capital they had. See J. R. Pole, *Foundations of American Independence: 1765–1815* (New York: Bobbs-Merrill, 1972), ch. 6. Nevertheless, Madison consistently treated the demands of debtors as an instance of the dangers posed by the propertyless.
77. To Thomas Jefferson, 24 October 1787, *Writings* 5:29.
78. *The Federalist*, No. 10, p. 60.
79. "Majority governments," 1833, Meyers, p. 526.
80. *The Federalist*, No. 10, p. 57.
81. *The Federalist*, No. 45, p. 309.
*82. "The aim of every political constitution is or ought to be first to obtain for rulers, men who possess most wisdom to discern, and most virtue to pursue the common good of the society" (*The Federalist*, No. 57, p. 384). See also *The Federalist*, No. 10, p. 62: "[T]o refine and enlarge the public views by passing them through the medium of a chosen body of citizens, whose wisdom may best discern the true interest of their country and whose patriotism and love of justice will be least likely to sacrifice it to temporary or partial considerations."
83. 21 February 1811, *Papers* 8:132–33 (my emphasis).
84. To Jefferson, 8 August 1791, *Writings* 6:59.
85. To Jefferson, 10 July 1791, ibid. 6:55.
86. To Thomas Jefferson, 8 August 1791, *Writings* 6:58.
*87. Madison thought the plan would make the least advantaged bear the greatest burden. The soldiers and farmers who had been forced to take government securities in payment, and forced to sell them at depreciated values out of need, would not be compensated, while the wealthy speculators would make an unjust gain.
88. "Parties," in the *National Gazette*, 23 January 1792, *Writings* 6:86 (second emphasis mine).
89. Ibid. (emphasis in original).
90. Farrand 2:123.
91. "Remarks on Mr. Jefferson's Draught of a Constitution," October 1788, Meyers, p. 58.
92. To Caleb Wallace, 23 August 1785, ibid., p. 49 (my emphasis).
93. Note on 7 August 1787 speech, 1821, ibid., p. 505.
94. Farrand 2: 204.
95. 23 August 1785, Meyers, p. 49.
96. Note during the convention for amending the constitution of Virginia, December, 1829, ibid., pp. 517–18.
*97. For example, that in theory every one has the right to all the property he can legally acquire, but in practice it is necessary for the harmony of soci-

ety and the material welfare of all for the property to be redistributed according to need.

98. To Caleb Wallace, August 23, 1785, Meyers p. 49.

99. Note during the convention for amending the constitution of Virginia, December, 1829, ibid., p. 517.

100. "Public Opinion," in the *National Gazette*, 19 December 1791, *Writings* 6:70.

101. Note during the convention for amending the constitution of Virginia, December, 1829, Meyers, p. 517.

102. To Jefferson, 3 October 1785, *Papers* 8:374.

103. "Remarks on Mr. Jefferson's Draught of a Constitution," 1788, Meyers, pp. 56–57.

104. To Washington, 16 April 1787, *Writings* 2:346.

105. *The Federalist*, No. 10, p. 59.

106. Ibid., p. 60.

107. *The Federalist*, No. 57, p. 384.

108. *The Federalist*, No. 10, p. 62.

109. Ibid., p. 60.

110. Ibid., p. 64.

111. *The Federalist*, No. 62, p. 419.

112. To William Barry, 4 August 1822, Meyers, p. 438.

113. To Caleb Wallace, 23 August 1785, ibid., p. 47.

114. To William Barry, 4 August 1822, ibid., p. 438.

*115. Madison did not explicitly make the argument that only property holders had a sufficient stake in society to be entrusted with a role in government. Only property holders could be trusted to feel a stake in the protection of property rights, which was essential for a stable society. But that is not the same argument.

116. Note to 7 August 1787 Speech, 1821, Meyers, p. 508.

117. To Thomas Jefferson, 9 December 1787, *Writings* 5:66.

118. To Thomas Jefferson, 19 February 1788, ibid., p. 101.

119. Farrand 2:124.

120. *The Federalist*, No. 54, p. 370.

121. Note to 7 August 1787 Speech, 1821, Meyers, p. 508.

122. *The Federalist*, No. 37.

123. Farrand 1:49.

124. Ibid., p. 50.

125. Ibid., 1:568; 2:553.

126. Farrand, 1:50.

127. Ibid.

128. Ibid., p. 136.

129. Ibid.

130. Speech in the Virginia Ratifying Convention, 11 June 1788, *Writings* 5:158.

131. *The Federalist*, No. 10, p. 63.

132. Ibid., p. 64.

133. Note on 7 August 1787 Speech, 1821, Meyers, p. 508.

134. Voters "would discriminate between real and ostensible property." Farrand 2:124.

135. Ibid., p. 123.

136. Farrand 1:585.

137. Note on 7 August 1787 Speech, 1821, Meyers, p. 508.

138. Farrand 2:203–4.

139. Ibid., p. 203.

*140. In his biography, *James Madison* (New York: Macmillan, 1971), Ralph Ketcham asserts that Madison voted against freehold suffrage (p. 221). But we know only that Virginia voted against it. Blair, Mason, and Randolph could have carried the state against Madison. Brant says that by early August, before the vote on suffrage, "Madison had seen the danger . . . of a persistent cleavage with him and Washington on one side, Mason, Randolph and Blair on the other" (Brant, *James Madison*, 3: 122). Brant also concludes that Madison voted with his state (neither he nor Ketcham cite any other source than the records of the debates). But he does not draw the same conclusions Ketcham does about Madison's position on property and the principle of consent. Since my interpretation of Madison's position is substantially different from Ketcham's, I think it is important to explain the basis for this difference. Ketcham says that Madison "bristled" at the suggestion of freehold suffrage. He says that "Morris raised the hoary fear that if the poor were enfranchised, they would sell their votes" (p. 220). I think it is clear that far from bristling, Madison raised some hoary fears of his own and took the opportunity to make an argument for freehold suffrage. Ketcham continues, "Madison added that though theoretically 'the freeholders of the country would be the safest depositories of Republican liberty,' he could not sanction departure from 'the fundamental principle that men can not be justly bound by laws in making of which they have no part.'" First, Madison does not say "theoretically," but "viewing the subject in its merits alone," and proceeds to show the very practical dangers of universal suffrage. He is not contrasting theory with practice, but what is best with what will be acceptable to the people. Second, the fundamental principle statement was offered only as an afterthought in a footnote. Indeed, it was this fundamental principle that Madison later referred to as a theory "which like most theories, . . . requires limitations and modifications" (Note during the convention to amend the Constitution of Virginia, December 1829, Meyers, pp. 517–18). Ketcham concludes, on the contrary, that Madison "consistently regarded the doctrine of consent as more vital than mere protection of property" (p. 221). I consider this misleading. Not only is Madison explicitly willing to "modify" the principle of consent in order to protect property, but for Madison there is no "mere" protection of property. The protection of property, as I have tried to show, is essential to stability, the public good, and the endurance of republican government.

141. Note to 7 August 1787 Speech, Farrand 2:204.

142. Farrand 1:421.

143. Ibid., p. 422.

144. Ibid., p. 152.

145. Ibid., p. 233.

146. Ibid., p. 423.

147. Ibid., p. 422.

148. Ibid.

149. Ibid., p. 423.

150. Note to August 7, 1787 speech, ibid., 2:204; "Remarks on Mr. Jefferson's Draught of a Constitution," October 1788, Meyers, pp. 58–59; Note on 7 August 1787 Speech, 1821, ibid: pp. 502–9.

151. Farrand 1:158.

*152. Ibid., p. 562. Madison's position was, of course, complicated by his concern to protect a particular form of property, slavery.

153. Farrand 2:35.

154. Ibid., p. 110.

155. Ibid. 1:108, King's notes.

*156. At this point the executive was to be elected by the legislature. Ibid., pp. 99–100.

*157. Election by the legislature was part of the Virginia Plan, but if Madison ever supported the idea, he soon changed his mind.

158. Ibid. 2:110–11.

159. Ibid., pp. 56–57.

160. Ibid.

161. Ibid., p. 65.

162. Ibid. 1:71.

163. 24 October 1787, Ibid. 3:132–33.

164. Ibid. 1:138.

165. Ibid.

166. Ibid. 2:74.

*167. Ibid. 2: 298. He later refined this scheme in his "Remarks on Mr. Jefferson's Draught of a Constitution" with the additional provision that "if either or both protest against a bill as violating the Constitution, let it moreover be suspended notwithstanding the overruling proportion of the Assembly, until there shall have been a subsequent election of the House of Delegates and a re-passage of the bill by 2/3 or 3/4 of both Houses, as the case may be. It should not be allowed the Judges or the Executive to pronounce a law thus enacted unconstitutional and invalid." Meyers, p. 65.

168. See the last sentence of the previous note.

169. Farrand 2:298.

*170. Ibid. 1:139.

*171. "He rather inclined to give it to the Senatorial branch, as numerous enough to be confided in—as not so numerous as to be governed by the motives of the other branch; and as being sufficiently stable and independent to follow their deliberate judgments" (ibid., p. 120).

172. Farrand 2:74.

173. Ibid. 1:97–98.

174. Ibid., p. 98.

175. Ibid. 2:77.

*176. Madison also wanted the Senate to serve as a national arbiter: he hoped that "being a firm, wise and impartial body it might not only give stability to the General Government in its operations on individuals, but hold an even balance among different States. The motion [to have senators' salaries come from the states] would make the Senate like [the Continental] Congress the mere advocates of state interests and views, instead of being the impartial umpires and Guardians of justice and general Good" (ibid., pp. 427–28).

177. To Washington, 16 April 1787, *Writings* 2:346–47.

178. Ibid., p. 346.

179. Ibid.

180. Ibid., p. 21.

181. Ibid. 2:440.

182. Ibid., p. 27.

*183. This was another reason the executive had to be strong, and why it had to be single rather than plural: the executive had to give the government sufficient energy to govern over an extended republic.

184. Farrand 2:27.

185. Ibid. 1:164–65.

186. Remarks on Mr. Jefferson's Draught of a Constitution, October, 1788, Meyers, pp. 65–66.

187. Farrand 2:27.

*188. The full dimensions of this undermining of republican principles will become clearer by comparison with Wilson and Morris.

189. Farrand 2:124.

190. Ibid.

Chapter 3

1. Farrand 1:533.

*2. "Political Inquiries," Gouverneur Morris Collection, Columbia University Libraries Special Collections, New York (hereafter cited as GMC).

This manuscript is not dated. However, a page identifying the contents mentions "Canal Reports," suggesting that the inquiries were written after 1800. Although this is well after the convention, I use these "Inquiries" as evidence of Morris's views at the time of the convention because I believe the "Inquiries" to be expositions of ideas which were basic to his political thought both before and after 1787. Until he left for France in December 1788, Morris found little time to write about his political positions or their theoretical foundation. There is therefore a good deal more material available from after 1787 than from before that date. I have used the later material when I believe it offers elaboration or clarification of ideas Morris expressed prior to or during the convention.

Morris's ideas did change. In his revolutionary fervor he held some of the "romantic ideas" that he was later pleased that Americans had been disabused of before 1787. At the time of the convention, he expressed a great deal of concern about protecting the people and a certain amount of faith in them, particularly in their ability to choose public officials. By 1800 he had shifted to an almost exclusive concern with controlling the people, and he expressed little faith in them. However, his basic ideas about the nature of political society, the division between the rich and the poor, the importance of protecting property, and the basic goals of government remained the same. It is therefore generally reasonable to use late statements to understand and document his most basic principles, but not his ideas about institutions.

3. Ibid.

4. *The Life and Correspondence of Gouverneur Morris*, ed. Jared Sparks, 3 vols. (Boston, 1832) 2: 291–92, March 7, 1793 (hereafter cited as Sparks).

5. "Political Inquiries," GMC.

6. Ibid.

*7. Ibid. Morris made a similar point ironically in a letter to Thomas Jefferson on a paper money scheme for France: "You will say, perhaps, that this measure is unjust, but to this I answer that in popular governments, strongly convulsed, it is a sufficient answer to all arguments, that the measure proposed is for the public good." February 13 February 1793, Sparks, 2:278.

8. "Politicial Inquiries," GMC.

9. Ibid.

10. Ibid.

11. Ibid.

12. Ibid.

13. Ibid.

14. Ibid. This, as I will show, is the right of property which Morris gave most emphasis to.

15. These articles are referred to in Sparks 1:519 as "Essays on the Finance,

Currency, and Inland Trade of the United States," in the *Pennsylvania Packet*, 1780. The *Pennsylvania Packet* was published in Philadelphia and is available at many university libraries, including The University of Pennsylvania and the University of Michigan.

16. Ibid., 4 March 1780 (my emphasis).

17. *Pennsylvania Packet*, 29 February 1780.

18. Ibid., 4 March 1780.

19. "To the legislators of New York State, A Public letter concerning land and property taxation," 1815(?), GMC.

20. "Observations on Finances: Foreign trade and loans," ca. 1780–81, GMC.

21. *Pennsylvania Packet*, 11 March 1780.

22. Farrand 2:344.

*23. *Pennsylvania Packet*, 15 April 1780. It is interesting to note that by 1816 Morris held the opposite view with respect to taxing land: he was opposed to taxing uncultivated land and urged that "if you will have a land tax, lay it on revenue" (To Moss Kent, 3 March 1816, Sparks 3:350). But I think that it can be argued that Morris's principle of encouraging productive use remained the same; he just saw the circumstances differently. In 1816 he saw vast tracts of western land that needed to be sold before they could be used productively: "While you offer millions of acres to sell, is it wise to threaten those who buy with an everlasting yoke of taxation?" (Ibid.) And in this case it was necessary to allow the wealthy to purchase vast tracts of land because only they had the resources to open it up for settlement. They would make a profit from their venture, but Morris did not fear their holding on to the land to monopolize it: "Some patriots (*sans terre* if not *sans culottes*) cry out, 'tax land speculators, and oblige them to sell. . . . ' As to selling, landholders gladly sell when they find purchasers" (To Rufus King, 26 January 1716, Sparks 3:343). Once again Morris urged that the actual effects of policy rather then moralistic sentiments should determine policy. "Take care, gentlemen patriots," he warned, "if taxing speculators should become fashionable, stocks may perchance be amerced. . . . Speculators, as such, are not respectable, but they are necessary; and in no case more than in the settlement of wild land. It has been tried to prevent accumulation of large tracts in few hands, by confining grants to small tracts, but experience has proved that until rich men purchase up these small tracts the country cannot be settled. It is in effect absurd to suppose that a person, with scarce a change of linen, can go two or three hundred miles to look out a farm, have it surveyed, travel back to the office for a patent, and, after spending time to get it, and borrowing money to pay for it, travel out a second time to the land, cut a road, and make a settlement" (ibid.).

24. *Pennsylvania Packet*, 23 March 1780.

25. Ibid.

26. Ibid., 11 April 1780.

27. Ibid, 29 February 1780.

28. Address to the Pennsylvania Assembly, 1785, GMC.

29. Notes on the form of a constitution for France, 1791, Sparks 3:481.

30. 2 January 1781, GMC.

31. *Pennsylvania Packet*, 23 March 1780.

32. To Robert Morris, 31 July 1790, Sparks 3:12.
33. To John Jay, 4 March 1789, ibid., 2: 65.
34. *Pennsylvania Packet*, 23 March 1780.
35. Ibid., 11 April 1780.
36. Address to the Pennsylvania Assembly, 1785, GMC.
37. To George Washington, 18 September 1790, Sparks 2:42.
38. To George Washington, 16 August 1790, ibid, 35.
*39. I think Morris would have found no difficulty in answering Patrick Henry's charge that: "You are not to inquire how your trade may be increased, nor how you are to become a great and powerful people, but how your liberties can be secured; for liberty ought to be the direct end of your government" (Quoted in Herbert Storing's introduction to *The Complete Anti-Federalist* [Chicago: The University of Chicago Press, 1981], p. 31). From Morris's perspective, not only did Henry's statement display a narrow understanding of the objects of government, but it showed a lack of understanding of the importance of America's strength and independence. To firmly secure the happiness of the people, including their liberty, America needed to be able to command the respect of other nations.
40. Address to the Pennsylvania Assembly, 1785, GMC.
41. To William Carmichael, 5 November 1792, Sparks 2:247.
42. To DeWitt Clinton, 19 February 1815, ibid. 3:336.
43. To William Carmichael, 5 November 1792, ibid. 2:246–47.
44. "Equality" comments on the rights of man, a reply to the Declaration of the Rights of Man by the London Corresponding Society, ca. 1796, GMC.
45. *Pennsylvania Packet*, 4 March 1780.
46. To the Legislators of New York State, 1818 (?), GMC.
47. To George Washington, 30 October 1787, Sparks 1:290.
48. To John Parish, 14 January 1803, ibid. 3:177.
49. Ibid. 1:23–25.
50. In 1806 he commented "Another disgusting trait of American manners is the insolent familiarity of the vulgar." But this was only to be found in "the lowest, worst educated, and truly contemptible part of the people . . . the great majority of that populace is made up of imported patriots, the off-cast and scum of other countries." *Notes on the United States* (Philadelphia: Office of the United States Gazette, 1806, 48 pages. Available at the University of Chicago and Harvard University Libraries, and at the New York Public Library.) p. 11.
*51. It is important to note that contempt for and hatred of the mob is not itself evidence of an antidemocratic or elitist attitude. Such renowned democrats as Tom Paine (see Eric Foner's *Tom Paine and Revolutionary America* [New York: Oxford University Press, 1976], ch. 3) and Thomas Jefferson shared Morris's feelings about the mob. In Jefferson's words, "The mobs of great cities add just so much to the support of pure government, as sores do to the strength of the human body." (*Notes on Virginia*, quoted in Stanley Katz, "Thomas Jefferson and the Right to Property in Revolutionary America," *Journal of Law and Economics* 19 (1976): 467–87). The question is what constituted a mob. In particular, it seems highly unlikely that Paine would have characterized the New York gathering of "a number of merchants and the

Body of Mechanics" (Carl Becker, *Political Parties*, quoted in Staughton Lynd, *Class Conflict, Slavery and the Constitution* [Indianapolis: Bobbs Merrill, 1967], p. 89) as a mob or felt inclined to speak of them as poor reptiles. What to some must have seemed the hopeful beginning of artisan participation in politics, looked to Morris like the stirrings of a mob.

52. Farrand 2:203.

53. To George Washington, 12 November 1788, Sparks 1:292.

*54. Morris reported the following conversation between a Frenchman and himself: every American "thinks himself equal to a king; and if, Sir, you should look down on him, would say, 'I am a man; are you anything more?' 'All this is very well; but there must be a difference of ranks, and I should say to one of those people, 'You, Sir, who are equal to a king, make me a pair of shoes.' 'Our citizens, Sir, have a manner of thinking peculiar to themselves. This shoemaker would reply; 'Sir, I am very glad of the opportunity to make you a pair of shoes. It is my duty to make shoes, and I love to do my duty. Does your King do his? But this manner of thinking and speaking is too masculine for the climate I am now in" (Diary, 1 March 1789, ibid., 1:296).

55. 10 January 1781, ibid., p. 267.

56. Farrand 1:512.

57. Ibid.

58. Ibid.

59. Ibid.

60. Ibid.

61. Ibid.

62. Ibid., p. 513.

63. Ibid.

64. Ibid., p. 514.

65. Ibid., p. 517.

66. Ibid., p. 514.

67. Ibid. 2:202.

68. To Robert Livingston, 10 October 1802, Sparks 3:172.

69. Farrand 2:202.

70. Ibid., 203.

71. To Robert Livingston, 10 October 1802, Sparks 3:172.

*72. Farrand 1:533. Morris's position on apportionment according to both wealth and numbers gave him a clear and consistent stand on one of the most delicate and contested issues of the structure of the House: the question of whether slaves should be counted for purposes of apportionment. Morris repeatedly argued that it was only by including wealth in the scheme of apportionment that slaves could be included on rational and consistent grounds: "If Negroes were to be viewed as inhabitants and the revision [of the principle of apportionment] was to proceed on the principle of numbers of inhabitants they ought to be added in their entire number, and not in the proportion of 3/5. If as property, the word wealth [in the phrase "apportionment on the basis of numbers and wealth] was right, and striking it out would produce the very inconsistency which it was meant to get rid of" (ibid., p. 604). Morris also took a strong moral stand against slavery.

73. Ibid., p. 583.

74. Ibid., p. 567.

75. Ibid. 2:52.

76. Ibid.

77. Ibid.

78. Ibid., p. 53.

79. Ibid.

80. Ibid., p. 29.

81. Ibid., p. 299.

82. Ibid., p. 300.

83. Ibid.

84. Ibid.

85. Ibid., p. 76.

86. Ibid.

*87. This would probably have been the case to some extent even in Morris's original proposal of confining the rich to the Senate. Since only those of "great personal property" were to be in the Senate, the men of "moderate fortune" would have been eligible for the House. It seems likely that Morris would have expected these men to be elected.

*88. In making these arguments Morris was in effect giving validity to the fears of some of the Anti-Federalists. In opposing the Constitution, they made just these points: In large districts, "a common man must ask a man of influence how he is to proceed, and for whom he must vote," and the only men with a chance of being elected are those "of conspicuous military, popular, civil or legal talents." (Patrick Henry, Melanchton Smith quoted in Storing, p. 44.) In their view, such a legislature would be undemocratic because the people themselves would never be elected to office.

89. *Observations on the American Revolution*, published by a resolution of Congress, 1779, in Pennsylvania Archives, Third Series, Vol. 7.

*90. Of course, this paradox was not peculiar to the people. It was in the nature of political liberty that it had to be restricted in order to be preserved.

91. "Political Inquiries," GMC.

92. Farrand 1:512.

93. Ibid., p. 583.

94. Ibid.

95. Ibid., p. 583.

96. Ibid. 2:222.

97. Ibid., p. 221.

98. *Notes on the United States*, p. 44.

99. *The Federalist* no. 51, p. 352.

100. To Robert Livingston, 10 October 1802, Sparks 3:172–73 (my emphasis).

101. Ibid., p. 172.

Chapter 4

1. Farrand 1:605.

*2. "As virtue is the business of all men, the first principles of it are written on their hearts, in characters so legible that no man can pretend ignorance of them." *The Works of James Wilson*, ed., Robert Green McCloskey, The John Harvard Library, 2 vols. (Cambridge, Mass.: Harvard University Press, Belknap Press, 1967), pp. 136–37. In 1790 and 1791 Wilson gave a series of lectures in which he presented the premises and principles of his theory of law and government. All quotes are taken from the law lectures unless otherwise noted. Pagination is consecutive through both volumes. Volume 2 begins on p. 441. (Cited hereafter as JHL *Works*.)

3. Ibid., pp. 133–34.

4. Ibid., p. 136.

5. Ibid., p. 213.

6. Ibid.

7. Ibid., p. 233.

8. Ibid., pp. 162–63.

9. Ibid., p. 163.

10. Ibid., p. 230.

11. Ibid.

12. Ibid., p. 129.

13. Ibid., p. 236.

14. Ibid., p. 592.

15. Ibid., p. 233.

16. Ibid., p. 232.

17. Ibid., p. 242.

18. Ibid. (my emphasis).

19. Ibid., p. 239.

20. Ibid., p. 235

21. Ibid.
22. Ibid., p. 240.
23. Ibid., p. 238.
24. Ibid., p. 272.
25. Ibid., Oration 1788, p. 777.
26. Ibid., pp. 777–79.
27. Ibid., p. 236 (quoting Cicero).
28. Ibid., p. 239.
29. Ibid., p. 159.
30. The state also has a duty of self-preservation; it has the duty to preserve "undissolved and unimpaired" the "association of individuals of which it is composed." Ibid., p. 154.
31. Ibid., Oration 1788, p. 777.
32. "Frugality and temperance: these simple but powerful virtues are the sole foundation, on which a good government can rest with security;" "the industrious alone constitute a nation's strength," Ibid.
33. Ibid., p. 778.
34. Ibid.
35. Ibid., p. 307.
36. Ibid., Oration 1788, p. 776.
37. JHL *Works*, p. 146.
*38. Ibid., p. 307. "In a serene mind, the sciences and virtues love to dwell. But can the mind of a man be serene, when the property, liberty, subsistence of himself, and of those for whom he feels more than he feels for himself, depend on a tyrant's nod." Ibid., Oration 1788, p. 776.
39. Ibid., p. 592.
40. The family "is the principle of the community; it is that seminary, on which the commonwealth, for its manners as well as its numbers, most ultimately depend. As its establishment is the source, so its happiness is the end, of every institution of government, which is wise and good." Ibid., p. 608. On noninterference, see ibid., pp. 602, 604.
41. Ibid., p. 592.
42. Wilson had planned to write a separate section on property rights. Unfortunately he completed only a fragment of that section. So we must piece his views together from his various remarks on the subject.
*43. Honor was also a personal preoccupation of Wilson's. He did not comment on the odd characterization of reputation as a right of man's "unrelated state."
*44. "Well may [character] be classed among those rights, the enjoyment of which it is the design of good government and laws to secure and enlarge: well does it deserve their encouragement and protection, for, in its turn, it assists their operations, and supplies their deficiencies" (ibid., p. 594). He also noted that "character may be considered as a species of property; but of all, the nearest, the dearest, and the most interesting" (ibid., p. 593). Here he quoted "the Poet of nature":

> Who steals my purse, steals trash.
> 'Twas mine; 'tis his; and has been slave to thousands;
> But he who filches from me my good name,
> Takes from that, which not enriches him,
> But makes me poor indeed.

45. Ibid., p. 719.
46. See text at note 48 below.
47. Ibid., Oration 1788, p. 775.
48. Wilson made this comment in the context of a discussion of foreign reprisals. Whether a nation establishes communal property or not, for the

purposes of reprisals, "the separate property of those citizens can neither be known nor discriminated by other states" (ibid., p. 275).

49. This is a tension that runs deep in the American tradition. I will return to it in subsequent chapters.

50. Ibid., p. 241.

51. Wilson articulated this classic view indirectly in his comments on the Saxons: "The freedom of a Saxon consisted in the three following particulars." The first was "in the ownership of what he had" (ibid., p. 401). And again, "We . . . have good reason for believing, that, among the Saxons, the smallness of their landed property was compensated by its independence. They were free men; and their law of property was, that they might challenge a power to do what they pleased with their own" (ibid., p. 717–18). This argument was one of many he planned to expand.

*52. Wilson offered a particularly interesting analysis of the classic description of this sphere: 'A man's house is his castle' was the expression, in times rude and boisterous, when the idea of security was founded only on its association with the idea of strength . . . In happier times, when the blessings of peace and law are expected and due—in such times, a man's house is entitled to an application more emphatic still—in such times a man's house is his sanctuary . . . Into this sanctuary, the law herself, unless upon the most urgent emergencies, presumes not to look or enter" (ibid., pp. 643–44). This certainly suggests the idea of private property as a realm of independence, a sphere of freedom from the interference of the state. In fact, however, it is not private property but domestic relations that define this protected sphere. It is not the ownership of the house, but "the favored spot in which a family reside[s]" which the law guards with "peculiar vigilance." The law recognizes a realm of private affairs in which it generally has no place. In Wilson's treatment, this realm coincides with, but is not constituted by, the ownership of a house.

53. Edmund C. Burnett, ed., *Letters of Members of the Continental Congress*, 8 vols. (Washington: Carnegie Institute of Washington, 1921–36), 14 February 1777 2:252. (Cited hereafter as Burnett).

*54. Wilson also hinted at two other rights of "property." In the context of other issues he suggested that there is a natural right of inheritance: "Corruption of blood is another principle, ruinous and unjust, by which the innocent are involved in the punishment of the guilty . . . A person attainted cannot inherit lands; . . . he cannot transmit them to any heir . . . This unnatural principle—I call it unnatural, because it dissolves, as far as human laws can dissolve, the closest and the dearest ties of nature . . . " (JHL *Works*, p. 633). He also hinted that there is some right to charity. "To bestow on another that reputation which he does not deserve, is equally profuse, and in many instances more unjust than to bestow on him that property, to which he is not, on the principles either of justice, *charity, or benevolence, entitled*" (ibid., p. 596, my emphasis).

*55. For example, referring to feudal land obligations, he says that land was "loaded with all the oppressive burthens of the feudal servitude—cruel, indeed; so far as the epithet cruel can be applied to matters merely of property" (ibid., p. 586). At another point, he suggested that what makes robbery a particularly serious crime is not that it is an attack on property, but that it involves an attack on the person: "Robbery is generally classed among the crimes against the right of private property; but somewhat improperly in my opinion. Robbery receives its deep dye from outrage committed on the person" (ibid., p. 642).

56. Ibid., p. 84.

57. Ibid.

58. "Each individual . . . engage[s] with all the others to join in one body, and to manage with their joint powers and wills, whatever should regard their common preservation, security, and happiness" (ibid., p. 171). The political association being thus formed, "some measures must be taken in order to regulate its operation . . . These measures involve the formation of government" (ibid., p. 172).

59. Ibid., p. 174.

60. Ibid., p. 77.

61. Ibid., p. 259. This idea, he says, is expressed in the preamble to the Constitution.

62. Ibid., pp. 78–79.

63. Jonathan Elliot, ed., *The Debates in the Several State Conventions on the Adoption of the Federal Constitution,* 5 vols., Burt Franklin Research and Source Work Series 109, reprinted from the edition of 1888 (New York: Burt Franklin Reprints, 1974) 2:432 (hereafter cited as Elliot).

64. Ibid., p. 433.

65. Ibid.

66. Ibid., p. 246.

67. Ibid., p. 577.

*68. As we shall see, Wilson did want and expect the federal judiciary to strike down unconstitutional laws passed by state legislatures. Indeed, he favored all kinds of restrictions on the states. But this general stance seems to reflect his view of the state legislatures not as the voice of the people, but as unreliable, bureaucratic subdivisions of government. I discuss this more fully in ch. 5. For his more complicated position on the role of the judiciary with respect to the Federal legislatures, see my discussion of the judiciary in Section V of this chapter.

69. Elliot 2:433.

70. JHL, *Works*, p. 573.

71. Ibid., p. 149.

72. Ibid., p. 72.

73. Ibid., p. 73.

74. Ibid., p. 406–7.

75. Ibid., p. 404.

76. Ibid.

77. Ibid., Speech 1789, p. 789.

78. Ibid., p. 73.

79. Ibid.

80. Ibid.

81. Ibid., p. 405.

82. Ibid.

83. Ibid., p. 313.

84. Ibid., Oration 1788, p. 778.

85. Ibid., p. 791.

86. Ibid., p. 406.

87. Ibid., p. 313.

88. Charles Page Smith, in *James Wilson: Founding Father 1742–1798* (Chapel Hill: The University of North Carolina Press for the Institute of Early American History and Culture, 1956), quotes from Wilson's notes of the "moot legislature" he held for his students on the question "should property be

represented in the legislature?" Smith also quotes one of the students paraphrasing Wilson: "Life, Character, The Rights of Conscience—these are the properties that ought to be represented" (p. 338).

*89. I shall take up these points in more detail in the last section of this chapter.

*90. When Wilson used the term "the people" he did not mean the people as opposed to the upper class; he did not set up such an opposition. Nevertheless, he intended the term to connote the common man, the ordinary citizen; he did not simply mean the American population. Thus the term is not literally exclusive, but when he used it he intended to emphasize that democratic government should be of, by, and for the common man.

91. Farrand 1:132.

92. Ibid., pp. 132, 359; 2:10–11.

93. Ibid. 1:605–6.

94. McMaster, p. 385.

95. Farrand 1:361.

96. Ibid., p. 133.

97. JHL, *Works*, p. 417.

98. McMaster p. 395.

99. Ibid., p. 394.

100. JHL, *Works*, p. 406, my emphasis.

101. McMaster, p. 230.

102. JHL, *Works*, pp. 75.

103. McMaster, p. 412.

104. JHL, *Works*, p. 406.

105. The plan was presented in the report of the committee of detail of which Wilson was a leading member (Farrand 2:201).

*106. "Having looked at the various provisions in the state constitutions we are well warranted, I think, in drawing this broad and general inference—that, in the United States, this right is extended to every free man, who, by his residence, has given evidence of his attachment to the country, who, by having property or by being in a situation to acquire property, possess a common interest with his fellow citizens; and who is not in such uncomfortable circumstances as to render him necessarily dependent, for his subsistence on the will of others" (JHL, *Works*, p. 411).

It is clear from this statement that Wilson did not consider the ownership of property the only basis for the independence necessary for an elector. The odd phrase "being in a situation to acquire property" presumably means not being so incapacitated as to preclude the possibility of acquiring property. Wilson probably also had incapacity in mind when he spoke of necessary dependence; his other statements make it seem unlikely that he meant all wage earners. In the same discussion, for example, he says that all free men should enjoy the rights of electors. I think Wilson considered his proposal to be the most liberal that would be acceptable both inside and out of the convention, and the only viable alternative to freehold suffrage.

Wilson also argued that the clause guaranteeing republican government to the states would prevent any radical restrictions on suffrage (McMaster, p. 344).

107. Farrand 2:203.

108. JHL, *Works*, p. 786.

109. Farrand 1:254.

110. JHL, *Works*, Speech 1789, p. 792.

111. Farrand I:544.

112. JHL *Works*, p. 320.

113. Ibid., p. 416.

114. McMaster, p. 231.

115. Farrand 1:80, 65.

116. Ibid., pp. 68, 69.

117. JHL, *Works*, p. 319.
118. Ibid.
119. Farrand 2:30.
120. JHL, *Works*, p. 293.
121. Farrand 1:98.
122. Ibid.
123. Ibid., p. 99.
124. Ibid., p. 100.
125. Ibid. 2:32.
126. Ibid. 1:103.

*127. I take his arguments in the law lectures to show a genuine change of opinion. If he had simply wanted to provide a defense for the Constitution as it stood, he need not have taken his argument as far as he did. Had he still genuinely considered an absolute veto to be preferable, I think he would have said so. He was comparing various constitutions and did not hesitate to say that he considered certain features of the Pennsylvania constitution preferable to those of the United States Constitution. In addition, his argument is entirely consistent with his political principles.

128. JHL *Works*, p. 323 (my emphasis).
129. Elliot 2:480–81.
130. JHL, *Works*, pp. 298–99.
131. Farrand 1:119.
132. Ibid., p. 253.
133. Ibid., p. 429.
134. JHL, *Works*, p. 297.

*135. Wilson also noted that because of their independence, the judges in Great Britain were able to defend private rights despite corruption in parliament (Farrand 1:253). There is, of course, a conventional rationale for Wilson's different stance toward factions in the legislature and the judiciary: even if it were legitimate for the legislature to make whatever general rules they liked regarding property, judges should be free from political pressure in applying those rules.

136. Ibid. 2:73.
137. McMaster, p. 357.
138. Ibid., p. 343.

*139. Ibid. The Constitution departed from Wilson's proposals for the judiciary only in that it provided for the concurrence of the Senate in the president's appointment of judges. Wilson accepted this as the next best alternative to a purely executive appointment.

140. Farrand 2:173, Wilson's notes of committee of detail.

*141. Wilson supported King's notion for a "prohibition on the States to interfere in private contracts" (ibid., p. 439). In his biography Smith also notes that authorship of the contracts clause (inserted in the committee of details' second draft) has been credited to Wilson. Smith's judgment is that "while there is no evidence definitely disproving Wilson's authorship, certainly no evidence exists to prove it" (pp. 247–48). I would note, in addition, that it seems entirely likely that Wilson would have inserted such a clause. Not only did he think that upholding contracts was extremely important economically, he saw the obligation of contract as part of the fundamental obligation to fulfill promises which makes society possible.

*142. Farrand 2:440. The contracts clause may therefore be seen as an extension to civil cases of the principle of prohibiting ex post facto laws. Dickenson pointed out to the convention that "on examining Blackstone's commentaries, he found that the terms 'ex post facto' related to criminal cases only; that they would not consequently restrain the States from retrospective laws in civil cases . . . " (ibid., 448–49).

143. Ibid., p. 439.
144. Ibid., p. 391.
145. Ibid.

*146. "He was not . . . for extinguishing these planets [state governments] as was supposed by Mr. Dickenson—neither did he on the other hand believe they would warm or enlighten the sun. Within their proper orbits they must still be suffered to act for subordinate purposes for which their existence is made essential by the great extent of our country" (ibid. 1:153). Wilson's attitude toward the state governments is an odd blind spot (discussed in ch. 5). Considering his emphasis on the connection between the people and their representatives, it is curious that he did not see that the state governments might have an advantage in this respect. But he consistently denied that there were any advantages to small election districts and even went so far as to deny that it mattered to the citizens at what level power was held: "A private citizen of a State is indifferent whether power be exercised by the General or State Legislatures, provided it be exercised most for his happiness" (ibid., p. 344). Wilson seems to have been certain that his plan for the national government would provide the intimate connection necessary between the people and their representatives, and that government on a smaller scale would only increase the disadvantages of popular government. He does not seem to have seen any advantage to local autonomous government in terms of the people's sense of responsibility for, and participation in, their government. In short, Wilson showed little understanding or appreciation of the advantages of federal government as such. He addressed his creative energies to the problems of a democratic national government, not to those of a federal republic.

*147. This role for juries is particularly appropriate in criminal cases where fact and law (e.g., intention) are interwoven and where the character and conduct of the witness and accused are essential: "Of all these, the jury are fittest to make the proper comparison and estimate . . . and their errors, except the venial ones on the side of mercy . . . are not without redress" (JHL, *Works*, p. 541).

148. Ibid., p. 74.
149. Ibid., p. 548.
150. Ibid.
151. McMaster, p. 283.

152. In January 1783, Wilson rejected the argument that depreciation was acceptable because it could be considered as a tax; in Wilson's view it was "the more oppressive as it fell unequally on the people." He also argued that if the paper currency were not backed by funds, "complete justice cannot be done to the creditors of the United States, or the restoration of credit be effected" Worthington Chauncey Ford, ed. *Journals of the Continental Congress 1774–1789* (Washington, 1904–1973), January 1783 25:867–68 (cited hereafter as Ford).

153. Burnett, 14 February 1777, 2:252.

154. Smith, *James Wilson*, p. 131.

155. For example, his argument against price controls is based on their inefficacy: "There are certain things, Sir, which [even] absolute power cannot do," and, if tried, will only bring the power "into contempt" (Ford 25:867–68).

*156. I think it is indicative of Wilson's primary concerns that the newspaper debate he apparently did enter was a controversy over the inadequacy of the Pennsylvania constitution of 1776. This was a debate over the proper implementation of the principles of democratic government. Smith, pp. 114–15.

157. McMaster, p. 228.

158. Ibid.

159. "On the Improvement and Settlement of Lands in the United States," 1790, Wilson Papers, Historical Society of Pennsylvania, Philadelphia. See also Smith, pp. 165–67.

160. Smith, p. 257.

*161. I shall take up the subject of the people's capacity for political responsibility shortly.

*162. He did make occasional references to differences between the states or regions, but the suggestion is that these are reconcilable. Smith cites a rare reference to the different economic interests, which also stresses their ultimate compatibility. "'If understanding is developed between agriculture, manufacturers and commerce, instead of mutual jealousy, mutual confidence between the three great interests will be the beautiful result,' he told his [law students]" (Smith, p. 337).

163. JHL, *Works*, p. 268.

164. Ibid., p. 789.

165. Ibid., p. 790.

166. Ibid., p. 577.

167. Ibid., p. 577–78.

168. Ibid., p. 578.

169. Wilson refers in particular to the redemption of depreciated public securities and promissory notes.

*170. Of course, the violation of property is implicit in the example of a highwayman. And Wilson, like Morris, is using the clear-cut injustice of taking property by force to bring out the injustice of refusing honest demands. But my point still stands: the purpose and thrust of Wilson's analogy is not to emphasize the iniquity of any violation of property rights, but to show the seriousness and "lowness" of a legislator using his power to perpetrate injustice.

171. Ibid., p. 578.

172. Ibid., p. 166. It is perhaps worth noting that this common analogy with the credit of a merchant had a force at the time which may not be immediately obvious today. James E. Ferguson, in his book on American public finance between 1776 and 1790, comments that "the most valuable asset of any merchant in an era when business was intensely personal—was a reputation for honesty and a scrupulous discharge of commitments." *The Power of the Purse: A History of American Public Finance, 1776–1790* (Chapel Hill: The University of North Carolina Press, 1961), p. 71.

173. JHL, *Works*, p. 578.

174. Ibid.

175. "Consideration on the Bank of North America," ibid., p. 833.

*176. Note that the whole society is responsible for the laws. The issue here as before is the relation of the society to its members, not the relation of the legislators as such to particular constituents, nor the relation of one group in society (e.g., the propertyless) to another.

177. Ibid.

178. Ibid., p. 834.
179. Ibid.
180. Ibid.

*181. Ibid., p. 835. It is important to see also that the obligation of contract which provides the analogy for the relation between the state and individuals derives its importance not from its relation to property rights (as Morris suggests), but from the fundamental social importance of promises and good faith.

*182. As I noted earlier, Wilson also thought the people's participation in the judicial process (through juries) had significant effects on their character and political responsibility. But he gave most attention to suffrage because it was the participation which provided the very basis of government.

*183. Although the Constitution as adopted provided for less direct participation than Wilson's preferred institutions would have, he clearly felt that the new system of government would foster participation in the essential ways.

184. JHL *Works*, Speech 1789, p. 788.

*185. "All the derivative movements of the government must spring from the original movement of the people at large. If to this they give sufficient force and a just direction, all the others will be governed by its controlling power" (ibid., Oration 1788, p. 778).

186. Ibid.

187. Ibid., Speech 1789, p. 788.

188. Farrand 1:387. On these grounds he considered it highly impolitic to render members of the national legislature ineligible to national offices (ibid. 2:288).

189. JHL, *Works*, p. 405.
190. Ibid.
191. Ibid., p. 315.
192. Ibid., A Charge to the Grand Jury, p. 823.
193. Ibid.
194. Ibid.
195. Ibid., Speech 1789, p. 788.

*196. The important qualification to this argument is that the development of this intelligence may take some time. It had obviously not been adequately developed in the confederation period.

Chapter 5

1. To Thomas Jefferson, 8 August 1791, *Writings* 6:58–59.

2. "If a faction consists of less than a majority, relief is supplied by the republican principle which enables the majority to defeat its sinister views by regular vote" (*The Federalist*, No.10, p. 60). He was confident that the result was that "where the power, as with us, is in the many, not in the few, the danger cannot be very great that the few will be thus favored" (To Thomas Jefferson, 17 October 1788, Meyers, p. 209).

3. See, for example, Farrand 1:132; 2:286, 632, 640.

4. Exceptions are the first clause, the slavery compromise, preventing congress from limiting importation until the 1808, and what may be described as basic terms of tax policy: no capitation or direct tax except in proportion to the census and no tax on articles exported from any state. The prohibition of

granting of titles of nobility may be seen as both a matter of republican policy and a protection against the abuse of power by legislators.

*5. The Senate was not, of course, what either Madison or Morris had wanted. It did not represent property as such, as Madison advocated, nor was it Morris's aristocratic preserve of the propertied. Most importantly, senators were to be appointed by the state legislatures with equal representation for each state. The reasons for this design (which both Madison and Morris opposed) had to do primarily with the relative power of large and small states and the role of state governments in the new federal system. While the need to check the folly and injustice of the people was not the concern lying behind the design, it was widely agreed that the smaller Senate would be a more elite body than the House and capable of providing the necessary check. *The Federalist*, No. 62, provided a half-hearted defense of the selection and representation of the Senate and then went on to a lengthy explanation of the advantages of a small body with a long term.

*6. Madison also saw the Bill of Rights in those terms: "Although it be generally true . . . that the danger of oppression lies in the interested majorities of the people rather than in usurped acts of the Government, yet there may be occasions on which the evil may spring from the latter source; and on such, a bill of rights will be a good ground for an appeal to the sense of the community." To Thomas Jefferson, 17 October 1788, Meyers, p. 207.

*7. Madison was happy to meet the demands of the Anti-Federalists by adding the Bill of Rights because he was confident that the basic structure was solid and would be unaffected by these additions: the amendments would make "the constitution better in the opinion of those who are opposed to it, without weakening its frame or abridging its usefulness, in the judgment of those who are attached to it." Quoted in Robert Allen Rutland, *The Birth of the Bill of Rights, 1776–1791* (London: Collier-Macmillan, 1969), p. 206. As the quotation in the previous note suggests, Madison came to see some salutary features in the Bill of Rights, but he did not see it as a basic part of the structure of the Constitution.

*8. For interesting arguments on these points see, for example, the essays by Stephen Holmes and the introduction by Jon Elster in *Constitutionalism and Democracy*, Jon Elster and Rune Slagstad, eds. (Cambridge: Cambridge University Press, 1988). One of the striking things about these arguments is that they seem inattentive to the question of whether the people are truly their own rulers. The problems of controlling government are different if one sees those in power as significantly distinct from those they are governing (the rulers vs. the ruled, as I noted in discussing Wilson). The arguments cited seem to me to presume that there is no such distinction one need be concerned with, that the project is simply facilitating the true and effective expression of the people's considered will. But, in fact, American democracy is complicated on that score. It is a democracy, but the people do not literally rule themselves. Even if one thinks that is desirable, the theory and justification of separation of powers must take that into account. See also Bruce Ackerman's thoughtful arguments in "The Storrs Lectures: Discovering the Constitution," *The Yale Law Journal* 93 (1984): 1013–1072.

9. Ibid.

*10. This special, all-encompassing usage is, however, strikingly absent in Wilson.

11. To Dewitt Clinton, 19 February 1815, Sparks 3:336.

*12. I say painful because the issue of slavery was at least an uncomfortable one even for those, such as Madison, who were prepared to provide protection for the institution. And, of course, as it is now trite to note, the Framers expressed their unease by avoiding the use of the word slavery in the Constitution.

*13. Freedom of conscience or religion is a useful contrast to highlight the ways in which property must be a matter of positive law, and thus a complex and problematic symbol of rights as limits to govenmental power. But Frank Michelman has reminded me that the image of freedom of conscience as a purely negative liberty, requiring only non-action by the state, is illusory—as all such images of legal rights are. There are real differences between property and freedom of conscience in the extent to which they can exist without state action in the form of legal definition and protection. Nevertheless, freedom of conscience does require protection, and the terms of that protection will be defined by the state. In addition, there are many governmental actions, from tax law to land use regulation, that will inevitably effect permissible practices of freedom of religion and thus will define its meaning.

It is interesting that Madison seems to have had some sense both of the distinction I draw between property and freedom of religion and of the requirement of affirmative protection that Michelman reminded me of: "Conscience is the most sacred of all property; other property depending in part on positive law, the exercise of that being a natural and unalienable right. To guard a man's house as his castle, to pay public and enforce private debts with the most exact faith, can give no title to invade a man's conscience, which is more sacred than his castle, or to withold from it that debt of protection for which the public faith is pledged by the very nature and original conditions of the social pact." "Property," *National Gazette*, 29 March 1792, Meyers, p. 244.

14. *The Federalist*, No. 10, p. 59.

15. To Edmund Randolph, 10 January 1788, *Writings* 5:79. The proposed Constitution was the particular subject he was referring to.

16. *The Federalist*, No. 58, p. 395.

18. Farrand 2:53.

17. *The Federalist*, No. 10.

19. "Unhappy state! Where talents excite Envy instead of inspiring Respect, where Defamation is the Reward of Merit, where Virtue meets the need of Folly, where it is dangerous to deserve and public Honors exclusively bestowed on worthless Minions become the true and indefeasible Titles to Contempt" ("Oration on Wealth," GMC, date and occasion unknown). The context for this outcry was an oration on the love of wealth, in which he argued that "there is an amiable Infirmity which may excuse" those who have turned their energies to material gain: "Shall we not rather pity than blame the Being who glows with a love of Fame but is cramped and shackled by the social institutions of a Country which leaves no Road to Distinction except through the Regions of Plutos?" (ibid).

*20. Morris spoke of the "high haughty and noble spirit which prizes Glory more than Wealth and holds Honor dearer than life." This spirit (in which national greatness was to be found) was "high—elevated above all low and vulgar considerations. It is haughty—Despising whatever is little and mean whether in Character Council or Conduct. It is generous—granting freely to the weak and to the indigent Protection and Support. It is noble—Dreading Shame and Dishonor as the greatest Evil esteeming Fame and Glory beyond all things human" (Oration, GMC, date and occasion unknown). One may allow for a certain amount of high-flown language here for oratorical purposes. But I think Morris took these noble (aristocratic) ideals very seriously. On the importance of the love of fame for the founders see the title essay in Douglass Adair's *Fame and the Founding Fathers*, ed. Trevor Colbern (New York: W.W. Norton and Co. for the Institute of Early American History and Culture, 1974). One of Adair's comments is particularly helpful in understanding the effect Morris expected this love of fame to have on the men of the upper class: "'The love of fame the ruling passion of the noblest minds' (Hamilton) thus transmuted the leaden desire for self-aggrandizement and personal reward into a golden concern for public service and the promotion of the commonwealth as the means to glory." I think this helps to explain the transformation Morris expected in men who would be senators for life—from men inclined to oppress the poor to wise and sagacious men who would guard against encroachments on all sides.

21. Farrand 1:512.

*22. Morris, as I noted earlier, thought of the elite as drawn from the well-off propertied class. But it is important to remember that Morris, like Madison and his other fellow Federalists, did not see classes as having a fixed composition. They wanted and expected men to move from one class to another according to their ability. It was not a man's class origins, but his class membership that was relevant to his role in government.

*23. To point out the limitations of an exclusively instrumental conception of political participation is not, of course, to say that the ends or purposes of that participation are irrelevant to its value or importance. Jon Elster makes the point that participation can only have the sorts of "intrinsic" values claimed for it if it is in fact a means to significant ends in *Sour Grapes: Studies in the Subversion of Rationality* (Cambridge: Cambridge University Press, 1983), ch. 2, s. 9. But the value of genuine self-governance presupposes the significance of the decisions at stake, namely decisions that affect one's individual and collective life.

24. On the issue of the nobility of republican government see Thomas L. Pangle, "The Federalist Papers' Vision of Civic Health and the Tradition Out of Which that Vision Emerges," *Western Political Quarterly* 39 (1986): 577–602.

25. Farrand 2:124.

*26. Discussing the Madisonian solution ("Democracy and the Federalist," *American Political Science Review*, 53(March 1959): 52–68) Martin Diamond says that "the mass will fragment into relatively small groups, seeking small immediate advantages for their narrow and particular interests." He does not give examples of these interests but he goes on to say that ". . . the lowly . . . must feel . . . sanguine about the prospects of achieving limited and immediate benefits." And "the gains must be real . . ." But from Madison's perspective these gains must be so small that they would never give even a hope of acquiring property (Note on 7 August 1787 Speech 1821, Meyers, p. 505). Could such gains keep the many divided? Diamond concludes that "Madison's solution to his problem worked astonishingly well. The danger he wished to avert has been avoided and largely for the reasons he gave." But I suggest that at least as important as the reasons he gave is the fact that the radically unequal division of property between the few who had all and the many who had none did not come to pass.

*27. "[I]n the present state of things the very best institutions have their imperfections . . . the imperfection incident to governments which are free . . . [is that] the people, at once subjects and sovereigns, are too often tempted to alleviate or to alter the restraints they have imposed on themselves." (JHL *Works*, p. 432). Wilson surely knew that, at least in 1787, laws affecting property were particularly susceptible to this temptation to legislate. It is not that Wilson was indifferent to the value of stability. He supported the stability-enhancing institutions of a bicameral legislature and an executive-judicial veto. But he did not accord stability a priority that made him focus on the people as a threat.

28. Richard Henry Lee, 28 April 1788, quoted in Storing 1:17.

29. Brutus, 18 October 1787, ibid. 2:371.

30. The Federal Farmer, 9 October 1787, ibid. 2:230.

31. Storing 1:18.

32. The Federal Farmer, 4 January 1788, ibid. 2:276.

33. *The Federalist*, No. 51.

34. Melancton Smith, 21 June 1788, Storing 6:160.

35. Ibid. 1:20.

36. The Federal Farmer, 13 October 1787, ibid. 2:251.

*37. Conditioned, I suspect, by our Federalist heritage, most of us think of participation in terms of electoral behaviour. But the Anti-Federalists had a broader view. Consider, for example, Storing's discussion of the Anti-Federalist demand for guarantees of jury trials: one "means by which the people are let into the knowledge of public affairs." He concludes that the "question was not fundamentally whether the lack of adequate provision for jury trial would weaken a traditional bulwark of individual rights . . . but whether it would fatally weaken the role of the people in the administration of government" (ibid. 1:19; Storing cites The Federal Farmer at 2:319–20). Storing does not, however, agree more generally with my interpretation of the Anti-Federalists' non-instrumental approach to political participation.

38. Storing points to another dimension of this issue in the Anti-Federalists' belief that government should foster religion and morals, "thereby making government less necessary by rendering 'the people more capable of being a law to themselves' " (ibid. 1:23; quoting Speech of Charles Turner at 4:221).

39. The Federalists, by contrast, believed that it was naive to think that Americans could be "relied upon to govern themselves voluntarily" (ibid. 1:71).

*40. Brutus, for example, argued that the relationship between citizens and their representatives necessary for a free republic is impossible on the scale proposed by the new Constitution. The representatives cannot adequately know their constituents: "in a large extended country, it is impossible to have a representation, possessing the sentiments, and of integrity to declare the minds of the people" and "if they do not know, or are not disposed to speak the sentiments of the people, the people do not govern, but the sovereignty is in the few" (ibid. 2: 369). Similarly, the people cannot know their representatives (ibid., pp. 370–71) and will neither have confidence in them, nor be able to effectively control them. See also the Federal Farmer who concluded that his detailed inquiry into the failings of the proposed constitutionalism proved that "we cannot form one general government on equal and just principles" (ibid., p. 236).

41. Storing persuasively describes the Federalist argument that "the means must be proportional to the end" and that "the end in the case of the general government is not capable of being limited in advance" (1:29).

42. This position is characteristic of the Anti-Federalist view: "To hold open to [the common people] the offices of senators, judges, and offices to fill which an expensive education is required, cannot answer any valuable purposes for them; they are not in a situation to be brought forward and to fill those offices; these, and most other offices of any considerable importance, will be occupied by the few. The few, the well born, etc. as Mr. Adams calls them . . . are generally disposed . . . to favour those of their own description" (The Federal Farmer, 12 October 1787, ibid. 2:249).

43. The Federal Farmer, 10 October 1787, ibid. p. 243.

44. See, e.g., Speech of Patrick Henry to the Virginia Ratifying Convention expressing fear of tyranny of ruling minority, 5 June 1788, ibid. 5:211.

45. The Federal Farmer, 4 January 1788, ibid. 2:276–77.

*46. Hamilton is the clearest exponent of this idea (see *The Federalist*, Nos. 17, 27), but a somewhat less stark version is present in Madison. He repeatedly insisted that what the people want is security and justice, and that they will ultimately not tolerate any government that fails to provide these values. What the people care most about is, in the end, not the process or structure of government, but its outcomes. And in particular, the outcomes that affect their security and prosperity. (Remember that the "justice" Madison invoked and never defined seems to be very largely ensuring to each his own, the secure preservation of rights—property in particular—whose proper content is not in question. See also Storing's discussion in his *What The Anti-Federalists Were For* (Chicago: The University of Chicago Press, 1981), pp. 41–42 and Forrest MacDonald, *Alexander Hamilton* (New York: W.W. Norton, 1982).

47. The Federalists did not in fact expect literal expropriation to be the means by which the poor would threaten the property of the rich. The threats they had encountered were of a different sort: the less obvious and therefore more dangerous incursions of depreciating paper currency and debtor relief. These were the threats the Constitution was designed to counter.

48. Storing 1:45–46.

*49. The Federalists did differ in their expectations about inequality. Noah Webster, for example, argued that "the inequalities introduced by commerce, are too fluctuating to endanger government. An equality of property, with a necessity of alienation, constantly operating to destroy combinations of powerful families, is the *very soul of a republic*" (ibid., p.46, quoting *Pamphlets on* *the Constitution of the United States, Published During Its Discussion by the People 1787–1788*, ed. Paul Leicester Ford [Brooklyn, N.Y.: Historical Printing Club, 1888], p. 59). Webster was characteristic of the Federalists in his emphasis on the fluidity of property: there would always be the rich and the poor, but there would be great mobility between the two classes. It is nevertheless fair to say that an expectation of a division between the rich and the poor was central to the Federalist position.

50. Remember that Madison doubted that harmony and consensus could ever be bought except at the expense of freedom; as long as there was freedom, there would be perceived differences of interest. The "various and unequal distribution of property" was the most enduring source of conflict, but not the only one. See *The Federalist*, No 10., p. 59.

*51. In *The Anti-federalists: Critics of the Constitution, 1781–1788* (Chicago: Quadrangle Books, 1964), Jackson Turner Main makes the point that there was some difference between the Anti-Federalists as a whole and their best-known leaders. Compared to the Federalists, most of the Anti-Federalists were not involved in commerce and were sympathetic to demands for paper money. But some of their leaders resembled the Federalists in these respects. One is left with the strong sense after reading Main that those who had actually had substantial experience with commerce favored the new Constitution, while those who had not, opposed it. There are, of course, different ways of thinking about this split (in addition to the question of whose interests were being served). It does suggest that those who knew something about commerce thought the Federalists were right about what commercial prosperity required. But that suggestion can easily be restated: the Federalists shared with the men of commerce their presuppositions about the requirements of the economy in a republic.

52. Of course this freezing was greatly facilitated by the rise of judicial review.

53. *The Federalist*, No. 51, pp.352–53.

54. Ibid., p. 353.

55. Fifth Amendment.

56. This claim for Madison's authorship is inferential. See Edward Dumbauld, *The Bill of Rights and What it Means Today* (Westport, Conn.: Greenwood Press, 1979). Dumbauld provides a table for sources of the provisions of the Bill of Rights showing that none of the states proposed a just compensation clause (pp. 160–65). Madison drafted the amendments proposed to Congress and Dumbauld describes this draft as "a distillate of the proposals emanating from the state conventions" (p. 36). But he then notes that "of the 32 items offered by Madison, two were apparently original" (p. 36, n. 12). Of those, only the just compensation clause was ultimately included in the Bill of Rights. Dumbauld suggests then that "Madison himself may have been responsible for the requirement of just compensation in connection with the exercise of eminent domain" (p. 53).

57. I discuss the issue of why the Anti-Federalists focussed less on property in "Democracy, Justice, and the Multiplicity of Voices: Alternatives to the Federalist Vision," Northwestern University Law Review 84 (1990): 231–48.

58. J. G. A. Pocock has been the most important exponent of "classical republicanism." See *Politics, Language and Time: Essays on Political Thought and History* (New York: Atheneum, 1973) and *The Machiavellian Movement: Florentine Political Thought and the Atlantic Republican Tradition* (Princeton, N.J.: Princeton University Press, 1975). On the debate generally, see (in addition to the authors cited below) Stanley Katz, "The Origins of Constitutional Thought," In *Perspectives in American History*, III (Cambridge, Mass: Charles Warren Center for Studies in American History, 1969), pp. 474–90; John P. Diggins, *The Lost Soul of American Politics: Virtue, Self-Interest and the Foundations of Liberalism* (Chicago: University of Chicago Press, 1984). I am engaging this debate in its current terms, and not considering the aptness of the term "republican" for one strain of American political thought. For a description of that problem and the tradition of "classical republicanism" see Thomas L. Pangle, *The Spirit of Modern Republicanism: The Moral Vision of the American Founders and the Philosophy of Locke* (Chicago: University of Chicago Press, 1988).

59. Lance Banning, "Jeffersonian Ideology," *William and Mary Quarterly*, 3d Ser., 43 (January 1986):3–19, pp. 11–12.

60. Ibid., p. 12.

*61. Joyce Appleby also disagrees with Banning with respect to the Jeffersonians: "Jefferson made sharp analytical distinctions in assessing how lines were drawn in 1800," and his language is that of a man "intent on making hard-edged divisions between himself and his opponents." "Republicanism in Old and New Contexts," *William and Mary Quarterly*, 3d Ser., 43 (January 1986): 20–34, p. 24. Of course, as Appleby suggests, not all the followers of Jefferson (or Madison) may have seen things so clearly. Her point is that the essence of what Jeffersonian republicanism had to offer rested on a deliberate differentiation from and improvement upon competing alternatives (associated with traditional political thought). My point about the Madisonian Federalists is the same (although, of course, the content of the two visions was different).

62. See, for example, the use of the republicanism debate in Hendrick Hartog's "The Constitution of Aspiration and 'The Rights that Belong to Us All' ": "A more republican vision of constitutional aspirations would have made participation in public life (civic virtue) the primary good to be secured by rights." *Journal of American History* 74 (December 1987): 1013–1034, p. 1018, n. 12.

63. Banning, "Jeffersonian Ideology," p. 18.

64. See Robert E. Shalhope, "Toward a Republican Synthesis: The Emergence of an Understanding of Republicanism in American Historiography" *William and Mary Quarterly*, 3d Ser., 29 (1972): 49–80.

65. Joyce Appleby, "The American Heritage: The Heirs and the Disinherited," *Journal of American History*, 74 (Dec., 1987): 798–813, at p. 801.

66. Ibid., p. 801.

67. Joyce Appleby, *Capitalism and a New Social Order: The Republican Vision of the 1790s*, (New York: New York University Press, 1984), p. 37.

68. Appleby, "Heirs and the Disinherited," p. 802.

69. Ibid., p. 799.

70. Isaac Kramnick, "Republican Revisionism Revisited," *American Historical Review* 87 (1982): 629–64, at p. 662.

71. Appleby, "Heirs and the Disinherited," p. 803.

72. "Interests and Disinterestedness in the Making of the Constitution" in *Beyond Confederation: Origins of the Constitution and American National Identity*, Richard Beeman, Stephen Botein, and Edward C. Carter II, eds. (Chapel Hill: University of North Carolina Press, 1987), p. 93.

73. Contrary to Robert Dahl's interpretation of Madisonian democracy as interest group pluralism in *A Preface to Democratic Theory* (Chicago: The University of Chicago Press, 1956).

74. *The Federalist*, No. 57, p. 384.

75. Beeman, et al, "Interests and Disinterestedness," p. 92, quoting *The Federalist*, No. 10.

76. Remember that traditional deference had been eroding. See Appleby, "The Heirs and the Disinherited," p. 799.

77. See Appleby, *Capitalism and a New Social Order*.

78. For Lance Banning's differing perspective on the Jeffersonians see "Jeffersonian Ideology."

79. Appleby, "Republicanism in Old and New Contexts," p. 32.

80. Ibid.

81. Ibid., p. 33.

82. Ibid., p. 25.

83. Ibid., p. 33.

84. The commitment to this order was shared despite differences among the Federalists in how clearly they saw this market economy (Morris had a particularly clear vision) and just what they thought it entailed (the role of agriculture vs industrialization, for example). For a particularly good discussion of Madison's ambivalent vision see Drew McCoy's *The Elusive Republic: Political Economy in Jeffersonian America* (Chapel Hill: University of North Carolina Press, 1980).

85. Appleby, "Republicanism in Old and New Contexts," p. 33.

*86. Madison's mixed language—sometimes emphasizing competing interests as the essence of politics but ultimately invoking a substantive concept of the public good—reflects an uneasy shift in the conception of the public good. J. E. Crowley provides an extremely interesting discussion of this shift in *This Sheba Self* (Baltimore: Johns Hopkins University Press, 1974). For example, he says, "The public interest consisted of the harmonious organization of the interests of autonomous, rational individuals. This harmony constituted the colonists' sense of community, and its vagueness made them all the more concerned about its preservation. The public interest could not be simply the sum of individual interests because it would then have an irrational basis. It was assumed that each society had a proper order, but in fact people knew only about the sources of that order—virtue and reason—and were confused about the nature of the order itself. Thus public good was often negatively defined as the absence of selfishness. It is impossible to give legitimacy to gain which came at the expense of others, because by definition such action violated the harmony of interests of the members of society. Self-respect required conviction of harmony between private pursuits and public interests" (p. 155).

*87. Madison's focus on stability and security rather than freedom may reflect some ambivalence about the volatility and ruthlessness of the modern market. But it is clear that he expected a dynamic economy with a great deal of individual mobility. I think it is likely that he, like modern exponents of the market such as Friedrich Hayek, treat security of expectations as an essential ingredient of the market and its freedom.

88. See Martin Diamond, "The Separation of Powers and the Mixed Regime," *Publius* 8 (1978): 33–43.

89. Appleby, "Republicanism in Old and New Contexts," p. 33.

*90. Wilson, of course, was an exception. He was interested in the character of the people and thought about it in the institutional terms of his fellow Federalists. He provides a different amalgam of ideas, and thus does not fit the contrast Shalhope makes between Madison, the rationalist, who wanted to change the structure of society, and John Taylor of Caroline, the evangelical, who wanted a rebirth of the spirit of the people within the existing structure (Shalhope, "Toward a Republican Synthesis," p.68). Like Madison, Wilson was interested in changing structure, but he was interested in its effect on character.

91. The campaign finance case, *Buckley v. Valeo*, 424 U.S. 1 (1976), is an example of how Madisonian notions of the entitlements of property and their alleged connection to liberty continue to interfere with our collective capacity to respond to the problems of the interpentration of economic and political power. (In chapter 6, I pursue the question of how concerns with problems such as economic power and participation have become highly visible, yet never integrated into the core of American political thought or public policy.)

*92. In the period 1800–1815, the term Federalist took on a slightly different meaning. The Federalist party, which lost power in the election of 1800, was not identical in personnel or position with the Federalists of 1787, although the connections were close. See Richard E. Ellis, *The Jeffersonian Crisis: Courts and Politics in the Young Republic* (New York: Oxford University Press, 1971), p. 342, n. 20. Nor was the party unified. Like the Republicans of the same era, the Federalists were split into moderate and extreme wings. I use the term Federalist in the specific sense of the Federalist party only when I pose it in direct contrast to the Republican party. This is particularly important to bear in mind when I speak of the Court's protecting the fundamentals of the Federalist vision. I do not mean that the Court was acting in the service of narrow party positions.

93. Letter to Thomas Jefferson, 17 October, 1788, Meyers, pp. 205–8.

*94. There remains the question of why the Federalists did not include a Bill of Rights in the Constitution in the first place. Most state constitutions had one. Wilson provided a not very convincing answer: the federal government, unlike those of the states, was one of designated powers only. It thus made no sense to list limits to a government which had not been granted the power to violate those limits. The Anti-Federalists were not persuaded, and it is hard to believe that this rather theoretical argument actually captures the reason for the omission. (Those sophisticated enough to see how the states had violated rights without formal violation of their constitutions could surely imagine the possibilities of abuse of the powers granted to the new government.) Madison provided substantive objections ranging from the fear that "a positive declaration of some of the most essential rights could not be obtained in the requisite latitude," to the more basic issue of inefficiency (ibid.). The most important reason is that the governmental structure that seemed dangerous and misguided to the Anti-Federalists, was for the Federalists the very means of securing rights. There remain two further questions. First, why did the Federalists include any prohibitions if the structure was the solution? One answer is that they included protections for those rights about which there was a clear consensus: jury trials for criminal cases, religious tests for any federal office or public trust, no ex post facto laws or bills of attainder. There was less uniformity on other protections whose omission the Anti-Federalists pointed to. Not all states had freedom of the press clauses, and the provisions for both civil juries and religious freedom varied from state to state. But the consensus argument does not seem wholly satisfactory because a consensus in favor of the Bill of Rights seemed to form virtually overnight. The second question we are left with is that raised by Robert Allen Rutland in *The Birth of the Bill of Rights: 1776–1791* (London: Collier-Macmillan Ltd., 1969). He suggests that the purpose of the 1787 convention was not the protection of civil rights: "The states alone protected civil rights; the rights of property formed another category, a category with many zealous guardians" (pp. 111–12). Did the Framers omit a Bill of Rights because they cared about protecting property, but not about civil rights? Rutland's distinction is somewhat misleading because property assumed its importance in part as an instance of the vulnerability of civil rights. But if we use Madison's parallel categories, we can restate the question: were the Federalists far more concerned about the rights of property than the rights of persons? Madison, of course, wanted to say no, while pointing out that in a republic the rights of property were at far greater risk than the rights of persons. In the end, as we have seen, the Federalists focused on protecting the rights particularly at risk, without seeing that their solutions created new dangers. The Constitution of 1787 was weighted toward the protection of property rather than other civil rights, and the Bill of Rights helped correct that imbalance. But it was a correction that left the Federalist structure intact.

*95. David Currie notes that the Court's holding that federal courts had the power to determine the constitutionality of *state* laws "passed almost unnoticed." Ware v. Holton 3 U.S. (3 Dall.) 199 (1796), *The Constitution in the Supreme Court: The First Hundred Years, 1789–1888*, (Chicago: University of Chicago Press, 1985), p.39. In the period I am discussing, the Court not only exercised the power of judicial review of both state and federal laws, but formulated the categories that justified that exercise. By the end of John Marshall's reign as chief justice the Court, the power of judicial review, and the sustaining categories of law and politics had become essential elements of the American constitutional system.

96. George Lee Haskins and Herbert A. Johnson, *The Oliver Wendell Holmes Devise, History of the Supreme Court of the United States, Volume II, Foundations of Power: John Marshall, 1801–15* (New York: Macmillan Publishing Co., Inc., 1981), p. 206. The book is divided into two distinct parts, the first written by Haskins, the second by Johnson. Hereafter I will refer to the book by the relevant author's name.

97. William Nelson, "The Eighteenth Century Background of John Marshall's Constitutional Jurisprudence," *Michigan Law Review* 76 (1978): 893–960 p. 931, quoting Daggett, *Sunbeams May Be Extracted From Cucumbers, But the Process is Tedious* (1799) (emphasis in the original); reprinted in *The Rising Glory of America: 1760–1820,* Gordon Wood, ed. (New York: G. Braziller, 1971), p. 184.

98. Johnson, p. 396. The quote continues, "Neither the limitations, nor the extent, of judicial power had been tested during the Federalist hegemony. . . . As it was staffed on March 4, 1801, the Supreme Court loomed as the major stumbling block to the entire Republican legislative program."

99. "The judiciary is now almost the only security left us—and it is at all times the most important branch of the federal government." Samuel Sewall to Theodore Sedgwick, 7 December 1800, Sedgwick I Papers, Massachusetts Historical Society.

100. Haskins, p. 222.

101. Nelson, "The Eighteenth Century Background of John Marshall's Constitutional Jurisprudence."

102. Haskins, pp. 215–34; Johnson, p. 397.

103. Johnson, pp. 415–32.

104. Johnson, pp. 650–51.

105. 5 U.S. (1 Cranch) 137 (1803), *American Constitutional Interpretation* by Walter F. Murphy, James E. Fleming, and William F. Harris, eds. (Mineola, N.Y.: The Foundation Press, 1986), p. 213–14, 216.

106. 5 U.S. (1 Cranch) 299 (1803).

107. For a description of the issues see David Currie, *The Constitution in the Supreme Court,* pp. 74–77.

108. *M'Ilvaine v. Coxe's Lessee* involved the right of a self-proclaimed British subject to inherit land in his native New Jersey. 8 U.S. (4 Cranch) 209 (1808).

109. David Currie notes that the absence of jurisdiction was not so clear. The Judiciary Act of 1789 gave the circuit courts "cognizance of all crimes and offenses cognizable under the authority of the United States." Ch. 20, ss 11,1 Stat.73,79 (repealed 1911). Justice Story argued that this provision "both gave the courts jurisdiction over nonstatutory crimes and empowered them to define those crimes according to the common law. United States v. Coolidge, 25 F. Cas. 619 (No. 14,857) (C.C.D. Mass. 1813). *Hudson,* not mentioning section 11, had appeared to deny both jurisdiction and lawmaking authority. See 11 U.S. (7 Cranch) at 34 ("The legislative authority of the Union must First make an act a crime, affix a punishment to it, and declare the court that shall have jurisdiction of the offence.") *The Constitution in the Supreme Court,* p. 94 n. 30.

110. Haskins claims (p.355) that both the Federalists and the Republicans (although not the bar) disapproved of federal common law crime. But see Stephen Presser, "A Tale of Two Judges: Richard Peters, Samuel Chase, and the Broken Promise of Federalist Jurisprudence," *Northwestern Law Review* 73 (1978): 26–111, pp. 46–48. He suggests that, at least in earlier years, the Federalists had been in favor of federal jurisdiction over common law crimes.

111. Nelson, "Eighteenth Century Background," p. 932, quoting *An Autobiographical Sketch by John Marshall,* J. Stokes Adams ed. (Ann Arbor: University of Michigan Press, 1937), pp. 9–10.

*112. William Nelson by contrast believes that judicial review at the end of the eighteenth century was believed "only to give the people—a single, cohesive, and indivisible body politic—protection against faithless legislators who betrayed the trust in them, and not to give judges authority to make law by resolving disputes between interest groups into which the people and their legislative representatives were divided." ("Changing Conceptions of Judicial Review: The Evolution of Constitutional Theory in the States, 1790–1860," *University of Pennsylvania Law Review* 120 (1972): 1166–85, p. 1172. I think this interpretation is inconsistent with the pervasive fears of majority oppression, based on real and anticipated divisions in society. This concern is expressed throughout the Constitutional Convention of 1787, in judicial opinions (see my discussion of Fletcher v. Peck below), and is clearly stated by Hamilton in the *Federalist Papers*, No. 78: "This independence of the judges is equally requisite to guard the Constitution and the rights of individuals from the effects of those ill humors which . . . sometimes disseminate among the people themselves . . . . "

113. 10 U.S. (6 Cranch) 87 (1810).

114. Ibid., 137–38.

115. Ibid., 143 (Johnson, J., concurring).

116. Haskins and Johnson, Part II.

117. Ibid., pp. 596–97 (emphasis in original).

118. 3 U.S. (Dall.) 386 (1798) edited in *American Constitutional Interpretation*, p. 87.

119. Ibid., p. 89 (emphasis in original).

*120. In fact, I think the view that law and politics are radically distinct is a mischaracterization of all law, including the common law. (See my discussion of changes in property law in chapter 6.) The fact that many people of good faith still hold to this vision of the strict apolitical quality of the common law gives me some pause about asserting Marshall's disengenuousness. But the pause is slight. In the context of all his actions and arguments at the time, I think he may well have believed that his interpretation of the Constitution was the best, perhaps in a sense the only acceptable one, but not that it had the straightforward, uncontested clarity he implied.

121. We have largely accepted the judiciary as the definitive interpretor of the Constitution and relied ever since Marshall on his law-politics distinction. As we shall see in chapter 6, we still face the problem of how to understand judicial review without that distinction.

*122. Of course, some of those judgments are inherent in the common law and thus have always been and remained with the courts.

123. Richard Buel, Jr., *Securing the Revolution: Ideology in American Politics, 1789–1815* (Ithaca: Cornell University Press, 1972), p. 98.

124. Ibid., pp. 97–105.

125. John Murrin, review of *Politics and the Constitution in the History of the United States, Vol. III: The Political Background of the Federal Convention*, by William Winslow Crosskey and William Jeffrey, Jr., in *New York University Law Review* 58 (1983): 1254–1271, p. 1265.

126. Murrin offers as examples that the Federal government did not use

its excise tax power and abdicated the explicit mandate to control monetary policy until after the Civil War. Ibid., pp. 1268–69.

127. See *Annals of Congress*, 11 February, 1790, pp. 15–19 and Brant, *Madison*, 3:292–300.

128. See Clinton Rossiter, *1787, The Grand Convention* (New York: The New American Library, 1968), ch. 9, on Madison's role in drafting the Virginia Plan and his success in establishing it as an agenda.

Chapter 6

1. Farrand 1:422.

2. Remember that Madison argued that even with an optimal distribution of land, not only would the majority be propertyless, but a significant minority unemployed.

3. As we have already seen, the Constitution implemented Madison's indirect controls on the people. In fact, the choices made at the convention achieve this control while remaining truer to Madison's aim of protecting the trilogy of rights, than Madison's own preferred plan. The convention rejected the direct preferences for property implicit in freehold suffrage and the representation of property in the Senate.

4. Meyers, pp. 10, 16.

5. Rutland tells us that, "no single issue among the various points covered by the [state] bills of rights caused so much discussion or legislative action as freedom of religion." Rutland, *The Birth of the Bill of Rights, 1776–1791*, p. 88.

6. Hannah Arendt, *On Revolution* (New York: The Viking Press, 1965), p. 238 (quoting Emerson).

7. Ibid., p. 284

8. As Wilson shows, one need not make the mistake of treating politics as the highest human activity to see an active role in collective self-governance as an important dimension of human potential.

9. Robert Dahl, *Preface to Democratic Theory*, p. 3; Sidney Verba and Norman H. Nie, *Participation in America; Political Democracy and Social Equality* (New York: Harper and Row, 1972), p. 2.

10. See Benjamin Barber, *Strong Democracy* (Berkeley: University of California Press, 1984); and Philip Green, *Retrieving Democracy* (Totowa, N.J.: Rowman and Allanheld, 1985). Jesse Jackson's campaigns can be seen as efforts to transform the nature of participation in the American political system, in particular to open it to those most thoroughly excluded.

11. Arendt, *On Revolution*, p. 241.

12. Ibid., p. 272.

13. This is not to say that representatives might not see their task as the pursuit of the public good (a point I will return to). But that pursuit does not characterize the *relation* between citizen and representative.

14. For Arendt's formulation of this issue see *On Revolution*, p. 256.

15. Ackerman, "Storrs Lectures," p. 1035.

16. Hendrik Hartog, "The Constitution of Aspiration and 'The Rights That Belong to Us All,'" *The Journal of American History*, Vol. 74, No. 3 (December 1987):1018 n. 12.

17. Garry Wills, "'New Votuhs,'" reviews of *The Best Congress Money Can Buy* by Phillip M. Stern; *Why Americans Don't Vote* by Francis Fox Piven and Richard A. Cloward; *Whose Votes Count?: Affirmative Action and Minority Voting Rights* by Abigail M. Thernstrom; and *Character: American Search for Leadership* by Gail Sheey. *New York Review of Books* 35 (18 August, 1988):3–5, at p. 3. Piven and Cloward offer an explanation for the twentieth century decline in voter participation in chapters 2 and 3.

Thomas Cavanaugh also notes, "The aggregate decline in turnout has been far from neutral in terms of class. It has tended to exaggerate the already pronounced class bias in participation patterns." "Changes in American Voter Turnout, 1964–1976," *Political Science Quarterly* 96 (Spring 1981): 53–65, p. 58. Numerous studies indicate that there is a positive correlation between social status—whether this is measured by level of education, income or occupation—and voter participation. See Verba and Nie, *Participation*.

18. Piven and Cloward (note 17) talk about the range of impediments to registration that various state governments have employed. See chapters 3, 4, and 6.

19. According to Wills, George Will "has argued that increasing the number of voters will just increase the amount of ignorance brought to the maintenance of 'good government'" ibid., (p. 3). Many of the Federalists would have shared this view.

20. Bruce Ackerman makes an interesting argument about another contribution of the American system: the separation of powers the Constitution implements insures that no branch of the government can unilaterally claim to be "We the people." The voice of democracy is a deliberately and constructively complicated one. See "Storrs Lectures."

21. Arendt, *On Revolution*, p. 230.

22. Ibid., p. 273.

23. Donald R. Matthews, "Legislative Recruitment and Legislative Careers," *Legislative Studies Quarterly* 9 (1984): 547–585, p. 548.

24. Roger Davidson and Walter J. Oleszek, *Congress and Its Members*, 2d ed. (Washington D.C.: Congressional Quarterly Press, 1985), p. 112. A survey of the background of all members of the House of Representatives from 1789 to 1960 concludes that "little change can be observed in the characteristics and experience of representatives before entry into House service." Allan G. Bogue, Jerome M. Clubb, Carroll R. McKibbin and Santa A. Traugott, "Members of the House of Representatives and the Process of Modernization, 1789–1960," *Journal of American History* 63 (Sept. 1976):275–300, p. 300.

25. David J. Rothman uses three categories to designate the class background of senators: elite, substantial, and subsistence. "Ordinary town lawyers, doctors and small merchants" comprised the substantial group. During the period 1869–1901 at least 42% of senators came from families of substantial social background. *Politics and Power: The United States Senate 1869–1901* (Cambridge, Mass.: Harvard University Press, 1966), p. 272.

26. See the Federalist Farmer, 4 January 1788, Storing 2:276.

27. *The Federalist*, No. 45, p. 309.

28. The top 0.5% of the population owns 25% of the country's wealth, the top 1% owns 34%, the top 10% owns 62%, the top 30% owns about 85%. G.

William Domhoff, *Who Rules America Now?* (Englewood Cliffs, N.J.: Prentice Hall, 1983), p. 42.

29. I suppose that it is also fair to say that those hostile to the welfare state would argue that Madison's fears have been realized, and that we are in a continuing struggle to hold at bay the unwise and unjust demands of the people.

30. On the progressives see Richard L. McCormick, "The Discovery that Business Corrupts Politics: A Reappraisal of the Origins of Progressivism," *American Historical Review* 86 (1981):247–74. "Had the muckrakers and their local imitators penetrated more deeply into the way that business operated and its real relationship to government, popular emotions might not have been so readily mobilized in support of regulatory and administrative agencies that business interests could often dominate" (p. 272).

31. Charles R. Beitz, "Political Finance in the United States," *Ethics* 95 (1984):129–48, p. 138.

32. "Any system for financing political competition must be governed finally by the aim of treating democratic citizens equally both as participants in political choice and as subjects of political decision. The main defect in much recent thought about the principled basis of campaign finance reform has been its failure to grasp the complexity of this aim" (Ibid., p. 146). See also pp. 141–46.

33. 424 U.S. 1 (1976).

34. Ibid., pp. 25–26.

35. Ibid., p. 57.

*36. Of course, some of the dissenters saw beyond these limitations. As always in American political thought, the dominant views are not monolithics; they coexist with contending alternatives.

37. Charles E. Lindblom, *Politics and Markets: The World's Political Economic Systems* (New York: Basic Books, Inc., 1977).

38. Appleby, "Heirs and the Disinherited," pp. 805–6.

39. John Rawls is the best known of the egalitarian theorists. As I read *A Theory of Justice* (Cambridge: Harvard University Press, 1971), he does not foreclose the possibility of major changes in the economic system. But he takes as his working model a market economy whose outcomes will be redistributed. Anthony Kronman is an important exception. He directly addresses the possibility of restructuring the legal rules that constitute the market, contract in particular. "Contract Law and Distributive Justice," *Yale Law Journal* 89 (1980):472–509.

40. For example, Owen Fiss's thoughtful argument in "Why the State," *Harvard Law Review* 100 (1987):781–94, is aimed at avoiding the problem of "politics dominated by the market." But he takes the market as given and suggests only minor adjustments in political institutions. For example, Fiss suggests that public hearings and offices of public advocacy in administrative agencies "will exert a countervailing force" against "the forces that dominate the social structure" (p. 792).

41. Ibid., p. 792.

42. "In hindsight, the Supreme Court's takings jurisprudence seems to have moved steadily from 1922 (citing Pennsylvania Coal Co. v. Mahon, 260

U.S. 393 [1922]) toward a highly nonformal, open-ended, multi-factor balancing method (citing, among other things, Penn Central Transportation Co. v. New York City, 438 U.S. 104 [1978]). In all the years between 1922 and 1987, however, the Court never once clearly applied the open-ended balancing test in favour of a takings claim and against a regulating government (distinguishing Loretto v. Teleprompter Manhattan CATV Corp., 458 U.S. 419 [1982] and Kaiser Aetna v. United States, 444 U.S. 164 [1979])." Frank Michelman, "Takings, 1987," *Columbia Law Review* 88 (1988):1600–1629, p. 1621.

43. C. B. Macpherson, "Human Rights as Property Rights," *Dissent* 24 (Winter 1977): 72–88, p. 77. Bernard Seigan provides an indirect confirmation of the ways in which protections for new rights, not conceived as property, are seen as standing in opposition to property rights: "When the courts attempt affirmative jurisprudence [the creation and protection of new rights requiring affirmative government action], they necessarily have to abandon their obligation to defend existing material rights." He wants property to work against, and certainly to take priority over, the new affirmative claims to welfare and equality. Bernard Siegan, *Economic Liberties and the Constitution* (Chicago: University of Chicago Press, 1980), p. 315.

44. On the shifts in meaning see Morton J. Horwitz, *The Transformation of American Law* (Cambridge: Harvard University Press, 1977): and Harry Scheiber, "Property Law, Expropriation, and Resource Allocation by Government, 1789–1910," *Journal of Economic History* 33 (March 1973): 232–51.

45. I shall comment shortly on whether recent instances of these rare cases are harbingers of a major shift in the Court's stance toward property.

46. West Coast Hotel v. Parrish (330 U.S. 379) is the conventionally recognized turning point.

47. Edwin S. Corwin, "The Basic Doctrine of American Constitutional Law," *Michigan Law Review* 12:(1914): 247–76, p. 255.

48. See David Currie, *The Constitution in the Supreme Court: The First Hundred Years, 1789–1888* (Chicago: University of Chicago Press, 1985), pp. 203–21. The picture is not quite as clear as under the Marshall years, but he concludes that "the overall impression conveyed by the contract cases of the Taney years is one of continuity with the Marshall tradition." He also quotes Benjamin F. Wright's conclusion that the contract clause was a "more secure and a broader base for the defense of property rights in 1864 than it had been in 1835." *The Contract Clause of the Constitution* (Cambridge, Mass.: Harvard University Press, 1938), pp. 62–63, 245–46.

49. See Currie, *The First Hundred Years*, especially p. 381, for notes on scholarly dispute on this point.

50. Scott v. Sandford, 60 U.S. (19 How.) 393 (1857), at 452 (per Taney).

51. Thomas Grey, "Substantive Due Process in the State Courts," paper presented at the American Political Science Association, September 1987.

52. For example, Webster as attorney in Wilkinson v. Leland, 2 Pet. 627 (1829), "If at this period, there is not a general restraint on legislatures, in favor of private rights, there is an end to private property. Though there may be no prohibition in the constitution, the legislature is restrained from acts subverting the great principles of republican liberty and of the social com-

pact" (pp. 646–47); and Story in an opinion for the Court, "That government can scarcely be deemed to be free where the rights of property are left solely dependent upon the will of a legislative body without any restraint. The fundamental maxims of a free government seem to require that the rights of personal liberty and private property should be held sacred" (p. 657). Quoted in Corwin, "Basic Doctrine," p. 253.

53. For the laissez-faire rhetoric, especially from the American Bar Association, see Benjamin R. Twiss, *Lawyers and the Constitution* (Princeton, N.J.: Princeton University Press, 1942). For the rhetoric of the 1820s see Merrill D. Peterson, *Life, Liberty and Property: The State Constitutional Conventions of the 1820s* (Indianapolis: Bobbs-Merrill,1966).

*54. Horwitz, *Transformation*. The practices in the different states perhaps were not as uniform as Horwitz presents them, but I think his claim about the judicial modification of the common law is clearly correct and is consistent with the findings of other legal historians, most notably Harry Scheiber. The most problematic parts of Horwitz's argument are about in whose interest these changes were made and how self-consciously. It is his bold and important claims about class bias that have drawn the fire of his critics. While I am generally sympathetic to his thesis, my argument here does not rely on the claims of class bias.

55. This is Horwitz's term.

56. Scheiber, "Property Law, Expropriation, and Resource Allocation," p. 243.

*57. Some of the nineteenth-century cases, eminent domain in particular, contain comments about the need to balance private rights and public good, and occasionally even a broad claim that property is always held subject to the needs of the community. But these comments do not amount to, nor lead to, an overall reevaluation or redefinition of property. The basic conception of, and rhetorical stance toward, property seem to remain the same, despite intermittent statements of contingency. The judiciary of the "economic due process" era was able to call upon the sacred tradition of property in part because the conception of property as a limiting value remained dominant despite practice and occasional pronouncements to the contrary.

58. Indeed, part of the difficulty is in precisely defining the groups who are alleged to have benefited and lost in the process. Horwitz's important book suffers from this problem. The patterns of development and distribution do seem to support the subsidy arguments made by both Horwitz and Scheiber. But the class structure of the distribution of legal benefits is not central to this part of my argument.

59. Whether the changes I have pointed to could be described as the result of the majority violating the rights of individuals is a more complicated question.

60. Bronson v. Kinzie, 42 U.S. (1 How.) 311 (1843) at 320.

61. For example, Charles River Bridge v. Warren Bridge, 36 U.S. (11 Pet.) 420 (1837); West River Bridge Co. v. Dix, 47 U.S. (6 How.) 507 (1848).

62. 10 U.S. (6 Cranch) 87 (1810).

*63. For example, Robert Gordon discusses the conflict in the thought of

Oliver Wendell Holmes "between law as an agent of freedom and law as an agent of collective good or natural necessity" in "Holmes' Common Law as Legal and Social Science," *Hofstra Law Review* 10 (1982): 719–46, p. 741.

It is important to remember that there was always something disingenuous about the Federalist vision. Not only was the meaning of property rights contested during the formation of the Constitution, but many of the Federalists were arguing for the rejection of older conceptions in the name of economic freedom and prosperity.

*64. The standard rejoinder to any claim of absolute property rights is to point out the acceptance of eminent domain and taxation as inhering in state sovereignty. Cooley et al. set out to define the limits to those apparent exceptions to the absolute rights of property, to transform them from exceptions to clearly defined contours of property rights. Eminent domain and taxation should not be exceptions or even limitations, properly speaking, but part of the boundaries property defines to the legitimate scope of government. See Clyde E. Jacobs, *Law Writers and the Courts: The Influence of Thomas M. Cooley, Christopher G. Teideman, and John F. Dillon upon American Constitutional Law* (Berkeley: University of California Press, 1954).

65. Lochner v. New York, 198 U.S. 45 (1905). The Court struck down, as a violation of freedom of contract, a law stipulating the maximum number of hours per week for bakers.

66. See Corwin's "Basic Doctrine" and my argument in chapter 5.

67. As I shall discuss later, it is a separate question whether restribution as such is now accepted as a public purpose.

68. Of course, as I argued above, the earlier presuppositions were given effect in some spheres and ignored in others. But they remained the ruling premises of constitutional law.

69. As Laurence Tribe puts it: "In *United States v. Carolene Products Co.*, 304 U.S. 144 (1938), the case in which Justice Stone's famous footnote 4 would later support increased judicial intervention in non-economic affairs, the Court declared that it would sustain regulation in the socioeconomic sphere if any state of facts either known or reasonably inferable afforded support for the legislative judgment. Even this limited scrutiny soon gave way to virtually complete judicial abdication. The Court became willing to resort to purely hypothetical facts and reasons to uphold legislation [citing Williamson v. Lee Optical Co., 348 U.S. 483 (1955)] or, as in *Ferguson v. Skrupa* [372 U.S. 726 (1963)], to uphold it for virtually no substantive reason at all." *American Constitutional Law* (Mineola, N.Y.: The Foundation Press, 1978), p. 450.

70. The current status of the contract clause is nicely captured in the statement of the majority in Keystone Bituminous Coal Association v. DeBenedictus, 107 S.Ct. 1232 (1987): "[I]t is well-settled that the prohibition against impairing the obligation of contracts is not to be read literally."

71. In addition to the articles cited below, see Carol Rose's insightful series of articles on the shifting meaning of property and its constitutional status, particularly "*Mahon* Reconstructed: Why the Takings Issue is Still a Muddle," *Southern California Law Review* 57 (1983–84): 561–99 and "Crystals and Mud in Property Law," *Stanford Law Review* 40 (1987–88): 577–610.

72. Berman v. Parker, 348 U.S. 26 (1954), at 32.

73. Poletown Neighborhood Council v. City of Detroit, Michigan, 304 N.W. 2nd, 455.
74. See Scheiber, "Property Law, Expropriation, and Resource Allocation."
75. 467 U.S. 229 (1984).
76. Midkiff v. Tom, 788 (9th Cir. 1983) at 798.
77. 467 U.S. 229 (1984) at 242. She also invoked the language of contemporary economics: the legislation was "a comprehensive and rational approach to identifying and correcting market failure."
78. Bruce Ackerman, *Private Property and the Constitution* (New Haven, Connecticut, 1977), p. 167. In Laurence Tribe's terms, the two issues of compensation and public use have been conflated. "The public's willingness to pay, expressed through the legislative process, would serve as proof that the public had in fact been the beneficiary of what otherwise appeared to be a forbidden transfer of property from one owner to another" (Laurence Tribe, *American Constitutional Law*, p. 458). Of course, if "public use" is defined by the legislative process, it no longer serves as a limiting requirement on the outcomes of that process. And it is this limit that property rights were traditionally proclaimed to be.
79. Ackerman, *Private Property and the Constitution*.
80. 260 U.S. 393 (1922).
81. Neal S. Manne, "Reexamining the Supreme Court's View of the Taking Clause," *Texas Law Review* 58 (1980):1447–73.
*82. I do not mean to adopt Ackerman's analysis in its entirety. There seem to be some unresolved problems with his categories. For example, we might expect a laymen to consider an 80% diminution in the value of property to be a clear violation of property rights, even if the only systematic way of accounting for such a diminution is in terms of a bundle of rights. I expect that a refusal to hold that such a diminution is a taking runs counter to the ordinary layman's understanding, even though no physical invasion is involved.
83. See Norman Dorsen and Joel Gora, "Free Speech, Property and the Burger Court: Old Values, New Balances" in *The Supreme Court Review 1982*, Philip B. Kurland, Gerhard Casper, and Dennis J. Hutchison eds. (Chicago: University of Chicago Press, 1983), pp. 195–241.
84. Buckley v. Valeo, 424 U.S. 1 (1976).
85. "The determination whether a state law unlawfully infringes a landowner's property in violation of the Taking Clause requires an examination of whether the restriction on private property 'forc[es] some people alone to bear public burdens which, in all fairness and justice, should be borne by the public as a whole.'" Robins v. Pruneyard Shopping Center, 447 U.S. 74 (1980), 82–83, quoting from Armstrong v. United States, 364 U.S. 40 (1960), 49.
*86. While it is startling to hear O'Connor say that the regulation of oligopoly is a classic use of police power, it is helpful to know that in this case the owners of the land to be expropriated were charitable trusts. Some of the impetus for the legislation seems to have come from major corporations and others who wanted to own rather than lease the downtown property of Honolulu. The case does not seem to be an instance of the poor using legislation to redistribute the property of the rich in their favor.

87. See the collection of articles on this issue in *Columbia Law Review* Vol. 88, No. 8 (December, 1988).

88. Keystone Bituminous Coal Association v. De Benedictus, 107 S. Ct. 1232 (1987)

89. Ibid., at 1240.

90. Ibid., at 1242, 1246. In justification Stevens quoted an earlier case stating that, "circumstances may so change in time . . . as to clothe with such a [public] interest what at other times . . . would be a matter of purely private concern." Block v. Hirsh, 256 U.S. 135, at 155 (1921), cited by Stevens at 1243.

91. *De Benedictus*, at 1249.

92. Ibid., at 1259.

93. Nollan v. California Coastal Commission, 107 S. Ct. 3141 (1987).

94. Radin, "The Liberal Conception of Property: Cross Currents in the Jurisprudence of Takings," *Columbia Law Review* 88 (1988):1667–96, p. 1677. As a condition for permission to build on beach front property, the commission required the owners of the property to permit public access across a strip of land beyond their seawall, adjacent to the mean high tide line that bounded their holding to the seaward side. *Nollan*, at 3150.

*95. Such an easement would constitute a "permanent physical occupation" if the house in question already existed. The majority did acknowledge that since the Coastal Commission could prohibit the building entirely, they could also substitute a condition for the prohibition. But in this case, the condition "utterly fails to further the end advanced as the justification for the prohibition. . . . The purpose then becomes, quite simply, the obtaining of an easement to serve some valid governmental purpose, but without payment of compensation." *Nollan*, at 3148. For a careful unpacking of the issues in this case see Michelman, "Takings, 1987."

96. Radin, "Liberal Conception," p. 1678.

97. In Richard Epstein's theory, compensation could be provided by a quid pro quo of direct benefit to those regulated, but not simply by an advancement of the public good. *Takings: Private Property and the Power of Eminent Domain* (Cambridge: Harvard University Press, 1985).

98. First English Evangelical Lutheran Church v. County of Los Angeles, 107 U.S. S. Ct. 2378 (1987).

99. Ibid., p. 3288.

100. Michelman, "Takings, 1987," p. 1619.

101. Ibid., p. 1601.

102. Ibid.

103. Loretto v. Teleprompter Manhattan CATV Corp., 458 U.S. 419 (1982).

104. Michelman, "Takings, 1987," p. 1608.

105. Ibid., p.1623.

106. Ibid., p.1624, quoting from *Irving* at 2083.

107. Ibid., quoting from *Irving* at 2083.

108. Ibid.

109. Radin for example sees an ominous trend in the 1987 cases combined with the 1982 holding in *Loretto* that a "permanent physical occupation" was a per se taking. "Perhaps we have the beginning of a trend toward conceptualism, both on the grand level of seeing a Platonic form of property [the

right to exclude as being an inherent part of the essence of property], and on the strategic level of willingness to engage in conceptual severance. If so, the trend is just beginning" ("Liberal Conception," p. 1684).

110. Michelman, "Takings, 1987," p. 1628.

111. In Ackerman's language, for example, property rights would be determined on the basis of some "comprehensive view," which is the basis for scientific policy making. Michelman, "Takings, 1987," p. 1628.

*112. In *Takings* Richard Epstein has tried to provide a principled basis for such calculation. He is unusual among the advocates of returning property to its status as boundary to state power in not basing his approach on property's thing-like quality. He acknowledges that virtually all legislation affects property rights. The relevant distinction is therefore not whether legislation involves some taking of a property interest or right, but whether such a taking is justified. He correctly identifies the problem. The difficulty he has in providing a solution may suggest why other defenders of property try to stick with some seemingly more graspable issue like when some *thing* has been taken.

*113. There is a connection between the literal concreteness of property as many people experience it, and the sense that property was vital to the republic, to individual freedom, to limited government. Although analytically there is a conflict between the notion of property as a literal thing and property as a boundary to governmental power, I think it is the concreteness of property that gives it its force as a concept which is seen as something more than a (rearrangeable) collection of legal entitlements. Property was seen as a specific, identifiable, knowable entity which held a special place in law, republican theory, and "society." Property was "something" which was important, which required and was entitled to protection, which could be threatened and whose destruction or violation would cause far-reaching damage.

It is as though property rights have remained infused with a natural rights quality long after natural rights theories were no longer generally accepted. Legal, as well as political, rhetoric implied that property rights gave effect to some pre-existing natural phenomenon—whose concreteness gave an intuitive certainty and substance to the legal construct. Lawyers' and judges' daily work with the mutability, variety, and multiplicity of property rights seemed (for at least 150 years) not to have shaken their sense that property rights were different from other legal entitlements and deserved a special and protected status.

114. Ackerman, *Private Property and the Constitution.*

115. "The Disintegration of Property," in Roland Pennock and John Chapman, eds., *Property: Nomos XXII* (New York: New York University Press, 1980).

116. The statement is from the district court judge in pretrial hearing, cited in the decision by the U.S. Court of Appeals, Steelworkers, Local 1330 v. U.S. Steel Corporation, 105 LRRM 2312, at 2324. The district court ultimately concluded that, "Unfortunately, the mechanism to reach this ideal settlement, to recognize this new property right, is not now in existence in the code of laws of our nation." 103 LRRM 2925, at 2931–2932.

117. Charles Reich, "The New Property," *Yale Law Journal* 73 (1964): 733–87.

118. Frank Michelman, "Property as a Constitutional Right," *Washington and Lee Law Review* 38 (1981):1097–1114, p. 1112.

119. Steven Munzer, "Control, Privacy, and Individuality in Justifications for Property," presented at the Jurisprudence Section, Convention of the Association of American Law Schools, Philadelphia, January 1982.

120. Richard Funston, "The Double Standard of Constitutional Protection in the Era of the Welfare State," *Political Science Quarterly* 90 (1975): 261–87. Not all arguments against the "double standard" of stricter protection for personal liberties than for economic liberties have this egalitarian thrust.

121. In addition to the "hints" in the cases discussed above, there are others in which Rehnquist has shown an inclination to use both property and contract to limit the scope of state power: Penn Central Transportation v. New York City, 438 U.S. 104 (1978); United States Trust Co. v. New Jersey, 431 (1977); Allied Structural Steel Co. v. Spannaus, 438 U.S. 234 (1978).

122. Goldberg v. Kelly, 397 U.S. 254 (1970).

*123. William H. Simon offers a different, but I think not conflicting, account of the paradoxical and destructive consequences of using the concept of property as the vehicle for reform: "With the disappearance of growth in the late 1970s, the liability of New Property as a liberal political vision became quite clear. The appeal to property rights simply backfired. In the 'zero sum society', the New Property rights of welfare recipients were perceived to conflict with the old property rights of investors and taxpayers, and the latter were considered better grounded in distributive considerations. The New Property provided no basis to challenge such notions." William H. Simon, "The Invention and Reinvention of Welfare Rights," *Maryland Law Review* 44 (1985): 1–37, p. 35.

The dimension of the New Property argument that Simon focuses on is the effort to legitimate welfare as a right. (And he is concerned not just with the argument Reich made in his article, but the uses to which that argument was put.) And most of his critique is aimed at the consequences and incoherence of trying to assimilate welfare to a classical model of rights. While I entirely agree with his judgement that property was a poor choice for capturing the aims of welfare reform, I think his emphasis on the substantive side of the issue misses part of what was valuable in Reich's argument and in the Court's adoption of it in *Goldberg v. Kelly*. *Goldberg* is best read as an effort to use the concept of new property to insist on certain procedural protection for welfare recipients. It had the potential (despite the serious drawbacks of the property metaphor) to generate a jurisprudence that was not about rights as a vehicle for reducing the power of the state, but about structuring that power so that it empowered the individuals dependent on the state. (I expand this argument in, "Reconceiving Autonomy: Sources, Thoughts and Possibilities," *Yale Journal of Law and Feminism* 1 [1989]: 7–36.) Simon makes the important claim that "the thrust of the administrative program is not to limit state power or discretion at all; it is simply to shift it around. In particular, the program tends to shift power from lower tier officials to upper tier officials and judges" (ibid., p. 34). But I think that is not quite fair to the potential of *Goldberg*. Even if enforced by the judiciary, greater participation by welfare recipients in the decisions that affect them could be a significant improvement in the welfare system. Constitutional protections for the new property could be taken to mean not the immunization of a particular distribution of benefits from legislative change, but requirements for autonomy-enhancing forms of bureaucratic decision making. The interesting question Simon raises is whether any invocation of property, even in a purely procedural context, will bring along with it the anti-redistributional (or immunization from change) notions traditionally associated with property. Ironically, in retreating from *Goldberg* the Court invoked not the static sanctity of the traditional image of property, but the startling suggestion that property is whatever the state says it is. (Simon also elaborates his arguments in "Rights and Redistribution in the Welfare System," *Stanford Law Review* 38 (1986): 1431–1516.)

124. Regents v. Roth, 408 U.S. 564 (1972).

125. Funston, "Double Standard."

126. The classic critique of the double standard is Robert McCloskey, "Economic Due Process and the Supreme Court: An Exhumation and Burial," in *The Supreme Court Review, 1962* (Chicago: University of Chicago Press, 1962).

127. Funston, "Double Standard," p. 262.

128. 405 U.S. 538 (1972), cited in ibid., p. 276. The case involved garnishment of the plaintiffs' credit union account. The issue was whether there was federal jurisdiction over cases involving property rights brought under Section 1982. This ruling provides a new avenue for judicial protection of property rights.

129. Ibid., p. 277.

130. San Antonio Independent School District v. Rodriguez, 411 U.S. 1 (1973); James v. Valtierra, 402 U.S. 137 (1971).

*131. There have, of course, been proponents of this position, from the Anti-Federalists' call for a republic with only moderate disparities of wealth, through the demand for "forty acres and a mule" for the former slaves, to the contemporary arguments by liberal academics that greater economic equality is necessary to make good on liberal claims. But none of these has prevailed, and virtually all claims for economic *entitlements* derived from civil or political rights have been strenuously and successfully resisted.

132. Macpherson, "Human Rights as Property Rights," p. 73.

133. Seigan, *Economic Liberties and the Constitution*, p. 310.

134. See Jennifer Hochschild, *What's Fair: American Beliefs About Distributive Justice* (Cambridge, Mass: Harvard University Press, 1981).

*135. There is a countervailing strategic benefit which I have not discussed. Attention drawn to the need to redefine property may have an important educative function. Redefining property may have the advantage of getting people to rethink their understanding of this basic right, rather than frightening them, as a frontal attack on private property would. It is hard to know how to weigh the dangers of inadvertantly giving additional support to traditional, inegalitarian, restrictive conceptions of property against the advantage of changing people's presumption about the nature of their basic rights.

136. The 1987 takings cases discussed above may constitute an effort by some of the justices to reestablish property as an effective boundary.

*137. This is, of course, based largely on impressionistic evidence. For example, the advertisements urging citizens to think of social security as something which is *theirs*, which they paid for, suggest that some people clearly think it is a forceful argument. The resistance to the idea of inheritance tax is another such indication. See generally Hochschild, *What's Fair*. For supporting survey data see: Dennis Chong, Herbert McClosky and John Zaller, "Patterns of Support for Democratic and Capitalist Values in the United States," *British Journal of Political Science* 13 (1983): 401–40; and Herbert McClosky and John Zaller, *The American Ethos: Public Attitudes Toward Capitalism and Democracy* (Cambridge, Mass.: Harvard University Press, 1984), chs. 4, 5, and 6.

*138. Frank Michelman has rightly reminded me that free speech may also serve this function. The parallel popular saying is, "It's a free country; I can say what I want." (Although my memory of schoolyard use is that the popular version focuses not on the government, but on one's fellow citizens.) At the academic and judicial level this vision of free speech as a boundary to governmental power merges in complex and troubling ways with property as boundary. As Michelman puts it: "In short, there remains among us the sense that a strong rule-of-law stance—a strong judicial defense of a flatly unbreakable line of defense against the democracy—is necessary *somewhere, at some point*; and why not, then at the point of freedom of the use of one's property holdings in exchange for the production of political speech." ("Possession v. Distribution in the Constitutional Idea of Property," *Iowa Law Review* 72 [1987]: 1319–50, p. 1347.)

There also seems to be a different kind of dissonance between popular belief and judicial practice in the case of free speech. With respect to takings, one might say that the Court provides *less* constitutional protection than would be popularly expected. (And whatever the convoluted quality of the legal arguments in *Nollan* and *First English* [see discussion above] it seems likely that the average person would have seen the challenged provisions as basic incursions on their property.) In free speech, by contrast, it seems that the Court provides "more" protection than the public expects. The recent flag-burning case is a dramatic example, and the rulings on pornography may be another. I do not know where *Buckley v. Valeo*, which involves both property and free speech, would fit. Efforts to control the political power of money are likely to have popular approval in general. But I think there is still a strong sense that "I can do what I want with my money, including (short of bribery) supporting candidates however I choose to." *Buckley* thus touches one of the many areas of an unresolved attachment both to increased equality and to the traditional image of property.

139. See, for example, Calder v. Bull, 3 Dall. 385 (1798).

140. Walter Lippman, quoted in Seigan, *Economic Liberties and the Constitution*, p. 330.

141. Reich, "The New Property," p. 777.

142. Charles E. Lindblom provides the best known contemporary statement of property as the allocation of state power: "Some people believe that wealth or property is the underlying source of power. But property is itself a form of authority created by government . . . The wealthy are those who enjoy larger grants of authority than most people do." *Politics and Markets*,

p. 26. The classic legal Realist versions of this argument are, Morris R. Cohen, "Property and Sovereignty," *Cornell Law Quarterly* 13 (1927): 8–30; and Robert L. Hale, "Coercion and Distribution in a Supposedly Non-Coercive State," *Political Science Quarterly* 38 (1923): 470–78.

143. As the conflict between conservatives and liberal egalitarians shows, the belief in the special relation between property and liberty is something quite different from the claim that there are many rights which cannot be enjoyed unless one's material needs are taken care of, and one is not subject to the power of another.

144. Michelman, "Property as a Constitutional Right," p. 1110.

145. Ibid.

146. Ibid., p. 1112.

147. "Mr. Justice Brennan: A Property Teacher's Appreciation," *Harvard Civil Rights—Civil Liberties Law Review* 15 (1980): 296–308, p. 306 as cited in Michelman, "Property as a Constitutional Right," pp. 1112–1113.

*148. Indeed it is part of the common law's claim to fame that its concept of property was divisible and abstract enough from a very early stage to allow for such useful concepts as trusts and remainder interests. The proposal in the Youngstown case that a community has a property claim on an industry that has "drawn the life blood" of the community is an instance of an effort to build on the less material elements of the traditional concept. (This is also, to use Macpherson's terms, not an exclusive right, but a right not to be excluded.) Thus the plaintiffs refer to their property claim as an easement (the most common instance of which is a right of way over another's property). This proposal was intended to meet a particular need, not to redefine all of property. While the Youngstown proposal is clearly at odds with other concepts of property (U.S. Steel's rights to use and dispose of its property), this seems to me to be the kind of stretching of the concept which would contribute only slightly to its disintegration. Precisely because it is less ambitious, it does not pose the problems for constitutionalism which the more complete redefinitions do.

149. The Realists' insights do not mean that it might not be useful to distinguish between modes and institutions of decision-making that we might call "law" and "politics." But those distinctions must be something other than what they are currently held out to be. It is one of the great puzzles of modern jurisprudence to figure out what valid distinctions might be, and how to restructure our understanding of the role of judges and of judicial review in particular once we cannot rely on the old distinctions.

150. G. Edward White, *Tort Law in America: An Intellectual History* (New York: Oxford University Press, 1980), p.158.

151. Ibid.

152. Ibid., pp. 158, 161.

153. Robert Gordon, Book review of *Tort Law in America, Harvard Law Review* 94 (1981): 903–18, at 918 (emphasis in original).

*154. I do not mean to suggest that CLS scholars are doing nothing more than reproducing the work of the legal Realists. For a particularly interesting argument about why no amount of mere demonstration of the nature of legal rights is likely to change people's attachment to the traditional concepts see

Peter Gabel, "The Phenomonology of Rights-Consciousness and the Pact of the Withdrawn Selves," *Texas Law Review* 62 (1984): 1563–99.

155. "*Lochner's* Legacy," *Columbia Law Review* 87 (1987): 873–919, at 882, emphasis mine.

156. *Ibid.*, p. 883.

157. *American Constitutional Law*, p. 447.

158. 424 U.S. 1 (1976), which I discussed in Section III of this Chapter.

159. 424 U.S. at 48–49 and see my discussion in Section III.

*160. "*Lochner's* Legacy," p. 884. Compare Tribe's discussion of Miller v. Schoene (276 U.S. 272 [1928]) in which the Supreme Court upheld a statute requiring owners of infected (but not ruined) red cedar trees to cut down their trees lest the contagion spread to a nearby apple orchard, where it would destroy the orchard's commercial value. The Court did not require compensation. Tribe notes that "*Miller* not only indicates that redistribution of property between private parties may be justified in the public interest. The decision also suggests that the state inevitably has a positive role to play, a role whose exercise in *either* direction will benefit some private actors while hurting others. For the Court opined that, if the state had done nothing and permitted disaster to strike the apple orchards, 'it would have been none the less a choice.' . . . The notion of a common law universe defining a 'natural' state of affairs without governmental interference was fading." *American Constitutional Law*, p. 446.

161. For a very thoughtful and detailed argument about the relevance of this illusory image of property for welfare jurisprudence, see William H. Simon, "The Invention and Reinvention of Welfare Rights," *Maryland Law Review* 44 (1985):1–37 and "Rights and Redistribution in the Welfare System," *Stanford Law Review* 38 (1986): 1431–1516.

162. "*Lochner's* Legacy," p. 885.

163. Ibid., p. 888. Also on this point see Paul Brest, "State Action and Liberal Theory: A Casenote on *Flagg Brothers v. Brooks*," *Pennsylvania Law Review* 130 (1982): 1296–1330.

164. Ibid., p. 889.

165. Ibid.

166. For example, Gabriel Kolko, the *Triumph of Conservatism: A Reinterpretation of American History, 1900–1916* (Chicago: Quadrangle Books, 1967).

*167. It is also destructive in other ways to which I will turn at the end of the Chapter.

168. This is Madison's phrase from *The Federalist*, No. 10, p. 58.

169. There are, of course, many variants of this vision. I am presenting the general features common to most. In most versions of liberal egalitarianism, economic inequality need not be abolished, but it must be compensated for or modified in ways which interfere with traditional property rights.

170. Perhaps it is an odd assymetry of rights and obligations that underlies the notion of charity or alms giving: there is a moral obligation to provide charity to the needy, but no true entitlement on their part to receive it. Not justice, but mercy compells alms giving.

171. Friedrich Hayek, for example, warns that the welfare state is a more insidious threat to freedom than socialism because its dangers are less appar-

ent and less easy to pin down and prevent. The welfare state is also a vague term without clear meaning or boundaries. *The Constitution of Liberty* (Chicago: University of Chicago Press, 1960), ch. 17.

172. In *Rodriguez* the Court did not actually have to face this question directly because they found that the facts of the case had not established that poor people lived in areas with a low tax base, and rich people in areas with a high tax base.

173. Harris v. McRae, 448 U.S. 297 (1980).

*174. This was Morris's fear. Once people take the idea of equal rights seriously, they will see that they cannot enjoy those rights equally as long as there are disparities of wealth. He thought proclaiming equal rights would inevitably be dangerous to property rights.

175. There was a flurry of articles explaining why the intrusion on private property entailed in telling a restaurant owner who he had to serve was in keeping with the traditional conception of property. See, for example, Neil Hecht, "From Seisin to Sit-In: Evolving Property Concepts," *Boston University Law Review* 44 (1964):435–66.

176. For an exploration of the depth of the changes in our constitutional system involved in judicial protection of Blacks, see Robert M. Cover, "The Origins of Judicial Activism in the Protection of Minorities" (*The Yale Law Journal* 91 [1982]: 1287–1316). Cover argues that "when the constitutional structure for political activity has been arranged to facilitate the pattern of oppression, judicial intervention will necessarily entail either inefficacy or a compromise of the constitutional structure itself" (p. 1304). I think there is a parallel argument about the transformations entailed in implementing equality in a constitutional system premised on the inequality of property. On "state action" see Paul Brest, "State Action and Liberal Theory: A Casenote on *Flagg Brothers v. Brooks*," *University of Pennsylvania Law Review* 130 (1982): 1296–1330.

177. Hochschild, *What's Fair*.

178. See John Hart Ely, *Democracy and Distrust* (Cambridge, Mass.: Harvard University Press, 1980).

*179. 304 U.S. 144, 152 n. 4 (1938). The footnote (excluding case references) reads as follows:

> There may be narrower scope for operation of the presumption of constitutionality when legislation appears on its face to be within a specific prohibition of the Constitution, such as those of the first ten amendments, which are deemed equally specific when held to be embraced within the Fourteenth . . .
>
> It is unnecessary to consider now whether legislation which restricts those political processes which can ordinarily be expected to bring about repeal of undesirable legislation, is to be subjected to more exacting judicial scrutiny under the general prohibitions of the Fourteenth Amendment than are most other types of legislation . . . .
>
> Nor need we enquire whether similar considerations enter into the review of statutes directed at particular religious, . . . or national, . . . or racial minorities, whether prejudice against dis-

> crete and insular minorities may be a special condition, which tends seriously to curtail the operation of those political processes ordinarily to be relied upon to protect minorities, and which may call for a correspondingly more searching judicial inquiry . . . .

The "process" theories rest primarily on the second and third paragraph. Indeed, they generally ignore the first paragraph. After all, some of the "specific prohibitions," like the contract clause and the Fifth Amendment prohibition against taking for public use without compensation, are substantive. Of course any focus on the first paragraph must account for why the specific prohibitions affecting property should receive less scrutiny than others.

*180. Bruce Ackerman has a persuasive account of why it was right for the Supreme Court to change its position in 1937: the political process, through a series of congressional and presidential elections had so clearly announced a deep and broad consensus in favor of the sort of legislation the Court had been striking down, that it amounted to a change in the meaning of the constitutional values at issue. In this case a special kind of political process determined the legitimacy of legislative outcomes. This thoughtful account also shows the flexibility of the American constitutional system. Basic changes in constitutional values can be initiated outside of either the courts or the formal amending procedures. Note, however, that Ackerman rejects the *Carolene Products* version of "process" theories. See "Beyond Carolene Products," *Harvard Law Review* 98 (1985): 713–46.

181. See Cass Sunstein, "Public Values, Private Interests, and the Equal Protection Clause," *The Supreme Court Review, 1983*, pp. 127–66; and "Naked Preferences and the Constitution," *Columbia Law Review* 84 (1984): 1689–1732; and "Interest Groups in American Public Law," *Stanford Law Review* 38 (1985): 29–87. He describes his conception of legitimate legislative decision-making as Madisonian. That is apt in some ways, but neglects the unresolved tension in Madisonian federalism between the public good and the representation of private interests.

182. An even starker example of a shift in what counts as a public purpose is desegregation. Once segregation was an acceptable public purpose; now the meaning of equality defines it as a prohibited objective.

183. William H. Simon offers very interesting examples of the efforts, from the time of the New Deal to the present, to disassociate welfare from redistribution. I think his overall picture offers strong support for my sense that there is no consensus on redistribution as a legitimate *goal* despite the well-established existence of a welfare state. "Rights and Redistribution in the Welfare System" and "The Invention and Reinvention of Welfare Rights," cited in n. 123.

184. For example, James Boyd White, "Law as Rhetoric, Rhetoric as Law: The Arts of Cultural and Communal Life," *University of Chicago Law Review* 52 (1985): 684–702.

185. Ackerman, "Storrs Lectures."

186. 347 U.S. 483 (1954).

*187. If we redefine the entitlements and privileges of property, we may also not only redistribute, but redefine the basic goods of society so that, in the end, economic equality as such will no longer be as important. (See C. B.

Macpherson, "The Rise and Fall of Economic Justice," in *The Rise and Fall of Economic Justice* (Oxford: Oxford University Press, 1985). I have not tried to present an argument for the desirable form of equality, but merely to point out the distortions that have followed from the particular vision of inequality that the Madisonian Federalists were wedded to. Once free of their vision, we can explore the desirable forms of equality and the forms of constitutionalism best suited to them.

188. Inequality in America has not, of course, taken the form Madison envisioned of a permanent propertyless majority. Economic inequality has, however, remained both a presumption and a feature of the system.

189. There is an interesting corroboration of my view of property-based independence as isolation in J. G. A. Pocock's analyses of the relationship between property and autonomy in seventeenth-century liberal thought: "The point about freehold in this context is that it involves its proprietor as little as possible in dependence upon or *even in relations with other people* and so leaves him free for the full austerity of citizenship in the classical sense." "Civil Humanism and its Role in Anglo American Thought," in *Politics, Language and Time* (New York: Atheneum, 1971), p. 91 (my emphasis).

190. I explore this notion of autonomy in "Reconceiving Autonomy: Sources, Thoughts and Possibilities," *Yale Journal of Law and Feminism* 1 (1989): 7–36.

191. See for example William H. Simon's description of the jurisprudence of welfare entitlement developed by social workers during and after the New Deal. "The Invention and Reinvention of Welfare Rights," cited in note 123.

192. The pure "process" theories are unacceptable not simply because they misunderstand our tradition, but because they would destroy rather than reshape its greatest strength.

*193. The Canadian Charter of Rights and Freedoms designates rights as basic values, but does not treat them as absolute limits. The very first section of the Charter says that it "guarantees the rights and freedoms set out in it subject only to such reasonable limits prescribed by law as can be demonstrably justified in a free and democratic society." There is also an "override" provision, Section 33, that permits legislatures to pass a law notwithstanding its violation of the Charter. The "notwithstanding" clause must be part of the bill and any law so passed ceases to have effect after five years (and thus would have to be passed again). It is possible, therefore, that Canada will generate a jurisprudence and a set of institutional practices that put into effect some version of the notion of rights that I have articulated.

194. I explore further the notion of law that is not boundary focused in "Law, Boundaries, and the Bounded Self," *Representations 30* (Spring, 1990):162–189.

195. For an extremely thoughtful discussion of "a revised ideal of legality," which explicitly makes the link to the shifting status of property see Frank Michelman, "Possession vs. Distribution in the Constitutional Idea of Property," *Iowa Law Review* 72 (1987): 1319–50. One of the most promising sources for this project of reconception is feminist theory. See for example, Martha Minow, "Foreword: Justice Engendered," *Harvard Law Review* 101 (1987): 10–95, Robin West, "Jurisprudence and Gender," *University of Chicago Law*

Review 55 (1988): 1–72, and "Love, Rage, and Legal Theory," *Yale Journal of Law and Feminism*: 1 (1989): 101–10.

196. See Margaret Jane Radin, "The Liberal Conception of Property: Cross Currents in the Jurisprudence of Takings," *Columbia Law Review* 88 (1988): 1667–96, Section II, for a very interesting argument that the rejects the old notion of autonomy and tries to provide a definition of what constitutional protections for property should look like under a new conception.

Index